CIVIL COURTS AND THE EUROPEAN POLITY

The Chapters collected in this book explore the place and role of judge-made private law in an emerging European polity. Examining case-law from the perspective of different theories and viewpoints, scholars and judges assess and reflect on the role of judges in civil cases for polity-building in Europe. The Chapters thus present a kaleidoscopic view on the dynamics of private law adjudication against a European backdrop. The book aims to add a private legal perspective to existing discourses in European constitutional law on Europe's political constellation. It aspires to enrich two debates – the first on the influence of fundamental rights in private legal relations, and the second on the constitutional dimension of European private law. The contributions are placed within a framework of five sub-categories or dimensions of judge-made European private law: politics of European private law adjudication, rights, remedies, representation and reflections of judges on specific cases.

Civil Courts and the European Polity

The Constitutional Role of Private Law Adjudication in Europe

Edited by
Chantal Mak
and
Betül Kas

•HART•
OXFORD • LONDON • NEW YORK • NEW DELHI • SYDNEY

HART PUBLISHING

Bloomsbury Publishing Plc

Kemp House, Chawley Park, Cumnor Hill, Oxford, OX2 9PH, UK

1385 Broadway, New York, NY 10018, USA

29 Earlsfort Terrace, Dublin 2, Ireland

HART PUBLISHING, the Hart/Stag logo, BLOOMSBURY and the Diana logo are
trademarks of Bloomsbury Publishing Plc

First published in Great Britain 2023

A catalogue record for this book is available from the British Library.

A catalogue record for this book is available from the Library of Congress.

Library of Congress Control Number: 2023932876

ISBN: HB: 978-1-50994-167-4
        ePDF: 978-1-50994-169-8
        ePub: 978-1-50994-168-1

Typeset by Compuscript Ltd, Shannon

To find out more about our authors and books visit www.hartpublishing.co.uk.
Here you will find extracts, author information, details of forthcoming events
and the option to sign up for our newsletters.

Acknowledgements

THE CHAPTERS ARE the elaborated versions of papers first presented at the final conference of the research project entitled 'Judges in Utopia' in Amsterdam in November 2019. The research project was funded by a Vidi grant of the Dutch Research Council, NWO, awarded to Chantal Mak in 2014 and hosted at the University of Amsterdam. The grant allowed us to invite a group of well-established experts and new, talented scholars in the field to discuss the role of judges in civil cases in a broad manner, examining case law in the light of different theories and viewpoints. They were joined by a number of judges, who reflected on their own experiences with the interaction of national and European law. We wish to express our gratitude to the contributors to this book, each of whom drew on their research or practical experience to provide a unique perspective on the role of civil courts in European polity-building, for their continuous collaboration, willingness to elaborate upon their papers and their patient engagement with our editorial comments. We are also grateful to the publishing team of Bloomsbury/Hart Publishing, especially Sinead Moloney and Sasha Jawed, for their enthusiastic support of this collection. Finally, we wish to thank the other team members of the 'Judges in Utopia' project for the inspiring collaboration: Anna van Duin and Laura Burgers, who both conducted PhD research within the project, and Fien de Ruiter, Ruby Kooter, Timo Zandstra and Vincent Stoop, who provided invaluable support as research assistants.

Contents

PART IV
REPRESENTATION

PART V
REFLECTIONS

Contributors

Laura E Burgers is an Assistant Professor of Private Law at the University of Amsterdam. She graduated from the University of Amsterdam with a Research Master in Public International Law and a BA in French Language and Culture. In 2020, she defended her PhD thesis dealing with the democratic legitimacy of judicial law-making in European private law cases on climate change. She is one of the experts in the United Nations programme Harmony with Nature on the rights of nature.

Fabrizio Cafaggi is a former Professor of Comparative Private Law at the University of Trento and the European University Institute and now judge at the Italian Council of State.

Michael W Dowdle is an Associate Professor at the National University of Singapore Faculty of Law. He was previously Visiting Chair in Globalization and Governance at Sciences Po in Paris, and a research fellow at the Regulatory Institutions Network (RegNet) at the Australian National University. He has also taught at the New York University School of Law, the University of Washington School of Law and the Centre for Transnational Legal Studies (CTLS) in London.

Francesca Episcopo is an Assistant Professor of European Private Law at the University of Amsterdam. She holds a degree in law *summa cum laude* from the University of Pisa (2014) and a Magister Juris from the University of Oxford (2016). She earned a PhD *summa cum laude* from the University of Pisa, with a dissertation on the meaning and normative value of the principle of effectiveness in the CJEU's case law (2019). She worked as a postdoc at the DIRPOLIS Institute, Scuola Superiore Sant'Anna (2018–21) and at the Law Department of the University of Pisa (2021–22). She was also an Emile Noël Fellow at NYU Law School (2020–22). She joined the Law Faculty of the University of Amsterdam in September 2022.

Giulia Gentile is a Fellow in Law at the LSE Law School. She holds a PhD from the Centre of European Law at King's College London, for which she was awarded the 2021 European Public Law Organisation PhD Thesis Prize. She is a qualified lawyer at the Italian Bar Association and gained legal experience, among other places, at the chambers of Judge Lucia Serena Rossi at the Court of Justice of the European Union and at the M&A Department of Clifford Chance (Milan).

Mateusz Grochowski is a Senior Research Fellow at the Max Planck Institute for Comparative and International Private Law and an Affiliated Fellow at the Information Society Project (Yale Law School). Previously he was a postdoctoral fellow at the New York University School of Law, the Buchmann Faculty of Law, Tel Aviv University and the European University Institute. He holds a title of Master of Laws (LLM) from Yale Law School. He serves as an editor for the *Journal of European Consumer and Market Law* and the *Rabels Zeitschrift für ausländisches und internationales Privatrecht*.

Monika Hinteregger is a Professor of Civil Law at the University of Graz. She is also the Director of the Centre of European Private Law of the University of Graz, Deputy Director of the Institute for European Tort Law of the Austrian Academy of Sciences and the University of Graz, and a board member of the Austrian Lawyers' Association (ÖJT) and the European Centre of Tort and Insurance Law (ECTIL). She is also a member of INLEX (International Expert Group on Nuclear Liability of the International Atomic Energy Agency).

Betül Kas is a postdoctoral researcher at Erasmus Law School of the University of Rotterdam. Previously, she was a researcher at the Private Law Department of the University of Amsterdam. She holds a PhD degree and an LLM in Comparative, European and International Laws from the European University Institute, an LLM in Globalisation and Law and an LLB in European Law from the University of Maastricht. As part of her doctoral research, she spent six months as a trainee at the CJEU. She serves as an editor for the *Maastricht Journal of European and Comparative Law.*

Cassandra CW Lange is a State Councillor at the Administrative Law Division of the Council of State of the Netherlands in The Hague. She is also a member of the Committee of the Rights of European Union of the Council of State. She is active in European judicial training projects, engaged in building bridges between the judiciary and academia to foster judicial dialogue between national and European courts, with a special focus on fundamental rights.

Chantal Mak is a Professor of Private Law, in particular fundamental rights and private law, at the University of Amsterdam. Her research focuses on the constitutional dimensions of private law, with particular interest for the influence of fundamental rights on judicial reasoning. This edited volume presents contributions to the final conference of her research project 'Judges in Utopia: Judicial Law-Making in European Private Law' (NWO Vidi 2014–2019).

Hans-W Micklitz is a part-time Professor of Economic Law at the Department of Law of the European University Institute. He has conducted study visits at the University of Michigan, Somerville College at the University of Oxford, Columbia University and the University of Helsinki as Finland Distinguished Professor. He held an Advanced Grant of the European Research Council (ERC) (2011–2016) on European regulatory private law and a grant from the Academy of Finland on the external reach of European private law (2015–2021).

Luca Ettore Perriello is an Assistant Professor of Private Law at Marche Polytechnic University, Ancona, where he teaches international contract law, commercial law and insolvency law. He has authored two books on liability for obesity and sham trusts, and many articles on European and comparative private law published in Italian and international journals. He serves as Chief Executive Editor for the *Italian Law Journal*. He is also a member of the European Law Institute (ELI) and the Italian Society of Private Law Scholars (SISDiC).

José María Fernández Seijo is a Magistrate of the Fifteenth Section of the Provincial Court in Barcelona.

JML (Anna) van Duin is an Assistant Professor of Private Law at the University of Amsterdam. After graduating from Leiden University (LLM in Civil Law, *cum laude*) and the University of Oxford (Magister Juris), she worked for more than six years as an attorney-at-law at Pels Rijcken. In October 2020 she defended her PhD thesis (*cum laude*) on effective judicial protection under Article 47 of the Charter of Fundamental Rights of the European Union in unfair terms cases before the CJEU, and the Spanish and Dutch civil courts.

Table of Cases

Court of Justice of the European Union

Opinions of the Advocate Generals at the Court of Justice of the European Union

European Court of Human Rights

Advisory Opinions of the European Court of Human Rights

Inter-American Court of Human Rights

National Case Law

Norway

Poland

Spain

1

Civil Courts and the European Polity
An Introduction

CHANTAL MAK AND BETÜL KAS

I. JUDGES IN UTOPIA

O F THE MANY possible ways in which to address the hopes and crises encompassed in the project of European integration, this book focuses on the role of judges in civil cases. This may, at first sight, not be an obvious choice. Civil cases typically concern a claim under dispute between two parties, be it on, for instance, payment of what was promised in a contract, compensation of damage or protection of property. In their reasoning on the legal merits of such cases, judges usually do not seem to pay much attention to the possible influence of their judgments on the ideas of the European Union (EU). However, upon a closer look, at least a part of the judgments in civil cases in a small way represent bigger questions on the relationship between Member States and the EU, the interaction among institutions, and the relations among individuals and communities in Europe. While these matters may often remain obscured by technicalities of private law, judges will have to determine their direction at the crossroads of different legal spheres, legal instruments and institutional settings. Each private legal judgment may, accordingly, be considered to not only answer the individual case, but to also offer a view on what Europe is and may become.

The chapters collected in this book explore the place and role of judge-made private law in an emerging European polity. They present a kaleidoscopic view on the dynamics of private law adjudication against a European backdrop. What this book aims to add to existing discourses in European constitutional law is a private legal perspective on Europe's political constellation. It aspires to enrich two debates – one on the influence of fundamental rights in private legal relations and the other on the constitutional dimension of European private law. In order to set the scene, this introductory chapter will outline these two parts of the theoretical framework for the understanding of the judicial role. Furthermore, it will provide a summary of the chapters and place them within the frame according to five sub-categories or dimensions: politics of European private law adjudication, rights, remedies, representation and reflections.

Metaphorically, we picture the protagonists of these inquiries as 'Judges in Utopia' for at least three reasons. First and foremost, our inspiration was Jürgen Habermas' assertion that human rights are at the basis of a 'realistic utopia' and provide a foundation for a just society in 'the institutions of constitutional states themselves'.[1] While Habermas' work does not specifically single out courts in civil cases, the chapters in this book add insights into the extent to which private law strengthens the protection of human rights across European countries through case law. Second, the metaphor of course goes back further, to Thomas More's *Utopia*.[2] Keeping away from the more controversial aspects of More's ideal society, authors were encouraged to develop 'utopian thinking' as a means of considering alternatives to the status quo of European private law and the ideas of justice it reflects.[3] Third, we were curious about the experiences of judges themselves and their thoughts on the European dimension of private law adjudication. 'Judges in Utopia' offered them a framework for reflection that transcends the national and the European dimensions of their tasks.

Before presenting the results of the exploration of the theme, it should be admitted that the overall, constructive approach to European integration that formed the starting point of our studies may perhaps seem too optimistic in light of the crises and challenges that the EU has faced in recent years. After the economic and financial crises of 2007–2008, the migration crisis and the COVID-19 pandemic, at the time of writing, the EU was under pressure because of the war at its borders. Issues of private law may, in this light, be seen as rather mundane affairs. It is the hope of the editors that we can place the case law within a bigger picture, inviting a reader when engaging with the chapters in this book to obtain a new understanding of the small contributions that we think private law can make and is making to the EU. Rather than sweeping statements, these are bottom-up contributions that on a case-by-case basis allow us to reimagine what Europe, despite its imperfections, stands for.

II. FUNDAMENTAL RIGHTS AND EUROPEAN PRIVATE LAW

The discourse on fundamental rights and private law has by now become mainstream in discussions on the development of rules and remedies on private legal relations in the interaction between the national and European levels.[4] Comparative studies of the role of constitutional rights in national private law[5] have been complemented by analyses of the influence of European fundamental rights on private legal questions.[6] Initially, these European influences mostly concerned the assessment of national legislation and adjudication against the European Convention on Human Rights (ECHR) by the European Court of Human Rights (ECtHR)

---

[1] J Habermas, 'The Concept of Human Dignity and the Realistic Utopia of Human Rights' in *The Crisis of the European Union: A Response* (Cambridge, Polity Press, 2012) 95, likely inspired by John Rawls. See also C Mak, ch 4 in this volume, section II.B.

[2] T More, *Utopia* (1516), full text available at: www.theopenutopia.org (edited and with an introduction by S Duncombe, 2012).

[3] M Loughlin, 'The Constitutional Imagination' (2015) 78 *MLR* 1, 13.

[4] For a recent discussion of these developments, see, eg, HW Micklitz, 'Constitutionalization, Regulation and Private Law' in S Grundmann, HW Micklitz and M Renner, *New Private Law Theory: A Pluralist Approach* (Cambridge, Cambridge University Press, 2021).

[5] A Colombi Ciacchi, G Brüggemeier and G Comandé (eds), *Fundamental Rights and Private Law in the European Union, Volumes I and II* (Cambridge, Cambridge University Press, 2010); OO Cherednychenko, *Fundamental Rights, Contract Law and the Protection of the Weaker Party* (Munich, Sellier, 2007); C Mak, *Fundamental Rights in European Contract Law* (Alphen aan den Rijn, Kluwer Law International, 2008).

[6] S Grundmann (ed), *Constitutional Values and European Contract Law* (Deventer, Kluwer Law International, 2008); H Collins (ed), *European Contract Law and the Charter of Fundamental Rights* (Cambridge, Intersentia, 2017); and contributions to HW Micklitz (ed), *Constitutionalization of European Private Law* (Oxford, Oxford University Press, 2014).

and national courts. In more recent years, decisions of the Court of Justice of the European Union (CJEU) on preliminary questions have also increasingly taken up human rights aspects of private legal matters, in particular after the EU Charter of Fundamental Rights (EUCFR) became legally binding in 2009. The CJEU's finding that all Charter rights may potentially have direct horizontal effect (*Bauer and Broβonn*)[7] is likely to encourage this trend even more.

At the same time, it should be recognised that cases in which either national constitutional rights or European human rights play a role is only a fraction of the number of private legal disputes that reach civil courts. Most private legal cases are not translated into the language of fundamental rights, but are resolved on the basis of the technical terms of national civil codes, statutes or judgments, where relevant in combination with provisions of the EU Treaties or Directives. A question thus remains: which cases should be 'constitutionalised' and for what reasons should they be turned into a matter of fundamental rights rather than technical private law?[8]

The *Aziz* case[9] has become a point of reference for many scholars in the field and it will not come as a surprise that it casts its 'lights and shadows'[10] over many chapters of this book. First, the case addresses the societal dimensions of a typical private legal procedure: the enforcement of Mr Aziz's mortgage contract, which eventually resulted in him and his family being evicted from their home, was representative for thousands of mortgage enforcement proceedings in Spain following the economic crisis that started in 2007. Although the far-reaching consequences for people having to leave their homes were broadly discussed in Spain, national law did not provide adequate remedies.[11] Second, the *Aziz* case demonstrates how the interaction of national courts in civil cases with the CJEU may affect the assessment of the effectiveness of remedies for homeowners: framing the mortgage enforcement as a question of the bank benefiting from unfair, one-sided standard terms in relation to a consumer, procedural lines in Spanish law did not hold up.[12] The CJEU's ruling that Spanish procedural law did not comply with the objectives of the EU Directive on Unfair Terms in Consumer Contracts[13] inspired a reform of national procedural law.[14] A bright side to the *Aziz* judgment may thus be found in the CJEU's somewhat hidden considerations on the fundamental importance of protecting the home as a reason for intervening in the procedural autonomy of a Member State. This is one reason why the *Aziz* judgment has attracted attention from those studying the influence of fundamental rights in private law.[15] In conversation with the national referring judge, the Court seems to open up space for the social dimension of contract law.[16] Eventually, however,

---

[7] Joined Cases C-569/16 and C-570/16 *Stadt Wuppertal v Maria Elisabeth Bauer and Volker Willmeroth v Martina Broβonn* EU:C:2018:871.

[8] HW Micklitz and N Reich, 'The Court and Sleeping Beauty: The Revival of the Unfair Contract Terms Directive (UCTD)' (2014) 51 *Common Market Law Review* 771, 801–02; H Collins, 'On the (In)Compatibility of Human Rights Discourse and Private Law' in Micklitz (n 6) 26, 58–59.

[9] Case C-415/11 *Mohamed Aziz v Caixa d'Estalvis de Catalunya, Tarragona i Manresa (Catalunyacaixa)* EU:C:2013:164.

[10] See Judge Fernández Seijo, ch 15 in this volume.

[11] S Nasarre Aznar, '"Robinhoodian" Courts' Decisions on Mortgage Law in Spain' (2015) 7 *International Journal of Law in the Built Environment* 127.

[12] JML van Duin, *Effective Judicial Protection in Consumer Litigation: Article 47 of the EU Charter in Practice* (Cambridge, Intersentia, 2022) 96–98, 155–61.

[13] Council Directive 93/13/EEC of 5 April 1993 on unfair terms in consumer contracts [1993] OJ L95/29.

[14] Ley 1/2013, BOE No 116, 15 May 2013, 36373.

[15] Micklitz and Reich (n 8) 800–01 speak of 'hidden constitutionalisation'.

[16] See I Domurath, 'Mortgage Debt and the Social Function of Contract' (2016) 22 *European Law Journal* 758, 766, reading the case law as presenting a more cooperative rather than an adversarial model for EU contract law.

the *Aziz* case also had its shadows, as Mr Aziz and his family did not benefit from the CJEU's findings: in appeal, only the standard default interest clause included in his mortgage contract was deemed to be unfair, and the outcome of the foreclosure proceedings was upheld.[17] This lesser-known dark side of the *Aziz* case, complemented by its brighter side, is a reason why the constitutionalisation of private legal questions in the interaction of national and European courts continues to deserve closer scrutiny.

III. PRIVATE LAW AND THE EUROPEAN POLITY

What 'constitutionalisation of private law' means is the second big question with which the chapters of this book engage. Considering the influence of fundamental rights reasoning on private legal cases as only one manifestation of this phenomenon, the inquiry is broadened to the question of what is being constituted through European private legal judgments. Accordingly, we turn to the idea of a European polity.

The term 'constitutionalisation' goes back to developments in the national laws of European countries, in which the inclusion of constitutional rights in the adjudication of private legal cases was given shape by embedding private legal orders in the norms and values of constitutional orders.[18] This limitation to the self-standing nature of private law is not uncontested.[19] It seems to have gained more ground in continental European systems that were under totalitarian or authoritarian rule at some point in the twentieth century (eg, Germany, Italy, Poland, Portugal and Spain) than in older continental European democracies (eg, France, Belgium, the Netherlands and Luxembourg) and non-continental European democracies (eg, the UK and the Nordic countries).[20] Despite the different intensity of constitutionalisation of private law, in national cases the private legal order still coincides with national borders. Accordingly, the political communities that are governed by a more or less constitutionalised national private law in principle coincide with the populations of nation-states.[21]

The Europeanisation of private law complicates this picture, insofar as it introduces fundamental rights that derive from the European level in national laws. In EU Member States, the ECHR and the EUCFR have arisen as sources for the constitutionalisation of private law in addition to national constitutional rights. Whereas the intensity of effects of national rights in private law is determined by national courts, two supranational institutions have a say in the interpretation and application of European fundamental rights: the ECtHR and the CJEU, respectively. As a consequence, the influence of European rights and judgments requires a rethinking of the political community or communities that can be related to the constitutionalisation of private law.

In public law, the EU's constitutional question has primarily been taken up in institutional terms. This involves the analysis of the type of entity that the EU is conceptually closest to: the nation-state, an international organisation or a *sui generis* category.[22] The nature of the

---

[17] Van Duin (n 12) 160–61; and Fernández Seijo, ch 15 in this volume.

[18] A Colombi Ciacchi, 'The Constitutionalization of European Contract Law: Judicial Convergence and Social Justice' (2006) 2 *European Review of Contract Law* 167, 167–68; HW Micklitz, 'Introduction' in Micklitz (n 6) 1.

[19] OO Cherednychenko, 'Subordinating Contract Law to Fundamental Rights: Towards a Major Breakthrough or towards Walking in Circles?' in Grundmann (n 6) 35–60.

[20] A Colombi Ciacchi, 'Judicial Governance in European Private Law: Three Judicial Cultures of Fundamental Rights Horizontality' (2020) 28 *European Review of Private Law* 931.

[21] G Comparato, *Nationalism and Private Law in Europe* (Oxford, Hart Publishing, 2014) 110–12.

[22] M Kumm, 'The Moral Point of Constitutional Pluralism: Defining the Domain of Legitimate Institutional Civil Disobedience and Conscientious Objection' in J Dickson and P Eleftheriadis (eds), *Philosophical Foundations*

European Constitution has in a somewhat similar manner been discussed in terms of one founded in a *demos*,[23] a self-standing cosmopolitan view or a dynamic reflexive form.[24] Furthermore, the relationship between national and EU legal orders and institutions has been addressed in terms of monism and pluralism, with theories of constitutional pluralism having become most influential.[25]

In private law, discourses on the constitutional dimension added by Europeanisation still seem somewhat more dispersed. Private legal scholarship took up the question of pluralism around the time that a Draft Common Frame of Reference was developed that promised to be a basis for more far-reaching harmonisation of private law on the European level.[26] Furthermore, developments in private law adjudication were linked to the debate on the EU's economic and social constitutions.[27] The constitutional discourse in private law thus gained a strong substantive dimension, especially in light of academic calls for an elaboration of a social justice agenda in EU legislation.[28] Given the fact that a more comprehensive codification of private law in Europe has not yet been realised, scholarship in the field does not seem to have fully explored the contributions that private law could make to a 'lasting constitutional settlement'.[29]

Although Europe does not have a constitution or a civil code[30] in any way similar to those that may be found in nation-states, both the discourses in public law and in private law still show a continuing concern with the political dimension of European integration and collaboration. Going back to the question of how a political community (or multiple communities) relates to private legal ordering, the EU presents a picture of a polity in the making, which is

---

of European Union Law (Oxford, Oxford University Press, 2012) 216–46; B de Witte, 'The European Union as an International Legal Experiment' in G de Búrca and JHH Weiler (eds), *The Worlds of European Constitutionalism* (Cambridge, Cambridge University Press, 2012) 19–56.

[23] Or multiple *demoi*; see K Nicolaïdis, 'The Idea of European Demoicracy' in Dickson and Eleftheriadis (n 22) 247–74.

[24] MA Wilkinson, 'Political Constitutionalism and the European Union' (2013) 76 *MLR* 191; M Loughlin, *Foundations of Public Law* (Oxford, Oxford University Press, 2010) 311.

[25] N Walker, 'The Idea of Constitutional Pluralism' (2002) 65 *MLR* 317; M Poiares Maduro, 'Contrapunctual Law: Europe's Constitutional Pluralism in Action' in N Walker (ed), *Sovereignty in Action* (Oxford, Hart Publishing, 2003) 501; M Kumm, 'Who is the Final Arbiter of Constitutionality in Europe? Three Conceptions of the Relationship between the German Federal Constitutional Court and the European Court of Justice' (1999) 36 *Common Market Law Review* 351. For further debate on these theories, see also N Krisch, *Beyond Constitutionalism: The Pluralist Structure of Postnational Law* (Oxford, Oxford University Press, 2010); M Avbelj and J Komárek (eds), *Constitutional Pluralism in the European Union and Beyond* (Oxford, Hart Publishing, 2012); JHH Weiler, 'Prologue: Global and Pluralist Constitutionalism: Some Doubts' in Weiler and de Búrca (n 22) 8–18. See also C Timmermans' review of the two aforementioned books, 'The Magic World of Constitutional Pluralism' (2014) 10 *European Constitutional Law Review* 349; J Baquero Cruz, *What's Left of the Law of Integration? Decay and Resistance in European Union Law* (Oxford, Oxford University Press, 2018), ch 3, 'Against Constitutional Pluralism'; and G Davies and M Avbelj (eds), *Research Handbook on Legal Pluralism and EU Law* (Cheltenham, Edward Elgar, 2018).

[26] L Niglia (ed), *Pluralism and European Private Law* (Oxford, Hart Publishing, 2013). For a more recent assessment of developments in theory and practice, see V Mak, *Legal Pluralism in European Contract Law* (Oxford, Oxford University Press, 2020).

[27] HW Micklitz, *The Politics of Justice in European Private Law: Social Justice, Access Justice, Societal Justice* (Cambridge, Cambridge University Press, 2018).

[28] Study Group on Social Justice in European Private Law, 'Social Justice in European Contract Law: A Manifesto' (2004) 10 *European Law Journal* 653. For a re-evaluation of the social justice dimensions of contract law in Europe, see D Caruso, '*Qu'ils mangent des contrats*: Rethinking Justice in EU Contract Law' in D Kochenov, G de Búrca and A Williams (eds), *Europe's Justice Deficit?* (Oxford, Hart Publishing, 2015) 367; M Fabre-Magnan, 'What is a Modern Law of Contracts? Elements for a New Manifesto for Social Justice in European Contract Law' (2017) 13 *European Review of Contract Law* 376.

[29] Study Group on Social Justice in European Private Law (n 28) 667.

[30] HW Micklitz, 'Failure or Ideological Preconceptions: Thoughts on Two Grand Projects: The European Constitution and the European Civil Code', EUI Working Paper LAW 2010/04.

governed by a compound of rules deriving from the European and national levels.[31] In some parts, the emerging polity can rely on quite extensive regulation of private legal relations through the constructive combination of Treaty provisions, Directives and national private laws. In other parts, the interaction of different types and sets of rules still poses challenges in light of the different underlying ideas of justice. As such, the polity-building dimension of private law may be said to encompass both the areas in which a constitutional settlement has been found and those in which the 'search of the European soul'[32] is ongoing.

IV. FIVE DIMENSIONS

In exploring the contributions of judge-made private law to the European polity, the chapters have been grouped according to five lines of inquiry: (a) the meaning and basis of polity-building in European private law; (b) rights; (c) remedies; (d) representation; and (e) reflections of judges on specific cases.

A. The Politics of European Private Law Adjudication

The chapters in Part I shed light on the different aspects of the politicisation of European private law adjudication. While private legal disputes are usually framed in highly technical terms, case law in specific areas undeniably touches upon politically sensitive questions. Betül Kas and Hans-W Micklitz's analysis in their chapter of the CJEU's case law in the field of consumer contract law makes clear what is at stake. Examining the more than 300 cases that the CJEU adjudicated upon preliminary references by national courts in the last 20 years, they trace the political aspects of European consumer law. The judicial assessment of seemingly technical disputes on credit and mortgage contracts and day-to-day consumer transactions can have much broader economic and societal implications than the facts of individual cases may suggest. As Kas and Micklitz show, this political dimension seems to become more apparent in collective conflicts with a strong societal dimension (eg, the mortgage cases) that require innovative legal solutions than in cases that are more firmly embedded in established legal doctrines. Tentatively, still, the authors demonstrate that CJEU-made private law can be considered an integral part of an emerging European polity, which builds on the interaction between the CJEU, the national courts, the national governments and the Euro-lawyers involved in and around the litigation.

The questions raised in this opening chapter go to the core of the debate on the constitutionalisation of private law in Europe, which concerns the different understandings of the nature and role of private law in relation to the constitution of political communities. The Europeanisation of private law has created new connections between individuals and groups in Member States: now they are not only part of political communities within their nation-States, but are also encompassed in the transnational community demarcated by EU consumer law. As Kas and Micklitz show, even passive consumers, who do not move from their place of

---

[31] C Eckes, *EU Powers under External Pressure: How the EU's External Actions Alter its Internal Structures* (Oxford, Oxford University Press, 2019) 5; C Eckes, 'The Court of Justice's Participation in Judicial Discourse: Theory and Practice' in M Cremona and A Thies (eds), *The European Court of Justice and External Relations Law* (Oxford, Hart Publishing, 2016) 183, 184.

[32] Kas and Micklitz, ch 2 in this volume.

residence, are affected by the European regulation of contracts allowing them to receive basic services and consumer goods. However, the fragmented manner in which the EU addresses questions of private law through targeted legal interventions does not make it easy to grasp the manner in which private law sustains a broader (consumption) polity.

In this sense, the constitutional dimension of private law on the EU level is quite different from that in nation-states. In the latter, codifications of private law were often fundamental to the constitution of the national political community, insofar as they provided a shared legal and political basis for the construction of national states.[33] In today's Europe, the sector-specific regulation of private legal matters results in a different dynamic. EU measures that affect private law are mostly justified on the basis of the combined objectives of redressing market failures and strengthening consumer protection. Accordingly, they target specific problems, such as unfair terms and issues relating to consumer sales. The picture of European private law that results is a patchwork one, which lacks a more coherent overarching general part.[34] As such, the constitutional dimension of European private law has to be imagined in different forms than that in nation-states.

The next two chapters, by Michael W Dowdle and Chantal Mak, engage in a dialogue on what could be a plausible theoretical explanation for the role of the judiciary based on different understandings of the constitutional nature of European private law. Dowdle proposes a 'doubly constitutional' role for contract law. According to his views, at the national level, contract law helps to constitute both the state and the market, insofar as it regulates market transactions and states are relying on markets to an increasing extent in order to fulfil their functions. Given the EU's even more prominent economic basis, Dowdle submits, the CJEU's relatively interventionist approach in cases like *Aziz*[35] can be explained by its reliance on contract law's role in sustaining both the European market and the EU's economic constitution. It is on this point that Dowdle and Mak differ: while they are in agreement that contract law has a state-constitutional or polity-building function, they hold different views on whether the CJEU's case law should be explained in terms of economic constitutionalism or rather a constitutionalism based on fundamental rights reasoning in private law. Mak proposes the latter, highlighting examples of case law of the CJEU and the ECtHR to show how a reading of private legal questions in light of fundamental rights opens up spaces for societal deliberations on the legal-political choices that are at stake in cases like *Aziz*. In her view, contributions of judge-made private law to the construction of a European polity do not relate only to market regulation, but also to the strengthening of the democratic dimension of European private law through inclusive deliberative processes. As the dialogue between Dowdle and Mak demonstrates, the view held on the constitutional role and nature of contract law – or, more broadly, private law – in a political community is thus decisive for understanding and guiding the work of judges at the interface of national and European law. In particular, their chapters provide starting points for further debate on the extent to which fundamental rights reasoning should be endorsed as a way of mediating this constitutional role (Mak) or rather give way to a more directly political reading of contract law's constitutional function (Dowdle).

The final chapter in Part I further elaborates on the CJEU's reasoning in private law adjudication and its relation to national courts in civil cases. Francesca Episcopo presents a critical

---

[33] S Rodotà, 'The Civil Code within the European "Constitutional Process"' in MW Hesselink (ed), *The Politics of a European Civil Code* (The Hague, Kluwer Law International, 2006) 115, 118; G Comparato, *Nationalism and Private Law in Europe* (Oxford, Hart Publishing, 2014) ch 4.

[34] AS Hartkamp, *European Law and National Private Law* (Antwerp, Intersentia, 2016) 143–45.

[35] *Aziz* (n 9).

reading of the Luxembourg Court's case law, indicating where judgments are in line with utopian ideals of judge-made private law and where they deviate from these. Focusing on the case law on effective judicial protection, Episcopo carefully deconstructs the Court's reasoning in order to show where constitutionalisation processes still fall short of presenting a clear image of the European polity. Notwithstanding the growing importance of Article 47 of the EUCFR (effective judicial protection) in private law, she contends, the case law still leaves many questions unanswered. These do not only regard the content and implications of Article 47, insofar as further clarification is needed of what constitutes effective private legal remedies. Perhaps more importantly, Episcopo argues, the question of what should be the basis for such remedies is not answered consistently. While the CJEU sometimes protects the right to effective judicial protection on its own merits, in other cases its reasoning seems primarily based on the effectiveness of EU law (*effet utile*). Accordingly, Episcopo submits, the CJEU's reasoning may be read as reflecting a 'latent ideology in the court's case law, strongly directed at ensuring the effectiveness of EU law by means of designing a supreme and self-referential legal system, even when hidden behind "fundamental rights-based" narratives'.[36] In order to obtain a better understanding of the case law, she suggests, a discursive reading on a case-by-case basis may clarify which questions the Court is seeking to answer and with which debates it is engaging. In this view, the role of national courts could be strengthened, insofar as a critical and discursive approach could serve to frame preliminary questions in such a way as to guide the debate. Complementing the discussion in the previous chapters on how the constitutional aspects of contract law should be understood, Episcopo thus adds insights into how the CJEU may be addressed in order to motivate it to develop a more consistent view on this constitutional dimension.

B. Rights

In Part II of this volume, the role of fundamental rights in shaping private legal relations is discussed on the basis of a core premise of European integration: the principle of non-discrimination. Two chapters examine the extent to which courts consider private actors, like public authorities, to be bound to this principle and how, in particular, freedom of contract is affected by fundamental rights reasoning in case law.

In her chapter, Betül Kas looks into the evolving balance between economic and social rationales in EU anti-discrimination law. She analyses a number of leading cases from the CJEU in order to obtain a better understanding of the manners in which fundamental rights have broadened and deepened the EU's protection against discrimination. In this context, the extent to which EU anti-discrimination law affects private legal relationships is still the subject of debate. Since EU law does not distinguish between public and private law, obligations under EU anti-discrimination law may in principle relate to both public and private actors. Thus, in theory, the freedom to choose with whom and on which terms to conclude a contract may be reduced to a vanishing point.[37] Kas traces the development of the CJEU's reasoning under EU anti-discrimination law in order to find out where case law draws the borderlines. She specifically focuses on the question whether and to what extent it requires

---

[36] Episcopo, ch 5 in this volume, section VII.
[37] H Collins, 'The Vanishing Freedom to Choose a Contractual Partner' (2013) 76 *Law and Contemporary Problems* 71.

profit-seeking businesses to act against the logic of the market in the interest of social inclusion. Placing the analysis in the key of the distinction between formal and substantive equality, as further conceptualised by Fredman,[38] Kas finds inconsistencies in the Court's approach. In judgments like *Feryn*[39] and *CHEZ*,[40] the CJEU embedded its reasoning in a substantive understanding of equality, which included considerations on participation in society and recognition of denigratory stereotyping behind certain statements or practices. The Court, however, took a very different approach in the cases of *Achbita*[41] and *Bougnaoui*,[42] which concerned the question of whether companies were allowed to prohibit employees from wearing religious symbols at work and, accordingly, dismiss female employees for wearing a Muslim headscarf. Adopting a formal notion of equality, the CJEU held that these kinds of company policies did not constitute direct discrimination, insofar as they prevented all employees from wearing visible signs of political, philosophical or religious beliefs. Such company policies could lead to indirect discrimination, the Court found, although this might be justified on the basis of a company's legitimate interest to project a neutral company image. Comparing the different cases, Kas concludes that the fundamental rights dimension of anti-discrimination law has not fully overtaken the initial economic rationale of EU law in this area. Nevertheless, it has provided more substantive protection in areas with a certain 'public-ness' about them, such as public statements in the employment sphere and the supply of energy services. The assessment of company policies concerning the right of employees to manifest their beliefs remains a complex issue on which the constitutionalisation of EU private law does not yet seem to have reached a final conclusion.

Equally addressing the balance between social and economic rationales in private law adjudication, Mateusz Grochowski's chapter shows how the non-discrimination principle may actually be strengthened by relating it to market freedom in consumer cases. He compares three recent judgments of supreme courts in different jurisdictions relating to the question of whether professional parties may refuse to conclude or perform a contract with a consumer on the basis of their religious or political convictions. His analysis shows similarities and differences in terms of how highest courts in different countries chose to frame the balance of fundamental rights in such cases. In the case of *Masterpiece Cakeshop v Colorado Civil Rights Commission*, the owner of a bakery argued that requiring him to create a cake for a same-sex wedding would violate his right to free speech by compelling him to exercise his artistic talents to express a message with which he disagreed and would violate his right to the free exercise of religion. The US Supreme Court affirmed that the baker could refuse to make a cake for a wedding of a same-sex couple and held that the Colorado Civil Rights Commission violated the Free Exercise Clause of the First Amendment by imposing a sanction on the baker for not accepting the customer's order.[43] In the case of *Lee v Ashers Bakery*, the UK Supreme Court relied on similar argumentation to find that a bakery could refuse to make a cake that would depict a statement in favour of the legalisation of same-sex marriage.[44] In contrast, in the case

---

[38] S Fredman, 'Substantive Equality Revisited' (2016) 14 *International Journal of Constitutional Law* 716.

[39] Case C-54/07 *Centrum voor gelijkheid van kansen en voor racismebestrijding v Firma Feryn NV* [2008] ECR I-5187.

[40] Case C-83/14 *'CHEZ Razpredelenie Bulgaria' AD v Komisia za zashtita ot diskriminatsia* EU:C:2015:480.

[41] Case C-157/15 *Samira Achbita and Centrum voor gelijkheid van kansen en voor racismebestrijding v G4S Secure Solutions NV* EU:C:2017:203.

[42] Case C-188/15 *Asma Bougnaoui and Association de défense des droits de l'homme (ADDH) v Micropole SA* EU:C:2017:204.

[43] *Masterpiece Cakeshop v Colorado Civil Rights Commission* 138 S Ct 1719, 201 L Ed 2d 35 (2018).

[44] *Lee v Ashers Baking Company Ltd and Others* [2018] UKSC 49.

of *National Public Prosecutor's Office v AJ (Printer from Łódź)*, the Polish Supreme Court held that a customer's order to print materials for an LGBT foundation could not be refused on the basis of the printer's individual beliefs.[45] Grochowski's analysis shows that an important factor in the balance made in the Polish judgment was that of the customer's freedom of contract and freedom of speech. Restrictions of this freedom could, in the view of the Polish Supreme Court, only be justified on the basis of objective religious reasons and not on the basis of the individual religious convictions of the printer. Considering the flipside of this line of reasoning, Grochowski submits that professional parties should not be allowed to refuse customers. His view is based on the idea that professionals who offer goods or services in a consumer market are under a 'public duty' not to discriminate among customers. Accordingly, the principle of non-discrimination limits the freedom of contract of those who are active on the consumer market in the sense that they may not refuse customers who accept their offer. According to Grochowski, it is justified to place limits on the professional's freedom to express their religious or ethical convictions by refusing to conclude or perform the contract. Thus, the comparative analysis of the judgments of the three Supreme Courts shows how a stronger emphasis on the public dimension of market activities of businesses may serve to prevent discrimination among consumers.

C. Remedies

Part III of the book contains a number of chapters that consider one of the most essential points of private law's contribution to the European polity, namely remedies, which in a broad sense can be understood to refer to legal means to assert rights or attain redress or relief. The authors in this part examine the remedies that European private law provides to those whose rights and interests have been adversely affected, and the ways in which these remedies are shaped in the interaction of national and European courts.[46] A particular focus is given to the influence of human rights reasoning in the development of new measures and institutional structures for enforcing legal rights, with a leading role for Article 47 EUCFR, being the most invoked Charter provision at the national level.

In her chapter, Giulia Gentile carefully maps and analyses the CJEU's case law on Article 47 EUCFR, thus casting light on what the norm has added to the understanding of effective judicial protection in the EU. Her overview demonstrates the breadth of the content of Article 47, impacting both procedural and substantive justice in the Member States: Article 47 has contributed to the safeguarding of procedural guarantees that allow individuals to ascertain and defend their right before courts, while from a substantive perspective, it has influenced the granting of effective remedies to redress violations of EU rights. Examining how Article 47 has influenced the division of competences between the Member States and the EU, Gentile considers the margin of discretion that has been left by the CJEU to national judges when indirectly reviewing the compliance of national procedural rules with Article 47 EUCFR via the preliminary reference procedure. Her study of the case law shows that there is no rigid margin of discretion and thus no fixed division of competences between the CJEU and the national

---

[45] *National Public Prosecutor's Office v AJ (Printer from Łódź)* Case II KK 333/17, published: OSNKW (Judgments of the Supreme Court, Criminal and Military Chambers) 2018, no 9, item 61.
[46] HW Micklitz, 'The ECJ between the Individual Citizen and the Member States: A Plea for a Judge-Made Law on Remedies' in HW Micklitz and B de Witte (eds), *The European Court of Justice and the Autonomy of the Member States* (Cambridge, Intersentia, 2012) 347.

courts. Instead, she reveals that there are various degrees of discretion, which are determined by two factors: the detailedness of the applicable procedural and remedial rules in EU secondary law and the enhancement of the system of remedies in the Member States under Article 19 of the Treaty on European Union (TEU). Particularly where Article 47 EUCFR and Article 19 TEU are invoked together, not only is the margin of discretion narrow, but the CJEU's interpretative powers are also pronounced. Finally, she uncovers how the case law on the essence of Article 47 EUCFR – constituting the provision's non-derogable core according to Article 52(1) EUCFR – reinforces the CJEU's role in depicting the EU's constitutional identity. In the absence of a clear judicial methodology that guides the identification of the core of Article 47, she observes that the CJEU appears to make 'strategic use' of the concept of essence, specifically with 'a signalling function, in order to highlight the importance of the violation of EU law' at stake.[47]

In her chapter, Anna van Duin further elucidates the 'signalling function' of Article 47 EUCFR by examining the provision's role in consumer debt collection cases that fall under the scope of the EU Directive on Unfair Terms in Consumer Contracts. Her analysis shows that Article 47 is not only employed by the CJEU to highlight systemic problems of the effective protection of EU rights, but may also empower national courts to trigger or support reform processes at the national level. She illustrates her argument by reconstructing the socio-legal background of the CJEU's judgment in *Finanmadrid*,[48] which arose out of one of the numerous preliminary references that were submitted by Spanish courts to address shortfalls in their national civil justice system that became painfully visible in the aftermath of the 2007–2008 financial crisis. The referring court in this case was asked by a financial institution to enforce an order for payment that was issued by a court registrar against a consumer-debtor without examination of the fairness of the contractual terms of the loan agreement. The CJEU held that the court must have the power to perform an *ex officio* control of the contractual terms as a last resort. However, it did not address the referring court's concerns regarding the protection of Article 47 EUCFR relating to a potential violation of the rights of defence of the consumer and, in general, the outsourcing of adjudicative competences to a court registrar. According to Van Duin, the national court's reference to Article 47 signified a call for change, which was subsequently addressed by the Spanish legislature and the Constitutional Court.[49] She suggests that the Spanish experience of an 'open constitutionalisation' of questions of judicial protection in consumer cases could inform judicial practices in other Member States, such as the Netherlands, where procedural bottlenecks have also surfaced in debt collection cases, but no discussion in constitutional terms took place.

In his chapter, Fabrizio Cafaggi presents an innovative view on the enforcement of EU rights through the interaction of administrative and judicial protection. He raises awareness of the fact that courts are not the only forum involved in the protection of rights in legal relationships between private parties by depicting the European institutional architecture as an 'enforcement triangle' that also encompasses administrative protection and alternative dispute resolution systems. He focuses on the rise of administrative enforcement, which, in his view: (i) has not emerged at the expense of, but as a complement to judicial protection; and (ii) may not diminish the level of legal protection. Their complementarity is explained with a view to

---

[47] Gentile, ch 8 in this volume, section III.A.

[48] Case C-49/14 *Finanmadrid EFC SA v Jesús Vicente Albán Zambrano and Others* EU:C:2016:98.

[49] Articles 552.1 and 815.4 of the Ley de Enjuiciamiento Civil; Ley 42/2015, de reforma de la Ley de Enjuiciamiento Civil; Tribunal Constitucional, judgment no 58/2016 of 17 March 2016, ES:TC:2016:58.

the different objectives and instruments of judicial and administrative protection. From an institutional perspective, the most pertinent difference relates to the fact that administrative enforcement usually focuses on the infringer, while judicial enforcement is driven by private actors, usually the victims of the violation. Looking at the instruments, the differences clearly emerge with respect to *ex ante* advisory powers and *ex post* cooperative enforcement through commitments and monitoring tasks that belong only to administrative enforcement. Sanctions and remedies are common to both administrative and judicial protection. Focusing on the latter instruments, Cafaggi shows that institutional and substantive coordination among national enforcers is key to ensure compliance with the right to an effective remedy, which, according to him, also applies to administrative enforcement, namely as part of the general principle of good administration. Currently, specific coordination rules are largely missing in EU legislation, which profoundly affects the effectiveness of EU law – such as in consumer and data protection – and may give rise to violations of the right to an effective remedy and procedural guarantees.

D. Representation

The chapters in Part IV are grouped under the theme of representation. These chapters in different ways may be read as addressing the potential for private law adjudication to recognise and include those affected by harmful actions of private actors in political communities.[50] For this purpose, all three chapters in this part examine case law on climate change and environmental pollution.

In her chapter, Laura E Burgers addresses the question of *who* is involved in judicial law-making processes. In particular, she investigates the representation of future generations in European private law climate change litigation. While political systems' short-termism fails to properly take the needs of future generations into account, legal sources at the international, European and national levels have recognised their relevance. Hence, Burgers raises the question whether the courts are fulfilling their legal duty to consider future generations in climate change litigation and how they approach the theoretical challenges posed by their representation. Specifically, she identifies four main challenges of future generation's representation discussed in political theory, namely the 'plurality problem', the 'non-identity problem', the 'authorisation problem' and the indeterminacy of climate change's exact implications as such. In her analysis of three case studies in which non-governmental organisations or individuals have challenged the failure of governmental authorities to take sufficient measures against climate change, she showcases how the problems re-emerge and are addressed in the reasoning of the courts and the parties. The ruling of the Hague Court of First Instance in the *Urgenda* case stands out for its readiness to accept the Urgenda Foundation's standing on behalf of future generations.[51] To some extent, the Oslo Court of Appeal in the *Arctic Oil* case also recognised future generations' relevance.[52] However, looking at the ruling of the Norwegian

---

[50] *cf* Nancy Fraser's distinction between the who, what and how of justice in transnationalised political (and legal) spheres; N Fraser, *Scales of Justice: Reimagining Political Space in a Globalizing World* (Cambridge, Polity Press, 2008) 12–29.

[51] Rechtbank Den Haag, 24 June 2015, NL:RBDHA:2015:7145.

[52] Borgarting Lagmannsrett, 23 January 2020, case no 18-060499ASD-BORG/03.

Supreme Court in *Arctic Oil*[53] and the CJEU's rejection of legal standing in the *People's Climate Case*,[54] Burgers concludes that the political system's short-term bias has not yet been fully outbalanced by the judiciary due to the latter's concern over overstepping the boundaries of its legitimate role within the separation of powers principle.

In his chapter, Luca Ettore Perriello broadens our perspective on *what* is and needs to be represented by investigating the interests that are implicated by litigation surrounding environmental damage. Specifically, his reconstruction of the *Ilva* case study highlights the political and legal complexities that have arisen in addressing the health-damaging pollution stemming from the operations of one of the largest steel plants in Europe. The Ilva plant in Taranto is of strategic importance for the Italian economy and a major employer in a region with high levels of unemployment. Perriello demonstrates how the *Ilva* case requires the courts to engage in a complex balancing exercise between health and the environment on the one hand, and production and employment on the other. He argues that the judicial treatment of the *Ilva* case has not yet resulted in satisfactory outcomes. While the Italian Constitutional Court gave priority to work over health instead of reconciling both rights,[55] the ECtHR found violations of the right to private life (Article 8 ECHR) and the right to an effective remedy (Article 13 ECHR), but refused to award damages, considering that the finding of the violations amounted to sufficient reparation for the moral damages suffered by the applicants.[56] Perriello advocates for the recognition of individual or 'reflected damages' in judicial practice, allowing individuals to claim compensation for the losses they have suffered with respect to their life, health and property as a result of environmental damage caused by private activities. According to him, the criticism levelled against reflected damages in scholarship is unwarranted and the Italian framework may be interpreted to offer more comprehensive reparation to the victims. Drawing to the unilateral role of Ilva in preventing damage and the irrelevance of Ilva's compliance with the permits granted to it, Perriello reasons that reflected damages should be awarded compensation through a strict rule of liability. Finally, looking at a variety of other instruments, he highlights and concludes that the desirability of civil liability lies in its potential to unfold significant preventive effects.

In the last chapter in this part, Monika Hinteregger examines *how* private law mechanisms can contribute to big societal questions such as climate change. She analyses the technicalities of private legal cases on climate change, showing both the limitations and possibilities for case law in terms of shaping the legal framework for addressing climate change. Specifically, she examines how courts could in the future approach the proof of a causal link for establishing tortious liability in climate change litigation. Establishing the proof of a direct causal link between greenhouse gas emissions by a specific private actor and the harm sustained is one of the key hurdles that must be overcome in order for a claim to be successful. Hinteregger demonstrates that the traditional methods of establishing causation – the 'but for' test of the common law and the 'conditio sine qua non' formula of the civil law systems – are not always suitable to ensure justice in individual cases. This has been recognised by the courts, which have shown their willingness to transgress the traditional boundaries of tort law doctrine in specific circumstances. In that respect, Hinteregger highlights cases where courts developed

---

[53] Noregs Høgsterett, 22 December 2020, case no 20-051052SIV-HRET.

[54] Case C-565/19 P *Armando Carvalho and Others v European Parliament and Council of the European Union* EU:C:2021:252.

[55] Corte costituzionale, 9 April 2013, no 85 (2014) *Foro italiano* I 441.

[56] *Cordella and Others v Italy* App Nos 54414/13 and 54264/15 (ECtHR, 24 January 2019) CE:ECHR:2019:0124 JUD005441413.

far-reaching strategies to alleviate the burden of victims that encountered difficulties in proving causality. Examples are the creation of the theory of market share liability by the US courts to deal with compensation claims for harm caused by the exposure to Diethylstilbestrol (DES),[57] the 'increased material risk of harm' test developed by the UK Supreme Court to facilitate compensation claims of workers who had been exposed to asbestos,[58] or the French Supreme Court's change of approach in terms of dealing with scientific uncertainty in relation to compensation claims brought by individuals who developed multiple sclerosis after having been vaccinated.[59] Based on these experiences, and considering that as climate change intensifies, dangerous weather events are becoming more frequent and severe, Hinteregger expects that the courts will in the future also see the necessity to adapt tort law doctrine to the challenges posed by climate change litigation. Although courts are faced with a difficult and challenging task in order to do so, Hinteregger claims that they can find at least some of the necessary instruments in existing tort law theory, such as in the concepts of minimal causation and proportionate liability.

E. Reflections

Finally, the academic exploration of the role of courts in the development of European private law is complemented by insights from legal practice in Part V of this book. In this part, two judges who in their daily practice deal with cases that combine elements of national and European law reflect on the judicial task and the strengths and weaknesses of the interaction with the European level of adjudication.

In her chapter, Cassandra CW Lange examines the self-understanding of 'the job of the judge' in the interplay between the national and European legal orders. Lange is a State Councillor at the Administrative Law Division of the Council of State of the Netherlands in The Hague, which is one of the highest instances in administrative cases. Previously, she practised as a judge in civil cases. Her chapter focuses on the influence that the right to effective judicial protection, as safeguarded by Article 47 EUCFR, can have on the ways in which judges understand their role. She contrasts two recent Dutch cases in order to illustrate the balance that judges need to strike in terms of fulfilling their tasks. On the one hand, in relation to the *Urgenda* climate case, which concerned a tort claim against the Dutch state aimed at enforcing its obligations to reduce greenhouse gas emissions, the question arose as to whether courts were overstepping the boundaries of their tasks by ruling on the executive branch's actions to tackle climate change.[60] On the other hand, in relation to a large number of cases concerning childcare allowances that were dealt with so severely that parents ended up in significant personal and financial difficulties, the question was raised as to whether the courts should have been more assertive in countering the effects of an excessively strict government policy against tax fraud. Lange finds a benchmark in Article 47 EUCFR for judges to assess where to strike the balance when establishing what effective judicial protection entails, which she deems of

---

[57] See, eg, the famous ruling of the Supreme Court of California in *Sindell v Abbott Laboratories* 607 P2d 924 (Cal 1980).

[58] *Fairchild v Glenhaven Funeral Services Ltd* [2002] UKHL 22, [2003] 1 AC 32.

[59] Cour de cassation 1re civ, 22 May 2008, no 05-20.317, Bulletin 2008, I, no 148; Cour de cassation 1re civ, 22 May 2008, no 06-10.967, Bulletin 2008, I, no 149. The CJEU confirmed the compliance of the French Supreme Court's approach with Council Directive 85/374/EEC concerning liability for defective products ([1985] OJ L210/29) in Case C-621/15 NW and Others v Sanofi Pasteur MSD SNC and Others EU:C:2017:484.

[60] Hoge Raad, 20 December 2019, NL:HR:2019:2006.

special importance in countries like the Netherlands, where a similar constitutional provision is (as yet) missing.[61]

Furthermore, Lange commends judicial training projects for allowing judges from different EU Member States to exchange experiences and emphasises the importance of judicial independence. Exploring the space created by Article 47 EUCFR for judges to shape remedies in cases with a European dimension, she carefully lists the questions that arise in this context: to what extent can judges set aside procedural rules or develop new remedies in order to safeguard effective protection? In which cases should judges be more active or creative to find remedies and in which cases should they wait for the legislature to step in? On the basis of insights from a recent opinion of two Advocates General in the childcare allowance cases[62] and the judgment of the Council of State,[63] she shows how Article 47 EUCFR may serve to offer some more leeway to judges in terms of providing effective remedies. Thus, the interaction of national law with European rights and principles can serve the process of balancing the different dimensions of the judicial task.

Finally, in his chapter, José María Fernández Seijo shares his reflections on 'the lights and shadows of the *Aziz* case', in which he was the national judge who submitted the preliminary reference to the CJEU on the compatibility of the Spanish law on mortgage enforcements with the EU Directive on Unfair Terms in Consumer Contracts.[64] According to him, considering previous case law, the ruling of the Court in *Aziz* cannot be considered a legal revolution, but rather was to be expected. Instead, the significance of *Aziz* lies in the socio-economic context out of which it emerged, namely a severe economic and financial crisis. As he explains, the ruling's effects outside the doctrinal realm were enormous, leading to a profound procedural reform in Spain and opening up an avenue for civil judges to protect millions of citizens affected by unfair terms in loan agreements. The 'lights' of the *Aziz* ruling have indeed been highlighted by numerous scholars. However, Fernández Seijo's reflections reach beyond the laudable story of the *Aziz* case. Instead, he chooses to narrate the personal story of Mr Aziz. Indeed, each preliminary reference to the CJEU arises out of a very concrete case and the story of Mr Aziz did not end happily. As recounted by Fernández Seijo, Mr Aziz was evicted from his home before the Court's ruling and the Advocate General's opinion were rendered. Thus, while the Advocate General's opinion was already a trigger for the Spanish courts to halt most of the ongoing enforcement proceedings, Mr Aziz could not achieve the same effect for himself and his family. All subsequent attempts of Mr Aziz to regain his home failed. The 'shadows' of the *Aziz* case thus leave Fernández Seijo with a bitter aftertaste.

The chapters by the two judges provide an additional layer to the study of the judicial role in an emerging European polity. They illustrate what are the potential benefits and limits of fundamental rights reasoning in European private law adjudication, showing how judges explore the space that these rights offer for creating new remedies and doing justice to different people and interests represented in the specific cases. They also highlight where tensions are perceived between the search for a just solution in the individual case and broader questions on the relationship between national and European ideals.

---

[61] A law proposal is currently pending that may partially make up for this omission by constitutionally entrenching the right to a fair trial; *Kamerstukken II* 2020/21, 35784, no 2, www.eerstekamer.nl/wetsvoorstel/35784_opnemen_van_een_bepaling.

[62] Raad van State, Opinion of the Advocates General, 7 July 2021, NL:RVS:2021:1468.

[63] Raad van State, 2 February 2022, NL:RVS:2022:285.

[64] *Aziz* (n 9).

Insofar as judge-made private law can be considered to be a part of the emerging European polity, in concrete cases this constitutional dimension of European private law manifests itself in the cooperation among courts on different levels of governance that contributes to the maintenance of a sphere for contestation and deliberation. In the case of the ECtHR, this influence can be quite direct, through the Strasbourg Court's assessment of the compliance of national legislation and adjudication with the Convention. More indirectly, the ECtHR's judgments also affect the legal systems of other states parties than the one addressed in the specific case by setting out an interpretation of Convention rights by which all have to abide. In the case of the CJEU and national civil courts, judicial conversations are mediated through the preliminary reference procedure. In the division of tasks between the European and national levels, the CJEU is responsible for the interpretation of EU law, whereas it is for the national courts to integrate this understanding of the law in the resolution of specific cases. The reflection pieces that conclude the book provide us with the viewpoints of two national judges on how they understand their role in this multi-layered setting.

Thus, the reflections of Judges Lange and Fernández Seijo offer invaluable insights into the ways in which national judges make connections with European law to find new solutions. They show which institutional and substantive questions judges encounter in this process. Furthermore, by sharing the stories of actual cases, these judicial reflections show glimpses of the reality of those, like Mr Aziz, whose personal circumstances were determined through the interplay of national and European rules. The reasoning of judges like Lange and Fernández Seijo in such cases connects the personal stories with communities that transcend the boundaries of the nation-state. In conclusion, therefore, their contributions complement the academic discourse that seeks to understand the role of civil courts in the European polity.

Part I

The Politics of European Private Law Adjudication

2

Judge-Made European Private Law and European Polity-Building

BETÜL KAS AND HANS-W MICKLITZ

I. TWO WORLDS APART

WHEN PUBLIC LAWYERS speak about the European Union (EU), the autonomous legal order or the constitutional legal order, they discuss to what extent the EU can be compared with a nation-state or whether it should be regarded as a *sui generis* institution. When private lawyers speak about the EU in constitutional language, they speak about the economic or social constitution, private law society or the constitutionalisation of private law. The purpose of this chapter is to bring the two strands of discourses together and to relate them to the phenomenon of judge-made European private law, which here is equated with the more than 300 judgments that the Court of Justice of the European Union (CJEU) rendered between 2002 and mid-2022 in the field of secondary European private law.[1] This chapter thus investigates whether the CJEU-made private law may be understood as an integral part of the process of European polity-building. Whilst the focus of the case law is on consumer issues,

---

[1] Overviews of the judgments that have been rendered between 2002 and mid-2018 can be found in HW Micklitz, 'Rechtsprechungsübersicht zum Europäischen Verbraucherrecht: Vertrags- und Deliktsrecht' (2006) *Europäisches Wirtschafts- und Steuerrecht (EWS)* 1; HW Micklitz, 'Rechtsprechungsübersicht zum Europäischen Verbraucherrecht: Vertrags- und Deliktsrecht' (2008) *EWS* 353; B Kas and HW Micklitz, 'Rechtsprechungsübersicht zum Europäischen Vertrags- und Deliktsrecht (2008–2013) – Teil I' (2013) *EWS* 314; B Kas and HW Micklitz, 'Rechtsprechungsübersicht zum Europäischen Vertrags- und Deliktsrecht (2008–2013) – Teil II' (2013) *EWS* 353; B Kas and HW Micklitz, 'Rechtsprechungsübersicht zum Europäischen Vertrags- und Deliktsrecht (2014–2018) – Teil I' (2018) *EWS* 181; B Kas and HW Micklitz 'Rechtsprechungsübersicht zum Europäischen Vertrags- und Deliktsrecht (2014–2018) – Teil II' (2018) *EWS* 241. We have collected and added the judgments that have been rendered between mid-2018 and mid-2022. These overviews are not published. It should be noted that our collection of case law is limited to 'judgments' of the CJEU. It is noticeable that the Court is increasingly making use of the possibility to reply to preliminary references by 'reasoned order' in the area of secondary European private law, specifically with respect to the Unfair Terms Directive 93/13/EEC ([1993] OJ L95/29). According to art 99 of the Rules of Procedure of the Court of Justice ([2012] OJ L265/1), the Court may reply by order when a preliminary ruling is identical to a question on which the Court has already ruled, where the reply to such a question may be clearly deduced from existing case law or where the answer to the question referred for a preliminary ruling admits of no reasonable doubt. In view of the increasing number of decisions, we had to exclude 'orders' from our overviews for practical reasons. For an interesting view as to what the increasing use of adjudicating orders may signify, see U Šadl, D Naurin, L López Zurita and SA Brekke, 'That's an Order! The Orders of the CJEU and the Effect of Article 99 RoP on Judicial Cooperation' (2020) iCourts Working Paper Series No 219: 'The findings suggest that the Court uses adjudicating orders to disengage from "local" problems and unilaterally terminate the conversations with resolute national courts.'

the judgments of the CJEU have legal effects far beyond the domain in the overall field of private law. This is true for two reasons. First, doctrinally many of the substantive questions affect small and medium-sized enterprises (SMEs) in one way or another and therefore raise the question whether consumer law can also serve as a standard for the protection of SMEs against large businesses. Second, and maybe more importantly, the kind of polity the CJEU is building is not limited to consumer law, but more generally to the private law 'field' in the meaning of Pierre Bourdieu, as we will develop below.

The chapter unfolds in three steps. The first is an elaboration of the conceptual and theoretical framework in which the idea of an EU polity needs to be embedded. This requires a deeper look into constitutional theories to justify why the link between CJEU-made private law and the European polity looks promising. This part will rely on three sources: *The Politics of Judicial Co-operation in the EU*,[2] *The Politics of Justice in European Private Law*[3] and the review article 'The European Union Project'.[4] The second step consists of the stock-taking and systematisation of the CJEU case law, which brings the debate down to earth as a counterpoint to high-flying constitutional theories. In the third step, these two – the theoretical strands and the realities of CJEU-made private law – are merged together with a view to clarifying the added value of the European polity paradigm in private law.

A. Constitutional Theories and the Missing Private Law

Ever since the CJEU held that the EU is governed by an autonomous legal order, later upgraded to a constitutional order, legal scholarship has debated how to classify the EU. This discussion has raised the question whether the autonomous legal order embraces private law. It must be recalled that the CJEU never used the same language with respect to private law. There is not a single case where the CJEU speaks about the 'autonomous European private law order'. In a handful of cases, the Court referred to 'general principles of civil law',[5] although this was not repeated in later rulings. European private law has developed in a piecemeal and unsystematic fashion through the adoption of secondary EU law regulating market activities in different sectors to serve various policy goals. Its implementation and categorisation within the national legal orders is left to the Member States. Hence, EU private law does not need to become part of the national private legal orders as defined by the Member States.[6]

The last few years have forcefully demonstrated the never-ending academic interest in the correct classification of the EU as a statutory or quasi-statutory body. In his review article of Pavlos Eleftheriadis' book *A Union of Peoples*,[7] Massimo Fichera provides for an insightful

---

[2] HW Micklitz, *The Politics of Judicial Co-operation in the EU: Sunday Trading, Equal Treatment and Good Faith* (Cambridge, Cambridge University Press, 2005).

[3] HW Micklitz, *The Politics of Justice in European Private Law: Social Justice, Access Justice, Societal Justice* (Cambridge, Cambridge University Press, 2018).

[4] HW Micklitz, 'The European Union Project, Review Article on J Dickson and P Eleftheriadis (eds), *The Philosophical Foundations of European Union Law*' (2013) 32 *Yearbook of European Law* 538.

[5] Case C-277/05 *Société thermale d'Eugénie-les-Bains v Ministère de l'Économie, des Finances et de l'Industrie* [2007] ECR I-6415; Case C-412/06 *Annelore Hamilton v Volksbank Filder eG* [2008] ECR I-2383; Case C-489/07 *Pia Messner v Firma Stefan Krüger* [2009] ECR I-7315; Case C-215/08 *E Friz GmbH v Carsten von der Heyden* [2010] ECR I-2947; Case C-174/12 *Alfred Hirmann v Immofinanz AG* EU:C:2013:856.

[6] For a recent account of the debate on the relationship between EU law and national private law, see OO Cherednychenko, 'Islands and the Ocean: Three Models of the Relationship between EU Market Regulation and National Private Law' (2021) 84 *MLR* 1294.

[7] M Fichera, 'Solidarity, Heterarchy, and Political Morality' (2020) 2 *Jus Cogens* 301.

account of the different strands in constitutional theory and legal philosophy to get to grips with the particularities of the EU. He distinguishes between the hierarchical and the heterarchical paradigms. Those who focus on the hierarchical paradigm must decide whether the national or the EU legal order is at the top of the hierarchy. Their approach is either state-centred or in one way or another federalist. Those who subscribe to a heterarchical paradigm reject both monism and dualism, and submit that the particularities of the EU cannot be caught in hierarchical categories.

Whatever the language used – the EU as a constitution, a supranational state or a polity – and whatever legal concept of the state and legal philosophy serves as the reference point (with Kelsen and Hart as key actors), it is striking that the role and function of private law in the understanding of the constitutional character of the EU is more or less absent, even if genuine private law categories are used, as Eleftheriadis does.[8] Maybe the gap is due to the fact that the whole idea of a Common Market and later on the Internal Market is implicitly based on the existence of private law that enables private parties to realise the four freedoms. The big theories focus on the EU as a constitution, on constitutionalism and on polity-building, notwithstanding the fact that since the 1920s, private law theory has discussed the idea of an 'economic constitution' and a 'private law society', a notion that had a strong impact on the conceptualisation of the EU in the political and theoretical discourse. Kaarlo Tuori is one of the few constitutional theorists who has taken up this strand in the 'many constitutions', where the economic constitution, but not yet the social constitution, forms a building block in his conceptualisation of the EU.[9]

However, what is true for the constitutional discourse is equally true for the private law discourse. There is not much connection between the grand constitutional theories on the one hand and the attempts of private lawyers to get to grips with private law beyond the nation-state on the other hand. The only connection between the two seems to be the 'economic constitution', where the problem of the EU legal order as a hierarchical order re-appears. When it comes to the heterarchical paradigm, private law theory focuses not so much on European private law as on transnational private law, of which the European legal order explicitly or implicitly forms an integral part. Rodotà showed how codifications of private law played an essential role in the constitution of a collective identity in the development of the nation-state and pictured its role 'in the transition from a Europe of the market to a Europe of the rights'.[10] Seen this way, the failure of the building of a European Constitution and a European Civil Code[11] rendered the making of a homogeneous European collective identity even more difficult.

One of the authors of this chapter has tried to conceptualise the heterarchical European private legal order by focusing on four constitutive parameters: self-sufficiency, convergence, hybridisation and conflict.[12] This conceptualisation of European private law comes close to an understanding of a legal order based on moral practical reasoning. The claim is that EU

---

[8] He refers to tort law and corrective justice as key elements of his conceptualisation of the EU as progressive internationalism; see P Eleftheriadis, *A Union of Peoples: Europe as a Community of Principle* (Oxford, Oxford University Press, 2020) chs 8 and 9.

[9] K Tuori, *European Constitutionalism* (Cambridge, Cambridge University Press, 2015).

[10] S Rodotà, 'The Civil Code within the European "Constitutional Process"' in MW Hesselink (ed), *The Politics of a European Civil Code* (The Hague, Kluwer Law International, 2006) 115, 121.

[11] HW Micklitz, 'Failure or Ideological Preconceptions – Thoughts on Two Grand Projects: The European Constitution and the European Civil Code' (2010) EUI LAW Working Paper 2010/04.

[12] See the ERC project on 'European Regulatory Private Law' at: www.cordis.europa.eu/project/id/269722/it.

private law is offering access justice and societal justice as unique values that hold the European private legal order together.[13] It is a heterarchical order of bits and pieces, because there is no central authority that holds all the power. This key position remains empty.[14] Our analysis of the CJEU-made private law and its impact on polity-building complements the overall picture.

B. Constitutionalisation of Private Law

For more than three decades, private law theorists have been discussing the constitutionalisation of private law, first at the national level and later at the European level. A clarification is needed for two reasons: first because of a possible link between the constitutionalisation of private law and the legal constitutional discourse on the EU, and second because the CJEU-made private law enjoys constitutional standing, at least if one subscribes to a hierarchical understanding of the EU, most clearly in the federal vision of the EU.

The constitutionalisation of private law is a dazzling term. First, constitutionalisation may mean the materialisation of private law through fundamental and human rights. This is by far the dominant discourse, particularly with respect to the idea that constitutionalisation should remedy justice deficits in private law, whether national or European. The CJEU's more recent move towards the recognition of the horizontal direct effect of fundamental rights in the EU Charter has even enhanced these expectations.[15] Second, the constitutionalisation of private law is enshrined in the idea of a private law society (*Privatrechtsgesellschaft*), as presented in Franz Böhm's social theory of an economic constitution for a nation-state.[16] In the EU, the idea of an economic constitution triggered a debate on the constitutional standing of the four freedoms and competition law. This is the second form of the constitutionalisation of private law. Third, constitutionalisation refers to the self-constitutionalisation of private law beyond the nation-state. This strand of the debate leads to transnational legal theories and suffers from differentiation between transnational private law and European transnational private law (with or without 'private').[17] Few attempts have been made to disconnect European private law from the broad strand of transnational legal theories in order to look for eventual distinctive features of European private law.[18]

Quite often, constitutionalisation is narrowed down to the analysis of CJEU judgments that refer explicitly or implicitly to human and fundamental rights. In the field of private law, these kinds of references are the exception to the rule, and it does not appear that the CJEU is ready to make extensive use of fundamental and human rights in private law decisions. The impact of the 'economic constitution' – as defined by Böhm and Mestmäcker – on private law is strong, but often neglected. The CJEU has endlessly interfered through the four freedoms into private legal relations and has thereby transformed private legal concepts, such as the legal subject, contract, tort, and remedies.[19]

---

[13] Micklitz (n 3).

[14] Micklitz (n 4) 551.

[15] Joined Cases C-569/16 and C-570/16 *Stadt Wuppertal v Maria Elisabeth Bauer and Volker Willmeroth v Martina Broßonn* EU:C:2018:871.

[16] F Böhm, 'Privatrechtsgesellschaft und Marktwirtschaft' (1966) 17 *ORDO: Jahrbuch für die Ordnung von Wirtschaft und Gesellschaft* 75.

[17] See A Beckers, HW Micklitz, R Vallejo Garretón and P Letto-Vanamo (eds), *The Foundations of European Transnational Private Law* (Oxford, Hart Publishing, forthcoming, 2023).

[18] An example is L Niglia (ed), *Pluralism and European Private Law* (Oxford, Hart Publishing, 2013).

[19] HW Micklitz and C Sieburgh (eds), *Primary EU Law and Private Law Concepts* (Cambridge, Intersentia, 2017).

But there is a loose end in the debate about the constitutionalisation of private law – one that matters in our examination of the CJEU-made private law in secondary European private law. As early as 1978, the ECJ held in *Simmenthal*[20] that not only primary EU law but also secondary EU law enjoys supremacy. In *Marshall*[21] the CJEU granted secondary EU law vertical direct effect. The struggle over the potential horizontal direct effect of EU directives is ongoing. Although the CJEU comes ever closer, to date it has rejected the horizontal direct effect of directives. The transfer of constitutional language to private law has triggered questions and resistance from the 1990s onwards. The key question was and is what it means for the national private legal orders if secondary EU law enjoys supremacy over private law. There is a huge amount of debate on this topic. It suffices to refer to G Teubner and C Joerges, who have amply shown how the hierarchical interference in the national legal systems leads to 'irritation' or 'diagonal conflicts'.[22]

We will stay away from the constitutional rhetoric and will instead connect the analysis to more recent strands in the search for the European soul, to which the CJEU-made private law can more easily be connected. There are three candidates: the role and function of private law in the building of a European society, the understanding of European private law as an epistemic community (or communities) and the linking of European private law to a European polity. For the purposes of clarification, the first two will be sketched out roughly before moving to the European polity, which seems to be the most promising and innovative avenue.

C. European Society, the Epistemic Community and Private Law

Putting private law into the limelight in the search for the European soul brings the idea of a 'private law society' back to the fore, which is enshrined in the idea of an economic constitution. Private law society – *Privatrechtsgesellschaft* – does not make much sense without explaining the background of Sinzheimer, Böhm, Mestmäcker and Schweitzer, the proponents (H Dagan and M Heller's liberal theory of contract)[23] and the critique (in M Hesselink's *Justifying Contract in Europe*)[24] or the much deeper conflict between Mestmäcker defending an economic constitution based on private autonomy and competition law, and Wiethölter's attempt to democratise the economy through law.[25] For our purposes, it might suffice to recall that the debate around the private law society and the economic (democratic) constitution is still a unique account in terms of developing a legal concept of society, an issue which is usually left to political science and sociology. Lawyers and even legal theory tend to refer to 'society' without trying to clarify what is meant. The essence of the concept is that private parties are the prime holders of the responsibility for societal order. What matters in our context is the

---

[20] Case C-106/77 *Amministrazione delle Finanze dello Stato v Simmenthal SpA* [1978] ECR 629.

[21] Case C-152/84 *MH Marshall v Southampton and South-West Hampshire Area Health Authority* [1986] ECR 723.

[22] G Teubner, 'Legal Irritants: Good Faith in British Law or How Unifying Law Ends up in New Divergences' (1998) 61 *MLR* 11; C Joerges, 'The Impact of European Integration on Private Law: Reductionist Perceptions, True Conflicts and a New Constitutional Perspective' (1997) 3 *European Law Journal* 378.

[23] H Dagan and M Heller, *The Choice Theory of Contracts* (Cambridge, Cambridge University Press, 2017); see also H Dagan, *A Liberal Theory of Property* (Cambridge, Cambridge University Press, 2021).

[24] MW Hesselink, *Justifying Contract in Europe. Political Philosophies of European Contract Law* (Oxford, Oxford University Press, 2021).

[25] See the contributions in G Grégoire and X Miny (eds), *The Idea of Economic Constitution in Europe* (Leiden, Brill, 2022), specifically HW Micklitz, 'Discussion: Society, Private Law and Economic Constitution in the EU' 380.

strong interaction between the 'law' (here private law) and the 'society', which is still very much conceived of in the national context.

When translated to the level of the EU, two strands stand out which embrace the (European) private law society: on the one hand, there is the understanding of competition and competition law as a constitutive part of a democracy,[26] which offers an innovative perspective on the interaction between private law and competition law in the European economic constitution; on the other hand, there are attempts to look at how the CJEU contributes to the building of a European society through law.[27] This debate has attracted the interest of political scientists and sociologists.[28] Vauchez goes as far as to say with regard to the EU that 'in the European Union, even more than anywhere else, there is no possible distinction between the "law" and the "society". There are no areas of Europe's politics, economics, bureaucracy or civil society that have not been produced or co-produced to some extent by lawyers'.[29] Whilst these are promising avenues to combine law and society, the question remains whether 'law' and 'society' can integrate the 'political' and constitute a European polity.

Before we move on to the 'polity', we have to clarify the relationship between society and epistemic community (or communities) – an idea or concept which does not originate in EU law but in transnational law.[30] Seen through the lenses of transnational legal theories, the EU becomes merely a variant of transnational law. Those who engage in the debate focus on private regulation and private ordering, on private actors who establish rules typically for particular business purposes or economic sectors.[31] Therefore, it might be more appropriate to speak of epistemic communities in the plural. We wonder what the idea of epistemic communities can add in terms of clarifying the meaning and importance of judge-made EU private law. There is a crucial difference between the European and the transnational legal order. European epistemic communities – provided they exist – look different from transnational epistemic communities. Beyond the nation-state and beyond Europe, transnational law is by and large to be equated with private regulation in institution-building and in shaping private transactions. The EU typically promotes regulation or co-regulation via secondary EU law. Moreover, and contrary to the global level, the CJEU has adjudicative power to interpret the law.

D. The European Polity

M Fichera has identified 'security' and 'fundamental rights' as meta-rationales of European constitutionalism.[32] This seems a high benchmark that requires connecting private law to

[26] E Deutscher, 'Of Masters, Slaves, Behemoths and Bees: The Rise and Fall of the Link between Competition, Competition Law and Democracy' (PhD thesis, European University Institute, 2020).

[27] G Comandé, 'The Fifth European Union Freedom: Aggregating Citizenship … around Private Law' in HW Micklitz (ed), *Constitutionalization of European Private Law* (Oxford, Oxford University Press, 2014); K Carr, 'Regulating the Periphery: Shaking the Core European Identity Building Through the Lens of Contract Law' (2015) EUI Working Paper LAW 2015/40.

[28] R Münch, 'Constructing a European Society by Jurisdiction' (2008) 14 *European Law Journal* 519; A Vauchez, *Brokering Europe. Euro-Lawyers and the Making of a Transnational Polity* (Cambridge, Cambridge University Press, 2015) 4.

[29] Vauchez (n 28) 4.

[30] J Klabbers, 'Setting the Scene' in J Klabbers, A Peters and G Ulfstein, *The Constitutionalization of International Law* (Oxford, Oxford University Press, 2009) 1.

[31] L Bernstein, 'Opting out of the Legal System: Extralegal Contractual Relations in the Diamond Industry' (1992) 21 *Journal of Legal Studies* 115; G Shaffer, 'Theorizing Transnational Legal Ordering' (2016) 12 *Annual Review of Law and Social Science* 231.

[32] M Fichera, *The Foundations of the EU as a Polity* (Cheltenham, Edward Elgar, 2018).

fundamental rights. If this is true, we are back to square one – back to constitutionalised private law. For the time being, it might suffice to start from a more general understanding of what a polity is and to link such an understanding to European private law. It remains for section III of this chapter to bring back the analysis of the CJEU-made private law to the broader picture of European constitutionalism. The European polity is being understood as an identifiable political entity with a collective identity, tied together through institutionalised social relations.

Whilst such a definition might come close to common sense in the field, there are many loose ends in relation to the idea of a European polity that reaches beyond public (constitutional) law. Three of the definitional elements are not necessarily connected to the perspective of the role of private law in polity-building – the notions of 'institution', 'political' and 'collective identity'[33] – although private law adds additional difficulties to the idea of a European polity. The difficulty is the implicit or explicit yardstick against which the EU is measured. The parameters for defining the polity are taken from the nation-state context and from nation-state-based constitutional theory. Shifting the perspective away from the nation-state brings quite a number of difficulties to the fore, which differ in terms of what is at stake – the institution, the political or the collective identity.

Could the EU be regarded as an entity which institutionalises social relations? The answer seems to be in the affirmative, although this chapter does not discuss whether the EU could be regarded as a supranational democratic entity. Judge-made private law points to the particular role and function of secondary EU law, and the role and function that private law plays within the European legal order. The *institutional* element does not pose insurmountable obstacles, as what holds true for primary EU law is by and large true for secondary EU law, perhaps with the exception of majority voting. *Simmenthal* was decided prior to the Single European Act of 1986, which introduced majority voting and thus facilitated secondary law-making. Although unanimity was no longer required, the CJEU continued to submit all directives adopted after 1986 to the doctrine of the supremacy of EU law and recognised the vertical direct effect of secondary EU law, whilst still rejecting horizontal direct effect – setting aside the doctrine of consistent interpretation. The limping institutionalisation of private law relations through the CJEU necessarily affects social relations. The institutional design leaves more space structurally for the Member States' courts in the preliminary reference procedure under Article 267 of the Treaty on the Functioning of the European Union (TFEU). The idea of a 'polity' seems to benefit from this opening as the interaction is less hierarchical than is the case in primary EU law.

But where is the *political* dimension in CJEU-made private law? It is easy to collate a long list of CJEU judgments that have a strong political dimension, beginning with *Van Gend en Loos*[34] and *Costa v ENEL*,[35] which laid the foundations for the autonomy of the European legal order, which was qualified in *Les Verts* as a constitutional order.[36] There are many landmark decisions in private law that have had a long-lasting effect on the understanding of rights,

---

[33] Stefano Bartolini is trying to get to grips with the many different understandings of the 'political' and of 'institutions': S Bartolini, *The Political* (London, Rowman & Littlefield International, 2018). In the EU context, identity is discussed much more often as an argument to defend national identity against EU intrusion.

[34] Case C-26/62 *NV Algemene Transport- en Expeditie Onderneming van Gend & Loos v Netherlands Inland Revenue Administration* [1963] ECR 3.

[35] Case C-6/64 *Flaminio Costa v ENEL* [1964] ECR 1141.

[36] Case C-294/83 *Parti écologiste 'Les Verts' v European Parliament* [1986] ECR 1339.

freedoms and remedies. However, there is no counterpart to *Van Gend en Loos* or *Costa v Enel* claiming the existence of 'a genuine and autonomous European private law order'. There is no big bang in private law and there is equally no inquiry similar to that of A Vauchez on the polity-building character of *Van Gend en Loos*.[37] Most of the private law judgments remain rather technical, even if technicality may hide politics.[38] Judgments in private law that came to the attention of the public and triggered political discussions in the democratic fora are the exception. In *Commission v France*,[39] the CJEU held that the Product Liability Directive aims at full harmonisation and restricts the competence of the Member States. The judgment triggered a resolution of the European Council with a forceful political critique on the assumption of full harmonisation, although without any long-lasting effects.[40] The vast majority of European private law litigation does not meet that benchmark. However, in line with Bourdieu, one may conceive of the private law litigation as a 'field'.[41] This would require the kind of research that looks not only into the judgments, but also into the key role played by the 'Euro-lawyers' within and outside the legal field under investigation independent of their particular role and function in the litigation.[42]

However, there is another way to introduce the political into European private law before the CJEU. One may understand the design of the preliminary reference procedure under Article 267 TFEU as a political mechanism, through the way it is constructed. The CJEU does not resolve a concrete dispute by applying EU law to the facts of the case, but provides guidance about the interpretation of EU law with *erga omnes* effect. This mechanism is opening a space for political action, at least in certain types of litigation, where the addressee of the CJEU's judgment is not necessarily the national referring court but the national legislature(s), the national society (or societies) or the EU institutions. In such conflicts, the parties could be understood as 'mandataire' of the collective interests, ie, of all those who are directly affected by the decision. Whether such a case reaches the European polity depends on the weight of the collective interest. A promising candidate for passing this threshold is public interest litigation. Here the claimant instrumentalises the preliminary reference procedure to bring high-level policy issues to the court.[43] On that basis, it looks as if the idea of a European political entity held together through social institutions allows for the integration of private law or at least particular forms of private litigation, such as mass litigation and public interest litigation.

However, what about the *collective* identity – is European private law part of a/the European collective identity or can it be or (maybe better) can it turn into something like a European polity? The founding fathers of the Treaty of Rome did not consider the role and function of private law in European integration. They relied on what F Wieacker termed the 'common heritage' of private law in Europe – individualism, legalism and intellectualism.[44]

---

[37] Vauchez (n 28) 116–50.

[38] D Kennedy, 'The Hermeneutic of Suspicion in Contemporary American Legal Thought' (2014) 25 *Law and Critique* 91.

[39] Case C-52/00 *Commission v France* [2002] ECR I-3827.

[40] Council Resolution of 19 December 2002 on amendment of the liability for defective products Directive [2003] OJ C26/2.

[41] P Bourdieu, 'La Force du droit. Élément pour une sociologie du Champ Juridique' (1986) *Actes de la recherches des sciences sociales* 3.

[42] The PhD thesis of B Kas could be understood as an attempt to apply the field theory in practice; see B Kas, '"Hybrid" Collective Remedies in the EU Social Legal Order' (PhD thesis, European University Institute, 2017).

[43] With a critical eye on the consequences for the legal profession, see HW Micklitz and Th Roethe, 'Public Interest Litigation, Legal Professionalism and the ECJ: Deciding a Case or Managing Politics?' in D Leczykiewicz et al (eds), *Liber Amicorum Stephen Weatherill* (forthcoming).

[44] F Wieacker, 'Foundations of European Legal Culture', translated and annotated by Edgar Bodenheimer (1990) 38 *American Journal of Comparative Law* 1.

The ambitious project of a European Civil Code did not progress beyond an academic draft. The attempt of the European Commission to develop at least a Common European Sales Law (CESL) so forcefully promoted by the European Parliament failed due to the resistance of six Member States. All that the EU has managed to achieve in the last three decades is a European private law of bit and pieces, composed of the horizontal consumer law, labour law and non-discrimination law, and the vertical law of the regulated market, complemented by a dense network of private international law on the place of jurisdiction, the applicable law and the recognition and enforcement of foreign judgments. A European private law of bits and pieces does not exclude the existence of a collective identity, although the identity might exist only in the fields where EU law is dense enough and it might be a divided identity, split between the national and the European.

Let us now investigate the CJEU-made private law and how the body of case law can be connected to the grand theories of European constitutionalism, here with a particular emphasis on the European polity.

II. THE BODY OF CJEU JUDGMENTS

Our collection of the CJEU's case law in European private law shows that the Court has rendered around 300 judgments in approximately 20 years.[45] The cases were selected through the 'advanced search' online form of the CJEU's website.[46] Our results are based on a double search: on the one hand, we conducted a narrow search by using the form 'references to case law or legislation' and by filling in the relevant secondary law instruments in the area of EU consumer law; on the other hand, we conducted a broader search by using the form 'text' to search all rulings containing the keyword 'consumer'. Among them, we selected the judgments that have relevance for private legal relationships between consumers and traders. We categorised the decisions according to the various fields of private law which have been Europeanised through secondary EU law since 1984: contract law (unfair terms, direct and distant selling, consumer sales and services), travel law (passenger rights, package travel and information on airfares), consumer credit, finance and insurance, product liability, consumer issues in European private international law (PIL) and alternative dispute resolution (ADR). Unfair commercial practices have been covered only as far as there is a strong connection to contract law.

In our analysis, each case was presented after the same scheme: the facts of the case, the arguments brought forward before the CJEU and an attempt to position the case in question into the *acquis communautaire*. Our analysis suffers from three major deficiencies. First, it does not examine the final judgment of the referring court or, where necessary, the reaction of the national legislature. Second, it does not investigate to what extent the cases have triggered a cross-border exchange between national courts and/or between plaintiffs/defendants on similar questions. Third, it does not investigate a potential triangular exchange between the CJEU, the referring national court and affected national courts in other Member States. Positively speaking, the way in which the analysis was built provides for a vertical insight into the interaction between the national court and the CJEU, and between the national law and the relevant parts of harmonised private law.

Although we are not able to systematically engage with all these questions in this chapter, we will present a refined analysis of the judgments rendered by the CJEU upon preliminary

---

[45] See n 1 for details.
[46] See www.curia.europa.eu/juris/recherche.jsf?language=en.

references by national courts in the last 20 years. We will base our analysis on the number of judgments per legal sub-field (section II.A), the spread between the Member States from which the references emerged (section II.B) and the type of conflicts behind the preliminary references (section II.C).[47]

A. The Number of Judgments per Field

The categorisation of the judgments according to the legislative instruments of secondary European private law shows that certain sub-fields stand out. About one-third of all judgments concern unfair standard terms. Specifically, 95 judgments deal with the Unfair Terms Directive 93/13.[48] The European law on unfair standard terms thus became established in a similar fashion to that in Member States with a long-standing tradition of judicial control, such as Austria, France and Germany.[49] In the area of travel law, we have collected 67 judgments. Air passenger rights have made a fast career. Most of the judgments in this area – 44 of them – concern Regulation No 261/2004.[50] Together, both sub-fields – unfair terms and travel law – cover over 50% of all judgments. They constitute self-standing areas of EU law. The same applies to European private international law, which historically lived its own life in commentaries and regular review articles. In this field, the Brussels I (Recast) Regulation stands out.[51] We have collected 24 judgments that deal with jurisdiction for disputes involving consumer rights under the Brussels I (Recast) Regulation, which are complemented by two recent rulings on the Lugano II Convention.[52] Only three judgments deal with questions on

[47] As indicated, our research shows that in the area of European private law, the Court has rendered around 300 judgments in approximately 20 years. In this renewed analysis of the empirical material, we are excluding judgments that were given in the context of infringement proceedings. As demonstrated by our overviews of the case law (n 1), their relevance as a source for CJEU judgments gradually decreased over time, while preliminary references have been constantly increasing. Our overviews reported in total about 21 judgments that resulted from infringement actions. Two further issues should be noted about the empirical material presented in sections II.A and B of this analysis: the (few) judgments that concern more than one legislative instrument or have joined references from the courts of several Member States have been counted multiple times. However, where judgments joined several references from courts of the same Member States, they have been counted a single time. For instance, the judgment in Case C-485/19 *LH v Profi Credit Slovakia sro* EU:C:2021:313 concerned the Directives on Unfair Terms and on Consumer Credit Agreements, and is thus counted twice with respect to the numbers of judgments per legal field. The judgment in Joined Cases C-146/20, C-188/20, C-196/20 and C-270/20 *AD and Others v Corendon Airlines and Others* EU:C:2021:1038, which joined one reference from an Austrian court and three references from the German courts, is counted as one reference from Austria and one reference from Germany with respect to the number of judgments per country.

[48] The judgments concern Council Directive 93/13/EEC of 5 April 1993 on unfair terms in consumer contracts [1993] OJ L95/29.

[49] HW Micklitz and N Reich, 'The Court and Sleeping Beauty: The Revival of the Unfair Contract Terms Directive (UCTD)' (2014) 51 *Common Market Law Review* 771.

[50] Regulation No 261/2004 on compensation and assistance to passengers in the event of denied boarding and of cancellation or long delay of flights [2004] OJ L46/1; seven judgments concern international air passenger rights under the Montreal Convention and one judgment under the Warsaw Convention; three rulings deal with Regulation (EC) No 1371/2007 on rail passengers' rights and obligations [2007] OJ L315/14; one judgment concerns Regulation (EU) No 1177/2010 of the European Parliament and of the Council of 24 November 2010 concerning the rights of passengers when travelling by sea and inland waterway [2010] OJ L334/1; five judgments concern Council Directive 90/314/EEC on package travel, package holidays and package tours [1990] OJ L158/59; and six judgments fall under Regulation (EC) No 1008/2008 on common rules for the operation of air services [2008] OJ L293/3.

[51] Regulation No 44/2001 on jurisdiction and the recognition and enforcement of judgments in civil and commercial matters [2001] OJ L12/1; Regulation (EU) No 1215/2012 of the European Parliament and of the Council of 12 December 2012 on jurisdiction and the recognition and enforcement of judgments in civil and commercial matters [2012] OJ L351/1.

[52] A total of 15 judgments concern Regulation No 44/2001 and nine judgments relate to Regulation 1215/2012. In addition, two recent judgments concern the Lugano II Convention on jurisdiction and the recognition and enforcement

the applicable law in consumer disputes.[53] Next to these largely self-standing areas, we can identify three fields that are gradually emerging: the area of consumer sales law, covering 41 judgments;[54] the rules on consumer credit agreements that were the subject of 23 rulings;[55] and liability for defective products comprising 13 judgments.[56] The remaining judgments are scattered among various areas, such as insurance, services (telecoms, energy, finance), non-discriminatory access to goods and services, and ADR.

B. The Number of Judgments per Country

Looking at the judgments concerning unfair terms, it is striking that 60% are based on preliminary references from three countries, namely Spain (26), Hungary (18) and Poland (13).[57] References from Central and Eastern European Member States play a crucial role. Together with Hungary (18), Poland (13), Romania (8), Slovakia (7), the Czech Republic (1) and Slovenia (1), 50% of these cases come from the new Member States (ie, those which joined the EU after the fall of the Berlin Wall). It is astonishing to see that preliminary references from the old Member States – France (5), Austria (3), the Netherlands (3), Belgium (2), Germany (2) and Italy (2) – together constitute the basis of less than 20% of the CJEU judgments on unfair terms. The courts of Lithuania, the Czech Republic, Slovenia, Greece, Croatia and Bulgaria have each submitted one reference in the last 20 years. Cyprus, Ireland, Luxembourg, Portugal, the UK, Malta, the Baltic States (except for Lithuania) and the Nordic countries (Denmark, Finland and Sweden) are not represented at all. Thus, all in all, the courts of 17 Member States referred a case to the Luxembourg Court.

The other fields show a very different spread. In the area of travel law, preliminary references of the German (19) and Austrian courts (14) – which make up about 50% of all

---

of judgments in civil and commercial matters, signed on 30 October 2007, the conclusion of which was approved on behalf of the European Community by Council Decision 2009/430/EC of 27 November 2008 [2009] OJ L147/1.

[53] Specifically, dealing with Regulation (EC) No 593/2008 of the European Parliament and of the Council of 17 June 2008 on the law applicable to contractual obligations (Rome I) [2008] OJ L177/6, and Regulation (EC) No 864/2007 of the European Parliament and of the Council of 11 July 2007 on the law applicable to non-contractual obligations (Rome II) [2007] OJ L199/40.

[54] Six judgments concern Council Directive 85/577/EEC to protect the consumer in respect of contracts negotiated away from business premises [1985] OJ L372/31; five judgments concern Directive 97/7/EC on the protection of consumers in respect of distance contracts [1997] OJ L372/31; 10 rulings concern Directive 1999/44/EC on certain aspects of the sale of consumer goods and associated guarantees [1999] OJ L171/12; 17 judgments involve Directive 2011/83/EU of the European Parliament and of the Council of 25 October 2011 on consumer rights, amending Council Directive 93/13/EEC and Directive 1999/44/EC of the European Parliament and of the Council, and repealing Council Directive 85/577/EEC and Directive 97/7/EC of the European Parliament and of the Council [2011] OJ L304/64; and three judgments deal with the compatibility of national consumer protection provisions with the free movement provisions. The latter were added even though they fall strictly seen outside the scope of secondary EU law.

[55] Council Directive 87/102/EEC of 22 December 1986 for the approximation of the laws, regulations and administrative provisions of the Member States concerning consumer credit [1987] OJ L42/48; Directive 2008/48/EC of the European Parliament and of the Council of 23 April 2008 on credit agreements for consumers and repealing Council Directive 87/102/EEC [2008] OJ L133/66.

[56] A total of 11 judgments concern Council Directive 85/374/EEC of 25 July 1985 on the approximation of the laws, regulations and administrative provisions of the Member States concerning liability for defective products [1985] OJ L210/29; one judgment concerns the interpretation of Council Directive 93/42/EEC of 14 June 1993 concerning medical devices [1993] OJ L169/1; Case C-581/18 *RB v TÜV Rheinland LGA Products GmbH and Allianz IARD SA* EU:C:2020:453, which deals with the compatibility of a contractual clause stipulated in a contract concluded between an insurance company and a manufacturer of medical devices with art 18 TFEU, was also added.

[57] In comparison to Spain and Hungary, Poland has been a latecomer – most preliminary references have occurred in the last five years.

judgments collected in that area – dominate. They are followed by Spain (7), Belgium (5) and the Netherlands (4). Few references stem from the UK (3), Portugal (3), Finland (3), the Czech Republic (3) and Ireland (2). Italy, Luxembourg, Sweden, Poland, Romania, Latvia and Cyprus have referred one case each. All in all, there are thus only four references from Central and Eastern European countries, namely three from the Czech Republic and one from Romania. As in the field of unfair terms, the CJEU's judgments are based on references from the courts of 17 Member States.

The 29 judgments that deal with consumer matters in PIL are dominated by references from Austria (11) and Germany (6), which together make up almost 60% of all judgments in that area. They are followed by the Czech Republic (4) and Italy (2). As in the area of travel law, the Czech Republic thus stands out from the other Central and Eastern European countries. Spain, Slovenia, Poland, Romania, Luxembourg and Croatia have each made one preliminary reference. Hence, the courts of 10 Member States have participated in that area.

In the area of consumer sales law, it emerges that Germany takes the lead with 22 references, accounting for more than 50% of all judgments in that area. This is followed by Austria (5), Belgium (4), Spain (3), Bulgaria (2), the Netherlands (2), the UK (1), Lithuania (1) and Estonia (1). Hence, in total, the judiciaries of nine Member States have referred questions to the CJEU.

The judgments on consumer credit agreement do not show clear tendencies. Poland has referred five cases, which is followed by four references from France and Slovakia. They are followed by Germany, Romania and the Czech Republic, each referring two cases. Italy, Austria, Belgium and Latvia have each submitted one reference. All in all, 23 judgments stemming from 10 Member States have been collected.

In the field of product liability, four references stem from Germany, three from France and two from the UK. Spain, Austria, Finland and Denmark have each submitted one reference. That means that the courts of seven Member States have participated in this field.

The overview shows that the judge-made European private law is based on an uneven spread of references from the courts of the Member States. Combining the insights from the six fields, leading in terms of preliminary references are the courts of Germany, Spain and Austria, followed by Poland, Hungary and Romania. Only the Maltese courts have not made use of the preliminary reference procedure during the examined period. Overall, using A Colombi Ciacchi's classification,[58] the courts of the old and the young continental European democracies are sitting in the driver's seat. They make extensive use of the preliminary reference procedure, thereby leaving a deep footprint on the making of European private law, whereas the courts of the Nordic insular democracies have rarely participated in the making of European private law.

C. Types of Litigation

Studying the summaries of the cases produces meaningful insights on the types of litigation which national courts are bringing before the CJEU. Three types can be distinguished, although there might be overlaps: first, collective conflicts with a strong societal dimension; second, conflicts with a strong national legal context; and, third, legal interpretational issues of relevance for the whole European private law.

---

[58] A Colombi Ciacchi, 'Judicial Governance in European Private Law: Three Judicial Cultures of Fundamental Rights Horizontality' (2020) 28 *European Review of Private Law* 931.

Up to now, the CJEU has twice had to deal with collective conflicts which arose in Germany and Spain, and the Central and Eastern European countries, and which have led to a whole series of references, where the CJEU was pushed to clarify its position and/or to react to developments in the Member States after its first judgment. The first is the *Heininger* saga, a €10 billion story.[59] After German reunification, German consumers in the former German Democratic Republic (GDR) were pushed to buy immovable property on the doorstep as credit financed investments. The investment scheme did not work, and the consumer investors ended up with overpriced property for which the rental income did not suffice to cover the mortgage. In *Heininger*, the CJEU held that the then Directive 85/577/EEC on doorstep selling grants an eternal right to withdrawal, thereby encouraging consumer/investors to get rid of their 'junk property' (*Schrottimmobilien*).

The second event was the financial crisis in 2007/2008. In Spain consumers had bought private property often at the limits of or beyond what they could afford. Both the banks and the consumers were relying on constantly rising housing prices. The crisis triggered a downward spiral. Consumers lost their jobs and could no longer pay their mortgages.[60] The CJEU's ruling in *Aziz* became a point of reference for demonstrating the potential of the Unfair Terms Directive 93/13 to alleviate the repercussions of the financial crisis on consumer debtors.[61] In Central and Eastern European countries, banks offered loans which were coupled to the Swiss franc. When the crisis resulted in the national currency being devalued, consumers found themselves confronted with a much higher debt than they had originally foreseen at the time of concluding the contract.[62] Almost all references from Spain, Hungary, Slovakia, Poland, Romania, Slovenia and the Czech Republic in the field of unfair terms have their origin in the effects of the crisis on mortgage contracts and consumer loans. Preliminary references invoking the Unfair Terms Directive 93/13/EC to deal with the consequences of the crisis have not yet subsided.

A less well-known collective conflict is the PIP scandal. For many years, the French breast implant manufacturer PIP used sub-standard industrial silicone gel instead of the required medical gel. When the fraud was discovered in 2010, millions of women across the world had already received sub-standard and potentially dangerous breast implants.[63] *Schmitt*[64] and *TÜV Rheinland*[65] demonstrate that EU law has not yet come to help the many women who received defective breast implants.[66] A further ongoing collective conflict is the *Dieselgate* scandal,

---

[59] Case C-481/99 *Georg Heininger and Helga Heininger v Bayerische Hypo- und Vereinsbank AG* [2001] ECR I-9945. The CJEU subsequently dealt with the conflict in Case C-350/03 *Elisabeth Schulte and Wolfgang Schulte v Deutsche Bausparkasse Badenia AG* [2005] ECR I-9215; Case C-229/04 *Crailsheimer Volksbank eG v Klaus Conrads and Others* [2005] ECR I-9273; and *E Friz* (n 5).

[60] F Gómez Pomar and K Lyczkowska, 'Spanish Courts, the Court of Justice of the European Union, and Consumer Law' (2014) *Revista para el Análisis del Derecho (InDret)* 4.

[61] Case C-415/11 *Mohamed Aziz v Caixa d'Estalvis de Catalunya, Tarragona i Manresa (Catalunyacaixa)* EU:C:2013:164.

[62] European Parliament, Briefing, 'Unfair Terms in Swiss Franc Loans: Overview of European Court of Justice Case Law', EPRS (European Parliamentary Research Service), author: Rafał Mańko, PE 689.361 – March 2021.

[63] B van Leeuwen, 'PIP Breast Implants, the EU's New Approach for Goods and Market Surveillance by Notified Bodies' (2014) 5 *European Journal of Risk Regulation* 338. See also P Verbruggen and B van Leeuwen, 'The Liability of Notified Bodies under the EU's New Approach: The Implications of the PIP Breast Implants Case' (2018) 43 *European Law Review* 394.

[64] Case C-219/15 *Elisabeth Schmitt v TÜV Rheinland LGA Products GmbH* EU:C:2017:128.

[65] *TÜV Rheinland* (n 56); on the ruling, see B van Leeuwen, 'The Scope of Application of the Free Movement Provisions and the Role of Article 18 TFEU: *Allianz*' (2021) 58 *Common Market Law Review* 1249.

[66] The Product Liability Directive 85/374/EEC could not be invoked due to the liquidation of PIP. In *Schmitt*, the Court held that the Medical Devices Directive 93/42/EEC did not regulate the conditions under which a notified body

which was uncovered in 2015 by the US Environment Protection Agency. Consumer organisations all over Europe have drawn attention to the fact that not all affected European car owners have been yet compensated.[67] The CJEU recently strengthened the position of consumers by clarifying that purchasers of diesel vehicles equipped with software which reduces the effectiveness of the emission control system at normal temperatures are entitled to rescind their sales contracts according to Directive 1999/44. Vehicles fitted with a prohibited defeat device do not show the quality which is normal in goods of the same type and which the consumer can reasonably expect. According to the Court, such a lack of conformity cannot be classified as 'minor'.[68] One could understand these two scandals as the third and fourth collective conflicts, which – unlike the previous two – have a pronounced transnational dimension.

The second category deals with consumer problems which have a very particular national background and where courts – quite often lower courts in the country – are invoking the Luxembourg Court to remedy national deficits with the help of European private law. Examples are jurisdiction and arbitration clauses in Spanish consumer contracts,[69] price increase clauses in German energy supply contracts[70] and dispute settlement procedures in Italy.[71] In Spain there was a fairly liberal policy on jurisdiction clauses, which barred consumers from pursuing their claims as they would have been obliged to travel to the business' residence. Price increase clauses in energy supply contracts provoked strong reactions from German consumers who wanted to get their money back.[72] While similar contract terms might exist in all Member States, they enjoy a particular economic, social and legal background in the country of origin. In Italy, access to court is easy and cheap, but consumer proceedings are lengthy, which acts as a deterrent. That is why dispute settlement procedures play a key role and the Italian legislator is at the forefront of promoting ADR by making access to court conditional on a prior attempt at an out-of-court settlement.

The third category is best categorised as legal technical, highly complicated doctrinal questions that provoke strong reactions in the respective legal community. From the range of fields, distant and direct selling, consumer sales and product liability stand out. For instance, if there

---

could be held liable for its potential failure to carry out the inspections of the manufacturer with sufficient skill and care. In *Allianz*, the Court clarified that the free movement provisions do not regulate the conditions of insurers' civil liability for harm caused by defective products.

[67] BEUC Report, 'Five Years of Dieselgate: A Bitter Anniversary', available at www.beuc.eu/publications/beuc-x-2020-081_five_years_of_dieselgate_a_bitter_anniversary_report.pdf; A Biard, 'Retour sur 6 ans de Dieselgate en Europe du point de vue des consommateurs' (2021) *Droit de la consommation – Consumentenrecht (DCCR)* 3.

[68] Case C-128/20 *GSMB Invest GmbH & Co KG v Auto Krainer GesmbH* EU:C:2022:570; Case C-134/20 *IR v Volkswagen AG* EU:C:2022:571; Case C-145/20 *DS v Porsche Inter Auto GmbH & Co KG, Volkswagen AG* EU:C:2022:572. In a pending preliminary reference, the Court has been asked whether EU law confers on an individual purchaser of a vehicle which does not comply with the emission limits laid down by EU law a right to compensation from the vehicle manufacturer, on the basis of tortious liability, and, if so, what method of calculating compensation must be established; see on this the opinion of 2 June 2022 of Advocate General Rantos in Case C-100/21 *QB v Mercedes-Benz Group AG, Formerly Daimler AG* EU:C:2022:420.

[69] Joined Cases C-240/98–C-244/98 *Océano Grupo Editorial SA v Roció Murciano Quintero and Others* [2000] ECR I-4941; Case C-168/05 *Elisa María Mostaza Claro v Centro Móvil Milenium SL* [2006] ECR I-10421; Case C-40/08 *Asturcom Telecomunicaciones SL v Cristina Rodríguez Nogueira* [2009] ECR I-9579.

[70] Case C-92/11 *RWE Vertrieb AG v Verbraucherzentrale Nordrhein-Westfalen eV* EU:C:2013:180; Case C-359/11 *Alexandra Schulz v Technische Werke Schussental GmbH und Co KG and Josef Egbringhoff v Stadtwerke Ahaus GmbH* EU:C:2014:2317.

[71] Joined Cases C-317/08–C-320/08 *Rosalba Alassini v Telecom Italia SpA, Filomena Califano v Wind SpA, Lucia Anna Giorgia Iacono v Telecom Italia SpA and Multiservice Srl v Telecom Italia SpA* [2010] ECR I-2213; Case C-75/16 *Livio Menini and Maria Antonia Rampanelli v Banco Popolare – Società Cooperativa* EU:C:2017:457.

[72] N Reich, '"I Want My Money Back": Problems, Successes and Failures in the Price Regulation of the Gas Supply Market by Civil Law Remedies in Germany' (2015) EUI Working Paper LAW 2015/05.

is no prescription period for the right to withdrawal in EU legislation, does this mean there is none?[73] How should the notion that the consumer can return a product bought online at 'no cost' be interpreted?[74] Does this mean that they can use the product without paying compensation for the use to the seller?[75] May consumers return a mattress purchased online even if they have removed the protective film or may the right of withdrawal be restricted for hygiene reasons?[76] Must the right of withdrawal be granted if the goods ordered are to be made to the consumer's specifications or are personalised, but have not yet been manufactured?[77] If the replacement of defective goods is the only remedy, is the seller obliged to remove the defective goods and install the replacement goods at his or her own cost?[78] Is a medical device a product and does it suffice to trigger liability if the medical device incorporated into the body is only potentially defective?[79] All these references and many more have in common that the outcome of the case depends on the interpretation of a particular legal concept. Typically, there are legal arguments for and against, and the technicality hides the deeper economic and social implications – how far does the right to return goods purchased online without cost reach? Who must bear the costs for a potential misuse or overuse during the return period? Should the producer of heart valves cover the surgery costs of a potentially defective product or are these costs left to be covered by health insurance, if at all?

III. ASSESSMENT OF THE CJEU JUDGMENTS

The remarkable rise of CJEU judgments in European private law is a phenomenon that deserves more consideration. What exactly is happening in the field of private law: is it still private law or is it a mixed field, intermingling public and private law, European and national? And how can the interaction between the national courts and the CJEU be qualified? Are the actors involved in the cases building a kind of judge-made European polity? To give a tentative reply, we will look more closely into three aspects related to the previously introduced three categories of 'fields', 'countries' and 'types of litigation', namely the scope of the polity (section III.A), participation in the polity (section III.B) and the politicisation of litigation (section III.C).

A. The Scope of the Polity

Is there a correlation between the number of CJEU judgments and the existence of a polity? And what is the private law polity? Is it the ensemble of the different fields that we identified? Is it European private law or consumer law? Or may it be more convincing and realistic to start from the existence of emerging sub-polities? Our empirical study can be understood to

---

[73] *Heininger* (n 59).

[74] Case C-511/08 *Handelsgesellschaft Heinrich Heine GmbH v Verbraucherzentrale Nordrhein-Westfalen eV* [2010] ECR I-3047.

[75] *Messner* (n 5).

[76] Case C-681/17 *Slewo – schlafen leben wohnen GmbH v Sascha Ledowski* EU:C:2019:255.

[77] Case C-529/19 *Möbel Kraft GmbH & Co KG v ML* EU:C:2020:846.

[78] Joined Cases C-65/09 and C-87/09 *Gebr Weber GmbH v Jürgen Wittmer, Ingrid Putz v Medianess Electronics GmbH* [2011] ECR I-5257.

[79] Joined Cases C-503/13 and C-504/13 *Boston Scientific Medizintechnik GmbH v AOK Sachsen-Anhalt – Die Gesundheitskasse and Betriebskrankenkasse RWE* EU:C:2015:148.

provide evidence of a sub-polity in the field of secondary EU consumer law. However, a word of caution is required. Are we really talking about consumer law only or are we talking about consumer law as private law, a field of law which intermingles the private and the public dimensions of EU law? The political dimension which is enshrined in the concept of a polity suggests a broader understanding, one that focuses on consumer law as an integral part of European private law.

Politicisation may take place independently of the number of preliminary references that have arisen in the legal field. *Heininger* stands for an extremely narrow bottleneck – the applicability of the Doorstep Selling Directive 85/577/EEC served to pave the way to questioning the legality of high value economic transactions. Looking back, however, it appears that the *Heininger* saga is the exception to the rule. European private law is compartmentalised. There is not much coherence between the different fields, despite the efforts of the EU legislature. A good example of this is all the information duties that are spread over different fields, but which are not interconnected. When it comes to litigation before the CJEU, it looks as if each field stands on its own. Such an understanding is underpinned by limited cross-references between the different fields.[80] The CJEU by and large conceives each field as a self-standing area of law, building its reasoning on prior cases. However, there are differences depending on the subject matter of the respective instrument of secondary EU law. The Unfair Terms Directive is particularly relevant as it covers goods and services, and because standard terms are omnipresent in consumer transactions. This might explain the high number of judgments on the Directive, although most of the references deal in variations with the economic consequences of the financial crisis. However, even the crisis did not suffice to bring together what belongs together. Mortgages and consumer loans are dealt with under the Unfair Terms Directive, leaving a marginal role for the Consumer Credit Directive, even if the deeper origin of both instruments is similar.[81]

Despite all the variations in the different fields and the very fragmented legal discourse and legal reasoning, the polity is held together through the addressee, which is the one in whose name and to whose benefit all the secondary EU law has been adopted. Here is the link to the consumer economy, to the consumption society and to the overwhelming importance of private consumption for the Internal Market. The 'consumption polity' is composed of two different types of consumers: the active consumer and the passive consumer. The prototype

---

[80] There are some exceptions. For instance, the Court applied its case law on the national judge's *ex officio* mandate developed under Directive 93/13 to consumer credit (Case C-429/05 *Max Rampion and Marie-Jeanne Godard v Franfinance SA and K par K SAS* [2007] ECR I-8017), distant sales (Case C-227/08 *Eva Martín Martín v EDP Editores SL* [2009] ECR I-11939) and consumer sales (Case C-32/12 *Soledad Duarte Hueros v Autociba SA and Automóviles Citroën España SA* EU:C:2013:637; Case C-497/13 *Froukje Faber v Autobedrijf Hazet Ochten BV* EU:C:2015:357). Another prominent example concerns the relationship between competition and contract law. In Case C-453/10 *Jana Pereničová and Vladislav Perenič v SOS financ spol sro* EU:C:2012:144 (more recently confirmed in Joined Cases C-776/19–C-782/19 *BNP Paribas Personal Finance* EU:C:2021:470, para 76), the Court held that the finding of an unfair commercial practice under Directive 2005/29/EC ([2005] OJ L149/22) is one element among others on which a court may base its assessment of the unfairness of the contractual terms under Directive 93/13, leading to a broader academic debate about the relationship of both instruments; see HW Micklitz and N Reich, 'AGB-Recht und UWG – (endlich) ein Ende des Kästchendenkens nach EuGH Pereničová und Invitel?' (2012) *Europäisches Wirtschafts- & Steuerrecht* 257.

[81] Recent preliminary references from Poland have asked the CJEU to take a more holistic perspective; see Joined Cases C-419/18 and C-483/18 *Profi Credit Polska SA v Bogumiła Włostowska and Others and Profi Credit Polska SA v OH* EU:C:2019:930; Case C-779/18 *Mikrokasa SA w Gdyni and Revenue Niestandaryzowany Sekurytyzacyjny Fundusz Inwestycyjny Zamknięty w Warszawie v XO* EU:C:2020:236; Joined Cases C-84/19, C-222/19 and C-252/19 *Profi Credit Polska SA and Others v QJ and Others* EU:C:2020:631; Case C-303/20 *Ultimo Portfolio Investment (Luxembourg) SA v KM* EU:C:2021:479.

of the active consumer is the traveller, the mobile citizen who constantly crosses borders and moves from one place to the other.[82] The high number of cases from many different countries of origin, though with a slight preference from the old Member States, in the field of travel law demonstrates the relevance of this group of mobile consumers. The second major group of 'mobile' consumers are the online shoppers. Since the adoption of the Distance Selling Directive 97/7/EC, the EU has strongly promoted the possibility of shopping online across borders. This mobility results from the broader perspective that EU law provides to consumers. The reality looks different and is often dominated by geo-blocking, where consumers are thrown back to the affiliation of the online seller in their country of residence.[83]

Conversely, there is the passive consumer who does not move. Most of the cases under review deal with all sorts of economic transactions concluded by the passive consumer 'at home'. A typical example here is mortgages and consumer loans. Both serve local needs – the financing of the home and/or credit financed investments tied to the local residence.[84] One might associate the different consumer types with Sousa's distinction of 'globalized localisms' and 'localized globalism'.[85] 'Globalized localism' is the active consumer and 'localized globalism' the passive consumer. Hence, globalisation is not bound to constantly moving around the world, but takes place at the most nitty-gritty consumer problem. Sousa helps to underpin the political dimension of the consumption process, regardless of whether the active or the passive consumer is concerned, and therefore the 'political' in the judge-made private law polity. It remains open as to whether the identified European consumption polity may become part of a broader judge-made European polity that allows for the (re)politicisation of consumption in view of the growing calls for more sustainable economic models.

B. Participation in the Polity

The construction of a judge-made European polity relies on the interaction between European and national actors within the framework of the preliminary reference procedure. The protagonists of the procedure are the national courts and the CJEU. However, their perspectives on the purpose of Article 267 TFEU clash easily. The preliminary reference procedure is designed to allow the CJEU to provide authoritative guidance on the interpretation of EU law. However, the referring court is seeking advice on how to solve a very concrete consumer case. There is thus a mismatch between the horizontal perspective of the CJEU, which is speaking to all Member States and all national courts, and the vertical perspective of the referring court, which is addressing the CJEU, but not necessarily the courts of the other Member States.[86]

---

[82] See the distinction in M Fichera, 'The Idea of Discursive Constituent Power' (2021) 3 *Jus Cogens* 159, 164 ff.

[83] In February 2018 the EU adopted the Geo-Blocking Regulation 2018/302 ([2018] OJ L60I/1), which prohibits restrictions on consumer access to e-commerce websites on the basis of their nationality or country of residence. The Commission's first evaluation report has shown that there were initial positive effects of the Regulation in improving the cross-border accessibility of traders' websites, but also that the Regulation has not yet reached its full intended effects (COM (2020) 766 final).

[84] While the fundamental rights flavour of the litigation in *Aziz* (n 61) might have contributed to the political attention the case raised, the CJEU did not really elaborate on the right to housing in the long stream of follow-up judgments. See I Domurath and C Mak, 'Private Law and Housing Justice in Europe' (2020) 83 *MLR* 1188; P Kenna and H Simón-Moreno, 'Towards a Common Standard of Protection of the Right to Housing in Europe through the Charter of Fundamental Rights' (2019) 25 *European Law Journal* 608; F Della Negra, 'The Uncertain Development of the Case Law on Consumer Protection in Mortgage Enforcement Proceedings: *Sánchez Morcillo* and *Kušionová*' (2015) 52 *Common Market Law Review* 1009.

[85] B de Sousa Santos, 'Globalizations' (2006) 23 *Theory, Culture and Society* 393.

[86] Micklitz (n 2) 446 ff.

This inherent mismatch in the institutional design of the preliminary reference procedure may hamper the process of EU polity-building via case law. On the one hand, the more the CJEU sticks to the horizontal perspective, the less useful the interpretation might be for the national referring court. In a worst-case scenario, the national court might be embarrassed by a 'useless' answer, which would deter it from using the preliminary reference procedure in the future. On the other hand, the more the CJEU is not only interpreting the law but also providing guidance on how the interpretation must be applied by the referring court to the facts of the case, the more the CJEU is engaging in a closed dialogue with the referring court, with the resulting danger of losing sight of the potential needs of all the other national courts and the national private legal orders. Although the Advocates General may act as 'catalysts' between the national courts and the CJEU, it has been suggested that they rarely meet the challenge of 'translating' between the different styles of communication.[87] A more (open and consistent) engagement with the comparative law method could potentially help the transposition of the preliminary reference into a horizontal European perspective.[88]

The preliminary reference procedure builds on a single institutional safeguard to open the litigation to other Member States, namely the opportunity of the governments to intervene before the CJEU based on Article 23(2) of the Statute of the Court of Justice of the European Union.[89] There is no empirical study which has analysed – quantitatively or qualitatively – the input provided by the Member States on the CJEU's case law in European private law. References to the interventions by the governments in the opinions of the Advocates General or the Court's judgments are neither complete nor systematic. Until 1994, it was possible to retrieve summaries of the Member States' observations from the Judge-Rapporteurs' reports published in the European Court Reports.[90] Today, it is necessary to directly request access to the written observations from the Member States to reconstruct a complete account of the arguments brought forward by the national governments.[91] A report by the Swedish Institute for European Policy Studies on the governments' interventions during the period from 1997 to 2008 shows that the Member States have taken the opportunity to intervene to considerably varying degrees.[92] The same applies to the area of European private law, where most Member States do not regularly present written observations or participate in the oral procedure, whereas the European Commission acts as a 'repeat-player' that is always providing input on what it believes to be the appropriate interpretation of EU law.[93] The differences in activity

---

[87] ibid 427, 448.

[88] On the use of comparative law by the CJEU, see K Lenaerts and K Gutman, 'The Comparative Law Method and the Court of Justice of the European Union: Interlocking Legal Orders Revisited' in M Andenas and D Fairgrieve (eds), *Courts and Comparative Law* (Oxford, Oxford University Press, 2015) 141, especially 145–50 on the role of the Advocate General in this respect.

[89] [2016] OJ C202/210.

[90] On the documentation of the Member States' observations, see P Cramér, O Larsson, A Moberg and D Naurin, *See You in Luxembourg? EU Governments' Observations under the Preliminary Reference Procedure* (Swedish Institute for European Policy Studies, 2016) 16–19.

[91] The CJEU recently undertook efforts to facilitate the public's access to its judicial activity. However, for the moment, only hearings from the Grand Chamber are broadcast to the public for a six-month pilot period; see 'Broadcast by Streaming of Hearings and the Handing down of Judgments and Opinions of the Court of Justice', Court of Justice of the European Union, Press Release No 63/22, Luxembourg, 22 April 2022.

[92] Cramér et al (n 90) 6 ff.

[93] On the difference between 'repeat players' and 'one shotters', see M Galanter, 'Why the "Haves" Come out Ahead: Speculations on the Limits of Legal Change' (1974) 9 *Law and Society* 95. According to Galanter, repeat players have the resources to engage in long-term litigation, which allows them to impact legal change. While studies have indeed suggested that the CJEU adheres to the Commission's position in most cases, different explanations have been put forward for this; see the overview in MP Granger, 'From the Margins of the European Legal Field: The Governments' Agents and Their Influence on the Development of European Union Law' in A Vauchez and B de Witte (eds), *Lawyering Europe: European Law as a Transnational Social Field* (Oxford, Hart Publishing, 2013) 55, at 59.

of the Member States may depend partly on the resources that the governments are ready to invest in the monitoring of and acting in EU judicial procedures, but also on how the handling of preliminary references is organised within government ministries and to what extent the conflict can be translated into the respective national environment.[94]

A fully fledged picture that covers the practice of all surrounding institutional dimensions would imply a considerable investment into the empirics of judicial cooperation in European private law. Our overviews of the case law do not come close to what would be needed in a perfect world. Still, the analysis throws doubts on whether the metaphor of national silos comes closer to reality than the ambitious language of the European polity. The Spanish courts and the courts of the new Member States have left a deep footprint on the development of the control of unfair terms under Directive 93/13/EC. The CJEU has not only given ever more concrete advice on the interpretation of individual standard terms, but has also shifted the focus from substantive to procedural control.[95] However, what do Spanish cases tell the other Member States about their law on unfair terms? The analysis of the Member States' observations, those of the European Commission and those of the parties would certainly help to clarify the role of the Euro-lawyers and to allow for some preliminary and tentative conclusions. However, a full picture would require all Member States to have provided input, which never happened in the private law cases here at issue.[96] On the other hand, it seems premature to conclude that silence – ie, no participation in the preliminary reference procedure – means that the absent Member States and their judiciaries are not surveying and monitoring the cases before the CJEU. For instance, it could be assumed that the Nordic countries very closely follow the CJEU, due to their long-standing commitment to consumer protection.[97]

In the absence of interactions within the institutional framework of the preliminary reference procedure, 'transnational social networks' may be able to give factual shape to the normative design of the procedure. Examples of this are the seminars of the European Academy of Law in Trier (Germany),[98] the European Law Institute in Vienna (Austria)[99] and the Centre of Judicial Co-operation in Florence (Italy),[100] which bring lawyers from all Member States (and beyond) together independently of their legal professions. In addition, there are networks between constitutional, administrative and civil/commercial law judges

---

[94] Cramér et al (n 90) 39–40. On the organisational aspect, see specifically Granger (n 93) 60–63, 66–68.

[95] On the CJEU's case law on procedural matters, focusing on the preliminary references emerging from Spain, see A van Duin, *Effective Judicial Protection in Consumer Litigation* (Cambridge, Intersentia, 2022). See also Van Duin's chapter in this volume, suggesting that the Dutch civil courts could learn from litigation in Spain.

[96] In the field of unfair terms, the highest number of participation, namely six governments, was reached in *Pannon* (Case C-243/08 *Pannon GSM Zrt v Erzsébet Sustikné Győrfi* [2009] ECR I-4713). It is striking that in many cases on the Unfair Terms Directive, only the government of the referring national court has been submitting observations. This also applies to the prominent *Aziz* case (n 61). Looking across the different fields, we found the highest number of participation by the Member States (namely 10 governments) in *Blödel-Pawlik* (Case C-134/11 *Jürgen Blödel-Pawlik v HanseMerkur Reiseversicherung AG* EU:C:2012:98). *Sturgeon* (Joined Cases C-402/07 and C-432/07 *Christopher Sturgeon and Others v Condor Flugdienst GmbH and Stefan Böck and Cornelia Lepuschitz v Air France SA* [2009] ECR I-10923) and *Pammer Alpenhof* (Joined Cases C-585/08 and C-144/09 *Peter Pammer v Reederei Karl Schlüter GmbH & Co KG and Hotel Alpenhof GesmbH v Oliver Heller* [2010] ECR I-12527) follow, with seven governments having submitted observations.

[97] T Wilhelmsson, 'The Emergence of Nordic Consumer Law and a Nordic Consumer Law Community and its Impact on Nordic Legal Unity' in HW Micklitz (ed), *The Making of Consumer Law and Policy in Europe* (Oxford, Hart Publishing, 2021) 171.

[98] See www.era.int.

[99] See www.europeanlawinstitute.eu.

[100] See https://cjc.eui.eu.

created by the judiciaries themselves,[101] and increasing (pre-litigation) cooperation between governments' legal agents has been observed.[102] However, the role and operations of such 'networks' – not to mention more informal/interpersonal contacts – remain largely opaque and unexplored. The claimed existence of a European polity must rely on the normative design of the preliminary reference procedure, independent of whether such exchanges take place. Yet, the tendency towards self-governance in judicial networks might lead to a closure which impedes polity-building.

C. The Politicisation of Litigation

The degree of politicisation of judge-made European private law differs in each case and depends on the type of litigation behind it. We distinguished three types in our study of the case law: collective conflicts with a strong societal dimension, conflicts with a specific national legal context and disputes on legal interpretational issues. Each type can be associated with a different actor, if not a different mindset. The potential of litigation to contribute to EU polity-building is pronounced where creative or innovative legal professionals translate collective conflicts into legal questions that are brought to the attention of the CJEU. In such cases, the political dimension of the preliminary reference is much more apparent than in situations where legal doctrine takes the lead. However, collective conflicts are the rarest type of litigation in European private law and a full investigation would require an analysis not only of the case law but also of all the Euro-lawyers involved in the cases.

In collective conflicts – such as *Heininger* (doorstep selling of credit-financed property), *Aziz* (mortgage enforcement proceedings) and *Schmitt* (the PIP scandal) – there is a social problem that raises the question of whether and to what extent litigation can contribute to finding societally acceptable solutions. This is the prominent field of public interest litigation. It requires innovative legal professionals – whether a practising lawyer who is defending the case or a judge who is delegating the dispute to the CJEU – who are confronted with a real-world problem, with people who suffer from a very concrete problem or with a broader societal and or political issue for which an acceptable legal answer has not yet been found.[103] The challenge for the legal professional is to find the best legal fit for the collective/societal problem at stake. It is striking that all the above-mentioned collective disputes concerned individual consumer litigants. Overall, consumer associations – at least formally – have not played a significant role in the case law on European private law. Clearly different from collective conflicts are the two other types of litigation, namely those with a strong national background and those raising legal technical doctrinal questions. Many – if not most – of the technical legal issues have been discussed in the legal doctrine prior to the dispute at issue. Legal scholarship had elaborated

---

[101] For an overview of the most well-known networks, see M de Visser and M Claes, 'Courts United? On European Judicial Networks' in Vauchez and de Witte (n 93) 75, 78–84; on judicial self-governance, see D Kosař, 'Beyond Judicial Councils: Forms, Rationales and Impact of Judicial Self-Governance in Europe' (2018) 19 *German Law Journal* 1567.

[102] Granger (n 93) 69–70.

[103] See, for instance, the account of José María Fernández Seijo – the national judge who submitted the preliminary reference in the *Aziz* case – in ch 15 of this volume. A further example, although from the field of EU environmental law, is the lawyer who devised the legal strategy in the *Janecek* case (Case C-237/07 *Dieter Janecek v Freistaat Bayern* [2008] ECR I-6221); see B Kas, 'Transforming the European "Legal Field" by Strategic Litigation' in L de Almeida, M Cantero Gamito, M Djurovic and KP Purnhagen (eds), *The Transformation of Economic Law: Essays in Honour of Hans-W Micklitz* (Oxford, Hart Publishing, 2019).

the meaning of the technical terms prior to the litigation before the CJEU – such as the right to return goods purchased online without cost, the remedies under the Consumer Sales Directive or the notion of defect in the Product Liability Directive – long before the case went to court and reached the CJEU. The lawyer in charge of the case or the judge involved could rely on legal doctrinal considerations. However, that does not necessarily facilitate a process of reflection and interaction on the economic and social implications that stand behind the technicality in the broader environment.

When it comes to private parties, the preliminary reference procedure puts the decision on who may participate in the procedure before the CJEU into the hands of the national legal orders. Private parties can submit an intervention only if they were already a party to the main national proceedings. Thus, in order to be able to reach the CJEU, the national requirements on legal standing play a crucial role. However, in European private law, contrary to environmental issues, legal standing never posed obstacles to testing the reach of EU law. It does not matter who the parties to the conflicts are, whether these are individual individuals, individuals as 'mandataire' for a good cause or non-governmental organisations, typically consumer associations, defending the collective interests of consumers.[104] However, what seems clear in theory might pose problems in practice. For instance, the procedural move in the law on unfair standard terms has brought the CJEU much closer to drawing a line between individual consumers and collective entities, let alone the link between the two. Several references, mainly from Central and Eastern European countries, bear witness to the difficulties that result from intermingling individual and collective interests.[105] Another example is *Asociación de Consumidores Independientes de Castilla y León*, in which the CJEU drew a sharp line between the position of consumer organisations and of individual consumers vis-a-vis traders. The Court clarified that the Unfair Terms Directive does not preclude national procedural rules under which actions for an injunction brought by consumer protection associations must be brought before the courts where the defendant is established.[106] A similar example is the famous *Schrems* case,[107] where the litigant collected 25,000 complaints on Facebook's infringement of privacy and data protection rights. The CJEU held that Mr Schrems could bring an individual action in Austria against Facebook Ireland, but that he could not benefit from the consumer forum as the assignee of other consumers' claims for the purposes of a collective action.[108]

Taking a more distant perspective and looking at the role of the various actors in shaping EU law more generally, there is a striking difference between the preliminary references from the old Member States and the new Member States, including Spain. In the former, the use and usefulness of EU law was discovered mainly through national legislation that imposed barriers upon trade. This applied to Germany in *Cassis de Dijon*,[109] Italy in *Zoni*,[110] the UK in

---

[104] Such a finding should not be conflated with the much more debated issue of collective legal actions such as the question whether all European consumers who suffered from *Dieselgate* could address the CJEU and seek compensation directly through a European-wide solution. The new Directive 2020/1828 on Representative Actions ([2020] OJ L409/1) introduces minimum standards at the national level, but provides only for rudimentary rules on a European-wide collective action.

[105] C Leone, 'The Missing Stone in the Cathedral: Of Unfair Terms in Employment Contracts and Coexisting Rationalities in European Contract Law' (PhD thesis, University of Amsterdam, 2020).

[106] Case C-413/12 *Asociación de Consumidores Independientes de Castilla y León v Anuntis Segundamano España SL* EU:C:2013:800.

[107] Case C-498/16 *Maximilian Schrems v Facebook Ireland Ltd* EU:C:2018:37.

[108] ibid.

[109] Case C-120/78 *Rewe v Bundesmonopolverwaltung für Branntwein* [1979] ECR 649.

[110] Case C-90/86 *Criminal Proceedings against Zoni* [1988] ECR 4285.

Sunday Trading[111] and France in *Keck*.[112] These cases were driven by business interests. In the latter, on the other hand, European private law was instrumentalised to combat hardship for which national private law lacked the tools to do so. Thus, although somewhat overstated, one might argue that in the old Member States, the market freedoms were used to strike down trade barriers, whereas in Spain and the Central and Eastern European countries, EU consumer law served to increase the level of social protection in the domestic legal orders. There are certainly inconsistences. Greek and Portuguese consumers were equally affected by the financial crisis, but there were no references from their respective courts. Instead, citizens addressed the European Court of Human Rights to contest measures implemented by their governments in response to the economic crisis.[113] The same applies to five financial companies, which – as a last resort to countering the CJEU's protective outlook – tried to challenge Hungarian legislation implementing the CJEU's case law on the Unfair Terms Directive 93/13 for violating their right to a fair trial (Article 6 ECHR).[114]

IV. ON THE WAY TO A EUROPEAN POLITY?

Bringing the 300 judgments of the CJEU into perspective raises many definitional issues – about the European Constitution, the role of private law in the European Constitution, the understanding of what private law means in the European regulatory context, the conceptualisation of the European society, the European epistemic community (or communities) and the European polity – and all this has to be analysed with a view to the particular role of the CJEU in the preliminary reference procedure. Based on our research, we tend to subscribe to the idea that EU law in general and EU private law in particular are apt to build and develop over time a European polity or perhaps more realistically European polities in different legal fields. However, such a finding rests on several ambitious assumptions – a holistic perspective on the interaction between the CJEU, the national courts, the national governments, the Euro-lawyers involved in the litigation and the key role of the law as the 'glue' (Vauchez) which holds the law, the society and the polity together.[115]

The overall process towards building a private law polity is certainly facilitated through the imperfect or incomplete constitutive elements of European private law – the claim of supremacy of secondary EU law over national private law coupled to the vertical (not the horizontal) direct effect of secondary EU law. The CJEU is thereby opening up space for interaction in a heterarchical image of private law, where Euro-lawyers in different roles and functions can interfere in the search for solutions which take the CJEU's interpretation into account, but without suffocating national adaptations.[116] The particular regulatory character of EU private law and its ambiguous nature in between public and private is an additional asset as it broadens the potential scope of Euro-lawyers, who may be public or private, EU-focused or concentrating on the national context. However, the problem in European polity-building results from the

---

[111] Case C-145/88 *Torfaen Borough Council v B & Q plc* [1989] ECR 3851.
[112] Case C-267/91 *Criminal Proceedings against Bernard Keck and Daniel Mithouard* [1993] ECR I-6097.
[113] C Kilpatrick and B de Witte (eds), 'Social Rights in Times of Crisis in the Eurozone: The Role of Fundamental Rights' Challenges' (2014) EUI Working Papers LAW 2014/05.
[114] *Merkantil Car Zrt v Hungary and Four Other Applications* App No 22853/15 (ECtHR, 20 December 2018).
[115] Vauchez (n 28) 6.
[116] G Tagiuri, 'How EU Law Politicises Markets and Creates Spaces for Progressive Coding' (2022) 1 *European Law Open* 390.

limited preparedness of the Euro-lawyers in the Member States and their national judiciaries to make constructive use of the space that the CJEU is opening up. There is a certain tendency for many of the 300 cases to be perceived as 'national problems' and to be referred to the CJEU in order to find a solution to a 'national' problem and not as a genuinely Europeanised issue, which might have an impact on all national orders in the Member States. As such, it might be safer, more realistic and conceptually wiser to speak of a European polity in the making, at least with regard to private law matters.

3

On the Doubly Constitutionalising Character of European Contract Law

MICHAEL W DOWDLE

I. INTRODUCTION

IN THIS CHAPTER, I want to develop a deeper explication of the European constitutional phenomenon identified by Chantal Mak in her essay 'First or Second Best? Judicial Law-Making in European Private Law'.[1] In that essay, Mak proposes that because the traditional functional specialisations that make up our understanding of the 'separation of powers' are predicated on a state-centric notion of constitutionalism, they do not translate into supranational political entities like that of the EU. For this reason, some incidents of what might appear to be illegitimate exercises in 'judicial activism' when performed by domestic courts should be regarded as normatively acceptable when performed by the Court of Justice of the European Union (CJEU). As she puts it:

> These considerations raise questions concerning the conceptions of democracy and democratic legitimacy in European private law. On the one hand, the central ideas remain participation and representation in law-making processes by those who will be governed by the resulting rules. On the other hand, it seems that the manner in which these ideals are realised in the multi-level sphere of European private law does not necessarily have to take the same institutional shape as in national constitutional orders, in particular as regards the division of powers between legislature and judiciary. A one-on-one translation of a conception of democracy from the nation-state level to the EU encounters difficulties – while the underlying ideas of participation and representation retain their importance, part of their meaning may be lost in translation if the division of powers in European private law is based on existing divisions of tasks among national legislatures and judiciaries.[2]

This, she concludes, is the case with the CJEU's treatment of European contract law. Even if the 'judicial activism' – what this chapter will refer to as 'interpretive freedom' – demonstrated by the CJEU in the area of contract law would generally be considered illegitimate (or anti-democratic) if engaged in by domestic courts, it should not be so regarded when engaged in by the CJEU because of the different institutional and political environment in which that court operates.

---

[1] C Mak, 'First or Second Best? Judicial Law-Making in European Private Law' in JM Mendes and I Venzke (eds), *Allocating Authority* (Oxford, Hart Publishing, 2018).
[2] ibid 233–34.

Mak's demonstration that the CJEU's interpretive freedom in the area of European contract law enjoys a distinct legitimacy is persuasive. But this chapter will argue that the reason she identifies as to *why* it enjoys such legitimacy is more debatable. In particular, she attributes it to the fact that political Europe in general suffers from a democratic deficit. By contrast, I will argue that it stems from the pronouncedly (but not uniquely) economic character of the 'constitution' of political Europe.

Before proceeding, I should define what I mean by a 'constitution'. As used in this chapter, a 'constitution' refers to that set of codified and uncodified ('unwritten') principles that 'constitute' a normative regulatory regime – ie, that bring it into being, allow it to persist, and make it visible.[3] In the political context, particularly that of the state, it is a device that 'creates ... a union',[4] both in terms of setting out that regime's organisational structure and in establishing a basis for its political, social and legal identity; it is not simply a device for delimiting a state's powers, for example, through the articulation of fundamental rights.

The state is the most paradigmatic manifestation of this kind of 'constitution',[5] and that will be our principal comparative referent in examining the 'constitutional' role that contract law plays in supranational Europe. I understand that many may object to the idea that there is a European 'constitution',[6] but such objections ultimately revolve around a denotational understanding of the term that is not relevant to this thesis. The point is that regardless of what you call it, the set of formal and informal principles that construct the political-legal regulatory entity called the 'European Union' resemble in their epistemic structure and interactions, and in their relationship to politics, those that are used to construct constitutional 'states', and that this resemblance helps explain and justify the interpretive freedom displayed by the CJEU in the realm of contract law. In order to better emphasise this resemblance, this chapter will therefore refer to the set of principles that construct – or 'constitute' – the political-regulatory entity called the 'European Union' as a 'constitution', in the sense that these principles both lay out the EU's organisational structure[7] and provide a possible foundation for the polity-building of 'political Europe'.[8]

Along these lines, it will be argued that the reason why the CJEU is able to engage in much more liberal interpretations than domestic courts in the area of the European law of contracts without provoking the legitimacy concerns associated with 'judicial activism' is due to the fact that contract law per se has a distinctive constitutional character that I will call 'doubly constitutionalising'. How is contract law 'doubly constitutionalising'? First, insofar as a state's private economy is concerned, the law of contract sets the principles that constitute the operation of the market – what we will call its 'market-constitutionalising' function.[9]

---

[3] *cf* G Teubner, *Constitutional Fragments: Societal Constitutionalism and Globalization* (Oxford, Oxford University Press, 2012).

[4] See, eg, Preamble to the US Constitution (1789) ('We, the people of the United States, in order to *create* a more perfect union ...' (emphasis added)).

[5] See generally MW Dowdle and MA Wilkinson (eds), *Constitutionalism beyond Liberalism* (Cambridge, Cambridge University Press, 2017). See also G Teubner, 'The Project of Constitutional Sociology: Irritating Nation State Constitutionalism' (2013) 4 *Transnational Legal Theory* 44.

[6] See N Walker, 'Not the European Constitution' (2007) 15 *Maastricht Journal of European and Comparative Law* 135.

[7] A Stone Sweet, 'European Integration and the Legal System' in T Börzel and R Cichowski (eds), *The State of the European Union*, Vol 6: *Law, Politics, and Society* (Oxford, Oxford University Press, 2003).

[8] See J Habermas, 'Struggles for Recognition in the Democratic Constitutional State' in *The Inclusion of the Other: Studies in Political Theory* (New York, John Wiley & Sons, 2018) 225–26, 203–36 (discussing 'constitutional patriotism').

[9] *cf* R Craswell, 'Contract Law: General Theories' in B Bouckaert and G DeGeest (eds), *Encyclopedia of Law & Economics*, vol III (Cheltenham, Edward Elgar, 2000) 18–20.

But at the same time, insofar as a state's political economy is concerned, contract law also works to structure a state's political-economic constitution[10] by establishing the 'constituting' principles that delineate that state's *national* economy and how it contributes to the state's political structure[11] – what we will call its 'state-constitutionalising' function.

Collectively, we will refer to the overall state-constitutional regime that is comprised of these two sub-constitutional regimes as a state's (or, in the case of the EU, 'Europe's') 'constitutional *system*'.

As noted above, contract law in general is intrinsically doubly constitutionalising, even insofar as state constitution systems are concerned. But, I will argue, it is particularly pronounced in the constitutional system of the EU due to the distinctly economic focus of that 'constitution'. For reasons that will be discussed below, it is the more pronouncedly *economic* character of the European constitutional system that serves to legitimate the CJEU's distinct interpretive freedom in the area of contract law.

My argument proceeds as follows. Section II explores contract law's 'doubly constituting' character, showing how it serves to help 'constitutionalise' both the state and the market. Section III then identifies the implications this has for our understanding of constitutionalism. The doubly constitutionalising character of contract law sits uneasily within conventional understandings of constitutionalism, and in particular with the separation of powers. This is because there is an innate paradox to the two sides of contract law's constitutional character: a kind of paradox that Gunther Teubner has famously termed a 'regulatory trilemma' and one that cannot be 'solved' via processes of legalisation, juridification and/or doctrinal articulation. This means that the constitutional character of contract law is always epistemically and intersystemically incomplete, and this sometimes demands that courts, when adjudicating contract law matters, engage in what Alec Stone Sweet has famously referred to as 'judicial politics'.[12] By contrast, as Stone Sweet shows, our conventional understandings of separation of powers cannot fit such judicial politics within its tripartite framework, even while such judicial politics are actually an essential part of a modern constitutional order. The principal way in which domestic court systems in civil law Europe have traditionally addressed the coherence problems stemming from contract law's doubly constitutionalising character is through the doctrine of good faith. But the use of that doctrine is problematic, in that it ultimately impedes the capacity of the state's larger constitutional system taken as a whole to 'regulate' how these two components of contract law's doubly constitutionalising character interact.

Section IV then explores the alternative response that has emerged in political Europe. This involves domestic courts delegating responsibility for addressing issues arising from the doubly constitutionalising nature of contract law to an alternative forum in which issues of 'judicial activism'/interpretive freedom are not such a normative concern, ie, the CJEU. This is because Europe's constitutional system has a particularly pronounced economic component to it. It is

---

[10] See H Collins, 'The European Economic Constitution and the Constitutional Dimension of Private Law' (2009) 5 *European Review of Contract Law* 71.

[11] See, eg, US Constitution, art 1, s 10, cl 1 (1789) ('No State shall … pass any … Law, or Law impairing the Obligation of Contracts'); see also US Constitution, art I, 8, cl 3 (1789) (giving the US Congress power '[t]o regulate Commerce with foreign Nations, and among the several States, and with the Indian Tribes'); *cf* HW Micklitz, 'On the Intellectual History of Freedom Of Contract and Regulation' (2015) 4 *Penn State Journal of Law and International Affairs* 14, 16–17, 21–25 (discussing the constitutional dimensions of the 'freedom of contract' doctrine in England, France and Germany).

[12] See A Stone Sweet, 'The Politics of Constitutional Review in France and Europe' (2007) 5 *International Journal of Constitutional Law* 69; M Shapiro and A Stone Sweet, 'The New Constitutional Politics in Europe' (2005) 2 *Comparative Politics: Critical Concepts in Political Science* 83.

therefore easier for the CJEU to identify and appeal to this aspect of Europe's constitutional system. This makes the CJEU's interpretive freedom with regard to contract law seem less 'activist'.

Finally, section V explores how all this may allow the CJEU to contribute to our broader understanding of the relationship between contract law and constitutional law more generally. As noted above, the doubly constitutionalising character of contract law is not unique to Europe; it is just distinctly visible there. That visibility allows the CJEU to provoke discourse on and investigation into the nature of that character – a discourse and investigation that is relevant to our understanding of how constitutionalism and contract law interact in all modern constitutional systems, not simply that of the EU.

II. THE CONSTITUTIONAL DIMENSIONS OF THE LAW OF CONTRACTS

Contract law has two constitutional dimensions: a 'market-constituting' dimension and a 'state-constituting' dimension. It is the presence of these *two* constitutional dimensions that gives contract law a distinctly 'doubly constitutionalising' character.

Exposing the constitutional dimensions of contract law requires us first to identify what constitutional law does. This requires that we first examine what it is that a state does, because, as noted above, state-domestic constitutional law is the quintessential paradigm for constitutionalism in general, and much of what so-called 'constitutional' law does is determined by what a state does and how it does it.

Along these lines, a state is, among other things, a regulatory device that converts individual power and autonomy into collective flourishing. Constitutional law governs this conversion by a variety of means. First, it determines what kind of (private) power will be admitted into this conversion process: can one use wealth to purchase votes? Can one use one's persuasive powers to threaten populist violence in order to get one's political way? Second, it determines the particular pathways by which different kinds of power flow within this conversion process: can the executive ignore a court pronouncement? Can a court nullify legislation on grounds of unconstitutionality? Finally, it determines the kinds of 'flourishing' this conversion must, may or may not work to promote or augment: can a state use its conversion processes to promote an individual's choice to purchase another as a slave, or by imposing limits on what can be reported in the media, or by forbidding cinemas from showing films on Sunday?

A. The First Constitutional Dimension of Contract Law: Contract Law as Part of the 'Constitution' of the Market

Like a state, a market is also a regulatory institution that works to convert individual power into collective flourishing. A particular cobbler may be the world's best and most efficient producer of shoes, but without a market for those shoes, she will likely starve to death. A (collective) market allows her to convert her limited (even if immense) individual capacity to make shoes into a capacity to possess the full diversity of resources necessary to pursue the kind of life she wishes to lead. It does this by promoting the capacity of choice. A slave relationship also allows one to convert one's individual capacities into material security, but that is a kind of security whose terms are dictated by another. A market, by contrast, allows one to convert one's power into material opportunities whose particular attributes and foci are determined by the individual herself.

Along these lines, contract law helps 'constitute' a market by allowing us to distinguish legitimate from non-legitimate ways of constructing an exchange. A market is ultimately a forum for economic exchange, and the 'contract' is the device that determines whether an exchange has in fact *validly* taken place: can a valid exchange be constituted where one withholds material information in extracting a promise? Does the promise have to be in writing? Does one bind oneself with a bare promise? Thus, insofar as a market is concerned, contract law is structurally analogous to what we are calling 'constitutional law'. This particular dimension of the constitutional character of contract will be called its 'market constitutionalising' function.

(To be clear, contract law is not the only legal phenomenon that works to constitute a market. In particular, property law is also a core component of a market's 'constitution' – albeit one that will not be of concern to this chapter.)

B. The Second Constitutional Dimension of Contract Law: Contract Law as Part of the Constitution of the State

But at the same time, markets – as fora for conducting economic transactions – are themselves constituent elements of a political state that are sometimes referred to in the collective as the state's 'economic constitution'. This is because the modern state in particular relies on markets to perform some of its most existential functions. For example, states create and use what Fernand Braudel called 'national markets' – markets whose rules, pricing structures, and supply and demand responsiveness are consistent across the entire geographical realm of that state and in which there are no barriers to entry to citizens of the state (ie, no local or regional protectionism)[13] – to provide national cohesion[14] and social and economic citizenship;[15] to generate political strength both domestically (such as through taxation)[16] and internationally;[17] and to supply politically essential goods to its citizenry (ie, goods that allow the state to maintain its political legitimacy).[18]

Contract law is used to determine, to a significant extent, how these essential state functions are to be realised.[19] For example, in cases in which the state relies on private markets to supply goods and services that are essential to a citizen's effective participation in the state – goods and services such as education, employment, medical care and public utilities[20] – contract

---

[13] F Braudel, *Civilization and Capitalism 15th–18th Century, Vol 3: The Perspective of the World* (Berkeley, University of California Press, 1992) 277–352, 365–69.

[14] See, eg, L Tribe, *American Constitutional Law*, 2nd edn (New York, Foundation Press, 1988) 417; R Collins, 'Economic Union as a Constitutional Value' (1988) 63 *New York University Law Review* 53.

[15] TH Marshall, 'Citizenship and Social Class' in S Lazar (ed), *The Anthropology of Citizenship: A Reader* (Chichester, John Wiley & Sons, 2013); A Sen, *Development as Freedom* (Oxford, Oxford University Press, 1999) 38–40.

[16] See, eg, CB Huat 'State-Owned Enterprises, State Capitalism and Social Distribution in Singapore' (2016) 29 *Pacific Review* 499.

[17] E Helleiner, 'Economic Nationalism as a Challenge to Economic Liberalism? Lessons from the 19th Century' (2002) 46 *International Studies Quarterly* 307.

[18] *cf* T Prosser, *The Limits of Competition Law: Markets and Public Services* (Oxford, Oxford University Press, 2005) 35–38 (discussing what he terms 'citizenship rights').

[19] *cf* MW Dowdle, 'On the Public-Law Character of Competition Law: A Lesson from Asian Capitalism' (2015) 38 *Fordham International Law* 301, 313–25.

[20] See generally Marshall (n 15).

law will often set out the terms that govern exchanges involving these good and services, thus ensuring that they are equally accessible to the citizenry.[21] It will prohibit certain kinds of private exchanges that are felt to corrode the state's moral legitimacy (eg, the purchase of slaves) or constitutional effectiveness (eg, monopolistic mergers that threaten the democratic character of the state).[22] It will carve out regulatory exceptions for kinds of contracts that are particularly conducive to the state's public policy objectives (eg, granting market monopolies in the form of intellectual property protection in exchange for product innovations that promote national competitiveness).[23] In this way, it is a part of the 'constitutional law' of the state – its 'state-constitutionalising' function.

III. IMPLICATIONS FOR 'CONSTITUTIONALISM'

Together, these two constitutional components of contract law are both essential parts of a state's 'constitutional system'. But their interplay fits uneasily within conventional understandings of constitutionalism, and in particular with the idea of separation of powers. This interplay can often result in what Gunther Teubner famously referred to as a 'regulatory trilemma': a condition in which divergence between state law and the social 'laws' of the market produce normative incoherencies in a state's overall constitutional system. Traditionally, in the context of contract law, domestic courts in civil law systems have used the doctrine of 'good faith' to negotiate this trilemma. But, as we shall see, this response is not without its problems.

A. The Problem of 'Separation of Powers'

The juridical interaction between the two constitutional components of contract law causes problems from the perspective of separation of powers. The doctrine of the separation of powers is fundamentally founded on the presumption that courts are normatively bounded by a demand for epistemic coherence and consistency, whereas legislatures are not. Legislatures are free to pass laws that continually contradict each other. It is ultimately the courts' job to massage such contradictions into that internally consistent normative and epistemic entity that is sometimes termed the 'rule of law'.[24] It is this drive for internal consistency that distinguishes the court's juridical function of legal 'interpretation' from the legislative function of 'law-making'.[25]

Critics may respond by pointing out that the distinction between law-making and law-interpreting is largely a myth. The internal normative consistency of law does not constrain judicial decision-making because judges can always construct arguments that present any decision as being determinately consistent with the existing body of legal norms – even where the norms of that system actually point in different directions, as they often do. This always gives judges inevitable leeway to 'make new law', regardless of what the formal separation of powers doctrine proclaims.

---

[21] *cf* T Prosser, *The Limits of Competition Law* (Oxford, Oxford University Press, 2005) 35–38.

[22] GS Becker, 'Competition and Democracy' (1958) 1 *Journal of Law and Economics* 105.

[23] WE Kovacic, 'A Regulator's Perspective on Getting the Balance Right' in RI McEwin (ed), *Intellectual Property, Competition Law and Economics in Asia* (Oxford, Hart Publishing, 2011).

[24] See, eg, J Raz, 'The Rule of Law and its Virtue' in *The Authority of Law: Essays on Law and Morality*, 2nd edn (Oxford, Oxford University Press, 2009).

[25] See also R Dworkin, *Law's Empire* (Cambridge MA, Belknap Press, 1986).

But in fact, complaints about what we today term 'judicial activism' can be found in many legal traditions, and have been around for over a millennium: Islamic law, for example, has been grappling with the issue of interpretive 'activism' since the tenth century CE (see, eg, 'the closing of the gate of *ijtihad*');[26] imperial Chinese jurists had been distinguishing appropriate from 'activist' judicial interpretations of law since the fourth century CE.[27] This suggests that rationally or irrationally, political populations across the globe and across the ages appear to believe that they can distinguish between an 'activist' judiciary and a non-activist judiciary. And while they may disagree about particulars, the universality and multi-millennial persistence of this perception as a socially meaningful tool for evaluating judicial performance suggests that such evaluations need to be taken seriously – at the very least, notions of judicial activism and judicial restraint appear to have a widespread social meaning that renders their normative dichotomy more than simply a metaphysical fantasy.

At the same time, even those legal cultures that especially shun interpretive activism also recognise that some degree of judicial responsiveness is a necessary component of justice.[28] The question is not how to rid ourselves of so-called judicial activism, but how to find the appropriate balance – an activity that this chapter will refer to as 'responsive adjudication'.[29] However, this is a question that simply does not resonate in traditional *constitutional* thinking: it is not a question for which the doctrine of separation of powers gives any analytic purchase. Thus, for example, while it is clear that courts in the classically civil law jurisdictions of Germany and France engage in what I call 'responsive adjudication',[30] at the *constitutional* level, both countries continue to cling to the French Revolutionary ideal that courts merely *apply* the law – an ideal that Jürgen Habermas famously captures in his concept of '[judicial] discourses of application', as distinguished from a more wide-ranging interpretive practice that he calls 'discourses of justification'.[31]

Another demonstration of the inability of the separation of powers to conceptualise what I call responsive adjudication can be seen in the historical evolution of England's law of equity. As is well known, the law of equity emerged when the Court of Chancery was given authority to ignore the legal rules of the common law when it felt that the application of such rules would result in injustice. But of course, that task would ultimately fail: by the seventeenth century, the law of equity was widely regarded as having become even more ossified and less responsive than the common law.[32] Thus, in both civil law and common law systems, our traditional constitutional understanding of the judiciary's role in a 'separation of powers' framework lacks the conceptual tools to encourage and regulate responsive adjudication.[33]

---

[26] See AM Emon, 'Ijtihad' in AM Emon and R Ahmed (eds), *The Oxford Handbook of Islamic Law* (Oxford, Oxford University Press, 2018).

[27] NP Ho, 'Chinese Legal Thought in the Han-Tang Transition: Liu Song's (d. 300) Theory of Adjudication' (2017) 35 *UCLA Pacific Basic Law Journal* 155.

[28] See, eg, H Merryman and R Pérez-Perdomo, 'Judges' in *The Civil Law Tradition: An Introduction to the Legal Systems of Europe and Latin America*, 3rd edn (Stanford, Stanford University Press, 2007).

[29] This term is obviously borrowed from Ian Ayres and John Braithwaite. See I Ayres and J Braithwaite, *Responsive Regulation: Transcending the Deregulation Debate* (New York, Oxford University Press, 1992).

[30] See K Zweigert and H Kötz, 'Courts and Lawyers in France' in *Introduction to Comparative Law* (trans T Weir) (Oxford, Clarendon Press, 1998); K Zweigert and H Kötz, 'The German Civil Code' in *Introduction to Comparative Law* (trans T Weir) (Oxford, Clarendon Press, 1998) 149–50.

[31] See generally H Baxter, 'Discourse Theory and the Theory and Practice of Adjudication' in *Habermas: The Discourse Theory of Law and Democracy* (Stanford, Stanford University Press, 2011).

[32] See JH Baker, *An Introduction to English Legal History*, 4th edn (London, Butterworths, 2002) 102–08.

[33] See also MC Dorf, 'Problem-Solving Courts and the Judicial Accountability Deficit' in MW Dowdle (ed), *Public Accountability: Designs, Dilemmas and Experiences* (Cambridge, Cambridge University Press, 2006).

B. The Regulatory Trilemma Caused by the Doubly Constitutionalising Character of Contract

Here is where the doubly constitutional nature of contract law becomes problematic. Let us recall that contract law both shapes the 'constitution' of the market and the constitution of the state. But these two constitutional functionalities introduce unavoidable internal normative inconsistencies into both contract law and the state's overall constitutional system. In a free market constitutional system, markets are largely autonomous from the state.[34] Being autonomous, they work to set their own constitutional norms, and there is no guarantee that these norms will be consistent with the norms set out by the constitution of the political state.

For this reason, the doubly constitutionalising character of contract law can introduce into the state's larger constitutional system what Gunther Teubner has famously termed a 'regulatory trilemma'.[35] As described by Teubner, a regulatory trilemma occurs when the regulatory norms of autonomous domestic law find themselves in conflict with alternative regulatory norms that have been constructed by and that constitute one or more of the autonomous social systems operating within that state (what this chapter will refer to as a 'societal constitution'). When this happens, it will produce one of three undesirable outcomes. One is what Teubner calls 'mutual indifference'. This occurs when the state's domestic law and a conflicting societal constitution simply ignore each other, each operating as if the other does not exist.[36] Another possible outcome is what Teubner calls 'social disintegration through law'. This occurs when the domestic law of the state 'colonises' the societal constitution, causing the latter to abandon its own, autonomously generated regulatory norms and instead conform with the alternative regulatory norms demanded by the state's domestic law.[37] A third possible outcome is what Teubner calls 'legal disintegration through society'. This occurs when the alternative regulatory norms of a societal constitution cause the state's domestic law to spontaneously evolve so as to serve the regulatory needs and expectations of that societal constitution rather than those of the state itself.[38] What makes this a 'trilemma' is that each one of these responses is problematic: mutual indifference corrodes the regulatory effectiveness of the political state; 'social disintegration through law' corrodes society's capacity to serve the social needs of its members; and 'legal disintegration through society' corrodes the legitimacy of state law by compromising its epistemic autonomy.

In the case of the doubly constitutionalising character of contract law, such a trilemma can be produced by conflict between the socially autonomous constitutional system of the market and the politically autonomous constitutional system of the state. So, for example, a 'black market' – a market that operates outside the regulatory reach of the constitutional state – can clearly be seen as a form of 'mutual indifference'.[39] 'Over-regulation' – wherein a state's constitutional-regulatory apparatus corrodes a market's ability to generate wealth and the

---

[34] See, eg, L Kaplow and S Shavell, *Fairness versus Welfare* (Cambridge, MA, Harvard University Press, 2002).

[35] See generally G Teubner, 'Juridification: Aspects, Limits, Solutions' in R Baldwin, C Scott and C Hood (eds), *A Reader on Regulation* (Oxford, Oxford University Press, 2012) 406–14.

[36] ibid 409–10.

[37] ibid 410–11.

[38] ibid 411–14.

[39] *cf* H de Soto, 'The Mystery of Legal Failure: Why Property Law Does Not Work Outside the West' in *The Mystery of Capital: Why Capitalism Triumphs in the West and Fails Everywhere Else* (New York, Basic Books, 2000).

opportunities that such wealth creates[40] – would be an example of what we might call 'market-constitutional disintegration through state', corresponding to Teubner's 'social disintegration through law'. And many would claim that what we might call 'state-constitutional disintegration through market', corresponding to Teubner's 'legal disintegration through society', can be perceived in the economic-ideological phenomenon known as 'neoliberalism',[41] in which the market's unfettered pursuit of capital accumulation – a core organisational logic of capitalist market systems[42] – corrodes a state's ability to provide social citizenship to its citizens.[43]

Conventional constitutionalism is ineffective in prescribing ways to regulate the constitutional trilemma produced by contract law. This is because the principal means through which the state regulates society is via a priori legislation. But a priori regulation is ill-suited for regulating the inter-constitutional conflicts produced by contract law's doubly constitutionalising character. Such a priori regulation simply gives rise to its own possibilities for a second-order regulatory trilemma, because it cannot dictate how an autonomous market society will respond after the fact to second-order, curative legislation: whether that society will respond by conforming to the state's law even without regard to the effect of such conformity on its own societal-constitutional order;[44] by 'socialising' the state's law to make it compatible with the market constitution at the expense of the legitimacy of the state's constitutional order;[45] or by simply ignoring that law.[46] So, paradoxically, the very act of trying to resolve a constitutional trilemma produced by contract law's doubly constitutionalising character by using state legislation itself simply works to move that trilemma to a new regulatory arena.[47]

Because legislation is unable to regulate regulatory-trilemmatic phenomenon, this leaves it up to the courts, which for the most part engage in *ex post* rather than a priori decision-making, to decide how to respond to inter-constitutional conflicts between contract law's two constitutional functionalities. But courts can only resolve *particular* litigatory incidents that produce this trilemma, they cannot use their legal-interpretative function to formulate a new precedent that can be used to resolve doctrinally a similar trilemmatic instantiation when it again arises.[48] Interpretive precedent and doctrine are themselves a priori in character, in that they establish abstract and autonomous regulatory norms that can themselves be catalysts for regulatory trilemmas. Using precedent or doctrine to seek to resolve *ex ante* a constitutional regulatory trilemma simply works to move that trilemma into a different constitutional realm: that of the judiciary. Thus, in addressing a litigatory dispute involving an inter-constitutional conflict between state-constitutional norm and a market-constitutional norm, the court often has no choice other than to step outside the traditional rule-based framework of adjudication.

---

[40] See F Hayek, *The Road to Serfdom* (Chicago, University of Chicago Press, 1944); *cf* Kaplow and Shavell (n 34).

[41] *cf* B Jessop, 'Putting Neoliberalism in its Time and Place: A Response to the Debate' (2013) 12 *Social Anthropology* 65.

[42] See, eg, M Weber, *The Protestant Ethic and the Spirit of Capitalism* (New York, Routledge, 2001 [1930]) 36, 116.

[43] See, eg, T Piketty, *Capital in the Twenty-First Century* (Cambridge, MA, Harvard University Press, 2014).

[44] *cf* Kaplow and Shavell (n 34).

[45] See, eg, MA Wilkinson, *Authoritarian Liberalism and the Transformation of Modern Europe* (Oxford, Oxford University Press, 2021); MA Wilkinson, 'The Reconstitution of Post-War Europe: Liberal Excesses, Democratic Deficiencies' in MW Dowdle and MA Wilkinson (eds), *Constitutionalism beyond Liberalism* (Cambridge, Cambridge University Press, 2017).

[46] See, eg, de Soto (n 39).

[47] *cf* K Polanyi, *The Great Transformation: The Political and Economic Origins of Our Time*, 2nd edn (Boston, Beacon Press, 2001 [1944]); see also F Block, 'Polanyi's Double Movement and the Reconstruction of Critical Theory' (2008) 38 *Revue interventions économiques/Papers in Political Economy* 1.

[48] See Teubner (n 35) 414.

In other words, by addressing such inter-constitutional conflicts, courts have no choice but to be 'activist',[49] in the way described by Mak in her analysis of the CJEU.

C. Domestic Responses: The Good Faith Doctrine

In civil law systems, courts generally respond to the innate threat of judicial 'activism' that stem from contract law's doubly constitutionalising character by using the doctrine of good faith. This doctrine allows the court to treat such normative conflicts as questions of fact specific to that case rather than general questions of law that are simply being provoked by the case. This, in turn, allows the courts to avoid complaints of judicial activism, which focus on issues of legal interpretation rather than fact-finding.

Along these lines, Martijn Hesselink well-describes how the doctrine of good faith is used to massage the inter-constitutional conflicts inherent in contract law, although he sees these conflicts as inter-ideological rather than inter-constitutional:

> Today, it is quite broadly accepted that contract law is best understood as being based on two funda-mental – and conflicting – ideas, i.e. autonomy and solidarity. The idea of autonomy is politically linked to liberalism ('the right') and its typical dogmas in contract law are the 'freedom of contract' and the 'binding force of contract'. The idea of solidarity, on the other hand, is politically linked to socialism ('the left') and its main dogmas in contract law are the 'duty of good faith' and the 'need for specific mandatory rules for the protection of weaker parties'.[50]

Although Hesselink's observation is framed in terms of political-ideological contradictions, his observation applies equally well to the role of good faith in negotiating constitutional contradictions. 'Freedom of contract' is one of the doctrinal pillars of 'market constitution-alism' in advanced capitalist state-economic systems. It is the foundation of the market's regulatory focus, articulating the foundational expectation out of which the market's consti-tutional autonomy is built, identified and operates. But at the same time, it sits uncomfortably in the context of a state's constitution, in which 'the need for specific mandatory rules for the protection of weaker parties' is a core component of both social and economic citizenship.[51] And, along these lines, in another essay, Hesselink expressly acknowledges the distinctly (if disguised) 'constitutional' dimensions of the good faith doctrine:

> In all systems objective good faith is usually regarded as a normative concept. Indeed good faith is often seen as the highest norm of contract law, or of the law of obligations or even of all private law. For that reason many provisions in the code which make no explicit reference to good faith are never-theless said to be based on it.

> Good faith is often said to be in some way connected with moral standards. On the one hand, it is said to be a moral standard itself, a legal-ethical principle; good faith means honesty, candour, loyalty et cetera. It is often said that the standard of good faith basically means that a party should take the interest of the other party into account. On the other hand, good faith is said to be the gateway through which moral values enter the law.

> ...

---

[49] See, eg, HLA Hart, *The Concept of Law*, 2nd edn (Oxford, Clarendon Press, 1961) 110 (arguing that certain kinds of judicial judgments can only be founded on 'social facts' rather than on legal rules).

[50] M Hesselink, 'The Horizontal Effect of Social Rights in European Contract Law' (2003) 1 *Europa e Diritto Privato* 11.

[51] See Marshall (n 15); see also Sen (n 15) 38–40.

[I]*n some systems good faith is regarded – and actually used by the courts – as a means through which the values of the Constitution enter into private law.* (Emphasis added)[52]

In this latter essay, Hesselink also describes how, as noted above, what insulates determinations of good faith from charges of judicial activism is that such determinations are portrayed as being fact-specific:

> It is generally agreed that a general good faith clause does not contain a rule, at least not one like most other rules in the code. It is not, like other rules, susceptive to subsumption since neither the facts to which it applies nor the legal effect that it stipulates can be established a priori. Good faith is therefore usually said to be an open norm, a norm the content of which cannot be established in an abstract way but which depends on the circumstances of the case in which it must be applied, and which must be established through concretisation.[53]

In sum, there appear to be two ways through which appeals to the legal doctrine of good faith shield domestic courts from complaints of 'judicial activism' when addressing the 'constitutional pluralism' provoked by contract law. The first is that, as described by Hesselink, they are not actually making new law, but are primarily engaged in a kind of decisionism – deciding cases on a case-by-case manner without regard to larger abstract doctrinal consistency.[54] The second is that the good faith doctrine allows the court to avoid challenging the legitimacy of state legislation. The case-specific nature of judicial determinations of good faith means that the reach of the state's legal authority in general rarely if ever becomes an issue.

However, judicial resort to the doctrine of good faith to address issues of contract law is not without its problems. First, because good faith derives from the private law – and in particular from the principal legal manifestation of the civilian private law, the Civil Code – its 'open norms' concern themselves primarily with the concerns of private law jurisprudence, particularly those implicit in the Code itself. It is therefore largely cognitively blind to the state-constitutionalising aspects of contract law and the trilemmatic paradox these aspects can introduce into contract law jurisprudence, and thus provides no assistance for evaluating which trilemmatic prong is nevertheless most legitimate or most appropriate for addressing the kind of conflict at hand. The more 'state-constitutional' aspects of contract law tend to be cabined in their own doctrinal boxes – such as consumer protection[55] – thus preventing jurisprudential communication between the two constitutional components of contract law.[56]

IV. AN ALTERNATIVE RESPONSE: FINDING A NEW FORUM FOR ADDRESSING THE DOUBLY CONSTITUTIONALISING CHARACTER OF CONTRACT – THE CJEU

As an alternative to invoking considerations of 'good faith' to address constitutional issues stemming from contract law, domestic courts in Europe have begun referring such issues to the CJEU. This is the phenomenon explored by Mak in her essay. As described above, she

---

[52] M Hesselink, 'The Concept of Good Faith' in AS Hartkamp, MW Hesselink, EH Hondius, C Mak and CE Du Perron (eds), *Towards a European Civil Code*, 4th edn (The Hague, Kluwer Law International, 2011) 620–21.

[53] ibid 622.

[54] See A Fischer-Lescano, R Christensen and M. Everson, '*Auctoritatis Interpositio*: How Systems Theory Deconstructs Decisionism' (2012) 21 *Social and Legal Studies* 93.

[55] cf HW Micklitz, 'Social Justice and Access Justice in Private Law' EUI Working Paper LAW 2011/02 (Florence, European University Institute, 2011) 7–8.

[56] ibid.

attributes this development to democratic deficiencies in the political constitution of Europe. But here it will be argued that the appeal of such referrals lies in the CJEU's distinctive ability to construct a theoretical-ideological framework for thinking about and debating how to balance the two dimensions of contract law's doubly constitutionalising character.[57]

A. An Example: Judicial 'Delegation' of Judicial Contract Law-Making in *Aziz v Catalunyacaixa*

In order to show how this is so, let us first examine a case in which a Spanish domestic court referred to the CJEU a dispute involving enforcement of a consumer mortgage: *Aziz v Catalunyacaixa* (the *Aziz* case)[58] – a case that Mak herself analyses in support of her argument.[59] In that case, a Spanish bank, Caixa d'Estalvis de Catalunya, Tarragona i Manresa, had imposed upon a customer, Mohamed Aziz, contract terms that allowed the bank to repossess the mortgaged property in the event of the mortgagee's failure to meet his or her monthly repayment schedule, regardless of how much of the mortgage he or she had already paid off. This in fact happened to Mr Aziz, who had been suddenly laid off due to the Global Financial Crisis. Such clauses were common in the mortgage contracts of Spanish banks, but the judge in the case, José María Fernández Seijo, nevertheless believed them to be patently unfair – at least in this particular instance. However, although he was assessed with deciding on the fairness – and hence validity – of the contractual term, Spain's civil procedure law gave another court responsibility for *enforcing* the repossession. And there was no avenue by which Judge Seijo could stay the enforcement proceedings in order to give him time to rule on the fairness of the contract.

This is a paradigmatic instance of a trilemmatic conflict between the market-constitutionalising and the state-constitutionalising dimensions of contract law. The bank's defence of the legal validity of its foreclosure provision was founded on freedom of contract, which as we saw above is one of the foundational principles of the market constitution. In contrast, Judge Seijo's scepticism regarding the legal validity of that provision was founded on concerns for providing meaningful public access to mortgage markets, concerns that resonate with state constitutional concerns regarding social citizenship.[60]

As noted above, Judge Seijo believed that the mortgage's enforcement terms were unfair and therefore void, but he lacked capacity to try to stay the enforcement proceeding himself using Spanish domestic law. He therefore referred a 'preliminary question' to the CJEU as to whether, in failing to allow for the stay of the enforcement proceedings against Mr Aziz pending determinations of the contract term's validity, Spanish law was in violation of EU standards for consumer protection as reflected in the Unfair Terms Directive.[61] In a ruling issued on 14 March 2013, the CJEU agreed.[62]

---

[57] *cf* JA Mayoral and AT Pérez, 'On Judicial Mobilization: Entrepreneuring for Policy Change at Times of Crisis' (2018) 40 *Journal of European Integration* 719.

[58] Case C-415/11 *Mohamed Aziz v Caixa d'Estalvis de Catalunya, Tarragona i Manresa (Catalunyacaixa)* EU:C:2013:164.

[59] Mak (n 1) 226–28.

[60] *cf* Micklitz (n 55).

[61] Council Directive 93/13/EEC of 5 April 1993 on unfair terms in consumer contracts [2013] OJ L95/29.

[62] *Aziz* (n 58).

Judge Seijo's appeal to the CJEU allowed him to bring the two components of contract law's doubly constitutionalising character into conversation with each other – something he could not have done on his own. In his words:

> From the beginning of the proceedings both the plaintiff and the defendant in their briefs – writ of summons and defence – have introduced elements of an economic, social and legal-political nature that transcend the strictly legal scope of the dispute and of the parties' claims.
>
> These factors intensified from November 2012 onwards, when the Opinion of the Advocate General at the Court of Justice of the European Union (CJEU) was published, in which she answered the questions referred to the CJEU from the perspective of Community law.[63]

On the one hand, Judge Seijo's referral, and the CJEU ruling, could be seen as 'activist'. The issue of enforcement was one that was not before him. Technically, it was one he had no authority to address. As further elucidated by Mak:

> [T]he question arises if the Spanish judge in the *Aziz* case may only have been paying lip service to established ideas of the division of powers between legislature and judiciary, while effectively having used the opening provided by the reference to 'the social reality at the time of application' in Article 3 of the Spanish Civil Code to redirect the outcome of the case. This form of interaction between national and supranational legislative and judicial institutions may raise criticism for not sufficiently respecting the principle of democracy underlying European (private) lawmaking. Rather than awaiting legislative intervention, the European and domestic judiciaries intervened in the Spanish national law of civil procedure and even provoked its reform. This may seem to be at odds with the idea of democratic legitimacy according to which EU citizens' voice in EU and national law-making processes is primarily guaranteed through the legislative process, not the judicial process.[64]

Nevertheless, as per Mak's general argument, the referral and the CJEU's subsequent ruling appeared to have provoked little concern regarding judicial activism. In fact, they provoked constitutional *reflection* rather than constitutional condemnation,[65] in that they induced sustained jurisprudential reflection on how the conflicting inter-constitutional concerns raised by this particular clause in the mortgage contract should be balanced. As noted by Judge Seijo:

> Without a doubt, the dissemination of this Opinion and the CJEU's judgment of 14 March 2013 have given the proceedings a dimension that by far exceeds the scope of the present case insofar as it coincided with an intense public debate – of a political, legislative, social and economic nature – that has prompted a process of legislative reform that has not yet come to an end.[66]

Further elucidation of Judge Seijo's observation is given by Fernando Esteban de la Rosa in 'The Treatment of Unfair Terms in the Process of Foreclosure in Spain: Mortgage Enforcement Proceedings in the Aftermath of the ECJ's "Ruling of the Evicted"':

> 'The Spanish system of foreclosure has suffered great changes as a consequence of the [CJEU's] *Aziz* Ruling. After this key judgment, Spanish legislation underwent a long awaited reform that in some ways failed to live up to social expectations ...

---

[63] Quoted in Mak (n 1) 228.
[64] ibid 231.
[65] See also P Gómez and K Lyczkowska, 'Spanish Courts, the Court of Justice of the European Union, and Consumer Law' (2014) 4 *InDret Revista para el análisis del Derecho* 2.
[66] Quoted in Mak (n 1) 228.

On the other hand, the role assumed by national judges in the application of the Ruling and in the development of subsequent judicial practice is noteworthy. While legislatively speaking, an attempt was made to formally adapt and save the existing system, the judicial branch placed more emphasis on using the *Aziz* Ruling to effect deep reform of the system, applying de facto solutions without legal norm, proposing progressive interpretations according to the doctrine established by the [CJEU] and referring preliminary questions to the [CJEU] to counter the new Spanish legislation. Even if it is difficult to agree with all of the changes judges in Spain are developing, the impact of the *Aziz* Ruling may be considered as very positive. The effects of the *Aziz* Ruling among judicial activists are still developing, and an answer to the many questions already raised by Spanish judges in the aftermath of the *Aziz* Ruling is much awaited. Pandora's box is now wide open.'[67]

Moreover, the CJEU's decision in the *Aziz* case affected contractual-constitutional jurisprudence not only in Spain, but in a number of other European countries as well.[68] In other words, in contrast to the good faith doctrine, the CJEU's judgment was indeed able to generate interconstitutional jurisprudential communication between market constitutionalism and state constitutionalism – not only within Spain, but also within the EU more generally.

Why might this have been the case? It is hard to see how this public acceptance of the scope of the CJEU's ruling, much less that ruling's enduring effect on European constitutional ideology, was catalysed by some democratic deficit in the constitutional system of the EU. Those institutions from which the democratic constitutional legitimacy, or lack thereof, of the EU are primarily thought to flow – namely the European Parliament, the European Commission, and the Council of the European Union – were of no normative or practical relevance to the case. The reason for this acceptance is better explained by some other aspects of the EU's constitutional framing. It is to this that we now turn.

B. Why the CJEU?

In order to understand why the CJEU's contract jurisprudence is able to overcome the doctrinal limitations found in the good faith doctrine of domestic courts, it helps to recount the distinctive trajectory of political Europe's 'constitutional' evolution. The modern economic levers of constitutionalism – such as competition law[69] and social citizenship[70] – only began to emerge in the North Atlantic countries in the late nineteenth century, largely in response to the emergence of the second industrial revolution, aka 'Fordism',[71] well after the orthodox constitutional dichotomy between 'public law' (of which state-constitutionalising law is a part) and 'private law' (of which market-constitutionalising law is a part) had become crystallised in American and European, and later in global, legal and constitutional thought[72] – a dichotomy

---

[67] F Esteban de la Rosa, 'The Treatment of Unfair Terms in the Process of Foreclosure in Spain: Mortgage Enforcement Proceedings in the Aftermath of the ECJ's "Ruling of the Evicted"' (2015) 2 *Zeitschrift für Europäisches Privatrecht* 388. See also SI Sánchez, 'Unfair Terms in Mortgage Loans and Protection of Housing in Times of Economic Crisis: *Aziz v Catalunyacaixa*' (2014) 51 *Common Market Law Review* 955.

[68] See S Nasarre-Aznar, '"Robinhoodian" Courts' Decisions on Mortgage Law in Spain' (2015) 7 *International Journal of Law in the Built Environment* 127, 137–38.

[69] See Dowdle (n 19) 374–84.

[70] See MA Glendon, 'Rights in Twentieth-Century Constitutions: The Case of Welfare Rights' (1994) 6 *Journal of Policy History* 140.

[71] See Dowdle (n 19) 325–27 (competition law); Marshall (n 15); Glendon (n 70) (social citizenship).

[72] This may be less the case with Germany, perhaps because its present constitutional jurisprudence only emerged during the second half of the twentieth century.

that continues to dominate our jurisprudential understandings to this day.[73] This in turn, as discussed in section III.C above in the context of the good faith doctrine, impedes recognition of the distinctly state-constitutionalising aspects of various forms of so-called private law, including contract law.[74]

However, the constitutional trajectory of political Europe has been different. The articulation of the constitution of political Europe – what is now the EU – emerged in the 1950s. Being a uniquely transnational, economic political-constitutional phenomenon, Europe's constitutionalising strategies focused much more prominently on constructing dynamics of economic constitutionalism (a focus foreshadowed by the German concept of ordoliberalism).[75] A particularly notable articulation of this understanding is found in the famous 'Schuman Declaration' that proposed the establishment of the European Coal and Steel Community, the forerunner to today's EU:

> Europe will not be made all at once, or according to a single plan. It will be built through concrete achievements which first create a de facto solidarity. The coming together of the nations of Europe requires the elimination of the age-old opposition of France and Germany. Any action taken must in the first-place concern these two countries.
>
> With this aim in view, the French Government … proposes that Franco-German production of coal and steel as a whole be placed under a common High Authority, within the framework of an organization open to the participation of the other countries of Europe. The pooling of coal and steel production should immediately provide for the setting up of common foundations for economic development as a first step in the federation of Europe, and will change the destinies of those regions which have long been devoted to the manufacture of munitions of war, of which they have been the most constant victims …
>
> By pooling basic production and by instituting a new High Authority, whose decisions will bind France, Germany and other member countries; this proposal will lead to the realization of the first concrete foundation of a European federation indispensable to the preservation of peace.[76]

Thus, in contrast to most state constitutional systems and the constitutional orthodoxies that dominate traditional Anglo-European constitutional discourses, political Europe has since its inception acknowledged rather than invisibilised the economic aspects of its constitutional order. In particular, it has historically been market access, rather than political access, that was the principal social benefit through which the political entity called Europe claimed its legitimacy of rule – a phenomenon that Hans-W Micklitz has well demonstrated in his study of Europe's distinct approach to 'access justice' (see below).[77]

This express recognition of Europe's economic constitutional character has made it much more acceptable for the CJEU to incorporate state-constitutionalising considerations into its contract law judgments. This is not to suggest that the CJEU's jurisprudential negotiation between the two constitutional dimensions of contract law is uncontroversial. For example, many criticise the CJEU's jurisprudential emphasis on issues of commodification at the

---

[73] See D Baranger, 'Uncovering the Foundations of Administrative Law?' in MA Wilkinson and MW Dowdle (eds), *Questioning the Foundations of Public Law* (Oxford, Hart Publishing, 2018).

[74] cf L Alexander, 'The Public/Private Distinction and Constitutional Limits on Private Power' (1993) 10 *Constitutional Commentary* 361.

[75] DJ Gerber, 'Constitutionalising the Economy: German Neo-liberalism, Competition law and the "New" Europe' (1994) 42 *American Journal of Comparative Law* 25, 69–74.

[76] Schuman Declaration of 9 May 1950. See generally F Larat, 'Present-ing the Past: Political Narratives on European History and the Justification of EU Integration' (2005) 6 *German Law Journal* 764.

[77] Micklitz (n 55).

expense of other social concerns.[78] But such opposition tends to be founded on the particular substance of that evolution – on its preference for a particular kind of economic constitutionalism – rather than on its interpretive liberties. By contrast, when the American Supreme Court adopted a similar, and similarly controversial, pro-market contract jurisprudence in the late nineteenth and early twentieth centuries, the principal American complaint was that it ignored the state-constitutional implications of that jurisprudence – ie, not so much that it was substantively wrong, but simply that it was too adventurous, given the constitutional constraints on the courts' responsibilities.[79]

V. POLITICAL EUROPE'S CONTRIBUTION TO CONTRACT LAW

So how does the argument advanced in this chapter compare and contrast with that advanced by Mak, and what difference might it make? Mak and I both agree that European contract law has a distinct state-constitutional dimension to it. Mak, however, locates that dimension in a realm of fundamental rights rather than that of economic constitutionalism.[80]

Relatedly, we disagree about what causes and perhaps justifies the CJEU's distinct, interpretive freedom in the realm of European contract law. Mak tentatively locates the cause and rationale for this activism in the democratic deficiencies of Europe's existing constitutional framework. In her last section in particular, she suggests that the activism of the CJEU might operate as structural compensation for the relative lack of democratic input with regard to European norm generation by the legislative or executive branches. One suspects that this focus might be because appeals to democratic legitimacy represent the principal (liberal) critique of claims of fundamental rights in general.[81] Her argument that the EU constitution is already and *innately* democratically deficient means that the influence of fundamental rights on European contract law is likely to have only minor negative impact on European democracy, thus removing one of the principal objections to their existence.

I, on the other hand, locate this interpretive freedom in the distinct constitutional character of contract law itself – in what I have called its doubly constitutionalising aspect. In contrast to Mak, I do not regard political Europe's democratic deficit as necessarily contributing to the acceptance of the CJEU's interpretive freedom. Rather, that acceptance is simply a product of political Europe's distinct recognition of the essential role that national markets play in the workings of its overall constitutional system,[82] a role that is largely, inadequately acknowledged in orthodox constitutional understandings of the relationship between the realm of public law vis-à-vis that of private law.

---

[78] See G Davies, 'The Consumer, the Citizen, and the Human Being' in D Leczykiewicz and S Weatherill (eds), *The Images of the Consumer in EU Law: Legislation, Free Movement and Competition Law* (Oxford, Hart Publishing, 2016); see also I Domurath, 'Mortgage Debt and the Social Function of Contract' (2016) 22 *European Law Journal* 758.

[79] See GE White, 'Revisiting Substantive Due Process and Holmes's Lochner Dissent' (1997) 63 *Brooklyn Law Review* 87.

[80] See also C Mak, *Fundamental Rights in European Contract Law: A Comparison of the Impact of Fundamental Rights on Contractual Relationships in Germany, the Netherlands, Italy, and England* (Alphen aan den Rijn, Kluwer Law International, 2008).

[81] See, eg, E Gill-Pedro, *EU Law, Fundamental Rights and National Democracy* (Abingdon, Routledge, 2018); see generally R Bellamy, *Political Constitutionalism: A Republican Defence of the Constitutionality of Democracy* (Cambridge, Cambridge University Press, 2007).

[82] *cf* M Loughlin and N Walker (eds), *The Paradox of Constitutionalism: Constituent Power and Constitutional Form* (Oxford, Oxford University Press, 2007).

As described above, European constitutionalism was originally framed in terms of markets, which gives it a unique perspective on the relationship between markets, economic constitutionalism and the construction of social-political solidarities. In this way, political Europe can make a distinct and important contribution to both 'contract law' and 'constitutional law'. The European constitution's pronounced recognition of its market-based components renders it particularly competent in developing a contract law jurisprudence that expressly recognises the contributions of that jurisprudence to modern constitutionalism.

What might such a jurisprudence look like? Like Mak, a number of other Anglo-European jurists – including Martijn Hesselink,[83] Hugh Collins,[84] Aurelia Colombi Ciacchi[85] and Olha Cherednychenko[86] – have explored the crucial role that fundamental rights play in European contract law jurisprudence. Such explorations resonate quite closely with how we tend to conceptualise constitutionalism as a kind of law (of which fundamental rights are a part).[87] The problem, as is well described in the work of Martin Loughlin, is that such legal conceptualisations of constitutionalism work to invisiblise the critical role that political and societal norms, practices and contestations play in constructing the regulatory workings of a state. Once we identify something as a fundamental right, we effectively remove it from further critical scrutiny, thus rendering its trilemmatic interactions with other key aspects of its constitutional *system* invisible.[88]

For the present at least, the better alternative for investigation into the multiple constitutional dimensions of contract law lies in what Loughlin has famously termed a 'political jurisprudence'. This is a jurisprudence that focuses on the symbiotic interrelationship between juridified constitutional *law* – and various political and social practices that interact with that law, in a way that allows for the development and continued refinement of a distinctly jurisprudential discourse that explores the constitutional-*systemic* implications of such practices and interactions.[89]

And in contrast to the legal jurisprudence that informs the fundamental rights approach to contract law espoused by Mak and others, political jurisprudence 'argue[s] that the relationship between law and authority can neither be presupposed nor assumed to rest on a set of universal values'.[90] Elsewhere, Loughlin states that: 'Political jurisprudence is the jurisprudence of experience … Suspicious of universal and abstract ways of thinking about law, political jurists focus on its local and concrete expressions.'[91] In this way, it somewhat resembles the pattern of judicial decision-making that Martijn Hesselink associates with the good faith doctrine:

> Good faith is therefore usually said to be an open norm, a norm the content of which cannot be established in an abstract way but which depends on the circumstances of the case in which it must

---

[83] See, eg, M Hesselink, 'The Horizontal Effect of Social Rights in European Contract Law,' in MW Hesselink, CE du Perron and AF Salomons (eds), *Privaatrecht tussen Autonomie en Solidariteit* (The Hague, Boom Juridische uitgevers, 2003) 119.

[84] See, eg, H Collins, 'On the (In)Compatibility of Human Rights Discourse and Private Law' in HW Micklitz (ed), *Constitutionalization of European Private Law* (Oxford, Oxford University Press, 2014).

[85] See, eg, A Colombi Ciacchi, 'The Constitutionalization of European Contract Law: Judicial Convergence and Social Justice' (2006) 2 *European Review of Contract Law* 167.

[86] See, eg, O Cherednychenko, *Fundamental Rights, Contract Law and the Protection of the Weaker Party: A Comparative Analysis of the Constitutionalisation of Contract Law, with Emphasis on Risky Financial Transactions* (Munich, Sellier European Law Publishers, 2007).

[87] See H Kelsen, *General Theory of Law and State* (Cambridge, MA, Harvard University Press, 1945).

[88] See M Loughlin, *Foundations of Public Law* (Oxford, Oxford University Press, 2010) 370–72.

[89] See M Loughlin, *Political Jurisprudence* (Oxford, Oxford University Press, 2017) 2.

[90] ibid 4.

[91] ibid 7.

be applied, and which must be established through concretisation. Most lawyers from a system where good faith plays an important role, will therefore agree that these differences in theoretical conception do not matter very much. Indeed, many authors are themselves not very consistent in their indication of the status of good faith. What really matters is the way in which good faith is applied by the courts: the character of good faith is best shown by the way in which it operates.[92]

But what the notion of political jurisprudence adds to Hesselink's description of domestic good-faith jurisprudence is an explicit investigation into the *constitutional* implications of contractual practices that have been called into question by the demand for good faith. We see this in Hans-W Micklitz's recent investigation into what he calls 'access justice', and what the notion of access justice contributes to Europe's constitutional order:

> The EU legal system was originally designed as an international treaty before the ECJ transformed the Rome Treaty into a genuine legal order based on enforceable rights. EU regulatory labour and consumer law, right from its beginning and with constant support from the ECJ, could be understood not only as integrating a social dimension into the market based project of European integration, but also to make sure that those who should benefit from the mandatory rules are also given access to the legal system. In this sense, access justice contains two elements, first breaking down the barriers which limit participation and access and second strengthening the position of consumers and workers with a view to enforcing their rights. With regard to the first category, access justice would require that all market participants, including consumers, must have a fair and realistic chance to enter the market, consume its products and use its services, as well as reaping the benefits of the market. Access justice in the second sense relates to the degree of justice the individual might gain after he or she has been granted access ...

> In sum: access justice means more than a formal guarantee to workers and consumers that they may have a theoretical chance in participating in the market and reaping the benefits of the market. This would be justice in the meaning of the libertarian concept. Access justice in the meaning of Max Weber, quite to the contrary, materialises the equity doctrine. The legal system is responsible for establishing tools which transform the theoretical chance into a realistic opportunity, thereby eliminating all sorts of barriers which hinder the assertion of the claim to access. This requires further deepening.[93]

Even more so than the paradox between autonomy and solidarity identified in section III.C above by Hesselink in his analysis of the jurisprudence of good faith – which he sees in terms of ideological rather than inter-constitutional conflicts,[94] Micklitz's dichotomy between the libertarian aspect of the law of contract and its equity aspect does indeed resonate with what this chapter calls the 'doubly constitutionalising' character of contract law. His libertarian aspect corresponds with how, in a free market society, contract law constitutionalises the market. At the same time, the EU's recognition as to how European contract law also '[integrates] a social dimension into the market-based project of European integration' by giving consumers 'a fair and realistic chance to ... *[reap] the benefits of the market*' (emphasis added) acknowledges the role that contract law plays in the construction (or 'constitution') of political Europe.

But while Micklitz's notion of 'access justice' shows the limitations of the fundamental rights approach to thinking about the doubly constitutionalising nature of contract law, nevertheless, at the end of the day, he, too, ends up retreating into the comforting embrace of rights-based conceptualisations: describing access justice as ultimately being comprised of

---

[92] Hesselink (n 52) 622–23.
[93] Micklitz (n 55) 23.
[94] Hesselink (n 50).

'individually enforceable rights'.[95] But what exactly he means by this is unclear: elsewhere he acknowledges that in fact these rights do not address themselves to the actual providers of access (who as primarily private entities lie beyond the direct reach of the EU's jurisdiction), but to the individual states that have legislative jurisdiction over such providers, resulting in what has been called by Norbert Reich 'rights without duties'.[96] Relatedly, he also notes that the EU's access justice therefore does not direct that the complainant actually be given access to those constitutionally critical markets or services from which she is being excluded (as is normally the case with substantive private law rights); rather, it merely demands that whatever exclusions she does suffer from simply be 'fair' and 'non-discriminatory'[97] (see also below).

So, what are the benefits of Micklitz's 'rights' of access justice? Micklitz characterises his rights-based conceptualisation of access justice as being what access justice looks like in its 'most outspoken form'. But he also acknowledges the existence of a 'less developed form' in which these what he calls '*so-called* rights' (emphasis added) are used 'to formulate policy guidelines or mere policy objectives which could and should nevertheless be taken into account by the courts'.[98] This, of course, was exactly the outcome of CJEU's ruling in *Aziz*. And maybe, rather than being its 'less developed form', this is actually access justice's most appropriate, albeit less 'outspoken' form. The sometimes competing and sometimes complementary interaction between the public and the private 'constitutional' aspects of 'the market' (and, by extension, of the law of contracts) is simply too complex to be *directly* regulated by courts using doctrinalised enforcement of substantive rights: such interactions will vary considerably from market to market, from class to class, and from place to place in ways that simply cannot be captured via reference to the *abstract* conceptualisations of 'fairness' and 'non-discrimination' that inhere in the orthodox jurisprudences of 'substantive rights' (consider, along these lines, the European Court of Human Rights' 'margin of appreciation' doctrine, which it uses to qualify how particular substantive fundamental rights should apply in the context of particular locales).[99] It is precisely through its ability to stimulate such 'policy formation', in contrast to the simple decisionism of the good faith doctrine, that access justice's distinct contributions to the doubly constitutionalising role of European contract law truly lie.

In sum, the doubly constitutionalising character of contract law thus simply does not lend itself to a jurisprudential construction built upon fundamental rights. The interacting constitutional orders do not resolve themselves into such a single, rationally coherent stasis. Instead, they exist in state of homeostasis – a more or less stable equilibrium in which new epistemic conflict is resolved, for the moment at least, 'politically' rather than through deductive extrapolation from a rational jurisprudential framework of fundamental principles.[100] Due to its history, Europe is more aware of this than most. This could well be political Europe's greatest contribution (to date) to our understanding of 'contract law' writ large.

---

[95] Micklitz (n 55) 25.

[96] N Reich, 'The Public/Private Divide in European Private Law' in HM Micklitz and F Cafaggi (eds), *European Private Law after the Common Frame of Reference* (Cheltenham, Edward Elgar, 2010) 56.

[97] Micklitz (n 55) 26.

[98] ibid 24.

[99] See generally OM Arnardóttir, '*Res Interpretata*, *Erga Omnes* Effect and the Role of the Margin of Appreciation in Giving Domestic Effect to the Judgments of the European Court of Human Rights' (2017) 28 *European Journal of International Law* 819.

[100] *cf* Dowdle (n 19) 349–60.

4

Reimagining Europe Through Private Law Adjudication

CHANTAL MAK*

I. PRIVATE LAW AND A EUROPEAN POLITY

IN TIMES OF COVID-19, Brexit, climate change, economic hardship and a migration crisis, an exploration of the utopian dimensions of European private law adjudication might seem slightly out of place. Dystopian accounts may seem to offer a more truthful picture of such uncertain times,[1] in which the idea of European unity is under pressure. The series of crises has highlighted a persistent lack of civic solidarity in addressing Europe-wide problems,[2] and it is not sure to what extent legal institutions can contribute to shared solutions. This is particularly urgent in civil cases that address specific effects of the developments, such as evictions following the collapse of housing markets in the wake of the economic crisis of 2008. How should courts in civil cases handle disputes among those who suffer the consequences of societal developments? To what extent might the reasoning of judges in private legal disputes on the validity of contract terms or on liability in tort law gain any broader meaning at all? And to what extent can and should national judges in civil cases be concerned with the development of a European polity that unites rather than divides those affected by the many crises?

This chapter addresses the question of to what extent judges in civil cases can and should contribute to the reimagination of a European political community.[3] Its focus lies on the way in which fundamental rights reasoning[4] may open up space for deliberations on the underlying

---

* The research for this chapter was made possible by a grant of the Dutch Research Council for the project 'Judges in Utopia' (NWO Vidi 2014–2019).

[1] Reflected in literature in such novels as M Atwood, *The Handmaid's Tale* (London, Vintage, 1996 [1985]) and *The Testaments* (New York, Nan A Talese/Doubleday, 2019) concerning women's rights; JM Coetzee, *The Childhood of Jesus* (London, Harvill Secker, 2013) on migration; and N Ammaniti, *Anna* (Turin, Einaudi, 2015), on a pandemic.

[2] J Habermas, *The Crisis of the European Union: A Response* (Cambridge, Polity Press, 2012) 3–4.

[3] In line with the idea of institutional imagination presented by R Mangabeira Unger, 'Legal Analysis as Institutional Imagination' (1996) 59 *Modern Law Review* 1.

[4] The concept of 'fundamental rights' here is broadly understood to include both supranational human rights standards and national constitutional rights. Although the differences in the scope and applicability of different rights are acknowledged, it is assumed that the formal basis of a certain right is not decisive for its possible influence on legal reasoning in private legal cases. The analysis focuses on substantive effects of fundamental rights in private legal cases and, accordingly, does not elaborate on formal-technical conditions for the applicability of such rights in the private legal context.

legal-political questions in private legal cases with a European dimension. Adopting a bottom-up perspective, both the interaction with norms deriving from EU law and those protected under the European Convention on Human Rights (ECHR) are included. Three high-profile cases will illustrate how judges have approached the differences between norms deriving from the European level and those embedded in national private legal orders. On the basis of the case law analysis, it will be submitted that the adjudication of disputes on the interface of national private law and European fundamental rights contributes to a process of polity-building, in particular by creating space for the inclusion of views that receive less attention in legislative processes.

Normatively, two premises underpin the analysis. First, it is postulated that solidarity among Europeans is something worth striving for.[5] Insofar as private law can contribute to this process, it can and should not be considered only in economic terms, but also in the light of its justice dimensions.[6] Second, it is assumed that the 'constitutionalisation of European private law' should not be limited to an investigation of the meaning of certain fundamental rights for specific private legal questions.[7] The question is rather to what kind of European 'constitutional settlement'[8] the adjudication of private legal disputes may contribute.

In the following, first, the place of civil adjudication in the European legal landscape will be determined and a theoretical framework for understanding the role of judges will be presented. In particular, I will contrast Michael W Dowdle's theory on the doubly constitutional character of contract law with the democratic theory of judicial law-making that I am developing. Second, an analysis of three cases will show how and to what extent judicial reasoning can be explained in the light of these two theories. On the basis of this analysis, the meaning of private law adjudication for the reimagination of a European political community will, in particular, be found in the extent to which private legal cases allow for the inclusion of affected individuals and groups in legal-political deliberations. As such, each case forms a building block for an inclusive European polity. It will be concluded that judges in civil cases can and should make a contribution to the process of European integration, especially when the legislature remains silent.[9]

---

[5] S Rodotà, *Solidarietà: un'utopia necessaria* (Rome/Bari, Laterza, 2014) 5–7; Habermas (n 2) 2–3.

[6] Study Group on Social Justice in European Private Law, 'Social Justice in European Contract Law: A Manifesto' (2004) 10 *European Law Journal* 653; D Caruso, '*Qu'ils mangent des contrats*: Rethinking Justice in EU Contract Law' in D Kochenov, G de Búrca and A Williams (eds), *Europe's Justice Deficit?* (Oxford, Hart Publishing, 2015); M Fabre-Magnan, 'What is a Modern Law of Contracts? Elements for a New Manifesto for Social Justice in European Contract Law' (2017) 13 *European Review of Contract Law* 376.

[7] The rich literature on this theme includes: OO Cherednychenko, *Fundamental Rights, Contract Law and the Protection of the Weaker Party: A Comparative Analysis of the Constitutionalisation of Contract Law, with Emphasis on Risky Financial Transactions* (Munich, Sellier, 2007); A Colombi Ciacchi, 'The Constitutionalization of European Contract Law: Judicial Convergence and Social Justice' (2006) 2 *European Review of Contract Law* 167; H Collins, 'On the (In)Compatibility of Human Rights Discourse and Private Law' in HW Micklitz (ed), *Constitutionalization of European Private Law* (Oxford, Oxford University Press, 2014). See also C Mak, *Fundamental Rights in European Contract Law: A Comparison of the Impact of Fundamental Rights on Contractual Relationships in Germany, the Netherlands, Italy and England* (Alphen aan den Rijn, Kluwer Law International, 2008).

[8] Study Group on Social Justice in European Private Law (n 6) 667; MA Wilkinson, 'Political Constitutionalism and the European Union' (2013) 76 *Modern Law Review* 191, 192–93.

[9] S Rodotà, *Il diritto di avere diritti* (Rome/Bari, Laterza, 2012) 96, referring to an earlier essay entitled 'Nel silenzio della politica i giudici fanno l'Europa'.

II. UTOPIAN THINKING IN EUROPEAN PRIVATE LAW ADJUDICATION

A. Judicial Utopias

The place of private law adjudication in the European legal order may be considered to be 'utopian' insofar as it is the subject of continuous reimagination, like Europe itself. In this sense, it has some affinity with Thomas More's *Utopia*,[10] although a comparison with that not uncontroversial ideal society will not be made here. In the context of legal theory, 'Utopia' may be considered as an imaginary 'view from nowhere'.[11] It is an ideal that may never be realised and as such offers an alternative worldview, a point of reference for considering changes to the status quo.[12] Utopian thinking allows for the imagination of new legal-substantive and institutional constellations to address societal developments, and thus, as Loughlin has submitted, the continuous process of constitutional imagination that creates political realities.[13] Utopian thinking is also prominent in the rise of fundamental rights protection, which transcends the level of nation-states in Europe.

While acknowledging critical views on fundamental rights utopianism, this chapter will explore the more constructive, emancipatory role that such rights may have in private law adjudication in Europe. Many authors have pointed to the problematic dimensions of the emergence of fundamental rights discourses, in particular regarding the international human rights movement. From a constitutional point of view, Loughlin questions the potential for human rights to change the status quo and instead sees a shift to their integration in existing schemes of governance.[14] From a legal-historical perspective, Moyn has observed that the turn to international human rights as a 'last utopia' does not seem to offer programmatic change[15] or address inequality in societies.[16] In contrast to such views, the analysis presented here agrees with a more constructive view of what human rights reasoning can contribute to polity-building. As Benhabib points out in reply to Moyn's historical account, politics and morality are not necessarily separated from each other in the interpretation and application of human rights.[17] She submits that, instead, we should see human rights as 'straddl[ing] a necessary line between morality and legality': they differ from moral norms, which transcend space and time, by

---

[10] T More, *Utopia* (1516), full text available at: www.theopenutopia.org (edited and with an introduction by S Duncombe, 2012). The name 'Utopia' is composed by the Greek *ou* and *topos*, literally meaning 'no place' (at xxxii).

[11] M Loughlin, 'The Constitutional Imagination' (2015) 78 *Modern Law Review* 1, 13. See also J Habermas, 'The Concept of Human Dignity and the Realistic Utopia of Human Rights' in *The Crisis of the European Union: A Response* (Cambridge, Polity Press, 2012) 71–100, who explains the development of human rights in utopian terms: 'Human rights constitute a *realistic* utopia insofar as they no longer paint deceptive images of a social utopia which guarantees collective happiness but anchor the ideal of a just society in the institutions of constitutional states themselves' (at 95). It may be noted that 'utopian thinking' may not only serve the development of law, but can also play a role in legal education; see D Kennedy, 'Legal Education and the Reproduction of Hierarchy' (1982) 32 *Journal of Legal Education* 591, 613–14.

[12] In line with the Rawlsian approach of theorising justice in terms of a 'realistic utopia', which presents an ideal for an 'achievable social world'; see J Rawls, *The Law of Peoples* (Cambridge, MA, Harvard University Press, 1999) 11–12. For a conceptual map of ideal and more realistic theories, see L Valentini, 'Ideal vs Non-ideal Theory: A Conceptual Map' (2012) 7 *Philosophy Compass* 654.

[13] Loughlin (n 11) 12–13.

[14] ibid 24–25.

[15] S Moyn, *The Last Utopia: Human Rights in History* (Cambridge, MA, Harvard University Press, 2010).

[16] S Moyn, *Not Enough: Human Rights in an Unequal World* (Cambridge, MA, Harvard University Press, 2018).

[17] S Benhabib, 'Moving beyond False Binarisms: On Samuel Moyn's *The Last Utopia*' (2013) 22 *Qui parle* 81, 86–88.

providing justiciable rights that can be invoked in specific jurisdictions.[18] In line with this view, and like Benhabib taking inspiration from Habermas' conceptualisation of human rights,[19] the present analysis looks into the potential of fundamental rights to contribute to a reimagination of private legal solutions to politically sensitive questions. This contribution is primarily found in case law, in which recourse to fundamental rights requires all actors involved in civil litigation to deliberate on the meaning of the core concepts of private law (freedom of contract, good faith, public policy) against the backdrop of moral and political questions raised by the specific cases. Such deliberative processes, for which European private law cases provide space, may contribute to the development of alternative answers to societal questions. The imagination of such alternatives may inspire the development of legal solutions by judges in civil cases, who are called upon to assess these questions in light of a transnational, European context.

An example can be found in the case law concerning the enforcement of mortgage contracts following the economic crisis of 2008, especially the Spanish cases that were referred to the Court of Justice of the European Union (CJEU).[20] Spanish law allowed banks to invoke mortgage contracts in accelerated procedures, on the basis of standard terms and conditions that one-sidedly favoured the interests of the banks as credit providers. Homeowners who found themselves in financial difficulties as a consequence of the crisis faced eviction after having failed to pay a few instalments, while not being able to repay the entire debt to the banks. In the landmark case of *Aziz*, the judge, who was asked to assess the fairness of the standard conditions that made such proceedings possible, rephrased the question in European terms.[21] He noted that homeowners could not effectively be protected under the EU Unfair Contract Terms Directive (UCTD)[22] if the outcome of an assessment of the bank's conditions could not halt the mortgage enforcement proceedings and eventual eviction.[23] The CJEU's confirmation of this observation resulted in important changes in the Spanish law of civil procedure, which was amended so as to enable the assessment of the fairness of mortgage conditions at the outset of the enforcement proceedings.[24] Given the emphasis that the Court placed on the protection of the home in *Aziz* and further judgments, this case law has been read as providing a form of 'hidden constitutionalisation' of contract law.[25] Moreover, both the Opinion of Advocate General Kokott and the CJEU's judgment sparked the debate on how to address the position of homeowners following the economic crisis.[26] For these reasons, the Spanish mortgage cases may serve as an illustration of the way in which alternative or utopian reimaginations of the legal framework may open up space for the development of new solutions.

---

[18] ibid 88.

[19] Habermas (n 2) 476–78.

[20] JML van Duin, *Effective Judicial Protection in Consumer Litigation: Article 47 of the EU Charter in Practice* (Cambridge, Intersentia, 2022). See also van Duin's chapter in this volume.

[21] Case C-415/11 *Mohamed Aziz v Caixa d'Estalvis de Catalunya, Tarragona i Manresa (Catalunyacaixa)* EU:C:2013:164.

[22] Council Directive 93/13/EEC of 5 April 1993 on unfair terms in consumer contracts [1993] OJ L95/29.

[23] *Aziz* (n 21) para 29.

[24] Ley 1/2013, BOE No 116, 15 May 2013, 36373.

[25] HW Micklitz and N Reich, 'The Court and Sleeping Beauty: The Revival of the Unfair Contract Terms Directive (UCTD)' (2014) 51 *Common Market Law Review* 771, 800–01; G Comparato and HW Micklitz, 'Regulated Autonomy between Market Freedoms and Fundamental Rights' in U Bernitz, X Groussot and F Schulyok (eds), *General Principles of EU Law and European Private Law* (Alphen aan den Rijn, Kluwer, 2013) 140. See also Van Duin's chapter in this volume. For a judicial perspective on the *Aziz* case, see Judge Fernández Seijo's chapter in this volume.

[26] Van Duin, *Effective Judicial Protection in Consumer Litigation* (n 20) 162–76.

While judicial interventions such as those in the *Aziz* case generally receive praise for offering solutions, they also encounter a critique of judicial activism.[27] Is the CJEU overstepping its competence within the European (private) legal order?[28] This critique relates not only to the interventions of European courts, but also to the approach of national courts in cases with a strong political dimension. Recent developments in climate change litigation illustrate the point: cases such as *Urgenda*, in which courts award claims for tort liability in relation to questions of climate change, based on ECHR rights, have received criticism for overstretching the boundaries of legitimate judicial law-making.[29] From an institutional perspective, it is questioned to what extent courts may be intervening in the sphere of competence of the executive and legislative branches.[30] Moreover, from a substantive point of view, the extent to which tort law can accommodate climate change questions is the subject of debate.[31] Thus, these cases raise the question of how judges should handle such politically sensitive questions. The analysis in the following sections will suggest that an answer may be found by moving away from the debate on judicial activism and trying to understand how the type of reasoning that emerges in the case law may be understood to be part of the role of judges in European private law.

B. Understanding Utopianism

In the following discussion, two ways in which the critique of judicial activism in European private law may be countered will be discussed and contrasted: first, Michael Dowdle's theory of 'responsive adjudication'; and, second, my proposal for a democratic framing of judicial law-making.

In his chapter in this volume, Michael Dowdle argues that contract law has a 'doubly constitutionalising' character, which can explain and justify the activism of the CJEU in the field of consumer contract law.[32] On the one hand, Dowdle submits, contract law enables and regulates market transactions. On the other hand, insofar as rules of contract law are enacted through public legal processes, contract law allows for the pursuit of public goals through markets.[33] This doubly constitutional function of contract law, then, facilitates political inclusion by giving citizens the freedom to use their economic resources to pursue ends of their own choice.[34] According to Dowdle's understanding of constitutionalism, courts handling contract cases cannot help but be activist, given the inherent normative inconsistencies between the state-constitution and the market-constitution that contract law upholds.[35] 'Responsive

---

[27] HW Micklitz, 'Mohamed Aziz – Sympathetic and Activist, But Did the Court Get it Wrong?' in A Sodersten and JHH Weiler (eds), *Where the Court Gets it Wrong* (European Constitutional Law Network, 2013), www.ecln.net/florence-2013.html.

[28] ibid 8; M Dawson, B de Witte and E Muir, *Judicial Activism at the European Court of Justice* (Cheltenham, Edward Elgar, 2013). On national courts, see A Beka, *The Active Role of Courts in Consumer Litigation: Applying EU Law of the National Courts' Own Motion* (Cambridge, Intersentia, 2018).

[29] LE Burgers, 'Should Judges Make Climate Change Law?' (2020) 9 *Transnational Environmental Law* 55, 57–58.

[30] ibid.

[31] M Hinteregger, 'Civil Liability and the Challenges of Climate Change: A Functional Analysis' (2017) 8 *Journal of European Tort Law* 238, 240; and see also Hinteregger's chapter in this volume.

[32] M Dowdle, 'On the Doubly Constitutionalising Character of European Contract Law', ch 3 in this volume, section IV.

[33] ibid section I.

[34] ibid section II.A.

[35] ibid section III.A.

adjudication', in this view, makes such inconsistencies visible and seeks to find a balance for interpretive activism.[36] According to this view, a justification for judicial activism may be found in a theory of 'judicial politics' rather than that of separation of powers.[37]

The second view, which I will defend here, is based on democratic theory.[38] While it shares some features with Dowdle's perspective, its underlying premises are markedly different. Like Dowdle's view, it asserts that the functionalities of courts not only comprise dispute resolution and norm generation, but also encompass a political dimension. In particular, the adjudication of politically charged questions of private law gives a voice to those whose interests may not have been heard or may have been overruled in legislative processes.[39] As such, case law may provide new rule-solutions or induce legislative action. However, in my view, the justification for this form of judicial law-making should rather be found in democratic reasons than in the constitutionalising function of contract law as defined by Dowdle. Judicial activism in European private law seems to be inspired both by the regulation of the market and by the deliberation of justice concerns that underlie regulatory frameworks.[40]

This theoretical framework, which will be further elucidated in the remainder of this chapter, builds on the dialogue between Jürgen Habermas and Nancy Fraser, combined with insights from European constitutional theory and private law theory. My main claim is that courts in civil cases do and should contribute to a transnational sphere of deliberation, which includes and mediates diverse legal-political views on the handling of private legal questions. In this way, courts provide space for the democratic development of new rules. While arguably attributing a more active role to courts in democratic constellations than Habermas does,[41] this theoretical view shares his idea on the role of public spheres. The possibility to discuss societal questions in a public space, encompassing debating rooms, cafés and (social) media, allows for these questions to be brought to the attention of legislative powers.[42] In my view, case law may help maintain such public spaces, insofar as it inspires debate.[43] Courts are not so much part of public space themselves – and hence distinct from the aforementioned fora – but rather contribute to the maintenance of a public sphere for deliberations on the societal questions underlying specific private legal disputes. Such deliberative processes are thus distinct from the judicial deliberations in the cases themselves, which provide a justification for the judgments. The link that I see is that, by including judicial reasoning on the societal aspects of cases – often in the language of fundamental rights – judgments contribute to the maintenance of the public deliberation on what the law should say. Importantly, judges do not have to follow

---

[36] ibid.

[37] ibid, referring to Ayres and Braithwaite.

[38] C Mak, 'First or Second Best? Judicial Law-Making in European Private Law' in JM Mendes and I Venzke (eds), *Allocating Authority* (Oxford, Hart Publishing, 2018).

[39] ibid 232–33; see also C Mak, 'Civil Courts as Constitutional Courts: Polity-Building through Private Law in Europe' (2020) 28 *European Review of Private Law* 953, inspired by the work of Habermas and Fraser.

[40] HW Micklitz, *The Politics of Justice in European Private Law: Social Justice, Access Justice, Societal Justice* (Cambridge, Cambridge University Press, 2018) 16–17.

[41] In his seminal work *Between Facts and Norms* (Cambridge, Polity Press, 1996), Habermas makes a distinction between 'discourses of justification' and 'discourses of application'. Judges should apply the existing law and, in principle, not enter into the justification of new norms (at 172). Judicial activism as discussed in the present chapter may seem to sometimes come close to a justifying logic of argumentation, especially in cases where national legislation is deemed to be non-compliant with European fundamental rights.

[42] ibid 373.

[43] On this basis, Laura Burgers submits that climate change litigation can be considered to be democratically legitimate; see LE Burgers, 'Justitia, the People's Power and Mother Earth: Democratic Legitimacy of Judicial Law-Making in European Private Law Cases on Climate Change' (PhD thesis, University of Amsterdam, 2020), https://hdl.handle.net/11245.1/0e6437b7-399d-483a-9fc1-b18ca926fdb5, 73–74.

public opinion, but while deciding on the legal merits of the case allows for much broader discourses on the issue at hand.[44]

Importantly, public spheres are inclusive; although publics composed many varieties, ranging from those attending a concert or theatre performance to Twitter or Facebook followers around the world, these spheres in principle remain 'porous' or 'permeable'.[45] All who will be governed by certain norms should thus be able to have a say in the development of these norms. Nancy Fraser's critical discussion of Habermas' work makes an important addition on this point, as she rightly observes that inclusive public opinion no longer overlaps with the borders of nation-states.[46] Accordingly – and this is of great relevance for the claim defended here – it is not primarily shared citizenship that defines a public, but rather common structures or institutions that affect people's lives.[47]

The following analysis will assess this theoretical claim that courts in civil cases should contribute to inclusive transnational deliberative spheres and thus the shaping of a political community. It will look into why and to what extent a democratic, public sphere theory of adjudication provides a convincing explanation and justification for judicial activism in European private law, in particular in comparison to Dowdle's view on contract law adjudication. However, before moving on to this analysis, it should first be briefly examined which types of cases involving the interaction of civil courts and the CJEU and the European Court of Human Rights (ECtHR) may be representative for such inclusive processes.

C. Judicial Conversations

The role of courts in maintaining deliberative processes in European private law combines aspects of judicial dialogue with judicial deliberations. The interaction of national courts with the CJEU and the ECtHR, as well as with courts in other countries, is often called a 'judicial dialogue'.[48] Through the interaction among courts, the interpretation of rules is clarified and questions of competence are handled. While this process is frequently characterised as one of conflict resolution,[49] the emphasis in the current analysis instead lies on legitimation through inclusion.[50] I submit that the interaction among courts on different levels of governance contributes to the maintenance of an inclusive public sphere, in which new legal solutions may emerge. To capture this dimension, and reduce the emphasis on conflicts of rules, I propose the term 'judicial conversations'. While a dialogue only involves two actors, a conversation mediated through the interaction of courts can likely include more than two speakers.

---

[44] For example, both the Opinion of AG Kokott (EU:C:2012:700) and the judgment of the CJEU in the *Aziz* case (n 21), which explicitly acknowledged the socio-economic context of the case, inspired debates on the handling of eviction cases after the economic crisis, both in Spain and in the transnational European sphere. See section III.B below.

[45] Habermas (n 41) 374.

[46] N Fraser, 'Transnationalizing the Public Sphere: On the Legitimacy and Efficacy of Public Opinion in a Post-Westphalian World' in N Fraser et al (edited by K Nash), *Transnationalizing the Public Sphere* (Cambridge, Polity Press, 2014) 30.

[47] ibid.

[48] A Arnull, 'Judicial Dialogue in the European Union' in J Dickson and P Eleftheriadis (eds), *Philosophical Foundations of European Union Law* (Oxford, Oxford University Press, 2012); A Torres Pérez, *Conflicts of Rights in the European Union: A Theory of Supranational Adjudication* (Oxford, Oxford University Press, 2009) 109 ff.

[49] G Letsas, 'Harmonic Law' in J Dickson and P Eleftheriadis (eds), *Philosophical Foundations of European Union Law* (Oxford, Oxford University Press, 2012) 91–92.

[50] cf Torres Pérez (n 48) 110–13.

Judicial conversations are shaped by the deliberations made in judgments, which are instrumental for developing answers to the questions posed in civil cases. They explain the line of reasoning and, in private law, the manner in which a balance is struck among the interests of the parties involved. Moreover, the legitimacy of judgments may be strengthened by the style of reasoning, for instance through the motivation of choices among different solutions.[51] Thus, judicial deliberations provide substance to the institutional interaction of courts.

In the following, three cases will be analysed that illustrate how judicial deliberations on politically sensitive topics are shaped in transnational judicial conversations in European private law – two involve the CJEU and one the ECtHR. In particular, it will be assessed to what extent deliberations that connect the national to the European dimension of private law may contribute to the inclusion of under-represented interests. Making these interests explicit in the conversations among courts, it will be shown, may clarify the legal framework or even induce legislative reform. The question is how this 'convening power' of courts may be explained. In the context of this chapter in particular, the two theories that were introduced in the previous section are explored: can judicial activism in European private law be understood as making visible the inconsistencies among state-constitutions and market-constitutions, as Dowdle submits?[52] And why might a democracy-based theory of judicial conversations offer a plausible alternative?

The cases have been selected on the basis of the debates they have raised among academics as well as, to a greater or lesser extent, a general audience. Furthermore, the aim has been to identify cases that are relevant to a larger number of European jurisdictions. Perhaps unsurprisingly, given these criteria, the selection comprises matters that go to the foundations of private law and have a clear fundamental rights dimension:[53] contracts on broadcasting rights for information of public interest (*Sky Österreich*), housing justice (*Aziz*) and surrogacy arrangements (*Mennesson v France*). It should be underlined that the aim of the analysis is not to give a full overview of case law or to advance the idea that there is one consistent approach to judicial conversations in European private law. Rather, it is attempted to show that there is more to the interaction of national and European courts in private legal cases than doctrinal aspects or an economic understanding of contract law. Analysing the cases in their social and political context, as well as their place in time in the private law debate, serves to substantiate the claim that the democratic, public sphere dimension of judicial conversations should be added to a theory of what courts do and should do in their handling of politically sensitive questions of private law.

III. THREE JUDICIAL UTOPIAS

A. Freedom of Information and Contract Law: *Sky Österreich*

Europa League football matches tend to attract a lot of public interest. The case of *Sky Österreich* concerned the business models that have been developed around television

---

[51] M de S-O-L'E Lasser, *Judicial Deliberations: A Comparative Analysis of Judicial Transparency and Legitimacy* (Oxford, Oxford University Press, 2009) 20–23; on the CJEU, see 349–52.

[52] *cf* Dowdle (n 32); see section II.B above.

[53] Note that these cases are meant as illustrations of judicial conversations in European private law. It is not the aim to give a full overview here, but rather to gain a better understanding of the process and the role of courts in the shaping of rules of private law in Europe.

broadcasting of these events and limitations to such models under EU law.[54] Sky had acquired an exclusive licence to broadcast Europa League matches in Austria in the seasons from 2009/2010 to 2011/2012 and provided viewers with access to a paid digital channel. A contract with the public broadcasting channel Österreichischer Rundfunk (ORF) initially stipulated that it would pay a price of €700 per minute for short news reports on the football matches. However, at the request of ORF, the Austrian media authority KommAustria determined that a possibility to present such short news report should be provided by Sky at the cost of providing access to the satellite signal, which in this case equalled zero.[55] In the appeal against this decision, the preliminary question was raised as to whether the European provision that led to this conclusion – Article 15(6) of the Audiovisual Media Services Directive – limited Sky's freedom to enjoyment of property as well as its freedom of contract in a disproportionate manner.[56] The CJEU held that there was no reason to doubt Article 15(6)'s validity, as the European legislature had struck a fair balance between Sky's freedom to conduct a business (Article 16 of the Charter of Fundamental Rights of the European Union (EUCFR)) and EU citizens' freedom of information and the freedom of media pluralism (Article 11 EUCFR).[57] The public interest in access to reports on Europa League football outweighed Sky's freedom of contract.

The case seems to fit Dowdle's view on judicial law-making, insofar as it makes visible inconsistencies between state-constitutions and market-constitutions. This comes to the fore when considering the case law of the German and Austrian Constitutional Courts, which was briefly referred to by the CJEU.[58] These Courts had determined that a right to broadcast short news reports free of charge was disproportionate and, accordingly, infringed the constitutional rights to professional freedom and protection of property. In his Opinion in the case, Advocate General Bot carefully examined the different balances struck by the CJEU and national courts, emphasising that each court has to consider the structure and objectives of the legal framework when assessing fundamental rights. Accordingly, he observed, 'it follows that the weighing of the different fundamental rights at stake does not necessarily call for the same response at national or EU level'.[59] Although the CJEU itself did not elaborate on this point, its judgment was in line with this observation, as it firmly placed the balance of Charter rights within the framework established by the Directive's objectives. While respecting the essence of the freedom to conduct a business, the Court observed, Article 15 of the Directive sought to guarantee access for the general public to information relating to events of high interest – that football matches qualify as such was not in question.[60] Interestingly, the Court, thus shaped a space for the 'social function' of the freedom to conduct a business.[61] With Dowdle, one could say that the reasoning in *Sky Österreich* visibly anchored the pursuit of a certain public interest within the EU's market-constitution.

Still, it seems that the constitutional dimension of contract law in *Sky Österreich* goes further than 'judicial politics'. The CJEU placed considerable emphasis on the importance of safeguarding the fundamental freedom to receive information and media pluralism in a 'democratic and pluralistic society' on the basis of Article 11 EUCFR.[62] Its reflections on the

---

[54] Case C-283/11 *Sky Österreich v Österreichischer Rundfunk* EU:C:2013:28.
[55] ibid paras 16–18.
[56] ibid paras 21, 24.
[57] ibid paras 59, 66–67.
[58] ibid para 23.
[59] Case C-283/11 *Sky Österreich*, Opinion of AG Bot, EU:C:2012:341, para 80.
[60] *Sky Österreich* (n 54) paras 49–52.
[61] ibid para 45.
[62] ibid paras 52, 66.

balance of fundamental rights accordingly took into account both the protection of the freedom of business and the interest of the general audience to have access to short reports on football events of high public interest. This democratic dimension seems even more present in the Advocate General's comparative exploration of the approaches chosen in the Council of Europe's Convention on Transfrontier Television, the case law of the ECtHR and the decisions of the German and Austrian Constitutional Courts.[63] Clarification of the relations of EU law to other European and national legal orders in this case served the demarcation of the 'democratic society' for which the CJEU was balancing the rights to information of public interest and the contractual freedom of exclusive rights-holders. In that sense, *Sky Österreich* provided a space for deliberation on a shared European direction.

The democratic dimension of these deliberations is further underscored by the discussion on the extent to which freedom of contract should be constitutionalised. In particular, the CJEU's later judgment in *Alemo-Herron*[64] has been widely criticised for giving too much weight to the essence of the freedom to conduct a business under Article 16 EUCFR.[65] Since the scope and meaning of this freedom, including the freedom of contract, are subject to continuous democratic reassessment, a strong constitutionalisation of a European 'essence' of Article 16 EUCFR is highly problematic.[66] Given the diverse understandings of freedom of contract in different national traditions, the definition of a European constitutional version of this freedom that may overrule national social policies likely lacks democratic support. Importantly, though, *Alemo-Herron* is seen as an 'aberration' between *Sky Österreich* and later judgments.[67] Its significance for the current analysis mostly lies in its contribution to the judicial conversation on the constitutional nature and limits of freedom of contract. As such, it remains of relevance for the shaping of a European political community.[68]

B. Unfair Contract Terms Control in the Housing Market: *Aziz*

The case law on Spanish mortgages that followed the 2008 economic crisis provides another example of judicial conversations on matters of notable legal-political significance. Like *Sky Österreich*, the individual cases arose against the backdrop of a fundamental debate on the balance that should be struck between the interests of different private actors. However, the stakes were much more personal for the debtors, as the object of the contracts were their homes. The aforementioned *Aziz* case is emblematic of how the interaction among civil courts

---

[63] Opinion of AG Bot (n 59) paras 73–80.

[64] Case C-426/11 *Mark Alemo-Herron and Others v Parkwood Leisure Ltd* EU:C:2013:521.

[65] J Prassl, 'Freedom of Contract as a General Principle of EU Law? Transfers of Undertakings and the Protection of Employer Rights in EU Labour Law' (2013) 42 *Industrial Law Journal* 434; J Prassl, 'Business Freedoms and Employment Rights in the European Union' (2015) 17 *Cambridge Yearbook of European Legal Studies* 189; S Weatherill, 'Use and Abuse of the EU's Charter of Fundamental Rights: On the Improper Veneration of "Freedom of Contract"' (2014) 10 *European Review of Contract Law* 167; M Bartl and C Leone, 'Minimum Harmonisation after *Alemo-Herron*: The Janus Face of EU Fundamental Rights Review' (2015) 11 *European Constitutional Law Review* 140.

[66] M Bartl and C Leone, 'Minimum Harmonisation and Article 16 of the CFREU: Difficult Times Ahead for Social Legislation?' in H Collins (ed), *European Contract Law and the Charter of Fundamental Rights* (Antwerp, Intersentia, 2018) 123.

[67] Prassl, 'Business Freedoms and Employment Rights in the European Union' (n 65) 190; Weatherill (n 65) 176.

[68] *cf* O Gerstenberg, *Euroconstitutionalism and its Discontents* (Oxford, Oxford University Press, 2018) 86–87, who observes that the case law was taken into account in subsequent legislative reforms.

allowed for a deliberation and reimagination of how the contractual relationships between banks and homeowners should be assessed.[69]

Again, Dowdle's perspective goes a long way towards explaining the 'judicial activism' with which the CJEU's *Aziz* judgment is often associated. Insofar as access to fair conditions for mortgage credit is essential for providing adequate housing, the judgment clearly established the links between market-oriented and social dimensions to the contractual relationship between bank and homeowner. The CJEU, following Advocate General Kokott, considered that it was problematic that there was no option under national law to halt mortgage enforcement proceedings while judicial review of the fairness of the contract terms was pending, since the only remedy available to the homeowner in the event of an eventual finding of unfairness of the terms would be monetary compensation.[70] In line with the concerns raised by the national judge who had referred the case,[71] the deliberations thus included a recognition of the tension between economic and social interests. If the CJEU were seen as a 'responsive' court in this saga,[72] one could say that its broad interpretation of the Unfair Terms Directive allowed for a deliberation of the approaches taken to mortgage and credit contracts in several Member States.[73]

However, the contribution of the judicial conversation on Spanish mortgages can hardly be detached in the debate on Europe's democratic and justice deficits.[74] While Dowdle's analysis convincingly explains why the market-constitutional dimension of contract law is more visible in the case law of the CJEU than that of national courts, it leaves this specific democratic concern unexplored. By focusing on the interaction between state-constitutions and market-constitutions, the model of national constitutionalism seems to be inadvertently transposed to the EU. As a consequence, the extent to which the EU's constitutional constellation may differ from national constellations is not fully taken into account. For cases like *Aziz*, this is problematic, insofar as a main concern raised by this case law is its democratic legitimacy: how can the interaction between the CJEU and national courts be explained, and to what extent can its impact on national legislative processes be justified?

The democratic theoretical framework proposed in this chapter seeks to address criticism on the type of judicial activism discerned in the *Aziz* judgment by fully engaging with the question of where boundaries to judicial law-making in European private law are and should be drawn.[75] From this perspective, it may be noted that the CJEU left the basis for its development of a remedy in the *Aziz* judgment implicit, relying on a legal-technical interpretation of the effectiveness of the UCTD. Thus, rather than establishing a fully developed view on the extent to which private legal questions should be constitutionalised, the *Aziz* case might instead be seen as a contribution to an ongoing conversation. In its judgment, the Court acknowledged the social dimension of the case, regarding the protection of the homes of Mr Aziz as well as many other homeowners in Spain. Yet, it refrained from addressing the fundamental rights

---

[69] See section II.A above.

[70] *Aziz* (n 21) paras 60–61.

[71] See Judge Fernández Seijo's chapter in this volume.

[72] Dowdle (n 32) section III.A.

[73] For comparative studies, see van Duin, *Effective Judicial Protection in Consumer Litigation* (n 20); M Józon, 'Judicial Governance by Unfair Contract Terms Law in the EU: Proposal for a New Research Agenda for Policy and Doctrine' (2020) 28 *European Review of Private Law* 909. From a point of view of democratic experimentalism, see Gerstenberg (n 68) 104; Mak (n 38) 236–37.

[74] Micklitz (n 27) 8–9.

[75] Mak (n 38) 221–23. See also Burgers (n 43) 52–57 and 271–80 on the boundaries of legitimate judicial law-making in climate change cases.

dimension of housing and, accordingly, left the relation between the UCTD and the EUCFR in the middle; as noted by Micklitz and Reich, *Aziz* could be read as 'hidden constitutionalisa-tion' of the private law debate.[76]

In later case law, the CJEU did more explicitly address the fundamental rights dimension of private legal relations. In judgments such as *Sánchez Morcillo*[77] and *Kušionová*,[78] it placed the financing of housing in the key of the Charter, although emphasis remained on the proce-dural dimension of effective judicial protection (Article 47 EUCFR) rather than a substantive elaboration of what a right to housing (Article 7 EUCFR) should entail in horizontal contrac-tual relationships.[79] Moreover, the Court's case law on the meaning of Charter provisions for private legal relationships expanded the potential reach of fundamental rights. In its judg-ment in *Bauer and Broßonn*, the Court held that Charter rights which are 'mandatory and unconditional in nature' may apply to private legal relations that fall within the scope of EU law.[80] As the Charter provisions that pertain to housing may not be able to fulfil these criteria, it remains to be seen which effects they may be inspire.[81] Still, tracing the developments in case law surrounding the *Aziz* judgment has shown how transnational judicial deliberations may shape the debate on housing justice in Europe. The fundamental rights dimension of the reasoning in these cases allowed for a broader debate on their socio-economic context.

C. Recognition of Children's Rights in the Balance with Immoral Contracts: *Mennesson v France*

Contrasting the interaction of courts under EU law with judicial conversations under the ECHR may serve to further substantiate the claim defended here on the democratic side to utopian reasoning in European private law adjudication. In fact, from a private law perspec-tive, both types of Europeanisation are of importance. Since cases arise from the private legal relations between the parties, the applicable rules of private law determine the scope for European influence. As we have seen, both EU Directives and Charter rights have gained increasing impact in defining freedom of contract in the interplay with national private legal orders. A comparison with similar effects of ECHR rights may further clarify the role of judi-cial conversations in this field.

The case of *Mennesson v France*,[82] on child–parent affiliation after surrogacy, illustrates well what is at stake. The case concerned the registration in France of the birth certificates of two children who had been born through surrogacy in California in the US. While surrogacy is allowed under Californian law, it is forbidden in France. Accordingly, contracts for surrogacy

---

[76] Micklitz and Reich (n 25) 800–02.

[77] Case C-169/14 *Juan Carlos Sánchez Morcillo and María del Carmen Abril García v Banco Bilbao Vizcaya Argentaria, SA* EU:C:2014:2099, para 35.

[78] Case C-34/13 *Monika Kušionová v SMART Capital, a.s.* EU:C:2014:2189, paras 45–47.

[79] I Domurath, 'Mortgage Debt and the Social Function of Contract' (2016) 22 *European Law Journal* 758, 766–67; van Duin, *Effective Judicial Protection in Consumer Litigation* (n 20) 107.

[80] Joined Cases C-569/16 and C-570/16 *Stadt Wuppertal v Maria Elisabeth Bauer and Volker Willmeroth v Martina Broßonn* EU:C:2018:871, para 85.

[81] I Domurath and C Mak, 'Private Law and Housing Justice in Europe' (2020) 83 *Modern Law Review* 1188, 1217.

[82] *Mennesson v France* App No 65192/11 (ECtHR, 26 June 2014), CE:ECHR:2014:0626JUD006519211; ECtHR (Grand Chamber) 10 April 2019, Advisory opinion concerning the recognition in domestic law of a legal-parent child relationship between a child born through a gestational surrogacy arrangement abroad and the intended mother, requested by the French Cour de Cassation, request no P16-2018-001.

are considered to be void as they infringe upon the French conception of *ordre public interna-tional*.[83] Since the French public authorities refused to register the children's birth certificates, the two girls remained US citizens and it was impossible to formalise the relationship with their French intended parents. In legal proceedings challenging this decision, the French highest court in civil cases, the Cour de Cassation, upheld this prohibition, considering that it was against the principle of inviolability of the civil status to give effect to a surrogacy arrangement.[84] The parents brought a complaint against the judgment to the ECtHR, based on an alleged violation of respect for their private and family life under Article 8 of the Convention.[85] While the Court did not find a violation of the parents' rights, it considered that the children's rights under Article 8 had been harmed. It emphasised the children's identity within French society depended on the recognition of the parent–child relationship.[86] Although it accepted France's discouraging policy towards international surrogacy, it held that the best interests of the children demanded that at least the biological relationship with their intended father should be recognised.[87] In a subsequent advisory opinion, which had been requested by the Cour de Cassation, the ECtHR further extended the children's right under Article 8 to the relationship with the intended mother, given the interest of the children of 'legal identifica-tion of the persons responsible for raising [them], meeting [their] needs and ensuring [their] welfare, as well as the possibility ... to live and develop in a stable environment'.[88] Although the ECtHR allowed states to choose which legal form to give to the recognition of the child–parent relationship, the Cour de Cassation eventually decided that the Mennessons did not have to go through the adoption procedure that would be required under national law: since the proceedings regarding their affiliation to the intended parents had already lasted for more than 15 years, in order to minimise the infringement of the children's rights under Article 8 ECHR, the Cour de Cassation ruled that the registration of their birth certificates should not be annulled.[89]

Of the three cases discussed in this chapter, *Mennesson v France* probably most clearly illustrates the differences between Dowdle's theory of the doubly constitutionalising func-tion of contract law and my democracy-based perspective. In particular, while we fully agree that contract law has a constitutional dimension, we appear to disagree on the place of non-economic factors in this dimension.

Dowdle's theory may explain why some legal systems, such as that of California, where the Mennesson girls were born, give precedence to contract law's facilitative economic func-tion – the market-constitution then aligns with an 'economic constitution' of the state. His theory could also explain why the French legal system takes a different approach and considers surrogacy contracts to lack validity – the open norm of 'public policy' allows for a judicial assessment of such contracts, which does not have to engage with the tension between the market-constitution and the state-constitution.[90] Considerations on the affiliation of the

---

[83] C Pavillon, 'Case 5: Surrogate Motherhood Contracts – France' in A Colombi Ciacchi, C Mak and Z Mansoor (eds), *Immoral Contracts in Europe* (Cambridge, Intersentia, 2020) 289.

[84] Cour de cassation 1re civ, 6 April 2011, no 10-19053, Bulletin 2011, I, no 72, in line with the case law of the Cour de Cassation that considers surrogacy contracts to infringe upon this principle as well as the principle of inalienability of the human body; Pavillon (n 83) 290; H Beale et al, *Cases, Materials and Text on Contract Law*, 3rd edn (Oxford, Hart Publishing, 2019) 670–74.

[85] *Mennesson* (n 82) para 43.

[86] ibid paras 80, 96.

[87] ibid paras 99–100.

[88] ECtHR, 10 April 2019 (n 82) para 42.

[89] Cour de cassation ass plén, 4 October 2019, no 10-19.053, paras 15–19.

[90] Dowdle (n 32) section III.C.

children in principle remain out of sight in this analysis, as they are not a matter of contract law.[91] It seems that neither the Cour de Cassation nor the ECtHR's judgments in the *Mennesson* case would be deemed to be activist in any way, since the courts did not have to engage with the question of whether surrogacy contracts should be allowed, but just handled the consequences of such arrangements under family law.

If my understanding of what Dowdle's theory would say about the *Mennesson* judgments is correct, then there is a clear contrast with my view on judicial law-making in Europe. In my 'utopian' theory, the interaction between the French court and the ECtHR provided a space for deliberation on the legal regulation of surrogacy. As many European countries deal with the question of whether to continue to prohibit surrogacy or rather to pragmatically facilitate the use of international 'baby markets' for their citizens,[92] the French case was of great importance for the debate on how to address the tension between national prohibitions and the affiliation of children born in countries where surrogacy is allowed. Although the courts have not managed to fully reconcile the interest of states to *ex ante* establish that surrogacy contracts should remain without effect with the best interests of the child that requires *ex post* affiliation, judicial deliberations have contributed to the broader, transnational debate. In particular, the judgments have given voice to the interests of children born as a result of surrogacy through the interpretation of Article 8 ECHR as well as a public debate on the case.[93] These insights are likely to affect further judicial as well as legislative decisions on surrogacy in Europe.[94]

IV. THE EUROPE-MAKING CAPACITY OF ADJUDICATION

In the previous sections, we explored three judicial utopias, representing three highly diverse areas of European private law: limits to freedom of contract of broadcasters aimed at providing a general audience with information on European football matches; judicial control of mortgage contracts in order to ensure housing justice; and looking past prohibitions on surrogacy contracts in order to enable the recognition of children's interests to be legally affiliated to their intended parents. As different as their substance and institutional setting were, the cases share several features. In particular, in each case, the interaction between a national court and a European counterpart – either the CJEU or the ECtHR – inspired deliberations that went beyond the economic basis of the contract at issue, in order to include social and political aspects. Moreover, the judgments gave a voice to those that are not often heard in legislative processes on the subject matter involved, respectively the European audience for

---

[91] MR Marella, 'The Old and the New Limits to Freedom of Contract in Europe' (2006) 2 *European Review of Contract Law* 257, 262.

[92] For an excellent introduction to this debate, see BC van Beers, 'Is Europe "Giving in to Baby Markets?" Reproductive Tourism in Europe and the Gradual Erosion of Existing Legal Limits to Reproductive Markets' (2014) 23 *Medical Law Review* 103; M Fabre-Magnan, *La gestation pour autrui* (Paris, Fayard, 2013). For a pragmatic perspective, see NF Bromfield and K Smith Rotabi, 'Global Surrogacy, Exploitation, Human Rights and International Private Law: A Pragmatic Stance and Policy Recommendations' (2014) 1 *Global Social Welfare* 123.

[93] See, for instance, this interview with Fiorella and Valentina Mennesson: 'Née d'une GPA: "Qui osera me dire: c'est horrible que tu existes ?"' *Le Parisien* (14 September 2018), www.leparisien.fr/societe/nee-d-une-gpa-qui-osera-me-dire-c-est-horrible-que-tu-existes-14-09-2018-7885803.php.

[94] In this context, it is interesting to mention that the Dutch legislature has proposed to regulate surrogacy through contract law in order to discourage international surrogacy and have a judicial check on the arrangements before the pregnancy. The pending proposal has already attracted a considerable amount of criticism, since it is contested whether the proposal can achieve its aims. See B van Beers and L Bosch, 'A Revolution by Stealth: A Legal-Ethical Analysis of the Rise of Pre-conception Authorization of Surrogacy Arrangements' (2020) 26 *New Bioethics* 351.

football matches in the CJEU in *Sky Österreich*, less affluent homeowners in the CJEU in *Aziz*, and children born as a result of surrogacy arrangements in the ECtHR in *Mennesson v France*. Thus, the interaction between national private law adjudication and the European level inspired new solutions for these individuals and groups.

Therefore, in conclusion, I would like to submit that the interaction between national courts in civil cases and the European level has a 'Europe-making capacity'.[95] The conversations among national and European courts open up inclusive deliberative spaces for debates on the underlying legal-political stakes of private legal questions. Judicial conversations in private law thus have the power to shape accounts of political (co-)existence that continuously allow for the imagination and reimagination of political reality in Europe, be it in relation to TV broadcasts, housing, reproductive treatment or other societal themes, such as climate change (*Urgenda*).[96] Each case provides a building block for a European polity.

A theoretical underpinning for the type of utopian thinking in adjudication that fuels this process was found in public sphere theory. Building on the dialogue between Habermas and Fraser, it is held that the interaction among national civil courts and the CJEU and the ECtHR maintains transnational public spaces for deliberation of societal questions. Thus, the judicial contribution to polity-building has a democratic dimension, which complements national and European legislative processes. Arguably, this theoretical view of judicial law-making in Europe can provide a more convincing or, in any case, more complete explanation of judicial conversations than Michael Dowdle's theory of 'responsive adjudication'. While Dowdle's theory gives a plausible explanation of the economic constitutional dimension of both national and European contract laws, its assertion that Europe's democratic deficit does not influence the interaction of national and European courts is, in my opinion, mistaken. Repairing a lack of democratic legitimacy, or even a justice deficit, is exactly what the CJEU and the ECtHR seemed to be doing when they gave a voice to the interests that had not been sufficiently taken into account in the legal framework for the cases at hand. This inclusive aspect of European private law adjudication is explained and made explicit by a public sphere theory as proposed in this chapter.

Thus, the question whether courts should be engaging in utopian conversations on European private law may be answered in the affirmative. As human rights needed a 'utopian gap in the temporal dimension' to develop into enforceable rights,[97] the process of European integration depends on realistic possibilities to reconcile national structures with overarching transnational deliberations. Private law adjudication, in some cases, may offer such utopian spaces needed for the constitutional imagination of Europe.

---

[95] Analogous to Loughlin's 'world-making' capacity of the constitutional imagination; Loughlin (n 11) 3.
[96] On the latter, see Burgers (n 29).
[97] Habermas (n 2) 93.

5

Deconstructing the CJEU's Jurisprudence to Enable Judicial Dialogue

FRANCESCA EPISCOPO*

I. INTRODUCTION

THE INSPIRING IDEA behind this book is that the continuous interaction between national courts, the Court of Justice of the European Union (CJEU or 'the Court') and the European Court of Human Rights (ECtHR) over cases involving the rights and duties of private parties can open up deliberative spaces in which to channel different conceptions of justice, leading towards a more democratic, solidaristic and fundamental-rights-based European Union (EU).

Under this view, national courts should use supranational instances to police and upgrade the laws of their own systems. Conversely, through fundamental rights litigation, they should bring national conceptions of justice into the regulatory stances of EU law, broadening its 'societal dimension' and leading to a constructive debate over the type of Europe we are striving for.[1] Overall, this process would contribute to the development of a self-standing and constitutionalised European private law (EPL).[2]

It is said that these processes have a descriptive and a normative relevance: they *are* already happening – as cases like *Aziz* and *Bauer* demonstrate[3] – and *ought to* be actively promoted.

---

* This is a revised and updated version of the paper presented at the 'Judges in Utopia' Conference, and I would like to thank all its speakers and participants for their comments and suggestions. I am also grateful to the participants of the 2020/2021 Emile Noël Forums for their engaging discussion on a draft version of the chapter. I am indebted to Chantal Mak and Betül Kas for their invaluable revisions. Any errors and mistakes are solely mine.
[1] For a distinction of the regulatory, social and societal dimensions of EPL, and their respective versions of justice, see HW Micklitz, *The Politics of Justice in European Private Law: Social Justice, Access Justice, Societal Justice* (Cambridge, Cambridge University Press, 2018).
[2] C Mak and B Kas, 'Civil Courts and the European Polity: An Introduction', ch 1 in this volume. See also L Burgers, A van Duin and C Mak, 'Judges in Utopia. The Transformative Role of the Judiciary in European Private Law' (2020) 28 *European Review of Private Law* 865; C Mak, 'Civil Courts as Constitutional Courts: Polity-Building through Private Law in Europe' (2020) 28 *European Review of Private Law* 953; C Mak, 'On Beauty and Being Fair: The Interaction of National and Supranational Judiciaries in the Development of a European Law on Remedies' in K Purnhagen and P Rott, *Varieties of European Economic Law and Regulation* (Cham, Springer, 2014) 823; C Mak, 'Hedgehogs in Luxembourg? A Dworkinian Reading of the CJEU's Case Law on Principles of Private Law and Some Doubts of the Fox' (2012) 20 *European Review of Private Law* 323. On the constitutionalisation of EPL, see, eg, HW Micklitz (ed), *Constitutionalization of European Private Law* (Oxford, Oxford University Press, 2014).
[3] Case C-415/11 *Mohamed Aziz v Caixa d'Estalvis de Catalunya, Tarragona i Manresa (Catalunyacaixa)* EU:C:2013:164; Joined Cases C-569/16 and C-570/16 *Stadt Wuppertal v Maria Elisabeth Bauer and Volker Willmeroth v Martina Broßonn* EU:C:2018:871.

In its normative dimension, the claim is commendable: it offers practical solutions to concrete problems by reconceptualising the interactions between legal systems, in a way that goes beyond positivist hierarchies, incentivises recursive and self-perfecting definitions of shared values and policy goals, and strengthens the constitutionalisation of EPL.[4]

Although sharable, it is important not to read the descriptive dimension of the claim too perfunctorily. While numerous cases signal such development,[5] others offer the antithetical account of a CJEU that is limitedly involved with justice and social matters, even when deciding on fundamental rights.[6] It should thus be subject to critical debate to what extent instances of judicial polity-building can be discerned in the Court's jurisprudence and how they relate to decisions that are clearly at odds with such an idea.

Indeed, this remark is not as pessimistic and defeatist as it sounds. If used constructively, a 'diffident' stance on the CJEU's case law allows us to better assess its lights and shadows, and envisage solutions that ensure the maximum protection of fundamental rights within private relations.[7]

For instance – and as will be discussed throughout this chapter – both the type and the level of effective judicial protection required by the CJEU for enforcing EU-based rights are often primarily directed to ensure the maximum realisation of EU law rather than a high level of judicial protection as such. This mismatch of rationales and goals could prevent the cross-fertilisation between legal systems, and could even lower the standard of protection set by Member States.[8] If – unlike what happened in *Taricco*[9] – national judges were to uncritically accept the notion of effective judicial protection adopted by the Court without realising the discrepancies which separate it from alternative conceptions present within national constitutions and the European Convention on Human Rights (ECHR), they may miss important opportunities for contributing to the development of EU law. The same applies to legal scholars, whose theoretical work substantially influences how the law is interpreted within and across jurisdictions.[10] Legal norms should thus be understood not as having a fixed, neutral and universal value, but rather as the product of ever-evolving interpretative practices performed by a plethora of legal actors, and whose content should be constantly checked and openly discussed.

For this purpose, a critical analysis of EPL is fundamental: it could help scholars to uncover ideologies driving the allegedly neutral and formalistic reasoning of the Court, question the

---

[4] I understand the normative claim underlying this book as: (i) an instrumental account of participative deliberation, where the open discussion is not simply an expression of political autonomy, but also a means to increase the likelihood of reaching a 'correct' decision; (ii) a strong form of legal pluralism, where systems coexist in a unordered way, and conflicts are solved through recursive mutual adjustments based on shared common values and mutual toleration; and (iii) a non-monist idea of legal interpretation, where judges adjudicate their cases according to what they deem the best possible solution in light of the interaction between systems, and in a way that increases the circulation of the model across different jurisdictions.

[5] See, eg, *Aziz* (n 3); *Bauer* (n 3).

[6] See, eg, Cases C-438/05 *International Transport Workers' Federation and Finnish Seamen's Union v Viking Line ABP and OÜ Viking Line Eesti* [2007] ECR I-10779; C-341/05 *Laval un Partneri Ltd v Svenska* [2007] ECR I-11767; Case C-426/11 *Mark Alemo-Herron and Others v Parkwood Leisure Ltd* EU:C:2013:521; C-399/11 *Stefano Melloni v Ministerio Fiscal* EU:C:2013:107.

[7] For instance, this could imply a redefinition of how national judges use the preliminary ruling proceeding and how they frame the referred question. Further considerations on this point are made in the concluding remarks of the chapter.

[8] See, eg, *Viking Line* (n 6); *Laval un Partneri* (n 6); *Alemo Herron* (n 6); *Melloni* (n 6).

[9] Cases C-105/14 *Criminal Proceedings against Ivo Taricco and Others* EU:C:2015:555; C-42/17 *Criminal Proceedings against MAS and MB* EU:C:2017:936.

[10] R Sacco, 'Legal Formants: A Dynamic Approach to Comparative Law' (1991) 39 *American Journal of Comparative Law* 1.

coherence and necessity of its decisions, as well as the broad consequences of its judgments,[11] and ultimately unlock the constructive path to judicial dialogue envisaged in the opening paragraph.[12]

Against this background, the chapter discusses the tensions at work within EU judge-made law to: (i) unveil questionable interpretative practices in the CJEU's jurisprudence; (ii) show how they are often used to perpetuate a self-referential and constitutionally thin judicial ideology; and (iii) suggest possible ways in which legal scholars can reveal such tendencies and guide national judges in their interaction with the CJEU in order to further enable the pluralistic and discursive development of a constitutionalised EPL.

To do so, it combines general attention for fundamental rights and constitutionally sensitive cases with a specific focus on the principles of effectiveness and effective judicial protection. This choice is determined by a twofold reason. First, with the adoption of Article 19 of the Treaty on European Union (TEU) and Article 47 of the EU Charter of Fundamental Rights (EUCFR or 'the Charter'), the two principles are increasingly used by both referring judges and the CJEU when interpreting EU law and reviewing national provisions, while scholars often view such developments as signifying an increased engagement with fundamental rights and social matters on the CJEU's side (see section III). Second, the 'ancillary' nature of the provisions makes them a privileged viewpoint for analysing the constitutionalisation of EPL, as they witness the enforcement and protection of primary entitlements, signalling *which* rights are protected, *when* and *how*.

In this context, section II sketches a roadmap to a critical analysis of the CJEU's case law, section III introduces the two principles and explains their role in the constitutionalisation of EPL, sections IV–VII assess their uses against the critical questions posed in section II to unearth the Court's judicial ideology, and section VIII shows how a deconstructive and discursive reading of these principles is instrumental to enabling a shared definition of EPL's policy and values.[13]

II. A METHODOLOGICAL ROADMAP

Critical legal theories aim at 'the disclosure of the actual origins, the social and economic functions, and the political and cultural entanglement of concrete legal solutions, modes of reasoning and argumentation, as well as the legal ideologies and theories legitimising them'. They strive to uncover factors and goals behind a given system or practice in order to

---

[11] HW Micklitz, 'Mohamed Aziz: Sympathetic and Activist, But Did the Court Get it Wrong?' in A Sodersten and JHH Weiler (eds), *Where the Court Gets it Wrong* (European Constitutional Law Network, 2013); HW Micklitz, 'Three Questions to the Opponents of the Viking and Laval Judgments' (2012) OSE Opinion Paper No 8.

[12] I am grateful to Rafał Mańko and Patricio Nazareno for their insights on the matter. For a (light) critical approach to EU law and scholarship, see L Niglia, 'Form and Substance in European Constitutional Law: The "Social" Character of Indirect Effect' (2010) 16 *European Law Journal* 439. For a stronger vibe, see S Rodin and T Perišin (eds), *The Transformation or Reconstitution of Europe: The Critical Legal Studies Perspective on the Role of the Courts in the European Union* (Oxford, Hart Publishing, 2018); the 'Special Issue on Critical Legal Theory and European Private Law', edited by MW Hesselink (2002) 10 *European Review of Private Law* 1; and MW Hesselink, 'Injustice in European Private Law' (2020) 41 *Yearbook of European Law,* https://doi.org/10.1093/yel/yeac005.

[13] Burgers, van Duin and Mak (n 2).

emancipate it from hidden ideologies and stem the replication of existing patterns of power.[14] While some typical methodologies may be found – deconstructionism, structuralism, decontextualisation etc – it is the very scope of the analysis that shapes the way forward. In our case, the analysis can be structured around three fundamental questions.

The first one asks how a given judicial trend contributes to the development of EU law and EPL. On a positivist account, this entails considering EU law and EPL: (i) not just in its original configuration, but also in its integration with national private law systems;[15] and (ii) in respect not just of the norms directly regulating the behaviours of private parties, but also of those norms guiding legal officials and pertaining to the interpretation and application of the law. However, from a more critical perspective, identifying how a judicial trend contributes to the development of EU law includes assessing the social, economic, political and institutional effects it causes, especially when contested issues are at stake. While cases like *Viking* and *Laval* are paradigmatic of the conflict between the national 'social' and the European 'access justice' (Zugangsgerechtigkeit),[16] a critical approach may help to detect less notorious judgments requiring Member States to revise their national systems of labour or social protection in order to meet the demands of the open market.[17] The same goes for the institutional dimension, which, once included in the picture, may shed new light on traditional accounts of the case law. For instance, the duty of consistent interpretation is commonly presented as a means of ensuring the effectiveness and judicial protection of EU rights, but was arguably introduced as a political compromise, where the German government fought to have domestic judges entrusted with balancing the enforcement of EU law and the socio-political choices underlying national legislation, without resorting to direct effect.[18]

The second question is whether the developments under analysis derive from a necessitated state of affairs or rather from discretional choices of the CJEU and, if so, which factors drive the Court's interpretation of the law. Most importantly, this should address not only the Court's final decision but also the very tools used for the purpose. Indeed, since EU law is composed of 'doctrines' conveying how broader principles are to be implemented, a critical analysis of judge-made EPL needs to inquire which of these doctrines constitutes the legal basis of the judgment and how legal reasoning is shaped as a consequence thereof. Far from a mere description, this step may help identify the overall rationales and goals at stake, as well as the judicial ideology to which the Court commits itself.

Finally, one should consider how the advancement of such goals sits within the peculiar structure of private law and private law adjudication. In particular, this involves asking, for example, where the responsibility of private parties for the implementation of EU law stand vis-a-vis that of public institutions; to what extent it can be translated within the dispute-resolution activity of the referring judges; and what type of constraints, if any, are set by

---

[14] R Mańko, 'Critique of the "Juridical": Some Metatheoretical Remarks' (2018) 11 *Latvijas universitātes žurnāls. Juridiskā zinātne* 24. For a paradigmatic expression of the critical school of thought, see, eg, D Kennedy, *A Critique of Adjudication* (Cambridge, MA, Harvard University Press, 1997).

[15] On pluralism in EPL, see, eg, L Niglia, *Pluralism and European Private Law* (Oxford, Hart Publishing, 2013); V Mak, 'Pluralism in European Private Law' (2018) 20 *Cambridge Yearbook of European Legal Studies* 202; and V Mak, *Legal Pluralism in European Contract Law* (Oxford, Oxford University Press, 2021).

[16] Micklitz (n 1).

[17] See, eg, Case C-209/03 *The Queen, on the Application of Dany Bidar v London Borough of Ealing and Secretary of State for Education and Skills* [2005] ECR I-2119; D Caruso and F Nicola, 'Legal Scholarship and External Critique in EU Law' in Perišin and Rodin (n 12) 233–34.

[18] Niglia (n 12).

private law and private law adjudication on the judicial development of EPL at the European and national levels.

While all these matters are of relevance for our purposes, a comprehensive analysis would exceed the space constraints of this chapter. In the following pages, I will mainly address the second issue, with only minor inroads into the first and third questions. In particular, I will consider the extent to which the principles of effectiveness and effective judicial protection – as resulting from the introduction of Articles 19 TEU and 47 EUCFR – foster the constitutionalisation of EPL, the institutional choices that may drive the CJEU's uses of the principle/right to an effective judicial protection (also in light of the horizontal nature of the cases involved) and the judicial ideology that such uses express.

III. EFFECTIVENESS, EFFECTIVE JUDICIAL PROTECTION AND THE CONSTITUTIONALISATION OF EPL

Effectiveness and effective judicial protection have always played a fundamental role in shaping the institutional architecture of the EU, as well as the rights and obligations private parties hold vis-a-vis public and private subjects. In EPL, the effectiveness principle is commonly understood as the specific limit to national procedural autonomy developed in *Rewe*: absent harmonised rules, it is for the Member States to designate the courts having jurisdiction and to lay down the procedural rules governing actions for safeguarding EU-based rights, provided that they are not less favourable than those governing similar domestic actions and do not render the exercise of these rights virtually impossible or excessively difficult.[19]

Article 19(1) TEU – 'Member States shall provide remedies sufficient to ensure effective legal protection in the fields covered by Union law' – is often seen as codifying this requirement, as part of the broader principle according to which the EU is primarily competent for establishing rights, while the national legal systems shall provide remedies and procedures for their enforcement and protection.[20]

As for the principle of effective judicial protection, its presence has long featured in the CJEU's jurisprudence. For instance, the doctrines of direct effect and consistent interpretation were based, inter alia, on the idea that national courts must ensure judicial protection to the rights which individuals derived from EU law.[21] Effective judicial protection emerged fully in *Johnston*, where the Court identified it as a 'principle of law which underlies the constitutional traditions common to the Member States [and is] also laid down in Articles 6 and 13 of

---

[19] Case C-33/76 *Rewe-Zentralfinanz eG and Rewe-Zentral AG v Landwirtschaftskammer für das Saarland* [1976] ECR 1989. The expression mirrors the one used in Case C-430/93 *Jeroen van Schijndel and Johannes Nicolaas Cornelis van Veen v Stichting Pensioenfonds voor Fysiotherapeuten* [1995] ECR I-4705, para 16, which the mainstream literature considers paradigmatic of the modern formulation of the standard: see, eg, M Dougan, 'The Vicissitude of Life at a Coalface: Remedies and Procedures for Enforcing Union Law before National Courts' in G de Bùrca and P Craig (eds), *The Evolution of EU Law*, 2nd edn (Oxford, Oxford University Press, 2009).

[20] See, eg, A Hartkamp, C Sieburgh and W Devroe, *Cases, Materials and Text on European Law and Private Law* (Oxford, Hart Publishing, 2017), 279. This division of competence was famously formulated by W van Gerven in 'Of Rights, Remedies and Procedures' (2000) 37 *Common Market Law Review* 501 and is the main rationale behind the 'extensive' reading of national procedural autonomy shared by many authors, including DU Galetta, *Procedural Autonomy of EU Member States: Paradise Lost?* (Berlin, Springer, 2011).

[21] Case C-26/62 *NV Algemene Transport- en Expeditie Onderneming Van Gend en Loos v Netherlands Inland Revenue Administration* [1963] ECR 3; Case C-14/83 *Sabine von Colson and Elisabeth Kamann v Land Nordrhein-Westfalen* [1984] ECR 1891.

the European Convention for the Protection of Human Rights and Fundamental Freedoms of 4 November 1950'.[22] With the adoption of the EUCFR, it was translated into a fundamental right, with Article 47 reading: 'everyone whose rights and freedoms guaranteed by Union law have been violated has the right to an effective remedy before a court of law'.

The introduction of Article 19 TEU and the binding nature of Article 47 EUCFR are often portrayed as leading to a new stage in the constitutionalisation of EU law and EPL. They are seen as shifting the significance of effectiveness and effective judicial protection from procedural norms used to assess Member States' judicial systems to 'more substantive principle[s] of a constitutional nature', which finalise the EU's transformation into a community that is fully respectful of the rule of law and fundamental rights.[23] Indeed, they: (i) allow the Court to shape a single code of procedure unifying the two-pillared judicial architecture into a coherent whole; (ii) consolidate both the EU's and the Member States' mandate to protect EU-based rights; and (iii) strengthen the legal positions of EU citizens, who now have an additional entitlement to receive an adequate level of judicial protection of the rights derived by the EU, for the realisation of which national judges are allowed (if not required) to develop remedies that 'upgrade' those originally set by national legislation.[24]

In EPL scholarship, the mainstream understanding of effective judicial protection was strongly shaped by the analysis made by Norbert Reich. According to Reich, despite 'not attach[ing] substantial new elements to the principle of effectiveness', Articles 19 and 47 do not merely restate the *acquis* based on national procedural autonomy, but also bolster its transformative potential, making it conform to the constitutionalisation of EPL. In a nutshell: EU rights that are sufficiently precise and unconditional require 'adequate protection'; if such protection is not granted by EU legislation, the effectiveness principle allows the CJEU to interpret EU law in a way that ensures the availability of more appropriate remedies. On their part, domestic courts must identify the applicable national remedy and measure it against the negative yardstick of effectiveness and equivalence; if the result is unsatisfactory, the effectiveness principle requires them to create new, 'hybrid' remedies allowing an *adequate* protection.[25]

Starting from similar premises, Hans Micklitz famously pleaded for the creation of judge-made remedies in order to rebalance the limited efficacy of social rights against economic liberties in EU law. In his view, improving the judicial protection of vulnerable subjects – consumers and employees – could compensate for the limited legislative intervention in the social rights field and the questionable management of the financial crisis by the EU Institutions.[26]

---

[22] Case C-222/84 *Marguerite Johnston v Chief Constable of the Royal Ulster Constabulary* [1986] 1651.

[23] A process arguably initiated in Case C-11/70 *Internationale Handelsgesellschaft mbH v Einfuhr- und Vorratsstelle für Getreide und Futtermittel* [1970] 1125 and Case C-294/83 *Parti écologiste 'Les Verts' v European Parliament* [1986] ECR 1339. See M Bonelli, 'Effective Judicial Protection in EU Law: An Evolving Principle of a Constitutional Nature' (2019) 12 *European Review of Administrative Law* 35.

[24] HW Micklitz, 'The ECJ between the Individual Citizen and the Member States: A Plea for a Judge-Made European Law on Remedies' in HW Micklitz and B de Witte (eds), *The European Court of Justice and the Autonomy of the Member States* (Antwerp, Intersentia, 2012) 347; N Reich, *General Principles of EU Civil Law* (Oxford, Oxford University Press, 2013); C Mak, 'Rights and Remedies: Article 47 EUCFR and Effective Judicial Protection in European Private Law Matters' in HW Micklitz (ed), *Constitutionalization of European Private Law* (Oxford, Oxford University Press, 2014); A van Duin, 'Metamorphosis? The Role of Article 47 of the EU Charter of Fundamental Rights in Cases Concerning National Remedies and Procedures under Directive 93/13/EEC' (2017) 6 *Journal of European Consumer and Market Law* 190; A Biondi and G Gentile, 'National Procedural Autonomy' in H Ruiz Fabri (ed), *Max Planck Encyclopedia of International Procedural Law* (Oxford, Oxford University Press, 2019).

[25] Reich (n 24). On the 'adequacy' threshold, see also van Gerven (n 20).

[26] Micklitz (n 24).

Over the last decade, these expectations were arguably met: Articles 19 and 47 have been increasingly used to interpret EU law and shape both the architecture of domestic judicial systems and the level of protection they offer within specific disputes.[27]

In the aftermath of the financial and migration crises, numerous preliminary references concerning the rights of consumers, investors and refugees triggered an evaluation of the obstacles set by national systems to judicial protection concerning judicial independence, legal aid, equality of arms, the right to appeal and to be heard, the relationship between judicial and administrative proceedings etc.[28] Against the rise of illiberal tendencies in some Member States, such scrutiny is also gaining a self-standing basis – ie, without the need to be triggered by a violation of substantive EU rights.[29]

At the same time, effective judicial protection has been used to shape national procedural autonomy, since domestic courts increasingly challenged national provisions under the *Rewe/Comet* framework, the *Johnston* effectiveness and Article 47, often in combination with one another. This phenomenon had a particularly strong relevance in the field of consumer law, where judges relied on effectiveness and effective judicial protection to overcome the procedural limitations precluding them from relying on Directive 93/13 to protect over-indebted and vulnerable consumers, eg, by assessing *ex officio* the unfairness nature of the term,[30] modifying the contractual agreement in the interest of the consumer[31] and suspending execution to account for the unfairness assessment.[32]

Finally, in fundamental-rights litigation, the domestic judges' duty to disapply incompatible national provisions, or interpret them in conformity with EU law, has been increasingly framed as part of their obligation to grant effective judicial protection, as an alternative or in combination to that of ensuring the effectiveness of primary norms. Paradigmatic of this is *Egenberger*, where the Court justified giving horizontal direct effect to Article 21 EUCFR as a way of granting an effective remedy under Article 47.[33]

---

[27] F Episcopo, 'The Vicissitude of Life at a Coalface: Remedies and Procedures for Enforcing Union Law before National Courts' in G de Bùrca and P Craig, *The Evolution of EU Law*, 3rd edn (Oxford, Oxford University Press, 2021), as well as the cases and literature cited therein.

[28] See, eg, Case C-625/11 P *Polyelectrolyte Producers Group GEIE (PPG) and SNF SAS v European Chemicals Agency (ECHA)* EU:C:2013:594; Case C-274/14 *Proceedings Brought by Banco de Santander SA* EU:C:2020:17; C-354/15 *Andrew Marcus Henderson v Novo Banco SA* EU:C:2017:157; Case C-752/18 *Deutsche Umwelthilfe eV v Freistaat Bayern* EU:C:2019:1114; Case C-64/16 *Associação Sindical dos Juízes Portugueses v Tribunal de Contas* EU:C:2018:117; Joined Cases C-542/18 RX-II and C-543/18 RX II *Review Simpson v Council and HG v Commissio n* EU:C:2020:232; Case C-272/19 *VQ v Land Hessen* EU:C:2020:535; Case C-223/19 *YS v NK* EU:C:2020:753; Case C-688/18 *Criminal Proceedings against TX and UW* EU:C:2020:94.

[29] Case C-824/18 *AB and Others v Krajowa Rada Sądownictwa and Others* EU:C:2021:153. For an example of an 'indirect' scrutiny, see Case C-279/09 *DEB Deutsche Energiehandels- und Beratungsgesellschaft mbH v Bundesrepublik Deutschland* [2010] ECR I-13849.

[30] See, eg, Case C-137/08 *VB Pénzügyi Lízing Zrt v Ferenc Schneider* [2010] ECR I-10847; Case C-618/10 *Banco Español de Crédito, SA v Joaquín Calderón Camino* EU:C:2012:349; Case C-472/11 *Banif Plus Bank v Csaba Csipai and Viktória Csipai* EU:C:2013:88; Case C-49/14 *Finanmadrid EFC SA v Jesús Vicente Albán Zambrano and Others* EU:C:2016:98; Joined Cases C-381/14 and C-385/14 *Jorge Sales Sinués and Youssouf Drame Ba v Caixabank SA and Catalunya Caixa (Catalunya Banc SA)* EU:C:2016:252; Joined Cases C-70/17 and C-179/17 *Abanca Corporación Bancaria SA v Alberto García Salamanca Santos and Bankia SA v Alfonso Antonio Lau Mendoza and Verónica Yuliana Rodríguez Ramírez* EU:C:2019:250; Joined Cases C-419/18 and C-483/18 *Profi Credit Polska SA v Bogumiła Włostowska and Others and Profi Credit Polska SA v OH* EU:C:2019:930.

[31] See, eg, Case C-26/13 *Árpád Kásler and Hajnalka Káslerné Rábai v OTP Jelzálogbank Zrt* EU:C:2014:282; Joined Cases C-482/13, C-484/13, C-485/13 and C-487/13 *Unicaja Banco, SA v José Hidalgo Rueda and Others and Caixabank SA v Manuel María Rueda Ledesma and Others* EU:C:2015:21.

[32] See, eg, *Aziz* (n 3); Case C-407/18 *Aleš Kuhar and Jožef Kuhar v Addiko Bank dd* EU:C:2019:537. On these topics, see A van Duin, ch 9 in this volume.

[33] Case C-414/16 *Vera Egenberger v Evangelisches Werk für Diakonie und Entwicklung eV* EU:C:2018:257. See also D Leczykiewicz, 'Horizontal Application of the Charter of Fundamental Rights' (2013) 38 *European Law Review* 479; Mak (n 24).

IV. A CRITICAL ANALYSIS OF EFFECTIVENESS AND EFFECTIVE JUDICIAL PROTECTION

While it is undeniable that reference to the 'subjective' and 'constitutional' dimensions of effectiveness and effective judicial protection, especially *qua* Article 47 EUCFR, enjoys a growing standing in the case law, the role attributed thereto within the constitutionalisation of EPL is open to discussion. This is not to say that the shift from a reasoning based on 'effectiveness of EU law' to one based on 'effectiveness of judicial protection' and the 'effectiveness of individual rights' did not take place or that it has no implications, but rather that the constitutional relevance and the social engagement often associated with it in private law scholarship may need to be re-evaluated and further contextualised.

First, in order to display a strong constitutional role, the right to an effective remedy and effective judicial protection needs to be framed accordingly. Yet, Article 47 is still in the process of development as far as the definition of its content and 'essential nature' is concerned.[34] Indeed, while the conditions set out in section III above are progressively being crystallised in the Court's jurisprudence, especially as far as the institutional profiles of the administration of justice are concerned, what constitutes an 'effective remedy' under paragraph 1 – which is of primary importance in the field of EPL – remains uncertain.

Moreover, the normative value of Article 47 risks being downplayed by the specific configuration of the Charter, where limitations are envisaged for fundamental rights, and under circumstances where it was not possible before. Indeed, the wording and interpretation of Articles 51–53 are such that an 'autonomous' Charter of rights may represent a stage of 'constitutional regress' compared to the moment in which the definition of the content and protection of fundamental rights was derived from the constitutional traditions common to the Member States.[35] Moreover, such a phenomenon may be particularly dangerous when referred to Article 47, as possible limitations – especially in the absence of a clear definition of its 'essence' – may further reduce the protection granted to the primary rights for which judicial protection is sought.

Second – and because of the above – it is difficult to determine whether the various manifestations of effective judicial protection elevate the scrutiny performed by the courts because of their own normative value or whether other considerations drive the courts' reasoning.

This is particularly true in the field of national remedies and procedures for the enforcement of EU-based rights, particularly for the interactions between *Rewe* effectiveness and *Johnston* effectiveness/Article 47.

In the Court's case law, these principles are linked in a blurred and inconsistent fashion.[36] In some cases, they are presented as distinct and autonomous, so that domestic remedies and procedures should not make it impossible or excessively difficult for individuals to exercise their EU-based rights, as well as to guarantee the minimum level of protection required by the general principle of effective judicial protection/Article 47.[37] In other cases, the *Rewe* test is

---

[34] On the difficulties of determining the 'essence' of art 47 CFR, see, eg, K Gutman, 'The Essence of the Fundamental Right to an Effective Remedy and to a Fair Trial in the Case-Law of the Court of Justice of the European Union: The Best is Yet to Come?' (2019) 20 *German Law Journal* 884; and G Gentile, ch 8 in this volume.

[35] D Leczykiewicz, 'The Charter of Fundamental Rights and the EU's Shallow Constitutionalism' in N Barber, M Cahill and R Ekins (eds), *The Rise and Fall of The European Constitution* (Oxford, Hart Publishing, 2019). On the unavoidability of balancing, see O Scarcello, 'Preserving the "Essence" of Fundamental Rights under Article 52(1) of the Charter: A Sisyphean Task?' (2020) 16 *European Constitutional Law Review* 647. For a practical example concerning the desired level of 'effective judicial protection', see, eg, *Melloni* (n 6).

[36] Episcopo (n 27) 285 ff.

[37] See, eg, Case C-12/08 *Mono Car Styling SA, in Liquidation v Dervis Odemis and Others* [2009] ECR I-6653; Joined Cases C-317/08–C-320/08 *Rosalba Alassini v Telecom Italia SpA, Filomena Califano v Wind SpA, Lucia*

portrayed as an expression of the broader principle of effectiveness of judicial protection, but it is uncertain under which framework compliance with EU law should be assessed: sometimes, the standard is directly identified in the *Johnston* effectiveness or Article 47,[38] while at other times *Rewe* effectiveness takes the lead.[39] Lately, the *Rewe/Comet* test has even been reframed to include an explicit reference to the Charter's fundamental right, stating that 'national law must observe the principles of equivalence *and the … right to an effective remedy, as laid down in Article 47*' (emphasis added).[40]

Against this backdrop, much has been written in an attempt to rationalise the relationship between *Rewe* effectiveness and *Johnston* effectiveness/Article 47. As anticipated, the principle of effective judicial protection and the right to an effective remedy are often presented as either an alternative and more demanding standard of protection, or as interpretative tools capable of intensifying the control under the *Rewe/Comet* test. Conversely, some authors compellingly argue that, regardless of whether *Rewe* effectiveness and *Johnston* effectiveness/Article 47 are autonomous or not, the latter adds little value to the scrutiny performed under the traditional equivalence-effectiveness test.[41]

Indeed, when discussing how much of an 'innovative potential' these particular manifestations of effectiveness bring, it may be useful to remember how, over the years, quite strong innovations in EU law and EPL – including the recognition of the *ex officio* power to review unfair contractual terms introduced in *Océano* – were accomplished by relying neither on *Johnston* effectiveness/Article 47 nor *Rewe* effectiveness, and secondary legislation was instead interpreted based on the need to ensure the application and enforcement of secondary legislation.[42] When 'subjective' versions of effectiveness and effective judicial protection were cited, they mostly featured as part of the legal provisions according to which directives ought to be interpreted, while the primary argument remained that of ensuring the 'effectiveness of European law' through, eg, the so-called '*effet utile* of direct effect'.

Against various attempts of rationalisation, the interactions between different manifestations of effectiveness and effective judicial protection are still difficult to untangle. Thus, the

---

Anna Giorgia Iacono v Telecom Italia SpA and Multiservice Srl v Telecom Italia SpA [2010] ECR I-2213. This solution is supported by the scholarship that understands effective judicial protection as a separate and more stringent standard, which can pave the way for the creation of new actions and remedies: Reich (n 24); K Havu, '"Adequate Judicial Protection" and Effective Application of EU Law in the Context of National Enforcement, Remedies and Compensation' (2015) 8 *Contemporary Readings in Law and Social Justice* 158; Bonelli (n 23); R Widdershoven, 'National Procedural Autonomy and General EU Law Limits' (2019) 12 *Review of European Administrative Law* 5.

[38] See, eg, Case C-432/05 *Unibet (London) Ltd and Unibet (International) Ltd v Justitiekanslern* [2007] ECR I-2271; Case C-268/06 *Impact v Minister for Agriculture and Food and Others* [2008] ECR I-2483; *DEB* (n 29).

[39] See, eg, Case C-61/14 *Orizzonte Salute – Studio Infermieristico Associato v Azienda Pubblica di Servizi alla persona San Valentino – Città di Levico Terme and Others* EU:C:2015:655; Case C-93/12 *ET Agrokonsulting-04-Velko Stoyanov v Izpalnitelen direktor na Darzhaven fond 'Zemedelie' – Razplashtatelna agentsia* EU:C:2013:432; J Krommendijk, 'Is There Light on the Horizon? The Distinction between "*Rewe* Effectiveness" and the Principle of Effective Judicial Protection in Article 47 of the Charter after *Orizzonte*' (2016) 53 *Common Market Law Review* 1395.

[40] Case C-495/19 *Kancelaria Medius SA v RN* EU:C:2020:431, para 17; Case C-176/17 *Profi Credit Polska SA w Bielsku Białej v Mariusz Wawrzosek* EU:C:2018:711; Case C-483/16 *Zsolt Sziber v ERSTE Bank Hungary Zrt* EU:C:2018:367.

[41] S Prechal and R Widdershoven, 'Redefining the Relationship between "*Rewe*-Effectiveness" and Effective Judicial Protection' (2011) 4 *Review of European Administrative Law* 31; M Bobek, 'Why There is No Principle of "Procedural Autonomy" of the Member States' in HW Micklitz and B de Witte (eds), *The European Court of Justice and the Autonomy of the Member States* (Antwerp, Intersentia, 2012); Episcopo (n 27).

[42] Joined Cases C-240/98-C-244/98 *Océano Grupo Editorial SA v Roció Murciano Quintero and Others* [2000] ECR I-4941. A paradigmatic example outside the realm of consumer law is Joined Cases C-6/90 and C-9/90 *Andrea Francovich and Danila Bonifaci and Others v Italian Republic* [1991] ECR I-5357.

actual impact of the 'subjective' dimensions of effectiveness – and Article 47 in particular – on the interpretation of EU law and the harmonisation of national remedies and procedures on EPL is uncertain, especially when assessed against the innovations achieved under the effectiveness of EU law. Indeed, judicial intervention is often based on the latter rather than on the former or – much more frequently – on an unsystematic combination of different versions of effectiveness This, of course, is not meant to downplay the importance of judicial strands such as that following *Aziz* on the protection of over-indebted and vulnerable consumers; it is only meant to stress that there is no binary relationship between the use of a particular type of effectiveness and the innovative dimension of the Court's judgments, or the standard of protection granted therein.

Indeed, the unclear relationship between these various manifestations of effectiveness and effective judicial protection causes two problems. How can we anticipate what it means that, in the specific case at hand, a right or a remedy must be made effective? How should we understand whether a matter should be framed as pertaining to *Rewe* effectiveness, *Johnston* effectiveness or Article 47?

V. MEASURING EFFECTIVENESS ...

The previous paragraph showed how the very margin of application of the effectiveness principle and the principle/right of effective judicial protection is uncertain and how, whenever they are used, their significance in shaping EPL is difficult to define.

This puts into question the European positivism and formalism – the approach according to which concepts, principles and doctrines within EU law are supposed to have a clear and defined meaning, and play a specific role in the interpreter's toolbox, setting them apart from one another – bringing us to analyse both the CJEU jurisprudence and EU law from a different viewpoint.

While various perspectives may offer useful insights, two complementary inquiries seem particularly promising: one relates to the *level* of effectiveness required and the other to the *type* of effectiveness used.

The principles of effectiveness and effective judicial protections do not seem to have a strong meaning and normative value, being defined on a case-by-case basis. This is a common problem: unlike rules, principles have a dimension of weight and need to be balanced against one another.[43]

However, while all principles may find different degrees of realisation, provisions referring to notions like 'effectiveness', 'adequacy' and 'proportionality' stand quite apart from others such as the principle of good faith or equality. Although all these principles have some degree of open texture, the former incorporates an idea of 'measure' that displays particularly high levels of indeterminacy.[44]

Indeed, effectiveness is not an ontological feature, but rather a property that the speaker attributes to an object and that is gradable by definition. Most importantly, it is: (i) vague,

---

[43] R Dworkin, *Taking Rights Seriously* (Cambridge, MA, Harvard University Press, 1977).

[44] On this matter – and for the considerations that follow – see F Episcopo, 'Judicial Law-Making and the Principle of Effectiveness in EU (Private) Law' (2019) 21 *Revista Catalana de Dret Privat* 53, 56 ff. On indeterminacy in the law, see, eg, T Endicott, *Vagueness in the Law* (Oxford, Oxford University Press, 2000). On the notion of 'open texture', see HLA Hart, *The Concept of Law* (Oxford, Oxford University Press, 1961).

because the semantic boundaries of the concepts are physiologically undetermined; (ii) essentially contestable, because attributing the property of effectiveness constitutes a normative judgment, which in turn depends on the ideology each subject adheres to; and (iii) ambiguous, because even if an agreement over its conceptual boundaries were found, what exactly is needed for something to be deemed effective depends on the very object to which the property in question is attributed. Thus, a plea for an effective application of substantive provisions, or an effective protection of the rights deriving thereof, says very little about the level of application or protection required: the latter is not predetermined, but depends on other factors influencing the desired level of effectiveness, which inevitably vary depending on 'what needs to be effective' and 'how much effective' we want it to be.

If assessed against the conditions of correctness set by argumentative and discursive theories,[45] the CJEU's use of effectiveness and effective judicial protection is questionable, as the Court often *assumes* that a certain level of effectiveness is needed, subtracting the definition of that threshold from the process of justification. Not addressing the question of why, how and to what extent something – such as a rule or a remedy – must be made effective, the Court presents its decisions as the outcome of a necessary interpretative procedure that is implicit in the very structure of EU law. Yet, the alternative is not between effective and non-effective rights, but among different *degrees* of effectiveness.

As section IV above demonstrated, *how much* effectiveness is needed does not necessarily depend on the parameters of the review – eg, *Johnston* effectiveness/Article 47, or a combination thereof – or on an unconditional strive for the advancement of judicial protection across the EU, but rather on the multiple considerations and circumstances which drive the CJEU's jurisprudence.[46] Indeed, a contextual analysis of the case law may show how the Court's scrutiny is strongly oriented by the legal, political and structural relevance of the substantive legal positions in need of judicial protection: procedural imbalances or bottlenecks are likely to be seriously addressed in cases dealing, for example, with obstacles in the field of consumer law, competition and state aid, precisely because of the importance of the interests at stake. Similarly, these impediments will be more directly addressed if they impair key features of the EU's institutional architecture, such as the domestic courts' capacity to raise preliminary questions.[47]

VI. ... AND CHOOSING AMONG DIFFERENT 'CAUSES OF ACTION'

The second issue relates to the *type* of standard against which national measures are analysed, and the assessment associated thereto.

Indeed, a critical assessment of the CJEU's case law mentioned in section III above uncovers an ambiguous overlap between the different specifications of effectiveness and effective judicial protection. What, then, drives the choice over the legal basis, which the Court adjudicates upon?

---

[45] See, eg, C Perelman and L Olberechts-Tyteca, *Traité de l'argumentation. La nouvelle rhétorique* (Paris, Presses universitaires de France, 1958); S Toulmin, *The Uses of Arguments* (Cambridge, Cambridge University Press, 1964); J Habermas, *The Theory of Communicative Action* (Boston, MA, Beacon, 1981); R Alexy, *Theorie der juristischen Argumentation. Die Theorie des rationalen Diskurses als Theorie der juristischen Begründung* (Frankfurt am Main, Suhrkamp, 1983).
[46] For a hermeneutical analysis of the steadying factors in the Court's jurisprudence, see G Beck, *The Legal Reasoning of the Court of Justice* (Oxford, Hart Publishing, 2013).
[47] Episcopo (n 27). On this point, see also Galetta (n 20).

Following the path set in section II, it may be useful to consider what would have happened had the Court used another notion of effectiveness in order to identify what legal conse-quences are enabled by the legal tools used in the context of adjudication. Indeed, in the field of national remedies and procedures, deciding to frame the matter as relating to the domestic measure's compatibility with *Johnston* effectiveness or Article 47, instead of the principles of equivalence and effectiveness, has three substantial implications in terms of the *type of scrutiny* enabled, relating to: (1) the positive or negative nature of harmonisation achieved; (2) the overall degree of its expansion; and (3) its reach in private disputes.

If effective judicial protection is used to solve a preliminary reference, either as a self-standing and autonomous standard or as a tool to interpret secondary law, national provisions are then assessed against EU law and arguably 'harmonised' EU law. This is a radically differ-ent frame compared to the one set by the *Rewe/Comet* test: here, *in the absence of EU rules on the subject*, it is for the domestic legal system of each Member State to designate the reme-dies and procedures governing the judicial protection of EU-based rights, provided that they comply with the twin principles of equivalence and effectiveness.

When the CJEU interprets substantive rights and duties as having a minimum content and, consequently, as requiring a certain type of legal and judicial protection, it engages in an incremental judicial harmonisation, defining new EU rules on the subject, regardless of whether this happens through the creation of new standards or their use for interpreting other provisions. Accordingly, when assessing the compatibility of national measures with EU law, the former is tested as 'falling within the scope of EU law',[48] and subject to EU 'procedural primacy', instead of being left to national procedural autonomy; the Court may thus consider it as directly precluded by EU law, even when the measure at hand does not constitute a specific implementation of the latter. The increased use of effective judicial protection therefore entails a fundamental expansion in the realm of harmonised law and a reduction of the areas of national remedial and procedural autonomy. Moreover, it triggers an assessment that is supposedly more stringent than the one performed under the *Rewe/Comet* framework, where a certain deference to national procedural autonomy still constrains the Court's evaluation.

Most importantly, this pattern also concerns the application of other effectiveness-based doctrines, going well beyond the alternative between *Rewe* effectiveness and the principle/right to an effective judicial protection.

Indeed, expanding the narrow definition given in section III, 'effectiveness' can first and foremost be described as the unwritten principle according to which EU law and its norms must be made effective and find concrete realisation at both the EU and national levels, and which is used by the CJEU to ensure that EU law has fully fledged legal effects by means of teleological and functional interpretation.

As such, this has both an autonomous and an instrumental bearing. It has a self-standing character when it directly justifies an effectiveness-based interpretation of primary norms, ie, rules that govern general societal conducts by constructing legal obligations and eventually the consequences associated with their breach. Conversely, it has an instrumental character when it constitutes the rationale behind the creation and expansion of other effectiveness-based principles and doctrines, such as primacy/supremacy[49] and direct effect – including quasi-horizontal direct effect,[50] incidental direct effect[51] and the *effet utile* of direct effect[52] –

---

[48] See Leczykiewicz (n 35).

[49] Case C-106/77 *Amministrazione delle Finanze dello Stato v Simmenthal SpA* [1978] ECR 629.

[50] Case C-36/74 *BNO Walrave and LJN Koch v Association Union cycliste internationale, Koninklijke Nederlandsche Wielren Unie and Federación Española Ciclismo* [1974] ECR 1405.

[51] Case C-443/98 *Unilever Italia SpA v Central Food SpA* [2000] ECR I-7535.

[52] Case C-453/99 *Courage Ltd v Bernard Crehan and Bernard Crehan v Courage Ltd and Others* [2001] ECR I-6297.

the duty of consistent interpretation, as well as the requirements of effectiveness and equivalence. Effectiveness is here used in interpreting EU law to justify the emergence of secondary norms, ie, rules that govern the definition of the law's validity and efficacy, the determination of its content, as well as the structure and functioning of adjudication in the European order.

Against this background, it is clear that a reasoning based on an 'external' review of national procedural autonomy is not only alternative to those based on Articles 47 and 19(1), but also to those based on the 'second-order' doctrines recalled above, as well as of proper European actions, like *Francovich* liability.[53] Indeed, it is significant that some of these cases, where the effectiveness-based interpretation of the Treaties grounded the recognition of new and 'autonomous' causes of actions, could have been framed as situations where the lack of a given remedy in domestic judicial systems was making it impossible or excessively difficult for European citizens to seek judicial redress and exercise their EU-based rights, under the traditional *Rewe/Comet* test.

This anticipates the second implication deriving from the peculiar standard of judgment, which may lead to 'strategic' choices on the part of the CJEU.

Indeed, reference to a specific version of effectiveness may be used to amplify the margin of intervention. While the need to ensure the effective realisation and judicial protection of EU-based rights is the common thread of all these doctrines and tools, inasmuch as they have different scopes of application and formal requirements, they may be easily used in combination with one another, compounding their respective effects.

The following progression is paradigmatic of the trend. Given a certain provision of primary or secondary law, the Court first recognises an EU-based right. It then extends its meaning and content through an effectiveness-based interpretation[54] and attributes to it specific features (such as the capacity to have direct effect) because the latter are deemed necessary to ensure the effectiveness of this right – if not that of EU law in general – its judicial protection, or even the realisation of the right to an effective remedy.[55] Moreover, the Court extends that right's application by means of the *effet utile* of direct effect, for example, including private parties among the addressees of the obligations imposed by EU law[56] or creating associated remedial rights, such as the right to receive compensation for breach of antitrust rules.[57] Eventually, *Rewe* effectiveness requires national procedural autonomy not to make the exercise of EU-based rights and freedoms impossible or excessively difficult, so that the specific conditions and procedures governing the remedial rights, or the specific expression that the latter assumes with national legal systems, are subject to the traditional constraints of national procedural autonomy.[58] Moreover, *Johnston* effectiveness and Article 47 EUCFR require domestic judges to further upgrade national remedies to ensure an *adequate* protection of the right in question.

Finally, and as anticipated, the choice over the type of effectiveness to be used for interpreting EU law, or indirectly reviewing national provisions, may affect the Court's capacity to expand the reach of EU law to cover horizontal relations.

Indeed, by referring to the 'subjective' versions of effectiveness, the Court may give a public law dimension to private adjudication, overcoming limits traditionally associated with

---

[53] *Francovich* (n 42).

[54] T Eilmansberger, 'The Relationship between Rights and Remedies in EC Law: In Search of the Missing Link' (2004) 41 *Common Market Law Review* 1199.

[55] *Van Gend en Loos* (n 21).

[56] Case C-415/93 *Union royale belge des sociétés de football association ASBL v Jean-Marc Bosman, Royal club liégeois SA v Jean-Marc Bosman and Others and Union des associations européennes de football (UEFA) v Jean-Marc Bosman* [1995] ECR I-4921.

[57] *Courage Ltd* (n 52).

[58] Case C-557/12 *Kone AG and Others v ÖBB-Infrastruktur AG* EU:C:2014:1317.

horizontal disputes. The Court's refusal to grant the requested protection may be seen as violating both their duty to ensure judicial protection pursuant to *Johnston* effectiveness and Article 19, as well as the claimant's fundamental right to an effective remedy, which has a broad scope of application and needs no further implementation, being directly effective in itself.

This pattern is clearly expressed in cases like *Egenberger* and *Bauer*.[59] In the former, the Court justified granting horizontal direct effect to Article 21 EUCFR as the only way of offering the claimant an 'effective remedy' under Article 47. In the latter, the horizontal application of Article 31 EUCFR – quite surprisingly read as encompassing a transmissible right to payment in lieu of annual leave – is derived from the need to ensure judicial protection to the right in question, without discussing whether private parties had any direct obligation under this provision. As a result, the Court managed to indirectly equate private parties with public entities, even if they were not directly charged with any specific obligation for the realisation of that right.[60]

However, while the horizontal application of fundamental rights is certainly a step in the direction of the constitutionalisation of EPL, and one that is to be welcomed, it is questionable to what extent private parties shall be obliged by duties and obligations based on EU law, and to what extent their conduct may be retrospectively qualified as illegal because the underlying national legislation was considered incompatible with EU legislation.

VII. UNEARTHING THE CJEU'S JUDICIAL IDEOLOGY

The considerations that we have made so far lead us to look beyond both the CJEU's 'functional formalism' and the positivists strive for its rationalisation, and rather frame effectiveness and effective judicial protection as decision-making, hermeneutical and justifying canons, which contribute, *inter alia*, to selecting specific doctrines upon which to adjudicate, based on the judicial reasoning that they enable.

But what is the *overall* effect? Is there an 'ideology' lurking in the background? The answer mostly depends on how we define ideology. Leaving aside the traditional understanding of the latter as a specific set of political preferences which individual judges display – which is typical of the American critics – we may give this notion at least two complementary definitions.[61]

In a narrow sense, ideology simply stands as a synonym of policy rationales or goals fostered by judicial interpretation. In this sense, if the Court adopts a functional and teleological interpretation of EU primary and secondary law, its ideology mirrors the policy goals underlying EU law itself: consumer protection, promotion of competition, market integration, legal integration etc.

However, if considered broadly, ideology also covers the judicial philosophy, which reflects the systemic understanding of the normative preferences and institutional constraints of the legal order.[62] In this sense, the CJEU may be seen as committed to a continuous strive for

---

[59] Cases C-555/07 *Seda Kücükdeveci v Swedex GmbH & Co KG* [2010] ECR I-365; *Egenberger* (n 33); *Bauer* (n 3).

[60] On these profiles, see Dorota Leczykiewicz, 'The Judgment in *Bauer* and the Effect of the EU Charter of Fundamental Rights in Horizontal Situations' (2020) 16 *European Review of Contract Law* 323.

[61] On the need to overcome the 'traditional' notion of ideology, see the contributions in Perišin and Rodin (n 12).

[62] MP Maduro, 'Interpreting European Law: On Why and How Law and Policy Meet at the European Court of Justice' in H Koch, K Hagel-Sorensen, U Haltern and JHH Weiler (eds), *Europe: The New Legal Realism* (Copenhagen, DJØF Publishing, 2010) 457, 460, as cited in T Càpeta, 'Ideology and Legal Reasoning at the European Court of Justice' in Perišin and Rodin (n 12), 96.

affirming the autonomy, supremacy and uniformity of the European legal order, and its effectiveness as such.

This view is often shared by legal scholarship, namely in studies on the constitutional advancement of EU law and in those relating to its constitutional and theoretical foundations.[63] While an exhaustive reconstruction of these theories would be beyond the scope of this chapter, two readings of the CJEU's case law may call for specific mentioning.

In a recent work,[64] Dorota Leczykiewicz criticised the CJEU for committing to a 'shallow' form of constitutionalism', as it prioritises constitutional values such as direct effect, supremacy, effectiveness, effective judicial protection and general principles of the EU, which directly and immediately contribute to the primacy, unity and effectiveness of EU law, over those of democracy, individual liberty and equality, respect of fundamental rights and constitutional identity, and proportionality of EU actions.[65] Most importantly, she highlights how, against all expectations, the role attributed to the EUCFR in the post-Lisbon jurisprudence either consolidates such shallow constitutionalism or leads to a constitutional regress. According to Leczykiewicz, the CJEU often uses the Charter as an 'autonomous source of fundamental rights' to depart from the constitutional tradition of Member States and the ECHR, which are merely cited when additional legitimation is needed. Through a questionable reading of Articles 51 and 52, it deploys fundamental rights as standards against which to review Member States' laws that do not immediately and directly fall within the scope of EU law, considers 'limitable' rights that were not treated as such when derived from the constitutional traditions common to the Member States, and varies its scrutiny depending on the object of the review, making its commitment to a true liberal theory of rights doubtful at least.

The idea of a CJEU that strategically uses its own source of fundamental rights, and its capacity to define their required level of protection, resonates with the considerations made by Justin Lindeboom on the Court's alleged theory of law and its philosophical foundation.[66] In reviewing the (in)famous Opinion 2/13, Lindeboom argued that the Court seems the primary concern in the Court's case law is the protection of the EU's legality – as well as its own prerogatives as an institutional actor. In this sense, it adopts the (Razian) idea according to which, in order to constitute a valid legal order, a normative system must claim supreme and comprehensive jurisdiction. All instances deriving from the EU's open nature – including the systems of judicial protection set by the ECHR or the Member States – need to be either scrutinised, to ensure that they are not applied whenever they would compromise the supremacy or effectiveness of EU law, or 'neutralised', ie, incorporated and transformed into (autonomous sources of) EU law.[67]

Both Leczykiewicz's and Lindeboom's claims show how the Court seeks to ensure the self-referentiality of the legal system and its monopoly in legal interpretation, eg, by defining its own version of fundamental rights and the relative system of protection and limiting the reference to other concurrent conceptions which could be found in national constitutional law and the ECHR, pursuant to a monist approach to the European legal system. While this is certainly not an exclusive picture – and cases of cross-fertilisation between different levels of the legal

---

[63] See, eg, the contributions in J Dickson and P Eleftheriadis (eds), *Philosophical Foundations of European Union Law* (Oxford, Oxford University Press, 2012).

[64] Leczykiewicz (n 35).

[65] Incidentally, it is quite significant that, in her characterisation of the two notions, Leczykiewicz considers both effectiveness and effective judicial protection as typical instances of a 'shallow' constitutionalism.

[66] Justin Lindeboom, 'Why EU Law Claims Supremacy' (2018) 38 *Oxford Journal of Legal Studies* 328.

[67] ibid.

system can be found – a monistic-based interpretation of the law is quite significant and needs to be taken into consideration. Overall, this may signal a latent ideology in the court's case law, strongly directed at ensuring the effectiveness of EU law by means of designing a supreme and self-referential legal system, even when hidden behind 'fundamental rights-based' narratives.

VIII. THE WAY FORWARD?

The previous sections show how a critical analysis of the CJEU's jurisprudence is necessary to account for the multiple dimensions and interests at stake within judicial harmonisation, setting the premises for a constructive discussion of what needs to be changed in order to foster the development of a self-standing, fully constitutionalised EPL.

While many facets of these claims require further debate, for the sake of this chapter, they may help us to identify two additional rationales lying behind the Court's uses of the principles of effectiveness and effective judicial protection.

First, arguments based on effectiveness are likely perceived as acceptable because of their allegedly technical and politically neutral nature. By invoking an unspecified need for effectiveness or claiming that no obstacles to the effectiveness of EU law are to be found, the Court presents its decisions as the necessary and automatic application of value-neutral and technical rules, whereas they reflect discretionary choices on the degree of realisation of the norm in question – a matter that, especially when concerning constitutionally sensitive issues, should instead be open to debate.

Second, other legal arguments, such as the need for coherence, uniformity, the respect of other legal principles and, most importantly, fundamental rights, may sometimes be used to strengthen or supplement the justification based on the principle of effectiveness, whenever the latter might not be perceived as convincing enough. Indeed, effectiveness-based arguments are often used to present solutions adopted to enforce EU law as if they were exclusively or predominantly aimed at ensuring the protection of subjective rights and freedoms or to add a subjective layer onto reasoning primarily based on other concerns. This partly explains why the reference to 'subjective' versions of effectiveness – such as *Johnston* effectiveness and Article 47 – plays such a strong rhetorical role in the Courts' justification. However, even specific manifestations normally associated with the effectiveness of EU law – such as the direct effect or its *effet utile* – may be portrayed as pertaining to the effectiveness of judicial protection, exploiting the 'family resemblance' that the various notions of effectiveness share with one another.[68]

Indeed, as a third point, very often the different versions of effectiveness used in EU law may belong to more discourses simultaneously. In *Van Gend en Loos*, *Costa* and *Simmenthal*, for example, the doctrine of direct effect is affirmed by saying that 'every national court must, in a case within its jurisdiction, *apply Community law in its entirety and protect the rights which the latter confers on individuals* and must accordingly set aside any provision of national law which may conflict with it, whether prior or subsequent to the Community rule' (emphasis added).[69] Here, the protection of individual rights was certainly part of the Court's concerns.

---

[68] Family resemblance constitutes 'a complicated network of similarities overlapping and criss-crossing', exhibiting the lack of boundaries among different uses of the same concept: L Wittgenstein, *Philosophical Investigations* (Oxford, Blackwell, 1974) para 66.

[69] *Simmenthal* (n 49) para 21. See also *Van Gend en Loos* (n 21), 13; Case C-6/64 *Flaminio Costa v ENEL* [1964] ECR 1141, 595.

However, the very structure and rationale of the judgments show that the CJEU was primarily interested in developing a system of private enforcement. By allowing European citizens to directly rely on a European norm before national courts – either obtaining the recognition of the entitlement they derive from it or merely excluding the application of national rules incompatible with the latter[70] – the Court ultimately ensured the effectiveness of European rules and that of the European legal system itself.

Focusing on the type of question that the CJEU seeks to answer may help to identify the type of discourse in which it is primarily engaging and whether its major object is, for example, the protection of subjective rights or rather of EU law in itself, such as by ensuring the autonomy of its own jurisdiction. In other words, regardless of the type of effectiveness concretely adopted, a discursive analysis of the case law can identify both the type of problem the Court seeks to address and the type of discourse it engages *ad abundantiam*. Therefore, it can show when the definition of the content, validity and efficacy of EU law, as well as the legal and judicial protection of EU-based legal rights, is solved in a way that realises the effectiveness of the legal order, which is intended as a system claiming exclusive and supreme authority within its jurisdiction.

Likewise, a discursive analysis of the case law makes it possible to discern when the protection of individual rights does not constitute a driving force in the Court's decision, but rather plays a strongly rhetorical role.

This account sheds new light on the effort to constitutionalise EPL through judicial dialogue.

By relying on a critical approach, legal scholars may improve the overall understanding of the Court's case law. Indeed, the analysis of effectiveness and effective judicial protection has shown how, even in the field of EPL, the two are often used to promote the integration of EU law while persuading the interlocutors of the opportunity and necessity of the Court's decisions, in a system where the precarious balance between different legal sources makes legitimisation and acceptance converge.[71] While the principles may be appreciated as leading to specific advancements in various sectors of law (such as consumer law), any attempt to give them a clear-cut meaning and normative value should come to terms with the fact that they are often used as instruments of governance: flexible gatekeepers that mould the division of competences between the EU and Member States, as well as the functions and limits of judicial activism at each level of the legal order.[72]

Therefore, the critical analysis could help identify the rationales that shape the Court's use of the various manifestations of effectiveness: from their rhetorical strength, framed as fundamental rights talk – which, however, does not necessarily guarantee an improvement of judicial protection across Europe – to their capacity of strategically selecting the 'formalism' best suited for pursuing the Court's integrationist agenda. In this sense, a critical approach could highlight potential abuses in the Court's interpretation of EU law, and push for a more coherent and transparent argumentation.

At the same time, such a reading may guide national judges in their role as interlocutors of the CJEU. First and foremost, it could raise awareness over the inconsistencies and limits of

---

[70] On the distinction between substitutive and exclusionary direct effect, see M Dougan, 'When Worlds Collide! Competing Visions of the Relationship between Direct Effect and Supremacy' (2007) 44 *Common Market Law Review* 931.

[71] Niglia (n 12). This point was also made in Episcopo (n 27) 306.

[72] M Accetto and S Zleptnig, 'The Principle of Effectiveness: Rethinking its Role in Community Law' (2005) 11 *European Public Law* 375.

the Court's alleged functional formalism and bolster the domestic courts' capacity to actively engage in a collective definition of what the law is – for example, by channelling it through 'constructive' preliminary procedures and pushing for the recognition of their instances at the European level.

Moreover, understanding the rhetorical dimension of effectiveness and effective judicial protection may help national judges to identify to what extent they are bound by the two principles. While Articles 19 and 47 require them to enforce EU law, fundamental principles common to Member States' constitutional traditions – pertaining, for example, to the separation of powers, the rule of law, equality and legal certainty – limit the judicial creativity associated with their mandate as decentralised European courts.[73] The solution to this impasse is sometimes framed on an ideological basis: the more one supports European integration and considers EU law as a source of positive harmonisation and innovation, the more effectiveness will be said to trump contrasting national principles and attribute a proactive role to domestic courts in its realisation. Yet, framing the problem as a matter of values and ideology creates additional issues, as it gives no practical guidance on the correct implementation of the two principles, leaving domestic courts to solve the matter in a heterogeneous way, possibly through solutions unsupported by either national law or EU law itself.[74]

However, the deadlock may be untangled, when picturing judicial interactions in terms of constructive dialogue within a pluralist legal order and differentiating among the different types of effectiveness involved. In particular, when the latter functions as a properly axiological principle, courts should try to implement it, adjusting it to national values of solidarity and justice, pursuant to the maximisation of fundamental rights' legal protection, based on a 'national' account effectiveness. Conversely, if – regardless of the version in which it manifests itself – effectiveness operates as a predominantly structural principle,[75] aimed at guaranteeing the maximum realisation of EU law, then judges should be cautious in their attempt to contribute to its realisation directly and autonomously. For example, it is questionable whether they should modify, via *corrective* interpretation aiming at fostering their *effet utile*, directives that have been correctly transposed, because this would alter choices legitimately made by national legislators.

A discursive and critical analysis could thus encourage national judges to also perform a strong and proactive role in their interactions with the CJEU through thoughtful preliminary questions and interlocutory mechanisms. The *Taricco* saga, where the Italian Constitutional Court introduced concerns over effective judicial protection of defendants in a discussion centred around the obstacles posed by national prescription periods to the effectiveness of EU law, is paradigmatic of such constructive exchange.[76]

Likewise, a discursive and critical analysis could also refine the *horizontal* application of the principles of effectiveness and effective judicial protection in determining the substance of EU-based rights and duties, and in shaping national systems of judicial protection. While both issues would require a more in-depth and careful inquiry, we may advance a few tentative considerations.

As discussed in section III, the effectiveness-based interpretation has often been used to determine both the rights that individuals are entitled to and the remedies available when the

---

[73] Episcopo (n 44), 56.
[74] ibid.
[75] T Tridimas, *The General Principles of EU Law* (Oxford, Oxford University Press, 2006) 3.
[76] *Taricco* (n 9).

latter are infringed[77] – a practice criticised for its lack of normative justification.[78] Critiques aside, concerns over justice and efficiency in private law adjudication and efficient regulation indeed beg the question of whether specific limits should be set to the use of effectiveness and effective judicial protection in private law disputes.

In this sense, Olha Cherednychenko suggested that the 'grammar' of a given EU law measure can signal its private or public-oriented nature, which 'may have important implications for the position of private parties at national level, for the ECJ activism in this context and ultimately for the measure's ability to realize policy goals'.[79] According to Cherednychenko, a measure should be considered more private law-oriented depending on how clearly it confers rights and remedies on private parties, and how strongly it displays an interpersonal dimension, as opposed to those that focus mainly on the relationship between regulators and regulatees and on the role of public authorities in securing compliance with the regulatory goals set therein. However, so the argument goes, public law measures may still have important implications for private parties: first, because Member States are obliged to provide individual or collective rights and remedies within their national systems and could potentially extend the 'private dimension' of the measure at hand; and, second, because the above-mentioned difference 'may be reduced by the ECJ to the extent that a certain public law-oriented directive also aims to protect the interest of private parties, the ECJ may interpret that (or a related) EU measure in light of the principle of effectiveness or effective judicial protection as to enhance its potential to provide for individual redress in national legal orders'.[80]

While this is certainly true, it should not be read as giving free rein to judicial interpretation.

On the one hand, private adjudication is mostly based on a 'reflexive' approach, according to which the principles to be applied in the case are those set in the applicable substantive law which, in turn, may be identified by reference to a pattern of internal coherence.[81] In cases involving EPL, this account of 'justice' necessarily reflects the peculiar multi-layered and competence-based feature of EU law, and the way it interacts with the laws of the Member States. The resulting rules – rights, duties, remedies and procedures – are both hybrid and contextual, as their configuration depends on how each silo of EU law combines with national rules, which, on their part, express the political, social, cultural and economic dimension of each Member State in the field.

Against this picture, a critical and discursive approach can, again, help in terms of distinguishing between the different dimensions of effectiveness and identify their normative force. While the 'autonomous' dimension of the right to an effective judicial protection should not be subject to different levels of realisation depending on the sector of law involved, in its 'ancillary' dimension – as a means of realising primary EU law rules – it is shaped by the underlying rationale of the silos and the importance of the interests at stake. If such context-dependency should not go as far as to shape the content and meaning of *Johnston* effectiveness and the right enshrined in Article 47, its capacity to mould *Rewe* effectiveness and other notions of

---

[77] P Rott, 'The Court of Justice's Principle of Effectiveness and its Unforeseeable Impact on Private Law Relationships' in D Leczykiewicz and S Weatherill (eds), *The Involvement of EU Law in Private Law Relationships* (Oxford, Hart Publishing, 2013).

[78] Eilmansberger (n 54).

[79] OO Cherednychenko, 'Rediscovering the Public/Private Divide in EU Private Law' (2020) 26 *European Law Journal* 26, 27.

[80] ibid.

[81] J Coleman, *The Practice of Principle: In Defence of a Pragmatist Approach to Legal Theory* (Oxford, Oxford University Press, 2003).

effectiveness is, in and of itself, less contestable. As Micklitz put it: 'Even if it is possible to deduce constitutionalized private law principles out of the case law, the question remains whether these principles are abstract enough so as to reach beyond the particular context in which they are developed. As there is no European constitutionalized law as such, constitutionalized private law principles remain bound to particular fields of EU law.'[82]

---

[82] HW Micklitz, 'European Regulatory and Private Law – Between Neoclassical Elegance and Postmodern Pastiche' in M Kuhli and M Schmidt (eds), *Vielfalt im Recht* (Berlin, Duncker & Humblot, 2022) 75.

Part II

Rights

6

The Societal Impact of EU Anti-discrimination Law

Widening and Deepening Equality in the Private Sphere

BETÜL KAS

I. INTRODUCTION

THE EU's EFFORTS of combating discrimination constitute one of the most visible policy areas of the EU's social justice and fundamental rights agenda. Equality and non-discrimination[1] are established constitutional principles of modern liberal democracies and the right to non-discrimination enjoys wide recognition in international human rights law.[2] However, in the EU, the principle of non-discrimination did not directly emerge out of the commitment to protect the human right to equality. EU prohibitions against discrimination have been initially framed as instruments to remove trade barriers and advance market integration.[3] Two historical events have heralded EU anti-discrimination law's normative evolution towards a human rights regime: first, on the basis of the 1997 Amsterdam Treaty, in 2000 the Council adopted several non-discrimination directives that extended the prohibition of discrimination to new areas (ie, beyond employment) and grounds (ie, beyond gender and nationality).[4]

---

[1] The terms 'equality' and 'non-discrimination' will be used interchangeably in this chapter.

[2] See, for instance, art 7 of the Universal Declaration of Human Rights; art 26 of the International Covenant on Civil and Political Rights; art 2(2) of the International Covenant on Economic, Social and Cultural Rights; art 14 of the European Convention on Human Rights and Fundamental Freedoms; the International Convention on the Elimination of All Forms of Racial Discrimination; and the International Labour Organization Convention No 111.

[3] The prohibitions of discrimination on the basis of nationality (now art 18 of the Treaty on the Functioning of the European Union (TFEU)), as well as of discrimination regarding pay between men and women (now art 157 TFEU) were included in the original EC Treaties in order to eliminate distortions of competition as a means to realise a single market. For a detailed reconstruction of the historical rationale of EU non-discrimination law and the human rights revolution brought by subsequent reforms, see R Xenidis, 'Transforming EU Equality Law? On Disruptive Narratives and False Dichotomies' (2019) 38 *Yearbook of European Law* e2; see also S Prechal, 'Non-discrimination Does Not Fall Down from Heaven: The Context and Evolution of Non-discrimination in EU Law' (2009) Eric Stein Working Paper No 4.

[4] In particular, Council Directive 2000/43/EC of 29 June 2000 implementing the principle of equal treatment between persons irrespective of racial or ethnic origin [2000] OJ L180/22; Council Directive 2000/78/EC of 27 November 2000 establishing a general framework for equal treatment in employment and occupation [2000] OJ L303/16.

The second event concerned the entry into force of the Lisbon Treaty in 2009, which incorporated the catalogue of human rights contained in the EU European Charter of Fundamental Rights (EUCFR) and in particular Article 21, which prohibits any discrimination based on numerous grounds into primary EU law.[5] Given the Charter's legal status, secondary EU law must be interpreted in compliance with the self-standing human rights standards contained therein.[6] However, even though EU anti-discrimination law has been considerably widened, deepened and framed as a fundamental right, criticism about its scope and standard of protection did not subside. The most tangible criticism from within the field relates to three grounds. First, EU law does not afford all protected grounds the same level of protection, leading to a hierarchy of discrimination grounds.[7] Second, in the absence of measures of social inclusion such as group-based positive action and a broader duty to accommodate, EU law is seen as being unable to defeat structurally embedded inequalities.[8] Third, EU anti-discrimination law is based on individual rights and lacks the necessary provisions on collective enforcement.[9] Deficiencies in the law's protective scope are perceived to demonstrate that the normative shift from economic orientation towards protection of human rights has not been fully realised yet.[10]

Against the background of EU anti-discrimination law's ambiguous normative underpinnings, the Court of Justice of the European Union (CJEU) has historically assumed a key role in strengthening and expanding the reach of the principle of non-discrimination.[11] Paradigmatic stories about the ability of EU law to improve the terms on which minority groups participate in society derive from such rulings as *Feryn*[12] and *CHEZ*.[13] While the former dealt with an employer's public statements about a recruitment policy excluding 'immigrants', the latter concerned the discriminatory conditions for the provision of electricity in districts inhabited predominantly by Roma. In both cases, the CJEU interpreted the prohibition of discrimination in line with a substantive conception of equality and took

---

[5] Article 6 of the Treaty on European Union (TEU). In addition, notably, before referring to the internal market in art 3 TEU, equality and respect for human rights, including the rights of persons belonging to minorities have been acknowledged among the foundational values of the EU in art 2 TEU.

[6] For a critical account of the influence of arts 20 and 21 EUCFR on the development of EU anti-discrimination law, see A Ward, 'The Impact of the EU Charter of Fundamental Rights on Anti-discrimination Law: More a Whimper Than a Bang?' (2018) 20 *Cambridge Yearbook of European Legal Studies* 32.

[7] E Howard, 'The Case for a Considered Hierarchy of Discrimination Grounds in EU Law' (2006) 13 *Maastricht Journal of European and Comparative Law* 445; M Bell and L Waddington, 'More Equal than Others: Distinguishing European Union Equality Directives' (2001) 38 *Common Market Law Review* 587.

[8] Xenidis (n 3) e36; see also S Fredman, 'Pasts and Futures: EU Equality Law' in A Bogg, C Costello and ACL Davies (eds), *Research Handbook on EU Labour Law* (Cheltenham, Edward Elgar, 2016) 391.

[9] The EU Directives rely on a so-called 'individual-complaint led model', which authorises collective actors to take legal action if they are acting 'either on behalf or in support of the complainant'; see art 7(2) of the Race Equality Directive 2000/43/EC; art 9(2) of the Framework Equality Directive 2000/78; art 17(2) of the Equal Treatment Directive 2006/54/EC ([2006] OJ L204/23); art 9(2) of the Directive 2010/41/EU on self-employed workers and equal treatment ([2010] OJ L180/1); art 8(3) of the Equal Treatment in Goods and Services Directive 2004/113/EC ([2004] OJ L373/37).

[10] However, as noted by Fredman, although the dichotomy between 'market-oriented rationale' and 'human rights approach' has framed the debate, both concepts lack further specification, allow for a variety of interpretations and are not necessarily mutually exclusive; see Fredman (n 8) 391.

[11] Xenidis (n 3) e10–e18; E Muir, 'The Transformative Function of EU Equality Law' (2013) 21 *European Review of Private Law* 1231, 1236 ff.

[12] Case C-54/07 *Centrum voor gelijkheid van kansen en voor racismebestrijding v Firma Feryn NV* [2008] ECR I-5187. The CJEU's ruling stimulated two follow-up rulings: Case C-81/12 *Asociaţia Accept v Consiliul Naţional pentru Combaterea Discriminării* EU:C:2013:275 and Case C-507/18 *NH v Associazione Avvocatura per i diritti LGBTI – Rete Lenford* EU:C:2020:289.

[13] Case C-83/14 *'CHEZ Razpredelenie Bulgaria' AD v Komisia za zashtita ot diskriminatsia* EU:C:2015:480.

account of the collective dimension of the discriminatory conduct.[14] Although these rulings were applauded for illustrating EU anti-discrimination law's transformative potential, the Court deviated from its favourable approach in subsequent cases about the wearing of headscarves by Muslim women at work, most prominently in *Achbita* and *Bougnaoui*,[15] which stimulated several follow-up preliminary references by national courts.[16] Seldom has a line of decisions by the CJEU raised such unanimous criticism.[17] The main explanation that has been offered for the Court's restrictive approach has been the sensitivity of the status of religion in Europe.[18] This perspective reinforces the so-called hierarchy of discrimination grounds, which means that some discrimination grounds and thus certain minorities enjoy a higher level of protection than others in the EU.[19]

This chapter will examine whether the public/private divide may play a role and provide an alternative explanation for the CJEU's diverging case law. Notably, all the aforementioned cases concern private legal relationships, namely between employer and employee or job applicant, or between service provider and consumer. EU anti-discrimination law's transformative potential is indeed most ambitious and pronounced in its regulation of interpersonal relationships, namely by impacting societal practices through the instillation of the non-discrimination norm in daily interactions.[20] However, in view of the traditional dichotomy between public and private law, the application of the non-discrimination principle to private legal relationships may to some extent still be considered controversial.[21] The public/private divide could therefore potentially obstruct the transformative potential of anti-discrimination law by shielding against a too expansive intrusion of constitutional norms into private dealings. Proposing a change of perspective from the right-holder to the duty-bearer, the chapter will determine based on the context of the previously mentioned cases whether there have been public or private elements that may explain the diverging reach of the duty of non-discrimination in the private sphere.

For that purpose, the chapter proceeds in the following way: section II will set the scene by giving an account of the discussion on the relevance of EU anti-discrimination law for the private sphere. Section III will reconstruct three case studies – *Feryn*, *CHEZ* and *Achbita* and their follow-ups – showing contradictions in the application of the non-discrimination principle in private legal relationships and distilling the different conceptions of equality underlying the rulings. Section IV will integrate the findings derived from the case studies with existing

---

[14] M De Vos, 'The European Court of Justice and the March towards Substantive Equality in European Union Anti-discrimination Law' (2020) 20 *International Journal of Discrimination and the Law* 62; Fredman (n 8) 408–12.

[15] Case C-157/15 *Samira Achbita and Centrum voor gelijkheid van kansen en voor racismebestrijding v G4S Secure Solutions NV* EU:C:2017:203; Case C-188/15 *Asma Bougnaoui and Association de défense des droits de l'homme (ADDH) v Micropole SA* EU:C:2017:204.

[16] Joined Cases C-804/18 and C-341/19 *X v WABE eV and MH Müller Handels GmbH v MJ* EU:C:2021:594; Case C-344/20 *LF v SCRL* EU:C:2022:774.

[17] For an overview of the criticism, see E Howard, 'Islamic Headscarves and the CJEU: *Achbita* and *Bougnaoui*' (2017) 24 *Maastricht Journal of European and Comparative Law* 348; and E Howard, 'Headscarves Return to the CJEU: Unfinished Business' (2020) 27 *Maastricht Journal of European and Comparative Law* 10.

[18] See the conclusions of R McCrea, 'Faith at Work: The CJEU's Headscarf Rulings' (2017) *EU Law Analysis*, www.eulawanalysis.blogspot.com/2017/03/faith-at-work-cjeus-headscarf-rulings.html; L Vickers, 'Religious Discrimination and Headscarves – Take Two' (2021) *Oxford Human Rights Hub*, https://ohrh.law.ox.ac.uk/religious-discrimination-and-headscarves-take-two/.

[19] S Jolly, 'Islamic Headscarves and the Workplace Reach the CJEU: The Battle for Substantive Equality' (2016) *European Human Rights Law Review* 672, 677; E Howard, 'Headscarves and the CJEU: Protecting Fundamental Rights and Pandering to Prejudice, the CJEU Does Both' (2022) 29 *Maastricht Journal of European and Comparative Law* 245, 260–61.

[20] Muir (n 11).

[21] See section II below.

theoretical accounts on the delineation of private duty-bearers under anti-discrimination laws. On that basis, section V will conclude by reflecting on the role that EU law confers on private parties in combating discriminatory attitudes prevalent in society.

II. NON-DISCRIMINATION IN THE PRIVATE SPHERE

The relevance of EU anti-discrimination law for the area of private law may be easily over-looked. EU legislation has given rise to a self-standing field of EU law, the development of which is closely scrutinised by legal experts and dealt with in specialised law journals, hand-books and volumes. The EU anti-discrimination directives provide for a specific regulatory framework encompassing notions and concepts that are foreign to the area of private law.[22] In addition, as is typical for the area of European (regulatory) private law,[23] it is a hybrid legal field that brings together private and public elements, thus distinguishing itself from the general contract law to be found in national codifications.[24]

As the EU anti-discrimination directives do not differentiate between public and private sectors, in the substantive areas covered, private actors are in principle placed under the same duties as public bodies.[25] EU anti-discrimination law therefore challenges the traditional understanding of the legal system as characterised by the divide between public and private law.[26] A strict divide between public and private law allows private parties to live their lives according to private preferences and free from the requirements of neutrality, equal concern and respect that in a liberal democracy are required from actions by the state. Private law has traditionally accorded a wide discretion for private choices. For instance, the principle of freedom of contract encompassing the choice of a contractual partner acknowledges that indi-vidual liberty is of paramount importance. Constitutional provisions guaranteeing liberty and privacy ensure that the private activities of individuals are not held to the same high standards of 'political correctness' as required from the conduct by the state.[27]

The existence of anti-discrimination laws is evidence of the fact that the boundary between private autonomy and public responsibility is no longer static. Its impact on private law becomes particularly evident in the restrictions that it imposes on the choice of contractual partners.[28] Looking at EU legislation, the following instruments are pertinent in guarantee-ing non-discriminatory access to the labour market and, for some protected grounds, to the consumer market: the EU Race Equality Directive, whose substantive scope encompasses

---

[22] Muir (n 11) 1245–49.

[23] G Comparato, 'What is European Regulatory Private Law? Stakes and Perspectives' (2018) *Revue internationale de droit économique* 123.

[24] N Reich, 'The Public/Private Divide in European Law' in HW Micklitz and F Cafaggi (eds), *European Private Law after the Common Frame of Reference* (Cheltenham, Edward Elgar, 2010); HW Micklitz, 'Rethinking the Public/Private Divide' in M Maduro, K Tuori and S Sankari (eds), *Transnational Law: Rethinking European Law and Legal Thinking* (Cambridge, Cambridge University Press, 2014); for a recent account of the role of the divide in EU private law, see OO Cherednychenko, 'Rediscovering the Public/Private Divide in EU Private Law' (2020) 26 *European Law Journal* 27.

[25] See, for instance, art 3 of the Equality Framework Directive 2000/78/EC and art 3 of the Race Equality Directive 2000/43/EC.

[26] Reich (n 24) 77 ff.

[27] H Collins, 'On the (In)Compatibility of Human Rights Discourse and Private Law' (2012) LSE Law, Society and Economy Working Papers 7, 32–35.

[28] H Collins, 'The Vanishing Freedom to Choose a Contractual Partner' (2013) 76 *Law and Contemporary Problems* 71; see also M Grochowski, ch 7 in this volume.

access to employment and to goods and services which are available to the public, including housing;[29] and the EU Equality Framework Directive, which applies to discrimination on the grounds of religion or belief, disability, age or sexual orientation, which covers only access to employment.[30] The prohibitions of gender discrimination are scattered among various directives. While Directive 2006/54/EC covers non-discriminatory access to employment,[31] Directive 2004/113/EC concerns access to goods and services, which are available to the public.[32] Seeking to avoid a too great interference with the freedoms of private parties, when it comes to access to goods and services, the Race Equality Directive and Directive 2004/113/EC specify that goods and services that are offered in the area of private and family life are excluded.[33]

The CJEU has repeatedly underlined that the directives constitute an expression, in the areas that they cover, of the general prohibition of discrimination laid down in Article 21 EUCFR.[34] By extending the vertical principle of equality to horizontal relationships between private parties, they can be considered to constitute a specific manifestation of the 'constitutionalisation of private law'.[35] However, instead of requiring a consistent interpretation of existing rules of private law with fundamental rights (indirect effect) or trusting the recognition of horizontal direct effect of constitutional provisions, anti-discrimination laws create their own causes of action against discrimination in certain areas.

Like the 'constitutionalisation of private law', the advent of anti-discrimination legislation in Europe has been feared to pose a serious challenge to private law's liberal core.[36] Specifically, private law scholars have denounced a virtue-based suppression of the freedom to choose a contractual partner and hence the end of private autonomy.[37] The extension of the anti-discrimination principle to relationships between private parties has not only been dreaded for imposing a specific type of moral conduct on private actors, but also for challenging an

---

[29] Article 3(1)(a) and (h) of the Race Equality Directive 2000/43/EC.

[30] Article 3(1)(a) of the Equality Framework Directive 2000/78/EC. A proposal for a new anti-discrimination directive that would extend Directive 2000/78 to, among other things, access to goods and services which are available to the public, including housing, has been pending since 2008 (COM (2008) 426 final).

[31] Article 1(a) of Directive 2006/54/EC.

[32] Article 3(1) of Directive 2004/113/EC.

[33] See recital 4 of Race Equality Directive 2000/43/EC: 'It is also important, in the context of the access to and provision of goods and services, to respect the protection of private and family life and transactions carried out in this context.' See also art 3(1) of Directive 2004/113/EC: 'this Directive shall apply to all persons who provide goods and services, which are available to the public ... and which are offered outside the area of private and family life and the transactions carried out in this context'. Recital 16 of the latter Directive gives specific examples of legitimate aims that may justify unequal treatment, for example, reasons of privacy and decency in cases such as the provision of accommodation by a person in a part of that person's home. The Commission's proposal for a new anti-discrimination directive on implementing the principle of equal treatment between persons irrespective of religion or belief, disability, age or sexual orientation explained that 'only professional or commercial activities are covered' and 'transactions between private individuals acting in a private capacity will not be covered: letting a room in a private house does not need to be treated in the same way as letting rooms in a hotel' (COM (2008) 426 final, 8).

[34] See, for instance, *CHEZ* (n 13) para 58 with further references to the case law.

[35] On the meaning and implications of the 'constitutionalisation of private law' in Europe, see C Mak and B Kas, ch 1 in this volume.

[36] For a summary of the criticism voiced against the application of constitutional rights to private law, see O Gerstenberg, 'Private Law and the New European Constitutional Settlement' (2004) 10 *European Law Journal* 766, 769.

[37] FJ Säcker, 'Vernunft statt Freiheit! – Die Tugendrepublik der neuen Jakobiner' (2002) *Zeitschrift für Rechtspolitik* 286; E Picker, 'Antidiskriminierungsgesetz – Der Anfang vom Ende der Privatautonomie?' (2002) *JuristenZeitung* 880; E Picker, 'Anti-discrimination as a Program of Private Law?' (2003) 4 *German Law Journal* 771; KH Ladeur, 'The German Proposal of an "Anti-discrimination"-Law: Anticonstitutional and Anti-Common Sense' (2002) 3 *German Law Journal* 1. Although such resistance has been particularly visible in the German discussion, it also includes voices from other Member States; see, for instance, ME Storme, 'De fundamenteelste vrijheid: de vrijheid om te discrimineren' (2005) 126 *Vivat Academia* 3; ME Storme, 'Freedom of Contract: Mandatory and Non-Mandatory Rules in European Contract Law' (2007) 15 *European Review of Private Law* 233, 247 ff.

ordo-liberal vision of the EU.[38] In the latter vein, it has been sustained that in the framework of a market economy, in the absence of a monopoly, competition alone may, on the one hand, punish discriminatory practices by private actors and, on the other hand, create new opportunities for those that have been excluded.[39] This viewpoint finds its roots in the attack launched against anti-discrimination legislation by certain scholars of the 'law and economics' movement in the US.[40]

The opposition against anti-discrimination laws never gained ground as a serious threat to the widespread consensus of the necessity of this type of legislation. However, the question whether the market may prevail over the prohibition of discrimination has continued to reappear in EU litigation, such as in the form of the question about whether consumer preferences may justify discriminatory business decisions by employers vis-à-vis employees or not.[41] In other words, should profit-seeking businesses be required to act against the market logic for the purpose of social inclusion? The following analysis of the case studies will show that the CJEU has not yet unequivocally settled this issue.

III. THREE PARADIGMATIC CASE STUDIES: *FERYN*, *CHEZ*, *ACHBITA* AND THEIR FOLLOW-UPS

This section will reconstruct three case studies that illustrate the impact of EU non-discrimination law in the private sphere. The analysis will examine the socio-political context and the facts of the cases, as well as the legal reasoning of the CJEU. The assessment of the judgments will place emphasis on the different conceptions of equality that are underlying the Court's reasoning. The discourse on anti-discrimination legislation is dominated by two principal conceptions of equality: formal equality and substantive equality. Formal equality articulates the Aristotelian formula that likes should be treated alike. It stresses neutrality and consistency by requiring the equal treatment of comparable situations and differential treatment of incomparable situations without guaranteeing any particular outcome. The formal approach to equality thus safeguards procedural justice stemming from consistent treatment.[42] The limitations of formal equality have provoked the development of concepts of substantive or distributive equality, which are, however, lacking a consistent core.[43]

Fredman has therefore proposed a multi-dimensional framework based on the multi-faceted nature of inequality and responsive to the social context of those who are disadvantaged. This influential framework will be adopted here to assess the CJEU's reasoning. Her practice-rooted approach includes four complementary and interrelated dimensions of substantive equality: to redress disadvantage (distributive dimension); address stigma, stereotyping, prejudice, humiliation and violence (recognition dimension); enhance social inclusion and political voice (participative dimension); and accommodate difference and achieve structural change (transformative dimension).[44]

---

[38] J Basedow, 'Freedom of Contract in the European Union' (2008) 16 *European Review of Private Law* 901, 921.

[39] ibid; see also Storme (n 37) 247, 248.

[40] R Epstein, *Forbidden Grounds* (Cambridge, MA, Harvard University Press, 1992); R Epstein, *Equal Opportunity or More Opportunity? The Good Thing about Discrimination* (London, Civitas Institute for the Study of Civil Society, 2002), https://civitas.org.uk/pdf/cs18.pdf.

[41] See in particular the case studies in section III.A (*Feryn*) and section III.C (*Achbita*).

[42] S Fredman, 'Substantive Equality Revisited' (2016) 14 *International Journal of Constitutional Law* 712, 716–19; C Barnard and B Hepple, 'Substantive Equality' (2000) 59 *Cambridge Law Journal* 562, 562–63.

[43] H Collins, 'Discrimination, Equality and Social Inclusion' (2003) 66 *Modern Law Review* 16.

[44] Fredman (n 42).

A. Discriminatory Public Statements in the Employment Sphere: *Feryn*

i. The Context of the Preliminary Reference

The genesis of the *Feryn* case[45] lies in an article published in a Belgian newspaper, reporting on the Belgian company Feryn NV, which specialises in the sale and installation of garage doors, which faced problems in finding the necessary workforce to install its doors in its customers' homes. The newspaper article reported that, according to Feryn's director, the reason for this difficulty was that the company's customers would refuse to allow Moroccans to enter their private homes.[46] The article provoked broad societal debate, as reflected by various subsequent statements made by politicians, trade unions, employer organisations and ethnic and cultural minority organisations in the media.[47] When Belgian national television contacted Feryn NV for an interview on the situation, the company's director emphasised the need to comply with the wishes of its customers in order stay in business, refuting to be a racist himself and pointing towards a wider problem in Belgian society.[48] Considering that Flanders – the place of the company's seat – was once home to one of the strongest far-right movements in Europe and anti-immigrant attitudes appear to persist in the region, this argument might have some truth to it.[49] The societal turmoil caused by the newspaper article pushed the Belgian equality body into action, which, after efforts to find an amicable settlement with Feryn failed, applied to the Belgian labour courts for a finding that Feryn applied a discriminatory recruitment policy.[50] While the Labour Court dismissed the action because of the hypothetical nature of the discrimination, the Appeal Court decided to refer the matter to the CJEU. The CJEU was asked whether public statements made by an employer concerning its recruitment policy may constitute direct discrimination under the Race Equality Directive 2000/43.[51]

ii. From a Formal to a Substantive Notion of Direct Discrimination

The crux of the case was that there was never any person identified whose job application was turned down by Feryn NV based on his or her ethnic origin. A formal approach to the prohibition of direct discrimination would suggest that such a situation is not covered. In the absence

---

[45] For a more comprehensive socio-legal reconstruction of *Feryn*, see B Kas, '"Hybrid" Collective Remedies in the EU Social Legal Order' (PhD thesis, European University Institute, 2017).

[46] 'Klanten hoeven geen Marokkanen' ('Customers Do Not Want Moroccans') *De Standaard* (28 April 2005), www.standaard.be/cnt/g2veep1s, translation provided by the Opinion of Advocate General Maduro in Case C-54/07 *Feryn* EU:C:2008:155, para 3.

[47] 'Vlaamse regering boos op discriminerend bedrijf' ('Flemish Government is Angry with Discriminatory Business') *De Standaard* (28 April 2005), www.standaard.be/cnt/dmf28042005_036: 'Both the Flemish Minister of Employment Frank Vandenbroucke (SP.A) and the Flemish Minister of Integration Marino Keulen (VLD) react with outrage to the fact that the company Feryn does not want any Moroccan employees. Unizo-topman Karel Van Eetvelt on the other hand fully supports the decision of the management of the company in Londerzeel.' See also 'Absurdistan in Londerzeel' *De Standaard* (29 April 2005), www.standaard.be/cnt/gl6eg28t.

[48] Translation provided by the Opinion of Advocate General Maduro in *Feryn* (n 46) para 4.

[49] Alexandra Brzozowski, 'Rise of Nationalist Parties Threatens to Stall Progress on Race Discrimination in Belgium' *EURACTIV* (31 March 2021), www.euractiv.com/section/non-discrimination/news/rise-of-nationalist-parties-threatens-to-stall-progress-on-race-discrimination-in-belgium; Othman El Hammouchi, 'Flanders' Dark Stain' *Politico* (17 October 2020), www.politico.eu/article/flanders-flemish-racism-belgium-immigrants-vlaams-belang.

[50] In line with art 6 of the Race Equality Directive, Belgium provides for more favourable protection of the principle of non-discrimination than the Directive by allowing the Belgian equality body to also initiate legal action if it is not acting on behalf of a specific complainant.

[51] Article 2(2)(a) of Directive 2000/43.

of a 'treatment' of an identifiable victim, or a specific comparator, the statements were merely words.[52] Such a reading is reinforced by the Directive's provisions on remedies and enforcement, which presume the identification of a complainant who claims to have been the victim of the alleged discriminatory conduct.[53] However, the Court expanded the scope of the notion of direct discrimination on the premise that the Directive aims 'to foster conditions for a socially inclusive labour market'.[54] According to the Court, this aim 'would be hard to achieve if the scope of Directive 2000/43 were to be limited to only those cases in which an unsuccessful candidate for a post, considering himself to be the victim of direct discrimination, brought legal proceedings against the employer'.[55] Thus, 'the fact that an employer declares publicly that it will not recruit employees of a certain ethnic or racial origin, something which is clearly likely to strongly dissuade certain candidates from submitting their candidature and, accordingly, to hinder their access to the labour market, constitutes direct discrimination'.[56] Hence, on the basis of the Directive's objectives, the CJEU endorsed a substantive reading of the prohibition of direct discrimination, focusing on the statement's role in entrenching disadvantage and exclusion (distributive and participative dimensions).[57]

Advocate General Maduro's opinion in the *Feryn* case reinforced this substantive perspective by emphasising the denigratory stereotyping behind the statements (which corresponds to the recognition dimension in Fredman's framework). Specifically, according to him, the social reality is that such statements have a humiliating and demoralising impact on persons of the origin targeted, not only to work for that particular employer at issue, but also to participate in the labour market more generally.[58] Rejecting the characterisation of such statements as being hypothetical discrimination, the Advocate General pointed to the actual effects of the employer's statement: 'By publicly stating his intention not to hire persons of a certain racial or ethnic origin, the employer is, in fact, excluding those persons from the application process and from his work floor. He is not merely talking about discriminating, he is discriminating. He is not simply uttering words, he is performing a "speech act".'[59] In addition, if such statements were excluded from the Directive's scope, it would allow employers to differentiate effectively between candidates on grounds of racial or ethnic origin, simply by publicising the discriminatory character of their recruitment policy as overtly as possible beforehand.[60]

iii. No Role for Customer Preferences

According to the Race Equality Directive, direct discrimination may be justified only in very limited circumstances, namely where the protected characteristic constitutes a genuine and determining occupational requirement.[61] The CJEU did not address the issue of whether customer preferences may justify the discriminatory behaviour of a private employer, thus

---

[52] De Vos (n 14) 67.
[53] Article 7 of the Race Equality Directive 2000/43.
[54] *Feryn* (n 12) para 23, referring to recital 8 of its preamble.
[55] ibid para 24.
[56] ibid para 25.
[57] Fredman (n 8) 409.
[58] Opinion of Advocate General Maduro in *Feryn* (n 46) para 15.
[59] ibid, para 16, with references to JR Searle, *Speech Acts: An Essay in the Philosophy of Language* (London, Cambridge University Press, 1969); JL Austin, *How to Do Things with Words* (Oxford, Oxford University Press, 1962).
[60] ibid para 17.
[61] Article 4 of Directive 2000/43.

negating their legal relevance. Advocate General Maduro addressed the matter directly, arguing that Feryn's contention was indeed 'wholly irrelevant': 'Even if that contention were true, it would only illustrate that "markets will not cure discrimination" and that regulatory intervention is essential.'[62] He reverted to the reasoning underlying the origin of EU anti-discrimination legislation, namely that of eliminating distortions of competition as a means to realise the internal market.[63] In particular, he reasoned that 'the adoption of regulatory measures at Community level helps to solve a collective action problem for employers by preventing the distortion of competition that – precisely because of that market failure – could arise if different standards of protection against discrimination existed at national level'.[64]

iv. The Follow-ups: Expanding into the Private Sphere

Two subsequent preliminary references from Romania and Italy dealt with comparable discriminatory statements broadcast in the media, but referring to job applicants' sexual orientation, thus falling within the scope of the Equality Framework Directive 2000/78. In its rulings, the CJEU confirmed that its reasoning in *Feryn* is transferable to the grounds protected by Directive 2000/78. The different factual constellations resulted in a further expansion of the reach of the principle of non-discrimination into the private sphere. In *Feryn*, when the discriminatory statements were uttered, the company was indeed seeking to recruit fitters as shown by a 'vacancies' sign that it placed on its premises, and the company's director making the statements had legal capacity to determine the company's recruitment policy. The CJEU's rulings in *Asociaţia Accept*[65] and *Rete Lenford*[66] clarified that the absence of these aspects does not prevent a finding of discriminatory conduct in the employment sphere. While the actual legal capacity of recruiting staff is not relevant, it must be established whether the person uttering the statements has or *may be perceived by the public* as having a decisive influence on the employer's recruitment policy.[67] In their assessment, the national courts must also consider the nature and content of the statements concerned and the context in which they were made, in particular, their public or private character, or the fact that they were broadcast to the public, whether via traditional media or social networks.[68]

In *Rete Lenford* the additional question arose as to whether 'mere statements which do not have, at the very least, the characteristics of a public offer of employment are protected by the freedom of expression'.[69] As noted above, while the anti-discrimination directives allow for direct discrimination to be justified only in very limited circumstances (namely genuine and determining occupational requirements), the Charter allows duty-bearers to invoke additional rights (in this case the freedom of expression in Article 11 EUCFR). The CJEU noted

---

[62] Opinion of Advocate General Maduro in *Feryn* (n 46) para 18, with reference to CR Sunstein, 'Why Markets Don't Stop Discrimination' in *Free Markets and Social Justice* (Oxford, Oxford University Press, 1997) 165.

[63] See section I, particularly n 3.

[64] Opinion of Advocate General Maduro in *Feryn* (n 46) para 18.

[65] *Asociaţia Accept* (n 12). *Asociaţia Accept* addressed the question whether a professional football club can be held responsible for the discriminatory public statements of an individual, who presents himself in public as being the 'patron' of the club.

[66] *Rete Lenford* (n 12). *Rete Lenford* dealt with the action against a lawyer who declared during a radio interview that he would not wish to recruit homosexual persons or to use the services of such persons in his law firm. For the background of the case, see V Passalacqua, 'Homophobic Statements and Hypothetical Discrimination: Expanding the Scope of Directive 2000/78/EC' (2020) 16 *European Constitutional Law Review* 513.

[67] *Asociaţia Accept* (n 12) paras 49, 51; *Rete Lenford* (n 12) para 44.

[68] *Rete Lenford* (n 12) paras 44–46.

[69] ibid para 26.

that freedom of expression is not an absolute right and that its exercise may be subject to limitations, provided that these are provided for by law and respect the essence of that right and the principle of proportionality. The Court found these conditions to be met, given that the limitations result directly from Directive 2000/78 and are applied only for the purpose of attaining its objectives, namely to safeguard the principle of equal treatment in employment and the attainment of a high level of employment and social protection (distributive and participative dimension).[70] The interference with the exercise of freedom of expression does not go beyond what is necessary to attain the Directive's objectives, in that only statements that constitute discrimination in employment and occupation are prohibited. The very essence of the protection afforded by that Directive in matters of employment and occupation could become illusory if such statements fell outside its scope because they were made in the context of an audiovisual entertainment programme or constitute the expression of a personal opinion.[71]

B. Non-discriminatory Access to Electricity: *CHEZ*

i. *The Context of the Preliminary Reference*

It is recognised that Roma living in segregated Bulgarian neighbourhoods are one of the groups that are particularly vulnerable in their access to energy. Access to electricity has not only been affected by the increasingly severe poverty among Roma and rising electricity prices after liberalisation, but, as illustrated by the situation in *CHEZ*, also by the less favourable treatment by providers of neighbourhoods mainly inhabited by Roma.[72] In the context of the challenges of Roma political representation, the Protection against Discrimination Act, which was adopted in 2004 to prepare for EU accession, has provided civil society organisations with a legal avenue to address some of the problems in the electricity sector.[73] One specific problem of unequal treatment reached the CJEU, namely the practice of former state electricity companies of installing meters to measure electricity consumption for consumers living in districts predominantly inhabited by persons of Roma origin at a height of between six and seven metres. In other districts, the meters were placed

---

[70] ibid paras 49–51.

[71] ibid paras 52–54. This question has been particularly controversial as demonstrated by the diverse criticism of the Court's approach: on the one hand, for favouring the protection of the right to non-discrimination over the freedom of expression – see J Miller, 'In a Tight Spot, the Court of Justice Delivers a Lopsided Judgment: *NH v Associazione Avvocatura per i diritti LGBTI* – *Rete Lenford*' *EU Law Live* (27 April 2020), www.eulawlive.com/op-ed-in-a-tight-spot-the-court-of-justice-delivers-a-lopsided-judgment-nh-v-associazione-avvocatura-per-i-diritti-lgbti-rete-lenford-by-jeffrey-miller; on the other hand, for implying that the freedom to engage in homophobic speech is protected as an aspect of the freedom of expression – see A Tryfonidou, 'Case C-507/18 *NH v Associazione Avvocatura per i diritti LGBTI* – *Rete Lenford*: Homophobic Speech and EU Anti-discrimination Law' (2020) 27 *Maastricht Journal of European and Comparative Law* 513.

[72] G Bogdanov and B Zahariev, *Access to Essential Services for Low-Income People: Bulgaria* (European Social Policy Network, European Commission, 2020) 15; D Mihaylova and M Iordanov, *Access to Electricity in Roma Settlements in Bulgaria* (Equal Opportunities Initiative Association, supported by a grant from the Open Society Foundations, Sofia, 2015) 30 ff; see also L Farkas, 'NGO and Equality Body Enforcement of EU Anti-discrimination Law: Bulgarian Roma and the Electricity Sector' in E Muir, C Kilpatrick, J Miller and B de Witte (eds), *How EU Law Shapes Opportunities for Preliminary References on Fundamental Rights: Discrimination, Data Protection and Asylum* (EUI Working Paper Law 2017/17) 35.

[73] Mihaylova and Iordanov (n 72) 30 ff; see also Farkas (n 72) 35.

at a height of 1.70 metres, thus making them accessible for normal visual checks by consumers. The practice, which was adopted between 1998 and 2000 and was not revised following the privatisation of the energy sector, was justified by the increased frequency of tampering with and damage to meters and by the numerous unlawful connections to the network in the districts concerned.[74]

Questioning the restrictive case law of the Bulgarian Supreme Administrative Court denying unlawful discrimination (in several cases on different grounds), the Bulgarian equality body – having a quasi-judicial function – submitted a preliminary reference on this matter in the case of *Belov*, which was, however, rejected by the CJEU.[75] Contrary to the opinion of Advocate General Kokott, the Court did not regard the Bulgarian equality body as a court or tribunal within the meaning of Article 267 of the Treaty on the Functioning of the European Union (TFEU). Two years after its judgment in *Belov*, the CJEU rendered a ruling on the merits of the issue due to a preliminary reference by the Administrative Court of Sofia in the case of *CHEZ*. The case arose out of a complaint lodged by Ms Nikolova – who ran a grocer's shop in one of the affected districts – with the Bulgarian equality body. Although, unlike the applicant in *Belov*, she was not of Roma origin herself, she considered that she was too suffering discrimination because of this practice. The equality body confirmed that Ms Nikolova had been discriminated against compared with the customers whose meters were in accessible locations. After the Supreme Administrative Court set aside the equality body's decision upon appeal by the defendant, the company lodged another appeal before the referring court against the equality body's fresh decision finding discrimination on a different ground. The referring court tended towards the view that Ms Nikolova suffered direct discrimination on ethnic grounds. While Ms Nikolova's claim was originally motivated by her private concern of being overbilled by the defendant, following the national court's decision to refer the matter to the CJEU, the Open Society Justice Initiative took on her legal representation in view of the potential to develop and impact EU discrimination law and policy.[76]

ii. Reinforcing the Substantive Dimension of Direct Discrimination

The Court's ruling is first of all marked by a broad interpretation of the scope of the Race Equality Directive 2000/43, which it substantiated in light of the Directive's objective, the nature of the rights which it seeks to safeguard, and in view of the fact that the Directive expresses the principle of equality as recognised in Article 21 of the EU Charter.[77] On that basis, the Court confirmed that 'access to goods and services', specifically the supply of electricity, includes the installation at the final consumer's property of an electricity meter.[78] In addition, the CJEU established that the protection of the Directive against 'discrimination on the grounds of ethnic origin' applies to persons such as Ms Nikolova, who, although not

---

[74] To allow consumers living in the affected districts to make an indirect visual check, the company undertook in its General Terms and Conditions to make available, free of charge and within three days of a written request by the consumer, a special vehicle with a lifting platform, by means of which the company's employees are able to read the electricity meters. However, this offer has not been taken up by consumers. The other option available to the consumer was to have an inspection meter installed at home, for which a fee must be paid. See the facts as set out in Case C-394/11 *Valeri Hariev Belov v CHEZ Elektro Balgaria AD and Others* EU:C:2013:48, paras 19 ff and *CHEZ* (n 13) paras 21 ff.

[75] *Belov* (n 74).

[76] Farkas (n 72) 40.

[77] *CHEZ* (n 13) paras 42, 56.

[78] ibid para 43.

themselves a member of the ethnic group concerned, suffer, together with them, less favourable treatment on account of a discriminatory measure.[79]

Differently to Advocate General Kokott, who argued that there was no direct discrimination,[80] the CJEU adopted – like in *Feryn* – a purpose-oriented interpretation of the prohibition of direct discrimination, thus emphasising its substantive dimension.[81] The Court pointed out that the presence of inhabitants who are not of Roma origin in the district at issue does not in itself rule out that the contested practice was imposed on account of the Roma origin shared by most of that district's inhabitants.[82] The Court found no difficulty in establishing a 'comparable situation' even though persons of non-Roma origin were also affected in the region at stake, while, in districts generally not affected, there were also persons of Roma origin residing. All final consumers who are supplied by the same supplier within an urban area, irrespective of the district in which they reside, must be regarded in a comparable situation.[83]

In order to establish direct discrimination, the Court held, it is relevant whether the practice has in fact been imposed for reasons of an ethnic nature.[84] The evidence which may be taken into consideration by the Bulgarian courts includes, in particular, the fact that the practice at issue has been established only in districts which have Bulgarian nationals of Roma origin as the majority of their population.[85] Also, the fact that the company has asserted in various cases before the Bulgarian equality body that the damage and unlawful connections are mainly due to persons of Roma origin is capable of suggesting that the contested practice is based on ethnic stereotypes or prejudices (Fredman's recognition dimension).[86] The Bulgarian court also has to take account of the compulsory, widespread and lasting nature of the practice complained of. That practice affects without distinction all the inhabitants of the district concerned, irrespective of whether their individual meters have been the subject of abuse and, as the case may be, who has committed that abuse. Thus, the practice at issue may be perceived as suggesting that the inhabitants of that district are, as a whole, considered to be potential perpetrators of unlawful conduct (Fredman's recognition dimension).[87] All in all, the Court makes clear that the practice amounts to unfavourable treatment to the detriment of the inhabitants concerned on account of both its offensive and stigmatising nature (Fredman's recognition dimension) and the fact that it is extremely difficult or even impossible for them to check their electricity meters for the purpose of monitoring their consumption (Fredman's distributive dimension).[88]

iii. Justifying Indirect Discrimination

If the Bulgarian court were to hold that the practice does not amount to direct discrimination, the Court observed that that practice could constitute indirect discrimination. Assuming

---

[79] ibid para 56.

[80] Opinion of Advocate General Kokott in Case C-83/14 *CHEZ* EU:C:2015:170, paras 80–88, in particular para 86: 'As far as can be seen, the contested practice therefore affects consumers whose electricity is supplied by CHEZ in the Gizdova mahala district solely by reason of their status as local residents. It is not as inextricably linked to their ethnic origin as pregnancy is to a person's sex, as entitlement to an old-age pension is to a person's age or as living in a registered partnership is to their sexual orientation.'

[81] Similarly, see de Vos (n 14) 67.

[82] *CHEZ* (n 13) para 75.

[83] ibid para 90.

[84] ibid para 76.

[85] ibid para 81.

[86] ibid para 82.

[87] ibid para 84.

[88] ibid para 87; see Fredman (n 8) 412.

that the practice has been carried out with the sole aim of responding to abuse committed in the district concerned, it would be based on apparently neutral criteria while affecting persons of Roma origin in greater proportions, giving rise to a disadvantage in particular for those persons compared with other persons not possessing such an ethnic origin.[89] With respect to a possible justification of indirect discrimination, the Court noted that protection of the security of the electricity transmission network and the due recording of electricity consumption constitute legitimate aims,[90] which may justify the practice at issue, provided that the company can prove that abuse has in fact been committed and that a risk of such abuse remains.[91] The Court left it to the Bulgarian court to examine whether other appropriate and less restrictive measures existed for resolving the problems encountered.[92] If no other measure as effective as the practice complained of exists, the referring court will have to determine whether the disadvantages caused by the practice at issue are disproportionate to the aims pursued and whether that practice unduly prejudices the legitimate interests of the persons inhabiting the district concerned.[93] According to the Court, the practice seems to be disproportionate in light of the offensive and stigmatising nature of the practice in question (recognition dimension) and of the fact that it has, without distinction and for a very long time, denied the inhabitants of an entire district the possibility of monitoring their electricity consumption regularly (distributive dimension).[94] Notably, unlike the opinion of Advocate General Kokott, the Court makes no mention of the condition that equally suitable measures to achieve those aims must be 'at a financially reasonable cost'.[95] However, the Advocate General also ultimately recognised that when it comes to the proportionality assessment, when balancing the conflicting interests, '[p]urely economic considerations must take secondary importance and recourse must possibly be had to less cost-efficient measures than installing electricity meters at an inaccessible height'.[96]

C. Muslim Headscarves at Work: *Achbita* and *Bougnaoui*

i. The Context of the Preliminary References

With the large influx of Muslim immigrants that the EU experienced, the Muslim headscarf has become a subject of major controversy. Several European countries have implemented or discussed bans to wear a headscarf in public.[97] Studies have shown that attitudes towards Muslims wearing a headscarf are significantly more negative than towards Muslims in general.[98] Also employers' behavioural responses to job applications are influenced by the wearing of a headscarf. Field experiments reveal that women with a migration background are less likely to

---

[89] ibid paras 106, 107.
[90] ibid para 114.
[91] ibid para 116.
[92] ibid paras 120–22.
[93] ibid para 123.
[94] ibid paras 125–27.
[95] Opinion of Advocate General Kokott (n 80) para 130.
[96] ibid para 134.
[97] For a reconstruction of the origins of the debate in Europe, see R Grillo and P Shah, 'Reasons to Ban? The Anti-Burqa movement in Western Europe' MMG Working Paper 12-05, 12 ff.
[98] JAC Everett, FMH Schellhaas, BD Earp, V Ando, J Memarzia, CV Parise, B Fell and M Hewstone, 'Covered in Stigma? The Impact of Differing Levels of Islamic Head-Covering on Explicit and Implicit Biases toward Muslim Women' (2015) 45 *Journal of Applied Social Psychology* 90.

be invited for a job interview in Germany and the Netherlands if they wear a headscarf in their job application photograph.[99] A study based on interviews with Muslim women in Britain shows that an intersectional perspective captures Muslim women's challenges in employment as being shaped by the combination of gendered, ethnic and religious stereotypes to which they are exposed.[100]

The so-called 'headscarf debate' reached the CJEU owing to two preliminary references on the Framework Equality Directive 2000/78/EC. The Belgian Court of Cassation and the French Court of Cassation asked the CJEU to assess prohibitions on the wearing of religious symbols in the context of private employment. The cases concerned women who lost their jobs for refusing to remove their Islamic headscarves while at work. In *Achbita*, the employer had an internal rule in place – first unwritten, later written – that prohibited the wearing of any visible signs of political, philosophical or religious belief at work.[101] In *Bougnaoui*, an employee was requested to stop wearing a headscarf when sent on assignment to customers after a customer informed her employer that her wearing of the headscarf had upset some of their employees and requested that there should be 'no veil next time'.[102] In both cases, the women, supported by the Belgian equality body and an association for the protection of human rights respectively, brought legal actions against their former employers alleging discriminatory conduct on the ground of their religion. Their claims that the dismissals constituted discrimination on the ground of religion or belief were rejected by the lower courts.

ii. A Formal Approach to Direct Discrimination

The CJEU adopted a formal interpretation of the prohibition of direct discrimination. It clarified in *Achbita* that an internal rule preventing an employee from wearing a headscarf at work did not amount to direct discrimination if that rule refers to visible signs of political, philosophical or religious beliefs and thus covers any manifestation of such beliefs without distinction. According to the Court, such a rule must be regarded as treating all workers of the company in the same way, by requiring them, in a general and undifferentiated way, to dress neutrally.[103] Having answered the referring court's question about direct discrimination in the negative, the Court noted that 'it was not inconceivable' that the referring court might conclude that the rule in question was indirectly discriminatory if the internal rule puts, in fact, persons adhering to a particular religion or belief at a particular disadvantage.[104] The judgment was criticised for ruling the existence of direct discrimination categorically out. On the one hand, it has been argued that the Court should have chosen a different comparator –

[99] M Fernández-Reino, V Di Stasio and S Veit, 'Discrimination Unveiled: A Field Experiment on the Barriers Faced by Muslim Women in Germany, the Netherlands, and Spain' (2022) *European Sociological Review* 1; D Weichselbaumer, 'Multiple Discrimination against Female Immigrants Wearing Headscarves' (2020) 73 *ILR Review* 600.

[100] M Tariq and J Syed, 'An Intersectional Perspective on Muslim Women's Issues and Experiences in Employment' (2018) 25 *Gender, Work and Organization* 495. The preliminary reference by the Labour Court of Hamburg in *WABE* (n 16) presented the CJEU with the opportunity to assess whether bans on the wearing of religious clothing and symbols at work could constitute discrimination on the ground of gender (para 33). However, the CJEU refused to deal with that issue because gender discrimination does not fall within the scope of Directive 2000/78/EC, which is the only EU law instrument that the preliminary questions explicitly referred to (para 58). Hence, not surprisingly, the Court also did not address the argument raised by the applicant that such an internal rule may constitute discrimination on the ground of ethnic origin (para 30). On this point, see Howard (n 19) 254–55.

[101] *Achbita* (n 15) paras 10–21.

[102] *Bougnaoui* (n 15) paras 13, 14.

[103] *Achbita* (n 15) paras 29–32.

[104] ibid para 34.

for instance, not other employees who wanted to express their religion or belief through the wearing of religious symbols at work, but an employee who does not manifest any belief would have been the correct comparator.[105] On the other hand, the ruling deviates from the substantive interpretation in *Feryn* and *CHEZ*. In particular, instead of merely taking account of a formal consistency of treatment, it was expected that the Court would determine whether the practice was based on stereotypes and prejudice (recognition dimension) to decide whether direct discrimination was at stake.[106] However, the Court abstains from questioning why an employer would adopt a neutrality policy if it was not for the (presumed) preferences (or stereotypes and prejudices) of its customers, which is subsequently also reflected in the Court's uncritical acceptance of the existence of a legitimate aim.[107]

iii. Justifying (Indirect) Discrimination

In *Achbita*, the Court concluded that in principle, the aim on the part of an employer to project an image of neutrality must be considered legitimate.[108] It reinforced this conclusion with reference to the freedom to conduct a business under Article 16 EUCFR, which, according to the Court, weighs in favour of the employers' wish to project an image of neutrality towards customers, 'notably where the employer involves in its pursuit of that aim only those workers who are required to come into contact with the employer's customers'.[109] However, the Court stressed that such an internal rule can only be seen to be appropriate when it is part of a neutrality policy that 'is genuinely pursued in a consistent and systematic manner'.[110] Whether this was the case in relation to Ms Achbita was left for the national court to decide.[111] The judgment gave notably stronger guidance on the question whether the ban at issue was necessary by finding that if it were the case that it covered 'only G4S workers who interact with customers ... the prohibition must be considered strictly necessary for the purpose of achieving the aim pursued',[112] though it finally indicated that the national court must also assess whether, 'taking into account the inherent constraints to which the undertaking is subject, and without G4S being required to take on an additional burden, it would have been possible for G4S, faced with such a refusal, to offer her a post not involving any visual contact with those customers, instead of dismissing her'.[113]

In *Bougnaoui*, the Court affirmed that a generally applicable ban on all visible signs of religious, philosophical or political beliefs would be indirectly discriminatory and referred to the guidance given in *Achbita* for the assessment of the justification of such a policy.[114] The Court left it to the national court to ascertain whether Ms Bougnaoui's dismissal was

---

[105] Howard, 'Islamic Headscarves and the CJEU' (n 17) 352. The latter comparator was chosen by Advocate General Sharpston in her Opinion in Case C-188/15 *Bougnaoui* EU:C:2016:553, para 88. For a discussion of the right comparator, see also J Mulder, 'Religious Neutrality Policies at the Workplace' (2022) 59 *Common Market Law Review* 1501, 1509 ff.

[106] Howard, 'Islamic Headscarves and the CJEU' (n 17) 354. On this, see also the Opinion of Advocate General Kokott in Case C-157/15 *Achbita* EU:C:2016:382, para 55.

[107] Howard, 'Headscarves Return to the CJEU' (n 17) 13.

[108] *Achbita* (n 15) paras 37–39.

[109] ibid para 38.

[110] ibid para 40.

[111] ibid para 41.

[112] ibid para 42.

[113] ibid para 43. De Vos (n 14) sees in this point that 'the ruling does contain seeds of a substantive religious accommodation' in 'an otherwise formal approach to non-discrimination' (at 79). On the other hand, the Court was criticised for not considering the 'denigrating effect' of such a measure; see Mulder (n 105) 1515.

[114] *Bougnaoui* (n 15) paras 32, 33.

based on her non-compliance with such a general internal rule. If that was not the case, then it would be necessary to address the referring court's question, namely, whether compliance with a customer's wish that the employee abstains from wearing a headscarf at work could be seen as a 'genuine and determining occupational requirement' that could justify a directly discriminatory practice.[115] The Court pointed out that only in very limited circumstances can a characteristic related to religion constitute a genuine and determining occupational requirement.[116] The wish of a customer not to be served by someone wearing a headscarf does not meet this requirement, which must be objectively dictated by the nature of the occupational activities concerned or by the context in which they are carried out, not by subjective considerations.[117]

iv. The Follow-ups: Strengthening the Role of Fundamental Rights

Two preliminary references from courts in Germany – the Labour Court of Hamburg and the Federal Labour Court – presented the CJEU with an opportunity to clarify and expand on its earlier rulings. Both cases dealt with employees that were prohibited from wearing a headscarf based on their religious beliefs at work. In *WABE*, a company running nurseries introduced a neutrality policy prohibiting employees in contact with customers the wearing of any visible signs of political, ideological or religious beliefs. *Müller* dealt with the internal rule of a company operating chemist shops that banned the wearing of any prominent and large-scale signs of religious, philosophical and political convictions. This policy aimed to preserve neutrality and avoid conflicts between employees, because conflicts had happened in the past.[118]

The Court confirmed its formal interpretation of direct discrimination. Although the Court recognised that the application of an internal neutrality rule encompassing all political, philosophical or religious beliefs is capable of causing particular inconvenience for workers wearing religious clothing, that has no bearing on the finding that such a rule does not establish a difference of treatment based on a criterion that is inextricably linked to religion or belief.[119] According to the CJEU, on that basis, the situation in *WABE* is different from that in *Müller*. A rule that prohibits only the wearing of conspicuous, large-sized signs is liable to have a greater effect on people with religious, philosophical or non-denominational beliefs which require the wearing of a large-sized sign, such as a head covering, and may therefore constitute direct discrimination.[120]

Most notably, the CJEU clarified the justification test for indirect discrimination, which has been considered too loose in comparison with the approach taken with respect to other discrimination grounds.[121] While the CJEU confirmed that the employer's desire to display neutrality towards its customers is a legitimate aim that is covered by the freedom to conduct a business in Article 16 EUCFR, particularly if it only applies to workers who come into contact with customers, it added that the employer must however demonstrate that there is a genuine need for such a policy.[122] Specifically, customers' wishes may be taken into account if they

---

[115] ibid para 34.
[116] ibid para 38.
[117] ibid para 40.
[118] *WABE* (n 16) paras 22 ff.
[119] ibid para 53.
[120] ibid paras 72, 73.
[121] Howard, 'Islamic Headscarves and the CJEU' (n 17) 359 ff; M Bell, 'Leaving Religion at the Door? The European Court of Justice and Religious Symbols in the Workplace' (2017) 17 *Human Rights Law Review* 784, 792 ff.
[122] *WABE* (n 16) paras 63, 64.

are legitimate and relate to their rights. As an example, with respect to *WABE*, the CJEU referred to the rights of parents, set out in Article 14 EUCFR, to ensure the education and teaching of their children in accordance with their religious, philosophical and teaching beliefs or their wish to have their children supervised by persons who do not manifest their religion or belief.[123] The CJEU distinguished this situation from the situation in *Bougnaoui*, where the employee was dismissed following a complaint by a customer and in the absence of a general neutrality policy as well as from *Feryn*, where the discriminatory conduct allegedly arose from the discriminatory requirements of customers.[124] Alongside that, the Court emphasised that the employer must prove that, without a neutrality policy, they would suffer adverse consequences given the nature of their activities or the context in which they are carried out.[125] Thus, employers must show that their policy is genuinely pursued in a consistent and systematic manner, and that the measures taken are limited to what is strictly necessary in view of the adverse consequences that the employer aims to avoid.[126] In relation to *Müller*, in the absence of direct discrimination, the Court confirmed that the prevention of social conflicts constitutes a legitimate aim that reflects a genuine need. However, it was less persuaded about its appropriateness. It questioned whether a neutrality policy could be pursued if not all visible manifestations of political, philosophical and religious beliefs were banned.[127]

The Court next clarified the impact of the EUCFR on the question of appropriateness within the objective justification analysis. The Court rejected the view of Advocate General Rantos that the Charter only plays a role in identifying legitimate aims,[128] and confirmed that the competing freedoms and rights can influence the assessment of necessity and appropriateness as well. Thus, the assessment of proportionality must aim at reconciling the requirements of the protection of the engaged rights, such as freedom of religion (Article 10), parental rights (Article 14), and the right to conduct a business (Article 16) and strike a fair balance between them.[129] Finally, with respect to the balancing of rights, the Court made clear that the Member States can take account of more favourable national provisions within the meaning of Article 8(1) of Directive 2000/78/EC. The EU legislature did not itself provide the necessary reconciliation between the various rights, but left it to the Member States and their courts to achieve that reconciliation.[130] Thus: 'Directive 2000/78 allows account to be taken of the specific context of each Member State and allows each Member State a margin of discretion in achieving the necessary reconciliation of the different rights and interests at issue, in order to ensure a fair balance between them.'[131] The Court concluded on that basis that national provisions protecting the freedom of religion – such as those making the justification of indirect religious discrimination subject to higher requirements – may be taken into account as provisions more favourable to the protection of the principle of equal treatment, within the meaning of Article 8(1) of the Directive.[132]

---

[123] ibid para 65.
[124] ibid para 66.
[125] ibid para 67.
[126] ibid paras 68, 69.
[127] ibid paras 76–77.
[128] Opinion of Advocate General Rantos in *WABE* EU:C:2021:144, para 103.
[129] *WABE* (n 16) para 84.
[130] ibid para 87.
[131] ibid para 88.
[132] ibid para 89.

IV. DEFINING PRIVATE DUTY-BEARERS IN EU ANTI-DISCRIMINATION LAW

The CJEU's divergent case law raised the question as to why certain discrimination grounds (ie, race and sexual orientation) enjoy a higher level of protection than others (ie, religion). A difference in protection depending on the protected ground at stake has indeed been imprinted in EU anti-discrimination law from its very beginnings.[133] However, from another perspective that does not focus on the right-holder but on the duty-bearer, we could also ask why certain private parties have wider-ranging duties than others. As described in section II, EU law regulates certain areas – employment and the sale of goods and services that are offered to the public – and thus the conduct of certain private parties, being employers, sellers and service providers. Although these areas are recognised to have a strong link with the internal market, and thus also lie within the EU's competences, the choice to regulate employment and access to goods and services offered to the public is also prevalent in other jurisdictions.[134] Thus, anti-discrimination laws generally preserve some scope for unrestricted private conduct.

The delimited scope of anti-discrimination legislation first of all raises the question about the principles that are determining the scope of a private sphere within which actionable claims against discrimination are unavailable. Collins has, for instance, posed this question in the following terms: if we agree that discrimination is morally wrongful, should the law not also prohibit 'parents to discriminate between their children by sending their sons to expensive schools whilst sending their daughters to be educated at cheaper, inferior schools'?[135] More narrowly construed, also within the areas regulated by legislation, only certain actors bear a duty of non-discrimination. Thus, even if these are controversial choices, an individual may lawfully choose not to buy a cake from a bakery run by a homosexual couple, get a haircut from a black hairdresser or apply for a job that implies working for a female boss.[136] Hence, an individual may be the bearer of anti-discrimination duties in one context (for instance, as an employer) and could hold a right to non-discrimination in another (for instance, as a consumer). In practice, anti-discrimination laws rely on two broad criteria to determine their scope of application: first, the relationship is defined as contractual or pre-contractual; and, second, the duty-bearer is the more powerful actor, ie, the person who controls access to the benefit envisaged by the contract.[137]

Collins has identified three frameworks that may justify and delimit the reach of the non-discrimination duty in the private sphere. First, anti-discrimination laws may not apply to certain private relationships or persons because their regulation is not required by the purpose of the law. For instance, the goal of social inclusion might be easily associated with employment and housing, thus explaining why the law might regulate the decisions of employers and landlords. However, Collins underlines that many theories suggest a foundation of the prohibition of discrimination in such broad principles (such as equal respect, positive freedom

---

[133] See the introduction in section I above.

[134] Exemplary is the US Civil Rights Act of 1964 that recognised the need to address more wide-ranging structures of segregation practised against African Americans that were not confined to state action. Harmful racist practices and institutional segregation were also taking place in the restrictions on access to transport, restaurants, clubs and to private sector employment. Subsequent legislation in the UK and thereafter the EU followed the approach set by the US.

[135] H Collins, 'Discrimination and the Private Sphere' in K Lippert-Rasmussen (ed), *The Routledge Handbook of the Ethics of Discrimination* (Abingdon, Routledge, 2017) 360.

[136] ibid.

[137] ibid 363, 364.

or access to valuable life opportunities) that the existence of any unregulated private sphere is rendered problematic.[138]

The second framework acknowledges that the purpose(s) of anti-discrimination laws may require a wider intervention in the private sphere, but restricts the scope of the law according to a proportionality test to prevent excessive interference with the negative liberty of the duty-bearers.[139] On that basis, Khaitan has developed an account that may explain the law's choice for certain duty-bearers. First, proportionality depends on the severity of the impact that the duty of non-discrimination has on the bearer's negative freedom. A person's interest in negative liberty is determined by the degree of its 'public' character. If a person has a more 'public' character, the imposition of the duty is more likely to be legitimate.[140] While employers have a public character because of the institutional power they enjoy in contemporary industrial societies, the typical retailer, service provider or landlord has assumed a degree of 'public-ness' by offering to serve the public generally, which dilutes privacy-based claims to negative liberty.[141] Second, the optimality of the choice of duty-bearer in furthering the goal(s) of anti-discrimination laws as such is decisive. If the law's aims are not supported or furthered to a significant extent, it is not an appropriate measure as its costs will probably exceed its potential benefits.[142]

While the second framework starts from a vertical perspective, the third framework takes a horizontal perspective through a balancing of competing rights. Limits to the regulated sphere are set by balancing the protected group member's right not to suffer discriminatory adverse treatment against the alleged perpetrator's rights or freedoms. A prominent example cited by Collins is the UK Supreme Court's decision in *Bull and Bull v Hall and Preddy*.[143] The Court held that a hotel owner's refusal to give a double-bedded room to a gay couple who were in a civil partnership amounted to discrimination on the ground of sexual orientation and that this protection by the law did not amount itself in a disproportionate interference with the owner's right to manifest their religion, having performed a balancing with the couple's right for respect for their sexual orientation.[144]

In the case studies that have been discussed in section III, the question of an unregulated private sphere did not arise as all situations were covered by the ambit of the EU non-discrimination directives. The defendants were employers and service providers that fall under the duty of non-discrimination in EU legislation. However, the standard of conduct required from the private parties involved notably differed. In *Feryn* and *CHEZ* the defendants were held accountable according to a substantive conception of equality, while in *Achbita* the standard of conduct was defined according to a formal reading of the duty of non-discrimination. Why is an employer making public statements about its recruitment policy subject to a higher standard than an employer adopting a neutrality policy? The discussion of the CJEU's rulings shows that all three strategies identified by Collins have been used by the Court to define the non-discrimination duty in the private sphere. Specifically, the first – purpose-oriented – approach is represented by the interpretation of direct interpretation in *Feryn* and *CHEZ*. The second approach focusing on the negative liberty of the duty-bearer is most visible in

---

[138] ibid 365.
[139] ibid 366.
[140] T Khaitan, *A Theory of Discrimination Law* (Oxford, Oxford University Press, 2015) 200.
[141] ibid 204, 206: 'A small employer with a single employee will be less public than a large factory employing thousands of workers. Where the landlord shares a house with the tenant, the negative liberty interest is stronger.'
[142] ibid 209.
[143] *Bull and Bull v Hall and Preddy* [2013] 1 WLR 3741.
[144] Collins (n 135) 366, 367; see also Collins (n 28) 71.

Rete Lenford when assessing the interference with the freedom of expression. A balancing of rights – the third approach – was proposed by the Court in *WABE*. However, the first limb of the second approach – the degree of 'public-ness' – might explain the varying standards of conduct defined by the CJEU. The factual situations of *Feryn* and its follow-ups have been standing out for the public context in which the statements have been uttered, which rendered them particularly damaging for the structuring of an inclusive labour market. *CHEZ* dealt with former state electricity companies and access to essential services, namely electricity. The presence of these elements of 'public-ness' might have given the CJEU reason to demand a higher standard of conduct, which in turn would show that the public/private divide still has a role to play in defining the obligations of private parties under EU anti-discrimination law.[145]

V. CONCLUSIONS

The examination of the case studies has shown how EU anti-discrimination legislation has transformed the resolution of disputes between private parties into an arena for the discussion of broader political questions on the integration of minorities in Europe. They thus constitute another example of the potential that lies in the introduction of EU fundamental rights in national private laws for provoking polity-building processes in Europe.[146] Although these processes have opened up a space for the discussion of social injustices and the contestation of established practices, they have not yet resulted in an unequivocal settlement of the role of private parties in combating discriminatory attitudes prevalent in society.

The CJEU's case law has not conclusively demarcated private parties' responsibility for addressing discrimination. On one side of the spectrum, there are the rulings in *Feryn* and *CHEZ*, which demonstrate how EU law employs private legal relationships as catalysts for the structuring of more inclusive and tolerant societies. A concern for substantive equality is predominant in both rulings. Employers and traders or service providers are rendered responsible for contesting stigma and stereotyping present in society, also at the cost of losing customers and profit. On the other side of the spectrum, there are the CJEU's succeeding rulings on employers' neutrality policies, which stand for a formal interpretation of the prohibition of discrimination. Instead of involving businesses in the fight against Islamophobia and negative stereotypes about Muslim women, employers have been conceded a broad leeway to adopt neutrality policies in the name of Article 16 EUCFR. The sole explanation that has been offered for the CJEU's restrictive approach in the cases dealing with the Muslim headscarf has been the sensitivity of the status of religion in Europe, which reinforces the existence of a hierarchy between different right-holders depending on the protected characteristic at stake.

Revisiting the traditional public/private divide and the rationales of identifying private duty-bearers has offered another explanation that becomes visible by examining more closely the context and the facts of the three case studies. The defendants in *Feryn* and *CHEZ* assumed a higher degree of 'public-ness' which was missing in the cases dealing with the

---

[145] Similarly, by looking at other areas of European private law, Cherednychenko has concluded that the CJEU's ability and willingness to engage in judicial activism is influenced by the public/private divide; see Cherednychenko (n 24) 45.
[146] Mak and Kas, ch 1 in this volume.

Muslim headscarf. While the employer in *Feryn* rendered discriminatory 'public statements' in the media, *CHEZ* dealt with the provision of a public utility, namely electricity. Similar elements were absent in *Achbita* and the rulings that followed the decision. Such a perspective shifts the focus from the status of the right-holder to the situation of the private duty-bearer concerned.[147] While such a change of perspective might not lead to an immediate difference in result, it could open a critical discourse on the extent to which EU anti-discrimination law has overcome the public/private divide and on defining more clearly the obligations of private parties in countering discrimination.[148]

[147] In this respect, the observation by N Reich that 'the imbalance between rights and obligations seems to be a fundamental one, written into the legal structure of Community law' appears pertinent; see N Reich, 'The Interrelation between Rights and Duties in EU Law: Reflections on the State of Liability Law in the Multilevel Governance System of the Union: Is There a Need for a More Coherent Approach in European Private Law?' (2010) 29 *Yearbook of European Law* 112, 120.

[148] Fittingly, as argued by Cherednychenko: 'Acknowledging the distinction between the "public" and "private law" grammar options in EU private law for descriptive and analytical purposes does not mean redrawing the strict line between these two areas of law. Rather, rediscovering the public/private divide along these lines would imply greater conceptual clarity, which is much needed in order to be able to choose the adequate means to pursue a particular policy goal and thus to improve the EU private law making.' See Cherednychenko (n 24) 30.

7

Freedom of Speech, Consumer Protection and the Duty to Contract

MATEUSZ GROCHOWSKI*

I. A MISSING LINK: CONSUMER PROTECTION AND FREEDOM OF EXPRESSION

AN AXIOMATIC PREMISE of today's European private law is its close connection with fundamental rights. Immense scholarly[1] and judicial efforts[2] have shaped the contours of this relation, and it eventually entrenched itself in the EU Charter of Fundamental Rights.[3] Despite this plethora of accounts, certain aspects of the liaison between fundamental rights and private law are still a riddle. One such area is the relationship between consumer protection and freedom of expression. In an interesting turn of events, three high courts on either side of the Atlantic grappled with this problem almost in parallel. First came the Supreme Court of the United States (SCOTUS) judgment in *Masterpiece Cakeshop v Colorado Civil Rights Commission* of 4 June 2018,[4] which was closely followed by the Supreme Court of Poland (SCOP) judgment in *National Public Prosecutor's Office v AJ* (known commonly as the '*Printer from Łódź Case*')[5] of 14 June 2018 and by the Supreme Court of the United Kingdom (SCUK) decision in *Lee v Ashers Baking Company Ltd and Others* of 10 October 2018.[6] All these decisions built on similar factual patterns and

---

*I am grateful to Martijn Hesselink, Ewa Łętowska and Daniel Markovits for discussions that substantially enriched this text.
[1] *cf* A Barak, 'Constitutional Human Rights and Private Law' in D Friedmann and D Barak-Erez (eds), *Human Rights in Private Law* (Oxford, Hart Publishing, 2001) 13.
[2] See C Mak, 'Civil Courts as Constitutional Courts: Polity-Building through Private Law in Europe' (2020) 28 *European Review of Private Law* 953, 959–64.
[3] *cf*, eg, H Collins, 'Building European Contract Law on Charter Rights' in H Collins (ed), *European Contract Law and the Charter of Fundamental Rights* (Cambridge, Intersentia, 2017) 1; D Leczykiewicz, 'Horizontal Application of the Charter of Fundamental Rights' (2013) 38 *European Law Review* 479; see also generally HW Micklitz (ed), *Constitutionalization of European Private Law* (Oxford, Oxford University Press, 2014).
[4] *Masterpiece Cakeshop v Colorado Civil Rights Commission* 138 S Ct 1719, 201 L Ed 2d 35 (2018).
[5] Case II KK 333/17, published: OSNKW (Judgments of the Supreme Court, Criminal and Military Chambers) 2018, no 9, item 61 (the full text is available at: www.sn.pl/sites/orzecznictwo/Orzeczenia3/II%20KK%20333-17.pdf). Like other European cases in the civil law tradition, Polish judgments are identified only exceptionally by parties to the proceedings or by nicknames. The commonly used labelling is based on the docket number and, if applicable, the place of publication (such as an official collection of judgments of the particular court). For the sake of coherence of citations across the chapter, the Polish case law will be referred to in the same pattern as the US and UK cases.
[6] *Lee v Ashers Baking Company Ltd and Others* [2018] UKSC 49.

addressed the same pivotal question: to what extent may the freedom to express one's moral or religious attitudes interfere with the obligation to enter into or perform on an agreement? But despite these parallels, each judgment developed a different argument about the juxtaposition of freedom of expression, consumer protection and market liberty.

The following remarks delve into the nature of both the parallels and the dissimilarities to explore some overarching ramifications of these decisions for fundamental rights and consumer law. The following analysis will proceed in three steps. The point of departure is a comparative analysis that asks how each court incorporated fundamental rights into its evaluation of business-to-consumer dealings. Tracing these strategies is necessary not only to better understand the essence of the reasoning developed in the opinion in each case, but also to better identify the common denominator of all three – the subject matter of the second part.

Against this background, a third layer of the analysis distinguishes between two interconnected issues of consumer protection. The first of these is the general relevance of freedom of expression as a consumer issue. While the classical tenets of consumer law rest on the framework of economic interests, the three high court judgments substantiate a non-economic side of consumption. The analysis in this chapter frames this as a 'missing link' between freedom of speech and consumer law in order to proceed towards the second question: how does freedom of speech – as a consumer value – intertwine with freedom of contract? In particular, this chapter seeks to discover the extent of the collision between a consumer's freedom of expression and a corresponding freedom on the side of the professional. And this leads to a related question: what impact may a balance struck between the consumer's and the professional's free expression have on freedom of contract? In particular, is free expression a permissible justification for selecting only particular consumers as contracting partners while rejecting others? For the purposes of this analysis, this text will introduce and develop the concept of a 'public duty' on the part of the professional. Proceeding through these stages, the chapter characterises the relationship between market freedom and freedom of speech, which is often overlooked in European scholarship, but is growing progressively more important for European consumer law.

II. A STORY IN THREE (AND A HALF) PIECES

The first element of this discourse (both chronologically and in terms of the order of argument) was set forth by the SCOTUS decision of 4 June 2018 in *Masterpiece Cakeshop*. Undoubtedly one of the most consequential decisions of the last decade, the judgment triggered an immense discussion over the intersection of different minority protections when they collide in a market environment.[7] SCOTUS confronted the question whether a professional baker who operates a pastry shop can refuse to bake a cake for a same-sex wedding solely because of the sexual orientation of the would-be spouses.[8] The majority held that the bakery owner could refuse to render this service on the grounds of the free exercise of religion under the First Amendment

---

[7] For an in-depth analysis of the ramifications of *Masterpiece Cakeshop*, see ML Movsesian, 'Masterpiece Cakeshop and the Future of Religious Freedom' (2019) 42 *Harvard Journal of Law and Public Policy* 711, 722–49; M Murray, 'Inverting Animus: Masterpiece Cakeshop and the New Minorities' (2018) 2018 *Supreme Court Review* 57.

[8] *Masterpiece Cakeshop* was not the first instance where SCOTUS addressed discrimination through denial of a consumer contract; see the 1968 decision *Newman v Piggie Park Enterprises, Inc* 390 US 400 (1968).

to the US Constitution. Justice Kennedy, who delivered the majority opinion, observed that the First Amendment guarantees each individual the opportunity to express her views without any constraints imposed by a public authority – specifically, without a general prohibition against 'bas[ing] laws or regulations on hostility to a religion or religious viewpoint'.

SCOTUS identified the speech act in question as a creative expression by the bakery owner, part of whose business was decorating bespoke cakes in an artistic way. The court concluded that obliging him 'to create a cake for a same-sex wedding would violate his First Amendment right to free speech by compelling him to exercise his artistic talents to express a message with which he disagreed'. In other words, SCOTUS was concerned not directly with the ambit of religious freedom to which the baker was entitled, but rather with the scope of unlawful interventions into this freedom by the Colorado Civil Rights Commission, which had penalised the bakery owner. As will be further discussed below, this vertical setting entailed important ramifications for balancing freedom of speech and equal treatment.[9]

A decision in the UK followed shortly after the SCOTUS decision. In the judgment of 10 October 2018, the SCUK grappled with a refusal, by Ashers Baking Company of Belfast, to bake a cake featuring the slogan 'support gay marriage'. The cake was to be a part of a campaign promoting same-sex marriage, which at that time was still outlawed in Northern Ireland.[10] Although the consumer placed the order and paid for the cake in advance, the bakery owners declined delivery of a cake, explaining that they ran a 'Christian business'. Upon the consumer's complaint, the business owners found themselves accused of discrimination by the Equality Commission for Northern Ireland and were consequently sanctioned by a lower court with a fine that was upheld subsequently on appeal.

Against the specific factual background of the case, the majority (Lady Hale joined by the others) ruled in favour of the bakery owners, ascertaining their right to refuse to contract on the grounds of religious belief. The SCUK found no direct discrimination against the consumer since the refusal was not motivated by his sexual orientation, but solely by the content of the message to be put on the cake. As the court pointed out, by declining to deliver the cake, the bakery owners had exercised their right to object to a particular political view and had not acted against the person who expressed this view: 'The objection was not to Mr Lee because he, or anyone with whom he associated, held a political opinion supporting gay marriage. The objection was to being required to promote the message on the cake. The less favourable treatment was afforded to the message not to the man.'[11] Notably, Lady Hale's opinion relied in part on the SCOTUS decision in *Masterpiece Cakeshop*. Despite a few legal and factual differences between the two cases,[12] the UK court read it mostly as an expression of the same

---

[9] In the follow-up to *Masterpiece Cakeshop*, a number of similar cases were decided by the US courts: (1) After the 'original' SCOTUS case, the Masterpiece Cakeshop owner was involved in a series of lawsuits over his refusal to bake another cake, this time for a celebration of a gender transition. In 2021 the Denver District Court imposed a financial penalty on him. The appeal from this judgment is pending (www.edition.cnn.com/2021/06/18/us/jack-phillips-colorado-baker-discrimination-trnd/index.html). (2) In *Arlene's Flowers v State of Washington* (389 P 3d 543 (Wash 2017)), in which a florist refused to provide flowers for a same-sex wedding, the Washington Supreme Court found that the floral composition can be understood as neither an act of protected free speech nor as advocacy for same-sex marriages. In 2021 SCOTUS declined to hear this case (www.supremecourt.gov/orders/courtorders/070221zor_4gc5.pdf). (3) In *303 Creative LLC v Elenis* (currently pending), SCOTUS has to grapple with whether, in light of the freedom of speech, a designer of wedding websites may make a general statement on her website that she does not provide services to same-sex couples.

[10] The general recognition of same-sex marriages in the UK, which became effective as of 2014, was extended to Northern Ireland six years later.

[11] *Lee v Ashers Baking Company* (n 6) para 47.

[12] See section III below.

idea of there being a distinction between discrimination and refusal to endorse the expression of a certain viewpoint.[13]

Only ten days after *Masterpiece Cakeshop*, the Polish Supreme Court added another chapter to this story with its *Printshop* judgment of 14 June 2018. Despite intense domestic discussion, this case has rarely been reported in English-language sources, and hence it deserves a bit of a broader account. The dispute originated when a Polish non-governmental organisation (NGO) that advocates for the rights of non-heteronormative groups, LGBT Business Forum, ordered a placard featuring the name and contact details of the foundation.[14] The printshop refused to deliver the print and explained that it did not agree to contribute to promoting the LGBT movement. In the proclamation that followed, the printshop further substantiated this claim by asserting that in its refusal, it was following 'the Bible, morality and the conscience'.

This led to a criminal conviction of the printshop owner on charges brought by the public prosecutor under Article 138 of the Polish Code of Offences (CO),[15] which prohibits on financial penalty a refusal to sell goods or render services to a consumer without justifiable grounds.[16] The concept embedded in Article 138 CO dates back to the socialist economy of the 1970s, in which consumer protection had begun to emerge as a substantial problem for the centrally planned economy.[17] The original aim of the criminal sanction under this provision was to safeguard goals that the state-controlled economy prescribed for the consumer market. After the fall of communism and the re-institution of the market economy, Article 138 CO remained untouched in its wording. However, in the new political reality, it began to play a new role as a freestanding protection against discrimination in business-to-consumer contracts.[18] Although its practical relevance was almost negligible, it was sometimes invoked to protect vulnerable consumers who had been deprived of access to certain goods or services without justified grounds.[19]

---

[13] 'The important message from the *Masterpiece Bakery* case is that there is a clear distinction between refusing to produce a cake conveying a particular message, for any customer who wants such a cake, and refusing to produce a cake for the particular customer who wants it because of that customer's characteristics' (*Lee v Ashers Baking Company* (n 6) para 62). For a further comparison between both cases, see also M Burton, 'The Bakery as Battleground', *Verfassungsblog* (20 October 2018), www.verfassungsblog.de/the-bakery-as-battleground.

[14] For more on the case, see, eg, 'Court in Poland Rules against Printer who Refused Work from LGBT Group', *The Guardian* (14 June 2018), www.theguardian.com/world/2018/jun/14/court-in-poland-rules-against-printer-who-refused-work-from-lgbt-group; A Gajda, 'Refusal to Provide the Service Due to the Freedom of Conscience and Religion of the Service Provider in Poland' (2019) 10 *Przegląd Prawa Konstytucyjnego* 385, 389f.

[15] Act of 20 May 1971, Code of Offences (consolidated text: Journal of Laws of 2019, item 821 with further changes).

[16] In the exact wording: 'whoever, dealing professionally with rendering services … willingly and without a justified reason denies performance to which she is obliged is subjected to financial penalty'.

[17] *cf* A Wiewiórowska-Domagalska and M Grochowski, 'Consumer Law in Poland: Or There and Back Again' in HW Micklitz (ed), *The Making of Consumer Law and Policy in Europe* (Oxford, Hart Publishing, 2021) with further references.

[18] It should be noted that a similar provision is also contained in the Equality Act (Sexual Orientation) Regulations (Northern Ireland) of 2006, s 5(1) of which prohibits 'any person concerned with the provision (for payment or not) of goods, facilities or services to the public or a section of the public to discriminate against a person who seeks to obtain or use those goods, facilities or services (a) by refusing or deliberately omitting to provide him with any of them; or (b) by refusing or deliberately omitting to provide him with goods, facilities or services of the same quality, in the same manner and on the same terms as are normal in his case in relation to other members of the public or (where the person seeking belongs to a section of the public) to other members of that section'. Notably, however, despite quoting this provision in *Lee v Ashers Baking Company*, the SCUK did not build on the consumer discrimination argument, instead channelling its reasoning entirely towards freedom of speech and freedom of religion.

[19] See the cases listed by the Polish ombudsman: https://bip.brpo.gov.pl/pl/content/tk-uchylil-artykul-chroniacy-przed-dyskryminacja.

The *Printshop* case revived discussion about this provision, which so far had been a mostly dormant feature of legal doctrine. The judgment of June 2018 was the final word on a dispute that had occupied the lower courts, which had unequivocally found the business owner guilty of the offence. SCOP concurred, ascertaining that the printer had no justified grounds for rebuffing the consumer. The argument underlying this decision rested on balancing three values: the freedom to express religious views; the prohibition against discrimination on ethical grounds (along with the universal right to human dignity); and the freedom to engage in market activity (especially as realised through freedom of contract). In so doing, the Court clearly placed non-discrimination in the foreground, holding that an individual's expression of an ethical or religious attitude cannot trump it.[20] For a similar reason, market freedoms likewise could not supersede equality in serving all customers upon the facts of the case. According to SCOP, this view would prevail as long as the business party did not outright refuse to contract, but only sought an excuse for non-performance (as was the case with the printshop owner). In other words, the law in SCOP's view should protect the original choice of a consumer who could choose among several competing offers and ultimately opted for this particular printing service.

In the aftermath, the Constitutional Tribunal[21] reversed the final outcome of the proceedings.[22] But despite that intervention, the judgment of 2018 is a compelling instance of how values may be reconciled within the triangle of freedom of expression, market freedom and equal treatment. Notably, in balancing the rights at stake, the Court resorted to *Masterpiece Cakeshop* (not only to the majority opinion, but also to Justice Kennedy's dissent)[23] to conclude that in certain cases, religious identity may take precedence over equal treatment. This may be the case if a customer commissions a service that amounts to an artistic creation (such as a bespoke cake) that may engage the business owner's religious attitudes or ethical sensibility.[24]

---

[20] Moreover, referring to the facts of the case, the Court found that the roll-up placard in question had a purely informative character and did not express any statements contrary to Catholic Church doctrine. Thus, even more conspicuously, the denial of service by the printshop owner lacked legitimate grounds.

[21] Finally, the *Printshop* judgment of 2018 triggered a motion of the Polish Ministry of Justice to the Constitutional Tribunal to declare art 138 OC unconstitutional to the extent that it prohibits denial of performance without a justified reason (in particular, on ethical and religious convictions). The tribunal ruled in accordance with the application (judgment of 26 June 2019, K 16/17, Journal of Laws of 2019, item 1238). The decision was issued with the involvement of a judge whose appointment was subsequently questioned by the ECtHR in the *Xero Flor* decision of 7 May 2021 (App No 4907/18), with a consequent conclusion that a board comprising such a person does not constitute a legitimate court. Nonetheless, after reinstituting the proceedings, Polish courts (including the Supreme Court) acquitted the printshop owner in accordance with the Constitutional Tribunal's conclusion that Polish law does not penalise a conscience-based refusal to contract.

[22] In this way, the Supreme Court implicitly acknowledged an extremely broad 'conscience clause' for consumer contracts which allows one to refuse to make any contract by mere reference to subjective convictions of the seller or supplier; on this issue, *cf* E Łętowska, 'Tylnymi drzwiami ku uniwersalnej klauzuli sumienia? (uwagi na marginesie "sprawy drukarza" przed TK)' (2022) *Państwo i Prawo* 3.

[23] On the comparison between the *Printshop* and the *Masterpiece Cakeshop* judgments, see also A Śledzińska-Simon, 'O cukierniku i drukarzu, czyli o dwóch tradycjach praw człowieka' in R Balicki, M Jabłoński (eds), *Dookoła Wojtek ...: Księga Pamiątkowa poświęcona doktorowi Arturowi Wojciechowi Preisnerowi* (Wrocław, Wydział Prawa, Administracji i Ekonomii, 2018).

[24] Polish doctrine was divided along similar lines, putting freedom of religion in the foreground or opting for direct protection of these with consumers' economic rights. The former standpoint was taken by M Derlatka, 'Konstytucyjność zakazu odmowy świadczenia z art. 138 KW – na marginesie postanowienia Sądu Najwyższego z dnia 14 czerwca 2018 r., sygn. II KK 333/17' (2018) 12 *Prokuratura i Prawo* 119; the latter view was represented primarily by E Łętowska, 'Co naprawdę wynika z wyroku Sądu Najwyższego w sprawie Łódzkiego drukarza' in E Łętowska and J Zajadło, *O wygaszaniu państwa prawa* (Sopot, Arche, 2020) 77 (the text was originally published at: http://konstytucyjny.pl/co-naprawde-wynika-z-wyroku-sn-w-sprawie-lodzkiego-drukarza-ewa-letowska). The author concluded that art 138 CO 'is a provision intended to protect a client as a consumer, and not a provision that facilitates combatting unwanted ideologies'; on this standpoint see also Ł Mirocha, 'Polskie orzecznictwo w perspektywie wyroku w sprawie Masterpiece Cakeshop' (2018) *Forum Prawnicze* 65.

After these three episodes had played out, the European Court of Human Rights opened up a fourth – though still inconclusive – chapter to the story in *Lee v United Kingdom*, a follow-up case to *Lee v Ashers Baking Company*.[25] The plaintiff claimed that the SCUK decision infringed on certain provisions of the European Convention on Human Rights (ECHR), primarily the prohibition against discriminatory treatment (Article 14) connected with the rights to respect of one's private life, freedom of thought, conscience and religion, and freedom of expression (Articles 8–10). The Court dismissed the case on formal grounds, pointing out that the ECHR had not been raised in the domestic proceedings and hence finding that none of the UK courts had had an opportunity to take a position on it. This decision marks the last word – at least for the time being – in the judicial saga concerning freedom of expression vis-a-vis consumer protection in Europe.[26]

III. STRATEGIES OF INCLUSION

The picture sketched by the three supreme courts may be seen from a few vantage points. At the structural level, the judgments clearly illustrate the multiple ways in which fundamental rights may enter the realm of contract law. Juxtaposed against one another, the three judgments provide a unique insight into interactions between freedom of speech and market autonomy. With striking similarity, the three high court cases open a range of comparative issues concerning the concept of fundamental rights and their role on the market. This chapter limits its discussion of the three decisions mostly to the way in which they substantiate a more general problem: how does freedom of speech operate as a value in the consumer economy? But notwithstanding the general focus of the subsequent analysis, a few grounding comparative observations about the three cases are needed.

Each judgment grappled with a similar set of factual circumstances, the only meaningful difference being that while the US and UK cases did not clearly establish whether the matter was one of refusal to enter into a contract or a refusal to perform on a contract already entered into, the Polish court directly ascertained that an agreement had been made. But despite the apparent gravity of this distinction, its actual meaning for consumer rights seems mostly negligible. All three courts reached roughly the same conclusion about freedom of expression when confronted with non-discrimination: they all ascertained that as long as one's religious or ethical convictions are expressed through the design of a consumer good or service (in other words, as long as the contract performance entails a certain degree of creativity in voicing such statements), the business party may be entitled to abstain from the contract. This assertion or certain variations on it form the common conceptual and political denominator of all three decisions.

The question gets more complicated when the third element of this triad – market freedom – enters the picture. The US and UK decisions are utterly indifferent towards market freedoms; instead, they frame the entire problem as a tension between free expression (coupled with freedom of religion) and non-discrimination. The main reason why they miss this component seems to be twofold. First, they position fundamental rights differently vis-a-vis market freedom and freedom of contract. Since the early twentieth century, US courts have consistently confined themselves to the premise that contract law is politically neutral. The foundation of this approach is framed in SCOTUS's 1905 decision in *Lochner v New York*,[27] which adopted

---

[25] *Gareth Lee v United Kingdom* App No 18860/19 (ECtHR, 6 January 2022).

[26] On the questions left unanswered in *Lee v United Kingdom*, see N Alkiviadou, 'A Missed Opportunity for LGBTQ Rights', *Verfassungsblog* (10 January 2022), www.verfassungsblog.de/a-missed-opportunity-for-lgbtq-rights.

[27] *Lochner v New York* 198 US 45 (1905).

a laissez-faire version of freedom of contract that elevated it to the position of a fundamental right.[28] Although subsequent case law restrained this view,[29] freedom of contract in the US has maintained its strongly libertarian identity.[30] Under this assumption, contract law remains almost exclusively a domain of default rules, the principal role of which is to provide a legal framework to facilitate low-cost formation and performance of individual agreements.[31] This attitude is further enhanced by the Contract Clause in Article 10 of the US Constitution (the pivot for *Lochner* and subsequent case law), which prohibits state law interventions into contractual dealings. Consequently, market regulations are introduced beyond contract law as such – on the grounds of public law and administrative ordering.[32] At the same time, the US system notoriously rejects the horizontal effect of fundamental rights to an extent similar to what its European counterpart does: it limits the direct[33] effects of fundamental rights to the state–individual dimension only, perceiving them as a constraint on the exercise of public power.

All these elements can be clearly traced in the *Masterpiece Cakeshop* decision. Unlike the two other judgments, *Masterpiece Cakeshop* limits its focus to the relation between a cakeshop owner and the state agency charged with protecting fundamental rights. Hence, the case did not directly tackle non-discrimination in the horizontal (business-to-consumer) dimension. It focused instead on assessing whether the public enforcer of non-discrimination measures had overreached. In line with these premises, the problem was framed as a freedom of speech issue, and SCOTUS consequently focused on balancing these rights with the freedom not to be discriminated against on grounds of sexual orientation.

This attitude seems to have been prevalent also in framing the core legal question in *Lee*. The UK court clearly departed from a market-related context in terms of both freedom of contract and consumer protection. English law adopts the horizontal dimension of fundamental rights and does not refrain from also introducing them as limitations on the freedom of contract.[34] The lack of an upfront reference to economic liberty in *Lee* hence draws attention to other peculiar reasons, crucial amongst which seems to be the particular 'path-dependence' of the court's reasoning. From the outset, the plaintiff characterised the case as a fundamental rights dispute, which emphasised freedom of speech and freedom of religion while casting the issues of freedom of contract or economic freedom out of the picture.[35] The way in which the

---

[28] On *Lochner* in the US concept of market liberalism, see T Colby and PJ Smith, 'The Return of *Lochner*' (2015) 100 *Cornell Law Review* 527, 533–41.

[29] cf EF Paul, 'Freedom of Contract and the Political Economy of *Lochner v New York*' (2005) 1 *NYU Journal od Law & Liberty* 515, 549–50; DE Bernstein, '*Lochner v New York*: A Centennial Retrospective' (2005) 83 *Washington University Law Quarterly* 1469, 1507–09.

[30] So H Dagan and M Heller, 'Freedom of Contracts' (2013) Columbia Law & Economics Working Paper No 458, 3.

[31] MJ Trebilcock, *The Limits of Freedom of Contract* (Cambridge, MA, Harvard University Press, 1997) 15–17.

[32] See, eg, § 1-302(b) of the Uniform Commercial Code, which prescribes that only 'the obligations of good faith, diligence, reasonableness, and care' should be deemed mandatory in contract law.

[33] At the same time, however, a number of doctrinal accounts seek to justify an indirect or spill-over efficacy of fundamental rights in individual relations, including contracts (see, eg, H Dagan and A Dorfmann, 'Interpersonal Human Rights' (2018) 51 *Cornell International Law Journal* 361, 365–72; S Gardbaum, 'The "Horizontal Effect" of Constitutional Rights' (2003) 102 *Michigan Law Review* 387, 398–411.

[34] cf amongst many others H Collins, 'Private Law, Fundamental Rights and the Rule of Law' (2018) 121 *West Virginia Law Review* 1, 6–8; G Alpa, 'The Effect of Fundamental Rights on Contract Law in a Comparative Perspective' (2019) 30 *European Business Law Review* 301; and OO Cherednychenko, 'The Harmonisation of Contract Law in Europe by Means of the Horizontal Effect of Fundamental Rights' (2007) 1 *Erasmus Law Review* 37.

[35] This raises a more general question: to what extent does the protection in question pertain to the values actually at stake or (rather) to the values the parties declared to be relevant to the case? On a similar overlap (or mismatch) in the context of discrimination in employment, see N Reich, 'Effective Private Law Remedies in Discrimination Cases' in R Schulze (ed), *Non-discrimination in European Private Law* (Tübingen, Mohr Siebeck, 2011) 66–67.

fundamental rights milieu is framed in *Lee* seems a direct sequel to *Masterpiece Cakeshop*, which the SCUK majority discussed quite broadly in the final part of its opinion. It is of course impossible to determine the extent to which the US decision contributed to shaping the UK justices' legal arguments; nonetheless, the resemblance in reasoning between the two cases is striking.

The Polish case in turn builds on a different frame. As opposed to the two other decisions, it strongly accentuated freedom of speech and freedom of contract as consumer values, putting the 'market' dimension in the spotlight. This difference stemmed from the specificity of the legal backdrop of the case, which drew on a discrimination ban from a provision which directly limited a professional's freedom to pick and choose among clients. The ramifications for the ultimate conclusion in the *Printshop* case were significant; not only was the focus shifted away from protecting free expression, but the fundamental difference was also accentuated between the Polish case and *Masterpiece Cakeshop*. While the crux of the latter decision was freedom of artistic expression, the *Printshop* case concerned an 'ordinary' instance of consumer protection in which performing the printing service did not entail any artistic creation by the professional. After remarking generally on this, SCOP ascertained that refusing to render services on the grounds of religious convictions may constitute a 'justified reason' within the meaning of Article 138 CO (even if religious freedom conflicts with non-discrimination requirements).[36] However, this is possible only inasmuch as the specificity of the service itself conspicuously contradicts these values. Therefore, although SCOP's conclusion may seem diametrically opposed to the two earlier decisions, in essence all three decisions espouse the same general view of the juxtaposition between freedom of speech and non-discrimination in the consumer market.[37]

The Polish court concluded on this basis that the shop owner lacked a legitimate reason for refusing to print the poster. He was asked merely to print a ready-made graphic design which included only the logo and contact details of the NGO, and hence performing the service could not contravene his religious convictions. Since Catholic doctrine mandates equal and respectful treatment of sexual minorities, the printer's opposition did not rest on objective religious grounds and, furthermore, subjective convictions of the professional could not override the constitutional prohibition on discrimination. Nor could the professional resort to 'the principles such as freedom of contract and market freedom', as the shop owner refused to perform a service he had already agreed to perform.

The *Printshop* case thereby opened up an utterly new perspective on consumer protection, in that it appeals for a more precise understanding of the extent to which the sole fact of carrying on a business requires the businessperson (creates a 'public duty') to fill any order and to serve all comers[38] – and to what extent exceptions from this obligation may be justified on grounds of the professional's religious or ethical convictions. To answer this question requires

---

[36] Notably, SCOP profoundly reinterpreted art 138 OC, departing from perceiving it through the prism of a centrally planned economy. As the Court pointed out, in the present-day market economy, the provision was included in the system of anti-discrimination guarantees founded on the 1997 Polish Constitution (art 31), along with the ECHR and the EU Charter of Fundamental Rights.

[37] As observed in the scholarship: 'In fact the ruling of the Polish Supreme Court is not that far away from the seemingly different ruling of the US Supreme Court ... The US Supreme Court assumed that the cake in question, prepared upon an individual order, is a manifestation of the artist-craftsman's freedom of speech. It is hard to argue this way when it comes to a standardized service, a print of usual, neutrally-framed information materials.' See E Łętowska (n 24) 78.

[38] Notably, art 138 CO does not require that the obligation to render services results from a pre-existing agreement. According to the prevailing view among scholars (shared by SCOP in *Printshop*), the professional is obliged to render services solely because she runs a particular business and offers services to consumers.

a deeper look into the role of freedom of expression in consumer law and any further ramifications for market autonomy.

IV. THE OBLIGATION TO CONTRACT THROUGH FREEDOM OF EXPRESSION

A. Freedom of Speech as a Consumer Value

The three judgments discussed here revolve around the question of the extent to which a professional may distinguish among consumers justifiably on the basis of her freedom of speech. But these courts developed arguments that require one to look at the flipside: to what extent does autonomy in expressing one's views constitute an independent consumer good?

Quite importantly, in order to 'speak' through particular market conduct, consumers need not have included a clear statement in a good or service they have purchased. Depending on the circumstances, speech can also materialise through the placement of the order without any additional statements attached. This dimension became particularly clear in *Masterpiece Cakeshop*, a case in which producing the cake itself (which was not ordered to bear any specific label or motto) may have constituted a number of concurrent speech acts.

First, as SCOTUS pointed out, the cake may be understood as an object of artistic expression by the baker, and consequently the professional should be shielded from an obligation to use his skills and creativity to endorse values that contradict his religion.[39] Second, ordering a particular good or service may also be the consumer's way of expressing various messages. Such expression may take the form of direct statements (such as the phrase that was to be put on the cake in *Lee v Ashers*), but such messages may also be conveyed implicitly, through the good or service as such. In this way, producing the cake in *Masterpiece Cakeshop* can be understood as an expressive act (in this case, as part of the same-sex wedding celebration),[40] even though the cake did not feature an overt statement. Hence, as Justice Gorsuch noted, 'to suggest that cakes with words convey a message but cakes without words do not ... is irrational'.[41] Subsequent comments on this judgment in general approved of the idea that making a cake is an act of expression 'by itself',[42] while offering more precise yardsticks for identifying speech acts from amongst different kinds of choices in consumer transactions.[43] The cake in *Masterpiece Cakeshop*, it follows, could constitute a dual speech act that encapsulated messages by both consumer and professional. Despite a few caveats (because 'speech'

---

[39] Some commentators have pointed out that this conclusion was rather perfunctory and that the Court did not fully confront the fundamental question of what makes a cake (or any other consumer item, like an outfit or hairstyle) an act of expression – *cf* especially C Flanders and S Oliveira, 'An Incomplete Masterpiece' (2019) 66 *UCLA Law Review Discourse* 154, 160–64.

[40] See Justice Gorsuch (with Justice Alito concurring) in *Masterpiece Cakeshop*: 'Nor can anyone reasonably doubt that a wedding cake without words conveys a message. Words or not and whatever the exact design, it celebrates a wedding, and if the wedding cake is made for a same-sex couple it celebrates a same-sex wedding.'

[41] ibid.

[42] J Hart, 'When the First Amendment Compels an Offensive Result: *Masterpiece Cakeshop, Ltd v Colorado Civil Rights Commission*' (2019) 79 *Louisiana Law Review* 419, 427 ('baking a wedding cake is a message, even if the parties had not yet discussed the specific words and decorations ... As the Court of Appeals noted, the request was for a wedding cake that would "celebrate" their marriage – in other words, requesting a message').

[43] *cf*, eg, A Jensen, 'Compelled Speech, Expressive Conduct, and Wedding Cakes: A Commentary on *Masterpiece Cakeshop v Colorado Civil Rights Commission*' (2018) 13 *Duke Journal of Constitutional Law & Public Policy* 147, 156–59; and V Cappucci 'The Cost of Free Speech: Resolving the Wedding Vendor Divide' (2020) 88 *Fordham Law Review* 2585, 2602–10.

under the First Amendment has specific – and generally ample – meaning and is usually highly contextualised), *Masterpiece Cakeshop* poses a clear question: to what extent should a consumer's market choices be shielded as expressions of values and attitudes, even when not contained in an explicit message embedded in a good or service?

Given the trajectory of consumer law and EU consumer protection in particular, the answer to this question is not fully apparent. Traditionally, EU consumer law has been oriented primarily towards the economic dimension of consumer transactions. In this conventional setting, consumers were protected primarily from making ill-informed decisions about purchasing goods or services out of line with their economic needs. This view is value-neutral to the extent that it disregards other considerations or goods that may guide consumers in their economic decisions. In the market, consumer choices are clearly driven not only by purely economic incentives (especially the best price-to-quality ratio), but also by other considerations (as it seems, for example, to the 'free trade' movement).[44]

The three cases discussed above draw attention to another dimension of this issue: the extent to which consumers should be protected on grounds of the values they wish to communicate through their market choices. Only recently has freedom of expression started making its way into the foreground of EU consumer policy, triggered by a growing awareness of the new ways in which consumers are involved in the market under the influence of online platforms. More than ever before, the present-day consumer economy has embraced freedom of speech as one of its core values. Building on these three high court cases, one can give a more detailed picture of how free expression interacts with consumer protection and of the lessons to be learnt in terms of understanding and shaping EU consumer law.

B. Non-discrimination and the 'Public Duty'

In examining the link between market freedoms and the freedom to express one's views, which the supreme courts develop in diverse ways, one stumbles upon a more foundational issue: to what extent may participation in consumer markets impose a duty to contract on the part of the professional? Each of the three cases addresses this question to a varying degree, more or less directly, approaching it from either a freedom of expression or a freedom of contract perspective.[45] But the most straightforward question – one that stems from all the three judgments – is whether a professional enjoys unrestricted freedom in deciding with whom to contract.[46]

In all three judgments, non-discrimination was (directly or implicitly) revoked as a general constraint upon one's prerogative to refuse to contract with particular consumers. In this sense, fundamental rights may give rise to an actual obligation to contract on the part of the professional. This issue is a more detailed instance of the professional's 'public duty', a topic

---

[44] *cf* M Grochowski, 'European Consumer Law after the New Deal: A Tryptich' (2020) 39 *Yearbook of Consumer Law* 387, 407–411 with further references.

[45] This conflict pertains only to non-discrimination understood as a horizontal value, ie, as a prohibition of differential treatment at the individual–individual level, not as an individual–state relation; see also Reich (n 35) 57. At the same time, the essence of the dilemma is similar for those systems that do recognise the horizontal effect of fundamental rights ('Drittwirkung') and for those that consider fundamental rights to be horizontal values (as *Masterpiece Cakeshop* clearly illustrates – the public law prohibition on discrimination indirectly protects consumers' market autonomy).

[46] *cf* H Collins, 'The Vanishing Freedom to Choose a Contractual Partner' (2013) 76 *Law and Contemporary Problems* 71.

that was briefly introduced above:[47] by sole virtue of running a business, the business owner may not, without justification, abstain from contracting. Undoubtedly, solely disapproving of the values conveyed by a particular good or service does not vindicate rebuffing a consumer who is ready to treat. The same applies to contract performance: mere ethical dismay cannot justify any form of 'moral impossibility' of performance and hence cannot excuse breaking an agreement.[48]

Under this view, the only relevant question that might be asked is whether the subject matter of the agreement amounts to a performance that is illegal, objectively impossible (eg, due to material or workforce shortages) or unreasonable.[49] Outside of these conditions, the professional who has made a public promise to sell a good or render a service to all comers is bound by this offer. Consequently, as long as the consumer is responding to the offer so made, the professional cannot create any limits *ex post facto*. In particular, the law would bar a professional from invoking religious or ethical convictions as grounds for refusing to contract with a particular individual or a group. Such a refusal would not stand, either on the grounds of consumer identity (religious views, gender etc) or in relation to the values and opinions to be conveyed by the particular good or service (whether express or implied). Hence, the 'public duty' idea can be vindicated regardless of the market structure that underpins the particular transaction. Certainly, in a monopoly or oligopoly, discriminatory conduct may squeeze consumers out of the market completely, making it impossible for them to obtain a sought good or service.[50] Nevertheless, even competitive markets arguably demand full-fledged consumer protection against unjustified refusal to enter into or perform under an agreement.

The essence of 'public duty' rests on the assumption that participating in a professional capacity in the consumer market entails a different degree of universal duties than non-professional market activity. Solely by inviting consumers to treat (through setting up a website, opening a brick-and-mortar store or placing an advertisement in a newspaper), a professional makes an implied promise that all consumers who respond will be treated on an equal footing and, to the extent that is objectively possible and reasonable, receive the good or service they seek. Framed in this way, the 'public duty' idea is a tenet of the general right not to be discriminated against in social and market relations. Conversely, the universally binding nature of a professional's offer means that she cannot differentiate between customers without clear and objective grounds. All three of the jurisdictions discussed above recognise non-discrimination as a constraint on the freedom of market autonomy (understood as freedom to choose contractual partners).[51] As such, the ability to decide on one's contractual arrangements cannot supersede equal treatment and respect for the dignity of each market actor. In this sense, limits to the freedom *of* contract likewise apply to a more particular component of the same freedom: the freedom *from* contract[52] (ie, the liberty not to be bound by an agreement

---

[47] See section II above.

[48] On 'taste-based discrimination' see also AS Vandenberghe, 'The Economics of Non-discrimination' in Schulze (n 35) 13.

[49] For instance, a barber who refuses to perform service on an intoxicated client or a shop owner who denies entry to clients who pose a material health risk. The latter became particularly meaningful in the pandemic era, when the lack of a COVID-19 certificate could be a valid ground for rejecting a client to the benefit of other customers' security.

[50] See also LE Perriello, 'Discrimination Based on Sexual Orientation and Religious Freedom in European Contract Law' (2018) 4 *Italian Law Journal*, 639, 644; S Navas Navarro, 'Sex Discrimination in European and Spanish Contract Law' in Schulze (n 35) 259–60.

[51] *cf* E Picker, 'Anti-discrimination as a Program of Private Law?' (2003) 4 *German Law Journal* 771.

[52] See, eg, H Dagan and M Heller, *The Choice Theory of Contracts* (Cambridge, Cambridge University Press, 2017) 2.

and, in particular, to decline offers).[53] The 'public duty' idea limits freedom of contract on both counts.

C. Freedom of Contract as a Freedom to Speak?

A formal view on the freedom to enter into or abstain from contracts in the business-to-consumer setting can nonetheless be misleading when it comes to the 'public duty' to contract. This public duty is a specific form of the obligation to contract that touches upon a few much more profound layers of market freedom.

At a foundational level, a 'public duty' is not at odds with the freedom to (or not to) contract. On the contrary, it is a powerful instrument for safeguarding the essence of free choice in the market, understood as each market participant's prerogative to select the option that she considers optimal in the particular context. Naturally, one's preference for a particular good or service does not by itself entail the right to obtain it; only when a contract is formed does this become possible. However, at this point, the 'public duty' theory changes the simple understanding of freedom of contract, which conventionally correlated with a decision about engaging in a particular transaction. In the present-day consumer marketplace, the mechanics of contracting are discernibly different: individual consumers enter into agreements by responding to standing offers from professionals (such as to bake any cake or to print any banner or leaflet that a client might order).

In other words, a professional who makes an *erga omnes* promise to sell a good or render a service to any consumer who requests it cannot revoke it for reasons related to the message (or statement) that the particular good or service is going to convey. In this sense, the concept of a 'public duty' entails a practical consequence for freedom of expression on the professional's part: by protecting consumers' market autonomy, it limits the professional's prerogative to communicate her convictions by breaking a universal promise made to all potential customers.

In this sense, the essential question the three judgments ask is not *with whom* do we choose to contract? Instead it is *what values* do we introduce into the market and into social discourse in enacting our choice? In each of the supreme court cases discussed above, consumers were not simply denied a service; the denial was accompanied instead by a clear proclamation by the respective professionals that they disapproved of the values that the service was going to represent, turning the rejection from a purely market-driven act, such as when services are declined based, for example, on a lack of resources, into a decision that manifests ethical contempt – and one that (only as a spill-over) also has economic consequences for the consumer. At the individual level, being denied a service triggers additional transaction costs (the need to spend time and resources seeking another contractor to render the service) without guaranteeing that the next offer will not be more expensive. From a general perspective, denying contracts to certain consumers – if repeated and widespread – may lead entire clusters of clients to be excluded from the market for a particular good or service in that particular area.

Understood in this way, the 'public duty' concept uses market conduct (distinguishing between customers) rather than mere statements of ethical convictions in order to identify

---

[53] In this sense, merely refusing to enter into an agreement can be perceived in itself as a manifestation of the cakeshop owner's freedom of contract (see E Ruzzi, 'More Than Just a Cake: *Masterpiece Cakeshop* and the Future of Civil Rights' (2019) 1 *Roma Tre Law Review* 224, 225).

and target instances of discrimination.[54] In the three cases discussed above, the professionals explicitly asserted that they were denying service on the grounds that they did not support the equality of various sexual orientations, and in this way they created a clear premise for considering their conduct to be unjustified marketplace discrimination. But if the same professionals had given a fictional but seemingly objective reason for not rendering the service (flour shortage at the bakery) or had disclosed no reason at all, the answer should be the same. That is because market discrimination is oriented towards motives and not merely towards outcomes,[55] and as such the refusal to treat would be unlawful in all three scenarios. A 'public duty' asks whether it is permissible to differentiate among contract partners based on invalid premises for such distinctions.[56] From this perspective, the difference between cases in which a professional decided to disclose the actual reason for denying a service and those in which she lied or stayed silent may be significant for proving discrimination, but not for triggering it.

This issue also has a flipside: by protecting consumers from unjustified denial of services, the 'public duty' idea also clears a broader field for consumers to use the marketplace as a sphere for expressing their own views by making particular market decisions. The question of consumer choice as an instrument for following certain ethical convictions is not a novel one, and yet the three cases discussed above reveal a more specific layer of this issue: in all three, a consumer transaction turned into a battlefield where both parties used the instruments of contract law (offer, refusal and non-performance) as 'speech' devices in order to deliver certain statements of values and convictions. The outcome was that the courts were confronted with balancing the parties' rights to express themselves through market conduct. In this particular setting, the classical notion of consumer protection was intertwined with protecting the individual's autonomy to speak *in* and *through* marketplace dealings, and thus the freedom of contract was understood here not merely as a freedom to pursue one's economic interests, but also as a liberty to incorporate certain statements into market conduct.

As already indicated, certain values or views may be inherent in consumer choice, and to varying extents, this was also true of the three cases discussed above. From this perspective, it seems much easier to understand the core question that each high court grappled with: each attempted to address the extent to which market autonomy may provide a foundation for using contracts as devices of expression – and each sought ways to align the colliding interests of both parties, each of whom would have liked to 'speak' through their market decisions.

V. A TOOLBOX FOR EU CONSUMER LAW

Despite apparent misalignments, the three high court cases bear striking mutual resemblances. Their common denominator is the conundrum of freedom of speech and market autonomy each attempted to disentangle. Reconciling these values poses a substantial question for

---

[54] Thus, the concept of non-discrimination may be understood as an expression of collective morality, which excludes particular motives in deciding on the formation and content of an agreement (see also Vandenberghe (n 48) 13).

[55] *cf* ibid.

[56] In other words, the law prohibits discrimination encompassing both direct and indirect segregation upon unlawful premises – see, amongst many others, C Tobler, *Indirect Discrimination: A Case Study into the Development of the Legal Concept of Indirect Discrimination under EC Law* (Antwerp, Intersentia, 2005) 55–59.

consumer protection under EU law, which in its current form lacks a consistent conceptual framework for construing freedom of speech as a consumer value and balancing it against the other values and political goals that the EU endorses. Although freedom of conscience, freedom of speech, consumer protection and market freedom have been declared EU-protected fundamental rights,[57] neither scholarship nor case law has come up with a precise way to balance the first two against the latter two.[58] And so far, the idea that consumers pursue more than just economic goals in the marketplace and should be protected in terms of the message they want to express through a market decision has had little impact in EU consumer law.

The high court judgments shed light on this issue from three different perspectives, given the different domestic legal traditions of perceiving freedom of speech and various strategies for juxtaposing it against market freedoms. But at the same time, the common problem they all address reaches far beyond the question of consumer discrimination into the essence of consumer involvement in the market economy. Not only do the cases demonstrate that consumer protection goes beyond protecting economic interests, but they also provide a toolbox for reconciling the values that may collide in the form of 'speech acts' by consumers and professionals. As such, they also deliver parts of a toolbox that may be applied in order to reconcile and understand the interplay between these values. The concept of 'public duty' described above provides a partial answer to this question: a professional's offer on the market is binding as long as the contract is not precluded or unreasonable on objective grounds. Finding it unpalatable to serve or sell to an individual consumer – regardless of their identity or the nature of the requested good or service – does not justify revoking such a promise made to an indeterminate array of potential clients and customers.

This conclusion stems primarily from the general mechanics of making legally binding promises and thereby entering into agreements. However, from an EU law perspective, it is even clearer that consumer trust should be protected as a freestanding virtue,[59] and hence consumers should also be shielded from surprise at a seller or supplier who denies them based on individual ethical convictions. In this way, a general duty to make and perform under a contract – unless there is an objective reason to do otherwise – protects the predictability of a consumer's standing in the marketplace and prevents a fragmentation that would have consumers investing in the search for a particular professional who does not reject them for ethical reasons.[60]

Such an obligation to contract that stems from a professional's promise to the entire community of consumers obviously limits the professional's opportunity to express her views through market conduct. As such, the idea of a 'public duty' seems to provide a better response to the 'speech issue' in consumer contracts than the middle-ground solutions adopted by the US and UK courts. The situation in which the values a consumer expresses through a contract collide with the professional's reasons for not entering into such a contract should be resolved in favour of the consumer who chooses the particular professional as a contracting partner.

---

[57] See respectively arts 10, 11, 16 and 38 of the Charter of Fundamental Rights of the EU.

[58] In this context, see also the CJEU judgment in Case C-68/17 *IR v JQ* EU:C:2018:696, which addressed the limits of religious ethics as justification for differentiated treatment in employment.

[59] See, eg, CE de Jager, 'A Question of Trust: the Pursuit of Consumer Trust in the Financial Sector by Means of EU Legislation' (2017) 40 *Journal of Consumer Policy* 25, 27–36.

[60] This does not pertain to sectoral exceptions that may be introduced in domestic law for particular professions or services (eg, for bioethical reasons). Of course, each exception of this kind must meet the constitutionality criteria under domestic law as well as comply with EU law.

The business owner who decides to carry on a certain activity should in turn embrace the potential ethical concerns this activity may entail.[61]

In this way, consumers also enjoy a higher degree of protection of their market autonomy, understood as a freedom to realise one's needs and wishes in the most meaningful way. Undoubtedly, such a market liberty also embraces the possibility of using contracts as vehicles for pursuing certain values and ethical convictions (as long as such aims are themselves ethical and legal). In this regard, the three high court decisions provide a unique illustration of how freedom of speech and freedom of contract converge and diverge in consumer agreements.

---

[61] This idea also touches the position of employees who may be compelled to act against their conscience (eg, to print a leaflet promoting certain values or views) as a spill-over requirement of the 'public duty' incumbent on the employer. For further discussion of the values at stake, see, eg, JM Dieterle, 'Freedom of Conscience, Employee Prerogatives, and Consumer Choice: Veal, Birth Control, and Tanning Beds' (2008) 77 *Journal of Business Ethics* 191.

Part III

Remedies

8

Article 47 of the Charter of Fundamental Rights in the Case Law of the CJEU

Between EU Constitutional Essentialism and the Enhancement of Justice in the Member States

GIULIA GENTILE*

I. INTRODUCTION

J USTICE IS FOUNDATIONAL for any community. Without any promise of justice, individuals could hardly agree to cooperate and, ultimately, build societies. Crucial steps in achieving justice are an effective application of the law and the protection of rights, which both aim to grant to individuals the legal entitlements promised by the laws governing a society. Seen from another point of view, justice is the fulfilment of the social and legal arrangements on which a community is founded. It follows that the idea of justice is intrinsically procedural and substantive: on the one hand, it demands clear, participatory and transparent rules to enforce the law (procedural justice) and, on the other hand, it imposes to grant everything that the law has 'promised' (substantive justice). In this context, the guarantee that courts offer redress for violations of the law (including rights) via fair trials strengthens justice and ultimately the premises on which societies are construed. As Sir Arthur Conan Doyle rightly affirmed: 'It is every man's business to see justice done.'[1]

In the light of these observations, the judicial narrative on effective remedies and protection of rights enshrined in the EU general principle of effective judicial protection[2] is not surprising: it signals the willingness of the EU judicature to achieve justice in the Member States. Not surprising is also the exponential relevance of Article 47 of the EU Charter of Fundamental Rights (Article 47) in the enforcement of EU law at the national level. This article provides the right to an effective judicial remedy and a fair trial. Whereas the former right ensures that effective redress is available in the case of violations of EU rights,

*I am thankful to the editors of this volume, Chantal Mak and Betül Kas, for their helpful comments on this chapter. I am also grateful to Matteo Bonelli for his feedback.
[1] Arthur Conan Doyle, *The Memoirs of Sherlock Holmes* (London, George Newnes, 1893).
[2] Case C-222/84 *Marguerite Johnston v Chief Constable of the Royal Ulster Constabulary* [1986] ECR 1651.

the right to a fair trial imposes a series of procedural guarantees to access to courts and to conduct fair judicial proceedings. Article 47 *reaffirms* the principle of effective judicial protection.[3] As pointed out by Prechal,[4] the optimal relationship between Article 47 and the principle of effective judicial protection is of complementarity: when the former provision cannot be invoked, the Court can 'fall back' to the general principle. The (partial) codification of the principle of effective judicial protection in the Charter restates the importance of this right in the EU constitutional architecture.[5]

Interestingly, the EU case law illustrates that the more defined wording of Article 47 aids the Court of Justice of the European Union (CJEU) in painting the content of the principle of effective judicial protection. In *Associação*,[6] the *Tribunal de Contas* asked the CJEU to assess whether the principle of effective judicial protection was breached by national rules reducing the salaries of judges in Portugal. The CJEU interpreted this principle in the light of Article 47,[7] which protects the principle of judicial independence. This case is a powerful example of the increasing prominence of Article 47 in scrutinising national laws.

Indeed, due to its link with the principle of effective judicial protection, Article 47 serves as a parameter for the CJEU to review national rules used to enforce EU law in the Member States. The scrutiny of national rules under Article 47 is qualitatively and quantitatively remarkable. Qualitatively, the scope[8] of Article 47 has proved to be extensive, 'capturing' not only rules used to enforce EU law *stricto sensu*, but also institutional design norms that *in abstracto* are related to the application of EU law.[9] Quantitatively, Article 47 has become the most invoked Charter provision at the national level, and preliminary references regarding this norm are increasing.[10] It is not an overstatement to say that Article 47 is almost 'omnipresent' in the EU judgments as a result of a growing number of preliminary rulings on that provision. The substantial amount of preliminary references concerning Article 47 reveals that national jurisdictions are actively engaging with the Luxembourg Court to identify the requirements stemming from that provision. In so doing, national judges utilise Article 47 to shape the way of granting justice in the areas covered by EU law via national procedural rules. The national application of Article 47 clearly reinforces the narrative on justice[11] initiated with the establishment of the principle of effective judicial protection by the CJEU. The scrutiny of the CJEU over national rules in the light of Article 47 of the Charter thus constitutes a topic of major constitutional interest, not least because of the repercussions of Article 47 as a fundamental right in the EU multi-level judiciary. Moreover, the EU case law is increasingly addressing the question of the essence of Article 47, thus laying down the foundations

---

[3] See Case C-348/16 *Moussa Sacko v Commissione Territoriale per il riconoscimento della Protezione internazionale di Milano* EU:C:2017:591; and Case C-243/15 *Lesoochranárske zoskupenie VLK v Obvodný úrad Trenčín* EU:C:2016:838.

[4] S Prechal, 'Effective Judicial Protection: Some Recent Developments – Moving to the Essence' (2020) 13 *Review of European Administrative Law* 16.

[5] S Prechal, 'The Court of Justice and Effective Judicial Protection: What Has the Charter Changed?' in C Paulussen et al (eds), *Fundamental Rights in International and European Law* (The Hague, TMC Asser Press, 2016) 152–153.

[6] See Case C-64/16 *Associação Sindical dos Juízes Portugueses v Tribunal de Contas* EU:C:2018:117.

[7] It should be noted that the Court also referred to art 19 of the Treaty on European Union (TEU); see para 32.

[8] Charter rights can be applied to scrutinise national measures whenever Member States are implementing EU law; see art 51 of the Charter.

[9] See Case C-619/18 *European Commission v Republic of Poland* EU:C:2019:531; *Associação* (n 6).

[10] Article 47 is amongst the most invoked provisions in the EU case law. See G de Burca, 'The Domestic Impact of the EU Charter of Fundamental Rights' (2013) 49 *Irish Jurist* (New Series) 49 ff; for more recent data, see E Frantziou, 'The Binding Charter Ten Years on: More Than a "Mere Entreaty"?' (2019) 38 *Yearbook of European Law* 73.

[11] See, among others, *Commission v Poland* (n 9).

of the EU constitutional essentialism. These issues are currently under-researched and beg for scientific observation.

In particular, three questions regarding the influence of Article 47 in the Member States' legal orders arise. First, what is the margin of discretion left to national judges under that provision when they enforce EU law? Second, what has Article 47 added to the notion of effective judicial protection developed under the homonymous EU general principle? Third, and consequently, what kind of justice does Article 47 enhance at the national level: procedural or substantive – or both? The chapter addresses these issues in turn and is divided into three main parts. Section II discusses the margin of discretion of national authorities under Article 47 of the Charter. Section III looks at how this provision has shaped the understanding of effective judicial protection in the EU and focuses on the content of Article 47.[12] Section IV considers the overall influence of Article 47 on the justice systems in the Member States.

II. THE INDIRECT JUDICIAL REVIEW OF NATIONAL PROCEDURAL RULES BY THE CJEU

Via the indirect judicial review carried through the preliminary ruling procedure, the CJEU contributes to the enforcement of EU law at the national level in cooperation with the Member States' courts. The Luxembourg judges offer the interpretation of EU law and draw the boundaries within which national courts can enforce EU law effectively. The rights to an effective remedy and to a fair trial included in Article 47 enhance the competence of the CJEU to oversee the national systems of enforcement of EU law, in compliance with Article 19 of the Treaty on European Union (TEU).[13] Seen from another perspective, Article 47 works as a general clause granting entitlement to an effective remedy and a fair trial when an EU right is breached, either by the state or by an individual.[14] The *Egenberger* case further established that Article 47 may apply in horizontal situations,[15] and thus brought this provision closer to its 'mother' right, the general principle of effective judicial protection.[16]

Article 47 is subject to the general provisions of the Charter, including Article 51 thereof.[17] Consequently, the scope of application of Article 47 is more limited compared to that of the general principle of effective judicial protection, which applies, instead, in all areas covered by EU law regardless of the existence of implementing measures.[18] In this respect, the CJEU has clarified that the Charter is invokable with regard to procedural rules used to

---

[12] As observed in the literature, a comprehensive study on the essence of the right to an effective remedy under art 52 of the Charter is still missing; see Prechal (n 4). Gutman has recently initiated a debate on the essence of the right to an effective remedy and to a fair trial under art 47 of the Charter; see K Gutman, 'The Essence of the Fundamental Right to an Effective Remedy and to a Fair Trial in the Case-Law of the Court of Justice of the European Union: The Best is Yet to Come?' (2019) 20 *German Law Journal* 884.

[13] C Mak, 'Rights and Remedies: Article 47 EUCFR and Effective Judicial Protection in European Private Law Matters' in HW Micklitz (ed), *Constitutionalization of European Private Law* (Oxford, Oxford University Press, 2014).

[14] In Case C-414/16 *Vera Egenberger v Evangelisches Werk für Diakonie und Entwicklung eV* EU:C:2018:257, para 78, the CJEU held that 'Article 47 of the Charter on the right to effective judicial protection is sufficient in itself and does not need to be made more specific by provisions of EU or national law to confer on individuals a right which they may rely on as such'.

[15] ibid.

[16] As established in Case C-144/04 *Werner Mangold v Rüdiger Helm* [2005] ECR I-9981, EU general principles may have a horizontal application.

[17] Article 51 of the Charter: '1. The provisions of this Charter are addressed to (...) the Member States only when they are implementing Union law.'

[18] See, eg, *Associação* (n 6), which is analysed below.

enforce EU law since they qualify as implementing rules under Article 51 of the Charter.[19] However, the Charter does not apply when national procedures implementing EU law cover situations that are not expressly envisaged under the original EU measure.[20] In other words, provisions included in a national implementing measure that 'go beyond' the scope of EU law will not fall under the umbrella of 'implementing measures' under Article 51. It follows that the notion of 'implementation of EU law' under Article 51 of the Charter is becoming more stringent[21] and covers only circumstances covered under the wording of EU (secondary) law. A more precise identification of the notion of 'implementation' would make it possible to better delineate the areas in which Article 47 may be relied on to scrutinise national rules.

More importantly, the scope of application of Article 47 of the Charter and the consequent margin of discretion of national courts in the enforcement of EU law impact the division of judicial competences in the EU. Indeed, when Article 47 is interpreted as not imposing specific requirements of effective judicial protection, Member States' judges remain 'free' to choose national procedural rules when applying EU law. On the contrary, when Article 47 is construed as requiring specific standards of judicial protection, national courts may have to adjust procedural rules to the conditions stemming from that provision under the guidance of the CJEU. From this angle, Article 47 is the compass of the effective enforcement of EU law and guides the cooperation between national courts and the CJEU in ensuring effective EU law application. The scope of Article 47 directly influences national procedural autonomy[22] and may therefore impose limits upon national authorities as to the shape and form of national procedural law.

This section demonstrates that there is a correlation between the source of the principle of effective judicial protection,[23] including the relevant sub-rights, and the margin of discretion left to the national courts. Notably, the CJEU acknowledges a relatively broad discretion for national courts when the sources used to scrutinise the compatibility of national procedural rules with EU law are Article 47 of the Charter alone (section II.A.i) or Article 47 jointly with a 'general' (ie, not sufficiently detailed) secondary EU law provision (section II.A.ii). Instead, the CJEU limits the discretion of national judges, with the corresponding higher likelihood that national law may be found to be incompatible with Article 47 of the Charter, when the source of effective judicial protection is a detailed EU secondary law provision (section II.B.i) or when Article 47 is applied with Article 19 TEU (section II.B.ii).

These different margins of discretion reflect the division of competences between the EU and the Member States. A broader leeway for national courts exists when the EU has not detailed the procedural rules applicable in the Member States. Instead, when the EU

---

[19] See section II.A.ii below.

[20] Case C-653/19 PPU *Criminal Proceedings against Spetsializirana prokuratura* EU:C:2019:1024, para 41.

[21] *cf* Case C-617/10 *Åklagaren v Hans Åkerberg Fransson* EU:C:2013:105.

[22] The principle of national procedural autonomy has received particular attention in the literature. See, for instance, A Biondi and G Gentile, 'National Procedural Autonomy' in *Max Planck Encyclopedias of International Law* (Oxford University Press), www.opil.ouplaw.com/view/10.1093/law-mpeipro/e1878.013.1878/law-mpeipro-e1878; M Bobek, 'Why There is No Principle of "Procedural Autonomy" of the Member States' in HW Micklitz and B de Witte (eds), *The European Court of Justice and the Autonomy of the Member States* (Antwerp, Intersentia, 2012).

[23] Eliantonio has addressed the relationship between EU secondary environmental law and the principle of effectiveness, including art 47. See M Eliantonio, 'The Relationship between EU Secondary Rules and the Principles of Effectiveness and Effective Judicial Protection in Environmental Matters: Towards a New Dawn for the "Language of Rights"?' (2019) 12 *Review of European Administrative Law* 95.

institutions have introduced distinct procedural rules, the discretion left to the Member States is correspondently limited. Additionally, it should be observed that the narrower discretion of national courts under the combined use of Article 19 TEU and Article 47 is in line with the well-established EU case law, according to which the CJEU has the interpretative monopoly in determining the implications of Treaty provisions, and therefore can direct national courts towards specific outcomes.[24] The following section will provide an overview of these four categories of the CJEU's jurisprudence and focuses on cases in which the impact of Article 47 on the discretion of national courts becomes especially evident.

A. The Broader Discretion of National Authorities Regarding National Procedural Rules

i. Article 47 as a Stand-Alone Parameter

As a first example, in *Toma*,[25] the preliminary question referred to the CJEU concerned the existence of a potential breach of the principle of equality of arms, a corollary of the general principle of effective judicial protection. The matter regarded a national rule requiring private parties to pay court fees and provide a guarantee when initiating an action against the state for restitution of taxes levied in violation of EU law. However, the same regime did not apply to public entities, which were exempted from that guarantee. The national court asked the CJEU to assess the compatibility of the procedural rule at issue with Article 47. The CJEU held that the national procedural rule complied with Article 47, as EU law (including the European Convention on Human Rights (ECHR) case law in the light of which Article 47 is interpreted)[26] did not provide any precise requirement regarding the enforcement of the principle of equality and the imposition of court fees.[27] In this sense, the scrutiny exerted by the CJEU was 'less strict' and recognised the broad discretion of the Member States as to the regulation of court fees.

Another case falling into this category is *Agrokonsulting*.[28] The background of the case was as follows. Under the applicable provisions, a company (Agrokonsulting) could only complain about decisions regarding agricultural aid before a central court and not the closest local court. Unwilling to go before the central court, Agrokonsulting relied on Article 47 to verify whether national rules offered an effective remedy to protect the EU-derived right to agricultural aid. The referring court considered this procedural norm as potentially hindering the effective judicial protection of EU rights. However, no EU secondary law provided for detailed rules on the seat of courts before which claims could be brought in this area of law. Consequently, in its decision the CJEU declared that the national procedural law at issue appeared to be compatible with Article 47.[29]

---

[24] For an account on the interpretative methods of the EU courts, see K Lenaerts and JA Gutiérrez-Fons, 'To Say What the Law of the EU is: Methods of Interpretation and the European Court of Justice' (2013) EUI Working Paper AEL 2013/9, 55 and ff.

[25] Case C-205/15 *Direcția Generală Regională a Finanțelor Publice Brașov (DGRFP) v Vasile Toma and Biroul Executorului Judecătoresc Horațiu-Vasile Cruduleci* EU:C:2016:499.

[26] See art 52(3) of the Charter.

[27] *Toma* (n 25) para 59.

[28] Case C-93/12 *ET Agrokonsulting-04-Velko Stoyanov v Izpalnitelen direktor na Darzhaven fond 'Zemedelie' – Razplashtatelna agentsia* EU:C:2013:432.

[29] ibid para 60.

Further examples of the broad discretion left to national courts under Article 47 are *Ordre des barreaux francophones and germanophone*[30] and *TX*.[31] In the first case, a national rule imposing VAT on lawyer services in Belgium, implementing Directive 2006/112/EC, was scrutinised in the light of Article 47 of the Charter. In the absence of detailed EU rules regulating costs for legal services, the CJEU considered that the national legislation at issue was compatible with Article 47 of the Charter.[32] Similarly, *TX*[33] indicates that Article 47 does not limit the discretion of Member States in regulating procedural rights where EU secondary legislation only achieves a minimum harmonisation. In particular, Member States remain free to adopt rules regarding the waiver of procedural rights of individuals, subject to compliance with the minimum requirements set in EU secondary legislation and case law. *TX* further suggests that the CJEU aligns rather faithfully with the minimum requirements on the waiver of defence rights identified in the ECHR case law,[34] in the light of which Article 47 should be interpreted.

ii. Article 47 and General EU Secondary Law Provisions

In *Texdata*,[35] the question concerned the compatibility of a national rule imposing periodic penalties on companies having failed to disclose annual accounts. The imposition of the penalty occurred without prior notice and with no possibility for the addressees to make their views heard. This legislation implemented Article 7(a) of Directive 2009/101, according to which the Member States should provide appropriate penalties at least in the case of failure to disclose accounting documents as required by Article 2(f) of Directive 2009/101. This norm includes a precise obligation (ie, the imposition of penalties for failure to disclose financial accounts); however, its implementation is left to the discretion of the Member States.

The CJEU used a manifest error threshold by stating that 'it does not appear that ... the imposition of an initial penalty of EUR 700 without prior notice or any opportunity for the company concerned to make known its views before the penalty is imposed impairs the substance of the fundamental right at issue'.[36] It observed that the penalty system did not impair the substance of Article 47, since the submission of a reasoned objection against the penalty decision rendered that decision inoperable and triggered an ordinary procedure under which there is a right to be heard.[37] Moreover, the CJEU took into consideration the fact that the penalty provided under national law contributed towards the achievement of an EU general objective, such as the effective disclosure of financial accounts. Also in this case, no secondary EU law provided for more detailed procedural rules and thus the national procedural rules were found to be compatible with Article 47 in the light of the broad discretion left to Member States in this area.

---

[30] Case C-543/14 *Ordre des barreaux francophones and germanophone and Others v Conseil des ministers* EU:C:2016:605.
[31] Case C-688/18 *Criminal Proceedings against TX and UW* EU:C:2020:94.
[32] Also, VAT legislation is one of the main examples of EU competence.
[33] *Criminal Proceedings against Spetsializirana prokuratura* (n 20).
[34] ibid paras 34–37.
[35] Case C-418/11 *Texdata Software GmbH* EU:C:2013:588.
[36] ibid para 85.
[37] ibid.

Another case falling into this category is *SC Star Storage*.[38] The CJEU was asked whether several provisions of Directive 92/13, read together with Article 47 of the Charter, should be interpreted as precluding legislation which makes access to review procedures of decisions of contracting authorities subject to an obligation to deposit beforehand a 'good conduct guarantee'.[39] The Court acknowledged that 'neither Directive 89/665 nor Directive 92/13 contains any provisions specifically governing the conditions under which those review procedures may be used'.[40] Subsequently, the CJEU went on to undertake a detailed scrutiny of how the provision of a guarantee could limit the right to an effective remedy. Notably, it evaluated the proportionality of this guarantee in relation to the objective it wishes to pursue, that is, the proper administration of justice.[41] It applied a deferential margin in favour of national legislation and affirmed that the guarantee did 'not go beyond' what is necessary to achieve the objective of combating improper actions. Thus, the national provisions in question were found to be compatible with Article 47 of the Charter and EU secondary law.

An additional example of the broad discretion left to national courts in enforcing EU law is the *Deutsche Umwelthilfe eV* case.[42] The factual background was as follows. A German official had consistently refused to comply with EU environmental law. The referring court sought to ascertain whether the first paragraph of Article 47 should be interpreted as empowering the national courts to order the coercive detention of office-holders involved in the exercise of official authority, in circumstances in which a national authority persistently refuses to comply with a judicial decision enjoining it to perform a clear, precise and unconditional obligation flowing from Directive 2008/50. As in *Texdata*, the EU secondary legislation in *Deutsche Umwelthilfe eV* required national authorities to provide penalties and left the implementation of this obligation to national authorities.[43]

The judgment found that when national authorities are implementing EU law, including the Aarhus Convention, they should comply with the principle of effective judicial protection reaffirmed in Article 47. Additionally, national courts should not only ensure the effectiveness of EU law objectives, but also balance the achievement of EU goals with the protection of EU fundamental rights – in that specific case, the right to liberty. The CJEU provided detailed guidance to national courts on the ways to ensure compliance with both the EU general objectives and fundamental rights; however, it acknowledged the ultimate discretion of national courts in achieving the final decision, taking into account all the above-mentioned factors. *Deutsche Umwelthilfe eV* held that compliance with EU fundamental rights is a precondition to the effectiveness of EU law objectives. Notably, national courts become primary guardians of EU fundamental rights: in this context, respect of Article 47 participates in a general balancing act carried out by national courts, which are delegated to guarantee both the respect of fundamental rights and the effectiveness of EU law.

It should be further observed that in *Deutsche Umwelthilfe*, the remedy at stake did not protect an individual right; on the contrary, the redress consisted in detention for an official having breached EU environmental law. In this sense, the 'remedy' protected the general

---

[38] Case C-439/14 *SC Star Storage SA and Others v Institutul Naţional de Cercetare-Dezvoltare în Informatică (ICI) and Others* EU:C:2016:688.

[39] Notably, arts 271a and 271b of the Government Emergency Ordinance No 34/2006.

[40] *SC Star Storage* (n 38) para 42.

[41] ibid para 53.

[42] Case C-752/18 *Deutsche Umwelthilfe eV v Freistaat Bayern* EU:C:2019:1114.

[43] It should be noted that art 30 of Directive 2008/50 ([2008] OJ L152/1) merely states that the penalties to be adopted must be 'be effective, proportionate and dissuasive'.

interest in the environmental protection guaranteed under Directive 2008/50. Article 47 is thus transforming into a truly systemic norm able to shape the application of remedies to protect the EU general interest in the Member States.[44]

Such an application of Article 47 brings to the fore the tension between views on fundamental rights as individual or collective tools of legal protection.[45] A traditional and consolidated standpoint is that fundamental rights seek to ensure human dignity and private legal positions.[46] Under this paradigm, the individual protection stemming from fundamental rights provides guarantees for private interests that could 'go lost' in the enhancement of the general interest. Could a traditionally (individual) fundamental right, such as the right to an effective remedy, be used as a norm to protect the general interest of a community to obtain clean air? The underlying reasons justifying the innovative use of Article 47 in *Deutsche Umwelthilfe eV* are valid and worthy of support. Nevertheless, a 'general-interest-oriented' application of Article 47 could deprive this norm of its nature as an *individual* fundamental right.

As will be discussed in the following section, the CJEU has identified a narrower discretion for national courts in the light of Article 47 of the Charter in other circumstances.

B. The Narrower Discretion of Member States in Relation to National Procedural Law

i. Article 47 and Detailed EU Secondary Procedural Law

As mentioned above, when Article 47 is invoked jointly with EU secondary law detailing more precise remedial and procedural rules, the discretion of national authorities is more limited when enforcing EU law. As a consequence of the scrutiny of national rules under Article 47 and secondary law, the procedural autonomy of the Member States is subject to more stringent restrictions: the requirements of Article 47 are coupled by detailed provisions of EU secondary, which further reduce the leeway available to Member States authorities in choosing procedures and remedies to enforce EU law. *Lesoochranárske, Sacko, VW* and *FMS, FNZ et al* provide useful illustrations in this regard.

In *Lesoochranárske*[47] an environmental association sought to intervene in a procedure for the granting of building permits in a protected area, but its request was dismissed. Subsequently, this association lodged an appeal against that decision. Following contradictory judgments on the right of the environmental associations to intervene in that procedure, the Slovak Supreme Court decided to stay proceedings and refer a question to the CJEU. In particular, the Slovak Court enquired whether national rules limiting the possibility for environmental associations

---

[44] Roeben has discussed the role of the EU principle of judicial protection as a meta-norm in the EU judicial architecture. See V Roeben, 'Judicial Protection as the Meta-Norm in the EU Judicial Architecture' (2020) 12 *Hague Journal on the Rule of Law* 29.

[45] See, among others, A McHarg, 'Reconciling Human Rights and the Public Interest' (1999) 62 *Modern Law Review* 671. For an opposite view, see D Meyerson, 'Why Courts Should Not Balance Rights against the Public Interest' (2007) 31 *Melbourne University Law Review* 873.

[46] Roeben has highlighted that the principle of effective judicial protection, traditionally conceptualised as a 'subjective right', has also acquired a 'general obligation' dimension under art 19 TEU: 'The animating idea of this fundamental right is to enforce individual rights and only rights. Right is a thick, value-bound concept, distinct from the formal completeness of the rule on which direct effect is based. The amended art. 19(1) of the Treaty on European Union (TEU) turns the subjective right into an objective obligation for Member States to ensure that their judicial systems provide effective judicial protection.' See Roeben (n 44) 31.

[47] *Lesoochranárske zoskupenie VLK* (n 3).

to intervene in environmental procedures were in breach of Article 47, Directive 92/43 and the Aarhus Convention. It should be observed that Articles 6 and 9 of the Aarhus Convention detail the procedural guarantees for third parties seeking to intervene in environmental procedures and specify the locus standi requirements.[48]

The CJEU held that while Member States are in charge of laying down the detailed procedural rules to enforce of EU environmental law, the combined reading of Directive 92/43 and the Aarhus Convention provided that the environmental association had a right to participate in the administrative procedure actively. The Court further specified that Article 9 of Directive 92/43 limited the discretion of the Member States in terms of shaping the procedural mechanisms to allow participation of the 'public'[49] in the judicial review of environmental permits. In the light of these factors, the Slovakian rules denying the status of participants to associations in the context of litigation on environmental permits were incompatible with the right to an effective remedy under Article 47 and the relevant EU secondary legislation.

The *Sacko*[50] case offers further insights into the possible limitations of the discretion of national authorities under a combined reading of Article 47 of the Charter and EU secondary law. This preliminary question arose in relation to an Italian national rule that empowered judges to dismiss manifestly unfounded appeals on international protection without hearing the applicant. The Court assessed with great intensity whether this norm was compatible with Directive 2013/32/EU, regulating the granting of international protection in the EU, and Article 47 of the Charter. In so doing, it identified several conditions to be respected in order to ensure compatibility of this national norm with Article 47. Among those, the addressee of the decision should have the opportunity to make his views heard at first instance; in addition, the report of the interview should be placed in the casefile. Therefore, while the national rule at stake was not contrary to EU law per se, the CJEU put conditions upon the application of that very procedural norm in order to comply with Article 47.

The CJEU is increasingly interpreting EU secondary law in the light of Article 47 of the Charter: *VW*[51] and *FMS, FNZ et al* are worthy of discussion in this respect. In the former case, the Court was asked to evaluate whether 'Directive 2013/48, read in the light of Article 47 of the Charter, allows Member States to derogate from the right of access to a lawyer, which must … be guaranteed to a suspect who has been summoned to appear before an investigating judge, on account of that person's failure to appear'. The Court found that the Directive provided an exhaustive list of conditions to allow such derogation and, therefore, the discretion of Member States was accordingly restrained. It followed that national authorities could not delay the right to access to a lawyer granted to individuals under Directive 2013/48 because the suspect or accused person has failed to appear. Any derogation from that right had to fall into one of the grounds included in the Directive. This was not the case in *VW*.

In *FMS, FNZ et al*,[52] Article 47 not only entailed a limitation of the discretion of the referring court, but also showed its 'creationist' power. The preliminary ruling request in that case regarded the right of individuals seeking asylum to obtain the review of administrative

---

[48] Environmental protection is among the EU's objectives under art 11 TFEU.

[49] See the definition under the UNECE Convention on Access to Information, Public Participation in Decision-Making and Access to Justice in Environmental Matters (Aarhus Convention).

[50] *Sacko* (n 3).

[51] Case C-659/18 *Criminal Proceedings against VW* EU:C:2020:201.

[52] Case C-924/19 PPU *FMS and Others v Országos Idegenrendészeti Főigazgatóság Dél-alföldi Regionális Igazgatóság and Országos Idegenrendészeti Főigazgatóság* EU:C:2020:367.

decisions amending the destination of a return decision. In its judgment, the CJEU affirmed that the features of the remedies provided in favour of asylum seekers under Article 13 of Directive 2008/115 should be determined in the light of Article 47. That provision entailed two requirements: that an independent body competent to review the decision of return should grant the remedies envisaged under Article 13, and that individuals should be able to challenge an administrative decision amending the destination of a return decision. The CJEU observed that the authority in charge of reviewing the administrative decisions in the case at hand was supervised by the minister controlling the police forces and, thus, the executive power. As a consequence, the principle of judicial independence, which stems from Article 47, was breached in its external aspect.

In addition, the CJEU held that Member States are not obliged to introduce specific actions to enforce EU law unless there is no remedy at the national level to protect EU rights. The same applies in the event that the national procedural rules consider a case based on EU law to be inadmissible. Therefore, Article 47 and Directive 2008/115 had to be interpreted as allowing an action to challenge an administrative act amending the destination of a decision of return. In *FMS, FNZ et al*, Article 47 was used to establish new remedies at the national level. Therefore, the creative aspect of the principle of effective judicial protection is also replicated under Article 47.[53] The CJEU may accordingly interpret this latter norm to impose obligations of results when it comes to granting remedies set out into EU secondary legislation.

ii. Article 47 of the Charter and Article 19 TEU

Recent jurisprudential developments have highlighted the essential role of Article 47 in the EU constitutional architecture, jointly with Article 19 TEU. This latter article provides the duty of Member States to grant 'remedies sufficient to ensure effective legal protection in the fields covered by Union law'. The judgment in *Associação Sindical dos Juízes Portugueses*[54] provided the CJEU with the opportunity to declare that the existence of effective judicial review in the Member States is part of the *essence of the rule of law* in the EU. Moreover, the Court interpreted the content of the principle of effective judicial protection laid down in Article 19 TEU in the light of the principle of judicial independence laid down in Article 47 of the Charter. Since the *Associação* judgment, the combined application of Article 47 of the Charter and Article 19 TEU has provided the legal basis to limit the discretion of national authorities to ensure effective remedies under EU law.

What is remarkable about this jurisprudence is that the duty to provide effective remedies in the fields covered by EU law, which is imposed by Article 19 TEU, gives significant leeway for the CJEU to impose specific obligations of result on the Member States. The difference between the reduction of national courts' margin of discretion under Article 19 TEU and under the combined application of Article 47 of the Charter and EU detailed secondary legislation is the interpretative activity of the CJEU. While under EU secondary legislation containing procedural rules, the CJEU requires Member States' authorities to achieve the results envisaged under that legislation, under Article 19 TEU, the CJEU exercises its interpretative powers to ensure that national courts grant 'effective remedies'. In this latter scenario, the CJEU is making use of its competence to interpret what the law is under the Treaties. *Commission v Poland* and *GAEC Jeannigros* exemplify this finding.

---

[53] Case C-432/05 *Unibet (London) Ltd and Unibet (International) Ltd v Justitiekanslern* [2007] ECR I-2271.
[54] *Associação* (n 6) para 36.

The judgment in *Commission v Poland*[55] came after the initiation of infringement proceedings against Poland for breaches of Article 19(1) TEU and Article 47. In particular, these violations occurred due to the judicial reform passed by the majority party in Poland, the PiS. Among the introduced innovations, members of the Supreme Polish jurisdictions were forced to retire. The CJEU found that the judicial reform hindered the principle of judicial independence, protected under Article 19 TEU and Article 47 of the Charter. In the reasoning of the Court, judicial independence is of cardinal importance as a guarantee that EU-derived rights will be effectively protected;[56] it is part of the essence of the right to an effective remedy and a fair trial, as well as a crucial aspect of the rule of law. Consequently, the CJEU held that, due to the link between Articles 19 TEU, Article 47 of the Charter and the rule of law, the remedies granted at the national level in the fields covered by EU law must comply with the principle of judicial independence. After the application of the appearance test developed in the ECHR case law,[57] the measures introduced in Poland were found to affect the independence of the judiciary and were thus in breach of Article 19 TEU, interpreted in the light of Article 47. *Commission v Poland* indicates that the right to an effective remedy under Article 47 requires Member States to satisfy certain standards of judicial independence when designing judicial bodies. As already seen in *Deutsche Umwelthilfe eV*, Article 47 may be used as a systemic norm to guide national authorities to provide effective remedies to protect the EU general interest, including EU founding values such as the rule of law.

In *GAEC Jeannigros*,[58] Article 47 read in the light of Article 19 TEU showed its potential to impose obligations of result and accordingly restrict the discretion of national courts when granting remedies. These provisions were invoked to assess the duty of national courts to adjudicate on disputes regarding product specifications' decisions. The matter was raised to the attention of the CJEU since the Commission had granted an application submitted by national authorities seeking a minor amendment to a product specification decision. Therefore, national courts were enquiring whether the pending disputes on the decision needed adjudication. The CJEU concluded that the finding that a court does not need to adjudicate on that matter after the amendment decision adopted by the Commission would 'compromise the effective judicial protection that that court is required to provide in respect of such applications for amendments'.[59] Allowing national courts to consider those disputes as settled would deprive individuals of the possibility to challenge the minor amendments introduced by the Commission.

It should be observed that in the recent judgment in *Repubblika v Il-Prim Ministru*[60] the CJEU has imposed obligations of effective judicial protection on national courts on the basis of a joint reading of Articles 2 and 19 TEU. In particular, the Court declared that Article 47 of the Charter and Article 19 TEU are different in nature: the former applies to protect rights deriving from EU law, while Article 19 'seeks to ensure that the system of legal remedies established by each Member State guarantees effective judicial protection in the fields covered by EU law'.[61] In so doing, the CJEU seems to separate the principle of effective judicial protection

---

[55] *Commission v Poland* (n 9).
[56] ibid para 58.
[57] For an analysis, see M Krajewski, 'The AG Opinion in the Celmer Case: Why the Test for the Appearance of Independence is Needed', *Verfassungsblog* (5 July 2018), www.verfassungsblog.de/the-ag-opinion-in-the-celmer-case-why-the-test-for-the-appearance-of-independence-is-needed.
[58] Case C-785/18 *GAEC Jeannigros v Institut national de l'origine et de la qualité (INAO) and Others* EU:C:2020:46.
[59] ibid para 37.
[60] Case C-896/19 *Repubblika v Il-Prim Ministru* EU:C:2021:311.
[61] ibid para 52.

enshrined in Article 47 of the Charter from Article 19 TEU, the latter provision being focused on structural elements of the justice systems of the Member States. This is a welcome development, which better distinguishes the role of Article 47 of the Charter and the principle of effective judicial protection – both being sources of fundamental rights in favour of individuals – from the structural obligations for the Member States' judiciaries required under Article 19 TEU. It remains to be seen whether the approach adopted in *Repubblika* will be followed in future cases.

We may conclude this part of the chapter with a metaphor. Article 47 is like a spider's web: it is apparently invisible, but, in reality, it seizes all national rules used (or that in principle can be used) to enforce EU law. The various degrees of discretion left to national court are the consequence of two factors: the detailedness of EU secondary procedural rules and the enhancement of the system of remedies in the Member States under Article 19 TEU. The subject matter or the competence of the EU does not seem to impact the margin of discretion left to national courts under Article 47.

III. THE CONTENT OF ARTICLE 47 OF THE CHARTER

Having discussed the discretion left to the national courts in the enforcement of EU law and the role played by Article 47 in this respect, we now move to the 'substantive' impact of Article 47 on national procedural systems. Another facet of the influence of Article 47 relates to its fundamental right dimension and the relationship with the principle of effective judicial protection: what has this provision added to the EU notion of effective judicial protection? The analysis of the content of this provision will cast light on this complex matter.

First of all, the implications of Article 47's dualistic nature constituted by the coexistence of the right to a fair trial and to an effective remedy require some clarifications. Under Article 47, the right to an effective remedy and the right to a fair trial are undoubtedly interconnected. The EU case law does not clearly differentiate between them. According to *Ordre des Barreaux*,[62] the right to an effective remedy is provided under the second paragraph of Article 47, which lays down the right to a fair trial. In other cases, such as *Ognyanov*,[63] the Luxembourg Court held that the right to a fair trial is enshrined in the second paragraph of Article 47 of the Charter, and thus suggested its separate identity from the right to effective remedies under the first paragraph of Article 47 of the Charter.

Regardless of the (somewhat unclear) CJEU case law on the content of Article 47, although linked, these rights serve different understandings of justice. On the one hand, the right to a fair trial reflects a bundle of procedural guarantees that allow individuals to ascertain and defend their right before courts. These guarantees incorporate, among other things, the reasonable duration of proceedings, and the independence and impartiality of the court.[64] Such procedural rights ensure the right to be effectively heard by an impartial and independent tribunal. On the other hand, the right to an effective remedy grants an effective redress for violations of rights. This latter right seeks to achieve corrective justice objectives by ensuring that those wronged are restored in their legal entitlements. On a more systemic level, the right to an

---

[62] *Ordre des Barreaux* (n 30) para 27.

[63] Case C-614/14 *Criminal Proceedings against Atanas Ognyanov* EU:C:2016:514, para 23.

[64] Legal aid, which is referred to in the third paragraph of art 47, is the condition to access a right to an effective remedy and to a fair trial.

effective remedy requires that justice be made in cases of unlawful conducts violating rights and freedoms deriving from EU law.

While the right to a fair trial is intrinsically procedural, the right to an effective remedy embodies a substantive view on justice. From a procedural point of view, the right to a fair trial protected by Article 47 guarantees that the decisions achieved by EU and national courts, as well as other entities, are 'procedurally sound', meaning that the participatory rights of the parties are respected. From a substantive perspective, the right to an effective remedy under Article 47 of the Charter contributes to effectively redressing violations of EU law, and protects EU derived rights and interests. In other words, the potential of Article 47 from a substantive justice perspective lies in the fact that it ensures the correction of instances of 'inadequate enforcement' of EU law. In so doing, the right to an effective remedy favours an 'upgrade' of national remedies to attain the objectives and the guarantees enshrined in EU law.[65]

The substantive justice dimension of the right to an effective remedy and its interplay with the (procedural) right to a fair trial becomes evident when one analyses the *Johnston* case,[66] which laid down the principle to effective judicial protection, the 'parent right' of Article 47. The facts of the case are well known: Ms Johnston sought judicial review of a decision adopted by the UK Secretary of State that prohibited her admission to the armed forces on the ground of her sex. While Ms Johnston could access a court and lodge a claim under the procedural guarantees existing under UK law (which granted her the right to access court and obtain a fair trial),[67] the applicable national rules excluded review by UK courts of decisions adopted by the UK Secretary of State. Therefore, Ms Johnston could not obtain an effective remedy to set aside that act and protect her Community-derived right not to be discriminated against on the basis of gender. The principle of effective judicial protection was introduced by the CJEU in that case precisely to overcome this gap in the judicial protection system in the UK, and thus to offer the chance to obtain a redress for violations of the Community right to equal treatment.

Johnston illustrates that compliance with procedural guarantees may not be sufficient to achieve substantive justice. At the same time, the centrality of a fair trial to attain substantive justice should not be understated. Without the promise that the parties of a dispute can equally and fairly contribute to the discovery of the 'truth', the possibility to ensure substantive justice is also negatively impacted. Procedural wrongs impede individuals to effectively participate in litigation; in turn, procedural injustices prevent everyone from obtaining what the law has 'promised' them. The right to an effective remedy is thus to be conceptualised as the consequence and the aspirational outcome of the right to a fair trial: the fair trial, and safeguarding the procedural guarantees and rights of the parties to the litigation are a precondition to obtaining an effective remedy. Through its potential to enhance *both* procedural and substantive justice, Article 47 becomes a central tenet in the achievement of EU objectives.

---

[65] For the concept of 'upgrading national remedies', see N Reich, '"I Want My Money Back": Problems, Successes and Failures in the Price Regulation of the Gas Supply Market by Civil Law Remedies in Germany' (2015) EUI Department of Law Research Paper No 2015/05.

[66] *Johnston* (n 2).

[67] According to Langford, the notion of a 'fair trial' may be traced in the UK legal terminology since the seventeenth century. This is reflected in a solid tradition of respect for procedural guarantees before UK courts. See I Langford, 'Fair Trial: The History of an Idea' (2009) 8 *Journal of Human Rights* 37. The concept of 'fair trial' is also one of the main aspects of the UK doctrine on natural justice. See EJ Sullivan, 'The Missing Link: Fairness, British Natural Justice, and American Planning and Administrative Law' (1979) 11 *Urban Lawyer* 75.

However, Article 47 rights are not unfettered prerogatives. The ECtHR case law on the right to be heard, in the light of which Article 47 of the Charter must be interpreted,[68] confirms that this latter article is not an absolute right.[69] The scope of Article 47 is influenced by Article 52 of the Charter, according to which Charter rights may be restrained subject to certain conditions. First, the limitation is to be provided for by the law. Second, it shall respect the essence of fundamental rights. Third, the limitation should comply with the principle of proportionality.[70] Fourth and finally, the limitation is to be necessary and should genuinely meet an objective of general interest recognised by the Union or needs to protect the rights and freedoms of the others.

A crucial element[71] under the test included in Article 52 of the Charter is the identification of the essence of the rights. A useful image to represent the concept of the essence is the pit of certain fruits: like the pit, the essence is what is left after 'consuming' the outside of the right. Charter rights may indeed be 'consumed' because of pressing EU general interests demanding sacrifices to individuals as to their fundamental entitlements or to protect a competing fundamental right.

All in all, the polymorph nature of Article 47 makes the task of identifying its essence challenging and complex. However, this exercise allows the CJEU to shed light on the non-derogable aspects of the judicial protection in the EU. The essence of Charter rights, including Article 47, is in fact shielded from legislative intervention and constitutes the core of fundamental guarantees in the EU constitutional space. A question arises: how does the CJEU identify the essence of Article 47?

The following section offers a discussion on the possible ways to extrapolate the essence of Article 47. Distinguishing possible methodologies for this purpose enables reflections on the breadth that the CJEU grants to the core of Article 47. Moreover, the identification of the essence of Article 47 entails consequences for the national procedural systems: the essence of Article 47 constitutes the inalienable minimum of judicial protection standards for the enforcement of EU law that national judges should always respect.

A. How to Identify the Essence of Article 47: An Analysis

First, it may be argued that, in the light of the 'multiple' sub-rights forming the content of the right to an effective remedy, the latter has no one single essence, but *multiple essences* belonging to the different sub-rights thereof. Therefore, there might be an essence to the (sub-)right to legal aid, an essence to the sub-right to a public hearing, and to all other sub-rights granted under Article 47. While this perspective would allow for enhanced logical clarity, two issues might arise: the need to identify multiple essences of the right to an effective remedy and, thus,

---

[68] Article 52(3) of the Charter.
[69] Joined Cases C-584/10 P, C-593/10 P and C-595/10 P *European Commission and Others v Yassin Abdullah Kadi* EU:C:2013:518, para 102; and, to that effect, Case C-560/14 *M v Minister for Justice and Equality Ireland and the Attorney General* EU:C:2017:101, para 33.
[70] For an analysis of the protection of the essence of Charter rights, see T Tridimas and G Gentile, 'The Essence of Rights: An Unreliable Boundary?' (2019) 20 *German Law Journal* 794.
[71] Under art 52 of the Charter, limitations to fundamental rights are subject to a more detailed test than that used by the ECtHR. See S van Drooghenbroeck and C Rizcallah, 'The ECHR and the Essence of Fundamental Rights: Searching for Sugar in Hot Milk?' (2019) 20 *German Law Journal* 904.

the potential fragmentation of this fundamental right and its essence. In the event that the latter approach were to be followed, the task of determining the essences of Article 47 would become highly complex for the CJEU.

Second, the essence of Article 47 might be interpreted as composed by *some sub-rights*. This approach would entail a selection of the most 'fundamental' elements of the EU notion of effective judicial protection as part of the essence of Article 47. Under this perspective, the challenge for the Court would be to determine the hierarchy of sub-rights and their relevant scope. This interpretation of the essence of Article 47 could appear more desirable than the previously outlined approach, insofar as it allows the Court to establish core sub-rights which should never be curtailed. Still, the question would remain as to how to identify the scope of the sub-rights forming the essence of Article 47, which should be accordingly shielded from legislative intervention.

A third potential approach would be to consider as essence of Article 47 the *essences of some sub-rights*. Under this conceptualisation, the essence of Article 47 would correspond to the essence of, for instance, the rights to an independent and impartial tribunal, and to legal assistance. In this manner, the CJEU would need to identify a series of essential contents of selected sub-rights, violations of which would lead to the breach of the very substance of Article 47. This judicial methodology would have the benefit of enhancing analytical clarity and identifying elements of Article 47 which cannot be derogated. In parallel, it requires the CJEU to create a hierarchy between sub-rights and their essences, by sacrificing others to possible total limitations. The same problems identified for the second approach would also apply in this case.

A fourth possible methodology would be to select a *single sub-right* as forming the essence of the right to an effective remedy. By having a single sub-right as the essence of right to an effective remedy, the Court would consider all other sub-rights as potentially subject to unlimited curtailment, while the core sub-right could never be restricted. Let us consider a potential scenario: the CJEU proclaims that the essence of the right to an effective remedy is the sub-right to a hearing. It would follow that all restrictions to this sub-right would breach the essence of Article 47 of the Charter and could not be justified under Article 52 Charter. This approach would have the benefit of clearly identifying the core of Article 47 of the Charter as opposed to its periphery. Nevertheless, this method might risk limiting the polymorph nature of Article 47.

A fifth possible way of interpreting the essence of Article 47 would be to identify *the essence of a single sub-right*. For instance, the essence of the right to an effective remedy would correspond to the essence of Article 47. Such approach might nevertheless excessively reduce the protection granted under Article 47. Thus, it is argued that this methodology is the least appropriate, as it might excessively limit the protection granted under Article 47.

A final method to interpret the essence of Article 47 might be a mix of the previous ones. The essence of that provision could be, for example, the right to an independent tribunal and the essence of the right to legal aid.

In the view of the author, the most viable approach would be the second, ie, pinpointing some sub-rights as the essence of Article 47. This methodology would make it possible to offer a series of non-derogable entitlements to individuals, while leaving room of manoeuvre for the CJEU as to the distinction between the periphery (derogable) and the core (underogable) of Article 47. In the light of the case law, it appears that the CJEU is applying this strategy, at least to a certain extent. The Court has indeed carved out, among other things, the principle of judicial independence and the existence of a remedy as part of the essence of Article 47 of the Charter.[72] Accordingly, the CJEU has shielded pivotal aspects of the EU notion of effective judicial protection from legislative intervention.

However, the Luxembourg judges do not follow a systematic approach as to the identification of the essence of Charter rights, including Article 47. In other words, the CJEU has not expressly clarified its approach as to the protection of the essence of Article 47 – eg, whether it sees the core of Article 47 as given by 'entire' sub-rights, or by the essence of sub-rights, or according to other approaches. Rather, the Court appears to employ the concept of essence with a signalling function, in order to highlight the importance of the violation of EU law. While the selective approach of the CJEU concerning the essence of Article 47 is an expression of the interpretative powers of the EU judicature,[73] a legitimate question is what principle(s) should guide the EU courts in drawing the boundaries of the essence of Charter provisions, including Article 47.

In this respect, it is submitted that the supreme values of the EU legal order may offer guidance in search of the essence of Charter rights. Not surprisingly, these values are also recalled in the preamble to the same Charter. The protection of the essence of Charter fundamental rights is in fact intrinsically linked with founding values of the EU, such as the rule of law and human dignity: the essence of Charter rights are those non-derogable individual entitlements that make the EU 'a society in which pluralism, non-discrimination, tolerance, justice, solidarity and equality between women and men prevail'.[74] The essence of Charter rights may therefore be conceptualised as all the 'faculties/rights' undeniably granted to individuals who are members of a society based on the values of Article 2 TEU.[75] It follows that the Court should ultimately consider the essence of Charter rights from the perspective of Article 2 TEU. In the event that the essence of Charter rights is not respected, the EU founding values would also be breached.

Applying these principles to Article 47, the identification of its essence would thus require the CJEU to answer the following question: what would be the sub-rights of Article 47 that, if annulled, would violate Article 2 TEU? In applying this test, the CJEU could identify the essential sub-rights of the rights to a fair trial and an effective remedy that form the unfettered constitutional underpinnings, and thus the identity, of the EU.[76]

Remarkably, the CJEU has recently begun to develop case law on the founding values of the EU as well as the essence of Charter rights. In so doing, the Court is laying the foundations to build the EU constitutional essence. In this jurisprudence, the connection between Article 2 TEU and the right to an effective remedy has been explored, insofar as the right to effective judicial review was declared to constitute the essence of the rule of law.[77] Nevertheless, when identifying the essence of Charter rights, Article 2 TEU does not currently play a primary role. This also applies for Article 47. The next section will illustrate these points.

---

[72] See Case C-216/18 PPU *LM* EU:C:2018:586; *Commission v Poland* (n 9).

[73] For an analysis of the interpretative powers of the EU judicature, see K Lenaerts, JA Gutierrez-Fons and F Picod, *Les Méthodes d'interprétation de la Cour de Justice de l'Union Européenne* (Brussels, Bruylant, 2020).

[74] Article 2 TEU.

[75] *cf* with A von Bogdandy et al, 'Reverse Solange: Protecting the Essence of Fundamental Rights against EU Member States' (2012) 49 *Common Market Law Review* 489 ff. The authors consider that the protection of the EU citizenship rights is intrinsically connected to the protection of the EU fundamental values.

[76] It is suggested that this test could apply to all Charter rights.

[77] *Associação* (n 6).

B. The Essence of Article 47 in the EU Case Law

In *Puškár*[78] the CJEU had to consider whether Article 47 of the Charter must be interpreted as precluding national legislation which makes the exercise of a judicial remedy by a person alleging a violation of his right to protection of personal data subject to the prior exhaustion of the remedies available before the national administrative authorities. In this case, the CJEU identified a limitation to the right to access to justice and assessed its lawfulness under Article 52 of the Charter. The Court held that the first part of the Article 52 test – ie, whether the limitation to the right was imposed for by the law – was respected. When assessing the respect of the essence, the Court considered that this requirement was also complied with: by imposing an additional step to the access to court, the national legislation at issue was enabling, instead of impeding, the exercise of the right stemming from Article 47. Subsequently, the CJEU considered compliance with the proportionality principle and delegated the duty to carry this assessment out to the national court. As in *Texdata*, in *Puškár* the Court also considered that the essence of the right to an effective remedy was not breached since national legislation was merely imposing *additional temporary steps* to the exercise of that right.

The *SC Star Storage* case[79] (discussed above) is a more unique than rare example of judgment in which the CJEU fully applied all steps of the test under Article 52 of the Charter. When assessing whether the essence of the right to an effective remedy was preserved, the CJEU considered the regime governing the good conduct guarantee, since it imposed a limitation to the right to an effective remedy. It affirmed that the fact that the guarantee would have been returned in any event, regardless the outcome of the litigation, did not hinder the essence of Article 47.[80] Having considered the protection of the essence of Article 47, the CJEU scrutinised the guarantee under the principle of proportionality, and concluded that it was proportionate.

It should be remarked that the CJEU has also identified the essence of Article 47 without recurring to the Article 52 test. For instance, in *Schrems*[81] the absence of judicial remedies under the Safe Harbour Agreement was seen as a flagrant violation of Article 47, entailing a breach of its essence. In *LM*,[82] *Associação*[83] and *Commission v Poland*,[84] the CJEU declared that the principle of judicial independence is part of the essence of the principle of effective judicial protection. In *Deutsche Umwelthilfe eV*,[85] the non-compliance with a judgment would be against the essence of the right to an effective remedy under Article 47.

In the light of these judgments, it is clear that there is no precise methodology to identify the essence of Article 47 under Article 52 of the Charter. The case law indicates that there is no analytical distinction between the essence of the right to an effective remedy and that of the right to a fair trial. The Court does not seem to privilege substantive or procedural justice aspects when it comes to protecting the essence of Article 47: a breach of the essence of the

---

[78] Case C-73/16 *Peter Puškár v Finančné riaditeľstvo Slovenskej republiky and Kriminálny úrad finančnej správy* EU:C:2017:725.

[79] *SC Star Storage* (n 38).

[80] There might be different arguments against this interpretation, such as the limited financial resources of the parties. Also, the relationship between the granting of this guarantee and the possibility to obtain legal aid is not clear.

[81] Case C-362/14 *Maximillian Schrems v Data Protection Commissioner* EU:C:2015:650.

[82] *LM* (n 72).

[83] *Associação* (n 6) para 45.

[84] *Commission v Poland* (n 9) para 58.

[85] *Deutsche Umwelthilfe eV* (n 42) para 35.

right to an effective remedy (Article 47(1) of the Charter) or to that of a fair trial (Article 47(2) of the Charter) is equally serious. Overall, the depiction of the essence of Article 47 is impressionistic and fragmented. The discovery of the essence of Article 47 occurs in the form of judicial 'enlightenments' and is strategically used by the CJEU to protect the rule of law in the Member States. The fuzzy use of the notion of essence by the CJEU may be considered as a form of judicial empowerment: the concept of essence is selectively applied to shield the scope of Article 47 from legislative intervention, or to guide EU and national authorities to adopt measures in order to protect crucial aspects of the justice system.

On the whole, Article 47 has added a more defined content and core to the understanding of effective judicial protection in the EU. Through its wording, Article 47 has transformed effective judicial protection into a (somewhat) more binding norm in the EU. Additionally, the identification of 'underogable' aspects of Article 47 has been progressively shaping the assessment of the compatibility between national rules and EU effective judicial protection. This methodology enhances the fundamental rights dimension of EU law enforcement in the Member States: it permits the balancing between the periphery of Article 47 with national policy objectives, while safeguarding the essential aspects of the EU understanding of effective judicial protection.

Having considered the influence of Article 47 on the discretion of national authorities and what this norm has added to the principle of effective judicial protection, this chapter will now offer some conclusive evaluations. In particular, it will reflect on how Article 47 has so far addressed questions of justice in the Member States.

IV. THE IMPACT OF ARTICLE 47 ON THE NATIONAL PROCEDURAL SYSTEMS: BETWEEN PROCEDURAL AND SUBSTANTIVE JUSTICE

The significant impact of Article 47 of the Charter on national systems emerges with regard to two elements. First, Article 47 has strengthened the competence of the CJEU to shape both procedural and substantive justice in the Member States. Procedurally speaking, the CJEU has contributed to regulate procedural rights and duties of the parties involved in litigation concerning EU law, by reference, among other things, to the right to a lawyer,[86] the right to be heard,[87] the right to intervene in environmental procedures,[88] and the level of court fees.[89] From a substantive justice point of view, Article 47 has influenced the granting of effective remedies and thus the possibility to obtain judicial protection following alleged violations of EU rights[90] or general interests.[91] Under Article 47, the content and the shape of the remedies and procedures used at the national level are tailored to the objectives pursued at the EU level. In this respect, Article 47 has been innovatively used as a legal basis for collective remedies, thus contributing to ensure the effective enforcement of EU general policy objectives. Overall, as the predecessor principle of effective judicial protection, Article 47 contributes to the hybridisation of remedies, which become polymorph creatures bearing both national and EU features.

---

[86] *VW* (n 51).
[87] *Sacko* (n 3); *Texdata* (n 35).
[88] *Lesoochranárske zoskupenie VLK* (n 3).
[89] *Toma* (n 25); *SC Star Storage* (n 38).
[90] *FMS, FNZ et al* (n 52).
[91] *Deutsche Umwelthilfe eV* (n 42).

Second, the underogable content of Article 47 has contributed to identifying essential aspects of the EU conception of justice.[92] Also in this respect, procedural justice and substantive justice in the Member States were both impacted. On the substantive side, *Schrems* has indicated that the absence of the possibility of effective remedies in the field of data protection runs counter to the essence of Article 47; similarly, *Deutsche Umwelthilfe eV* specifies that when a judgment issued by a national court on EU environmental matters is not enforced, this violates the essence of Article 47. These aspects aim to ensure that remedies may be effectively granted and that individuals may obtain protection of their rights or the EU general interest. In other words, individuals should be able to obtain everything that has been 'promised' by the law through effective judicial protection. On the procedural side, in *Commission v Poland* the CJEU has indicated that the essence of the right to a fair trial is the independence of the adjudicatory body.[93] Judicial independence has thus acquired a fundamental status among the procedural guarantees in favour of individuals involved in the enforcement of EU law, as it ensures that judges will enjoy equal distance from the parties involved in litigation and the state powers in the interpretation of the law. In the considered judgments, the protection of the essence of Article 47 was ultimately triggered to shield the rule of law and gradually build the constitutional identity of the EU.

It is therefore undeniable that Article 47 has empowered the CJEU to build a constitutional essentialist approach regarding effective judicial protection in the EU. Notably, the case law on the essential core of Article 47 contributes to a judicial narrative whereby the CJEU depicts the constitutional underpinnings of the EU. It is true that even before the entry into force of the Charter, the CJEU engaged in the analysis of the protection of the very substance of EU fundamental rights.[94] However, this exercise was not systematic or prominent. Article 47 has allowed the CJEU to progressively identify the 'noyeau dur' of an EU justice conception. The essence of Article 47 has also clarified what underogable entitlements individuals have with regard to the enforcement of EU law before the national authorities. In the light of the considered case law, it is evident that Article 47 partakes in enhancing justice for individuals and the achievement of objectives of general interests, such as the protection of the environment.

Moreover, the jurisprudence of Article 47 also influences national rights' enforcement. This spill-over effect is evident in case no 03542/2012 of the Italian Council State[95] where Article 47 was relied upon to 'rebrand' an extraordinary administrative action as judicial. The reconceptualisation of that action permitted the introduction of the right for the claimants to also obtain damages – normally not available for that type of administrative claims and only allowed for judicial actions. The impact of Article 47 on purely internal situations is a testament to the transformative power of the Charter as a source of fairness in the Member States.

V. CONCLUSION

This chapter has gathered novel findings as to the application of Article 47 of the Charter by the CJEU and its impact on national procedural rules. This provision works as an additional

---

[92] Domurath and Mak have offered interesting insights on the idea of justice under EU law concerning housing rights. See I Domurath and C Mak, 'Private Law and Housing Justice in Europe' (2020) 83 *Modern Law Review* 1468.

[93] *Commission v Poland* (n 9).

[94] *cf* Case C-4/73 *J Nold, Kohlen- und Baustoffgroßhandlung v Commission of the European Communities* [1974] ECR 491, para 14. For an analysis of the case law on the limitation of EU fundamental rights before the entry into force of the EU Charter, see Tridimas and Gentile (n 70) 802 ff.

[95] Parere Consiglio di Stato, Sezione II, 11 June 2018, no 1517.

tool guiding the cooperation between national and EU courts in the enforcement of EU law. In contributing to this endeavour, Article 47 has offered the legal basis for the CJEU's competence to significantly shape procedural rules and the judicial systems in the Member States, in particular with reference to the margin of discretion of national courts in enforcing EU law, the concept of effective judicial protection and the construction of an essential core of this right, and, ultimately, the enhancement of justice at the national level.

First, under Article 47 of the Charter, the CJEU has recognised a broad or a narrow discretion to national authorities in the application of national rules to enforce EU law. These different degrees of leeway for national authorities are determined in the light of the sources of EU law used to scrutinise national law. When the parameters to review national procedural rules are Article 47 of the Charter alone or general provisions included in EU secondary law, Member States will have a broader discretion in enforcing EU law. When, instead, national procedural rules are assessed not only in the light of Article 47 of the Charter but also under EU secondary law provisions which impose upon Member States more precise and tangible procedural duties, Member States have a narrower level of discretion. The same level of reduced discretion applies when Article 47 of the Charter is enforced with Article 19 TEU. These margins of discretions reflect the division of competences between the EU and the Member States when the EU legislature has (not) harmonised procedures and remedies, in parallel with the willingness of the CJEU to delineate the duty of national courts to provide 'remedies sufficient to ensure effective legal protection in the fields covered by Union law'.[96]

The chapter has further highlighted that Article 47 is detaching itself from its role of fundamental right, while becoming the legal basis for enforcing the EU general interest at the national level (eg, *Deutsche Umwelthilfe eV*). It was also demonstrated that the creationist nature of the principle of effective judicial protection is replicated under Article 47 of the Charter. Indeed, this latter provision allowed the introduction of new remedies not established at the national level (eg, *FMS, FNZ et al*). However, it should be observed that the recent *Repubblika* judgment has innovatively distinguished the scope of Article 47 of the Charter, which is applicable to redress individual rights' violations, from that of Article 19 TEU, which imposes structural obligations on the national judiciaries.

Second, the essence of Article 47 of the Charter is increasingly identified in recent cases, but the CJEU does not apply a clear methodology to identify the core of that provision. Rather, the Court makes strategic use of the essence of Article 47 in a twofold sense. On the one hand, the identification of essential features of Article 47 creates a shield from legislative intervention with regard to those aspects of judicial protection; on the other hand, the case law on the non-derogable core of Article 47 contributes to carving out the aspects of judicial protection which should always be respected by national (and EU) authorities. Overall, the depiction of the essence of Article 47 furthers the construction of the EU constitutional essentialism.

In conclusion, Article 47 is the factotum of the EU: it has enriched the EU conception of justice with a more prescriptive dimension and has strengthened procedural and substantive aspects of the judicial systems of the Member States. Article 47 is also intrinsically linked to the protection of the rule of law, and its interpretation and enforcement led to setting aside laws that *in abstracto* could hinder the application of EU law (eg, *Commission v Poland*). Article 47 continues to surprise us, and seems not to have any limits, also thanks to its links with Article 19 TEU.[97] Or should Article 47 instead have limits? This debate would require the attention of further research. Yet, so long as Article 47 makes it possible 'to see justice done', it will have achieved its purpose.

---

[96] Article 19 TEU.
[97] However, see the recent *Repubblika* case (n 60).

9

Justice in Times of Crisis

The Signalling Function of Article 47 of the Charter of Fundamental Rights in Consumer Debt Collection Cases

ANNA VAN DUIN*

I. CRISIS AS A CATALYST OF PROCEDURAL TRANSFORMATION

IN 2020, THE world was hit by a pandemic that disrupted society, including the justice system. Courthouses closed, making access to court physically impossible. If there is a silver lining, it is that new challenges gave rise to new opportunities, such as the digitisation of court proceedings.[1] Crisis as a catalyst of procedural transformation is a phenomenon that also occurred in the aftermath of the 2007/2008 credit crunch, in a different way. Civil courts in Spain, Poland, Hungary and other European Union (EU) Member States were confronted with large numbers of cases brought by credit institutions against (over-)indebted consumers. This triggered many preliminary references to the Court of Justice of the European Union (CJEU) on the meaning and scope of EU consumer law as well as the need for effective judicial protection, in particular and most urgently for vulnerable consumer-debtors. The referring courts questioned the adequacy of their own national legal framework, especially where the scope for judicial protection was limited. Examples can be found in the case law on mortgage enforcement and order for payment procedures.[2] The Unfair Contract Terms Directive (UCTD)[3]

---

*This chapter is based on part of the findings in my PhD thesis (defended on 23 October 2020, Cum Laude), which has been published under the title *Effective Judicial Protection in Consumer Litigation: Article 47 of the EU Charter in Practice* (Cambridge, Intersentia, 2022). The thesis explores the functions of art 47 in the context of the UCTD through a comparative analysis of the case law of the CJEU and civil courts in Spain and the Netherlands.

[1] Digital access to civil justice was accelerated by the COVID-19 crisis, although remote hearings created new difficulties as well. An example of a positive change brought about in the Netherlands is electronic communication with the courts. Due to the lockdown situation, there has been a heightened sense of urgency about the need to introduce digital case files. For an inventory of the response to the global pandemic in respect of civil justice, see HB Krans and A Nylund (eds), *Civil Courts Coping with Covid-19* (The Hague, Eleven International Publishing, 2021).

[2] See, eg, Case C-415/11 *Mohamed Aziz v Caixa d'Estalvis de Catalunya, Tarragona i Manresa (Catalunyacaixa)* EU:C:2013:164; Case C-169/14 *Juan Carlos Sánchez Morcillo and María del Carmen Abril García v Banco Bilbao Vizcaya Argentaria, SA* EU:C:2014:2099; Case C-49/14 *Finanmadrid v Albán Zambrano and Others* EU:C:2016:98; Case C-176/17 *Profi Credit Polska SA w Bielsku Białej v Mariusz Wawrzosek* EU:C:2018:711; Case C-495/19 *Kancelaria Medius SA v RN* EU:C:2020:431; Case C-485/19 *LH v Profi Credit Polska sro* EU:C:2021:313.

[3] Council Directive 93/13/EEC of 5 April 1993 on unfair terms in consumer contracts [1993] OJ L95/29.

proved to be one possible avenue, an 'indirect remedy',[4] to address structural imbalances in the civil justice system, both from a legal and a socio-economic point of view; 'a fountain of social justice in times of drought'.[5] As such, the Directive was a portal to the CJEU and the applicability of the EU Charter of Fundamental Rights (hereinafter EUCFR or 'the Charter').

Article 47 of the Charter safeguards the right to an effective remedy and a fair hearing before an independent and impartial tribunal established by law for (alleged) infringements of EU rights and freedoms, including the rights consumers derive from the UCTD.[6] In the context of the UCTD, the number of references to Article 47 in the CJEU's case law has increased over the past decade, which coincided with a wave of crisis-induced litigation. In this chapter, I will focus on one of the many different functions of a reference to Article 47: its signalling function in debt collection cases that fall, or can be brought, within the scope of the UCTD. This function is often overlooked in existing literature that focuses on the status of Article 47 in EU law, its scope of protection and legal requirements, as well as the question whether it entails (additional) positive obligations for the Member States and their national courts. In its signalling function, Article 47 does not immediately change the outcome of a case, which could make a reference to it seem merely ornamental. However, it may still be of significance where it puts the spotlight on a shortfall in judicial remedies or procedural safeguards, and implies an even more pressing need to address the consequences of a potential fundamental rights violation. Whilst its impact may be more indirect, it contributes to 'open constitutionalisation'[7] – ie, the explicit recognition of fundamental rights issues – and may lead to structural changes in the longer run.

Insofar as effective judicial protection as an EU fundamental right has become more manifest in judicial decisions, this is in line with the Charter's aim of strengthening the protection of fundamental rights in the EU by making these rights more visible. Visibility is not just symbolic; when a problem is framed as a fundamental rights issue, the case gets a constitutional dimension. The term 'constitutional' is used here in a narrow sense: it refers to the interpretation and application of EU law in accordance with fundamental rights. It is not (only) about a lack of consumer protection against unfair terms, but (also) about a potential infringement of one of the core components of Article 47, for example, where the right

---

[4] I Barral-Viñals, 'Aziz Case and Unfair Contract Terms in Mortgage Loan Agreements: Lessons to Be Learned in Spain' (2015) 4 *Penn State Journal of Law & International Affairs* 69, 71.

[5] D Caruso, 'Fairness at a Time of Perplexity' in S Vogenauer and S Weatherill (eds), *General Principles of Law: European and Comparative Perspectives* (Oxford, Hart Publishing, 2017) 346.

[6] Article 47 of the Charter is binding on national (civil) courts when they adjudicate disputes under the UCTD: see, eg, Case C-472/11 *Banif Plus Bank v Csaba Csipai and Viktória Csipai* EU:C:2013:88, para 29. The UCTD aims to protect consumers against unfair standard terms and conditions that have not been individually negotiated. Consumers have the subjective right to take legal action and request a court to examine whether a certain term of a contract to which they are a party is unfair: see, eg, Joined Cases C-381/14 and C-385/14 *Jorge Sales Sinués and Youssouf Drame Ba v Caixabank SA and Catalunya Caixa SA (Catalunya Banc SA)* EU:C:2016:252, paras 21 and 42. The Directive's system of protection is based on the idea that consumers are in a weak position vis-a-vis their professional counterparties – traders – in terms of knowledge and bargaining power. It aims to replace the formal contractual balance with an effective balance that re-establishes equality: see, eg, Case C-137/08 *VB Pénzügyi Lízing Zrt v Ferenc Schneider* [2010] ECR I-10847, para 47; *Sánchez Morcillo* (n 2) paras 22–24; Joined Cases C-154/14, C-307/15 and C-308/15 *Francisco Gutiérrez Naranjo v Cajasur Banco SAU, Ana María Palacios Martínez v Banco Bilbao Vizcaya Argentaria SA (BBVA), Banco Popular Español SA v Emilio Irles López and Teresa Torres Andreu* EU:C:2016:980, paras 53 and 55.

[7] HW Micklitz and N Reich, 'The Court and Sleeping Beauty: The Revival of the Unfair Contract Terms Directive (UCTD)' (2014) 51 *Common Market Law Review* 771, 801; F Della Negra, 'The Uncertain Development of the Case Law on Consumer Protection in Mortgage Enforcement Proceedings: *Sánchez Morcillo* and *Kušionová*' (2015) 52 *Common Market Law Review* 1009, 1024; HW Micklitz, 'The Constitutional Transformation of Private Law Pillars through the CJEU' in H Collins (ed), *European Contract Law and the Charter of Fundamental Rights* (Cambridge, Intersentia, 2017) 74.

of consumers to take legal action or to defend themselves is severely restricted or entirely excluded.[8] A reference to Article 47 in judicial decisions may signify a call for change, a transformation, of national (procedural) law. National civil courts may thus play a transformative role.[9] I submit that Article 47 can empower them in at least two ways. First, Article 47 emphasises their key position in the protection of EU (consumer) rights, which presupposes a genuine opportunity for consumers to exercise their rights *in court* and the possibility for courts to adjudicate those rights; ie, *justiciability* in a broad sense.[10] It reinforces a court-centred approach that goes beyond the effectiveness of specific instruments of EU law, like the UCTD. Second, Article 47 places the responsibility to ensure that effective judicial protection is available in practice and to set aside contrary provisions, if necessary, on the *judiciary*.[11] This turns Article 47 into a potential correction mechanism, even if the choice and design of remedies and procedures for the decentralised enforcement of EU law are primarily the prerogative of the Member States' legislatures.[12]

To illustrate the signalling function of Article 47 in this respect, I will single out one case: *Finanmadrid*.[13] A closer examination of the background of this case reveals it has a clear constitutional dimension (section II), even if the CJEU did not address the referring court's question regarding Article 47. The case touches on the role of civil courts in the EU legal order (section III), which crystallises in the field of unfair terms, but concerns a more fundamental issue: the balance between providing justice for both creditors, who seek to enforce their claims, and consumer-debtors, who may be in need of additional protection in light of their weaker position. A lack of procedural safeguards may aggravate inequalities between the parties.[14] The referring Spanish court in *Finanmadrid* mentioned Article 47 to indicate that the procedure at stake was flawed, which led to a debate about legislative reforms at the national level. Whereas the reference to Article 47 may not have been the *trigger* for these reforms, it was a clear *signal* that change was due. *Finanmadrid* shows how such a reference may enhance the visibility of systemic issues by flagging gaps and obstacles in, and creating space for, the effective judicial protection of EU (consumer) rights at the national level. This may inform judicial practices in other Member States too,

---

[8] Most requirements arising from art 47 of the Charter have been interpreted and construed judicially; see, eg, M Beijer, *The Limits of Fundamental Rights Protection by the EU: The Scope for the Development of Positive Obligations* (Cambridge, Intersentia, 2017) 309. To the extent that there is consensus, art 47 encompasses the right of access to court and an effective (judicial) remedy, the principle of equality of arms, the rights of the defence (in particular, the right to be heard), the right to legal aid and the right to adjudication within a reasonable time; see, eg, L Pech and D Sayers, 'Article 47 – Right to an Effective Remedy. D. Analysis. VII–VIII. Article 47(2)' in S Peers et al (eds), *The EU Charter of Fundamental Rights: A Commentary* (Oxford, Hart Publishing, 2014).

[9] See also C Mak, JML van Duin and LE Burgers, 'Judges in Utopia The Transformative Role of the Judiciary in European Private Law' (2020) 28 *European Review of Private Law* 865, 871.

[10] See also JML van Duin and C Leone, 'The Real (New) Deal: Levelling the Odds for Consumer-Litigants' (2019) 27 *European Review of Private Law* 1227, 1229. This understanding of justiciability is broader than the direct effect of (subjective) EU rights or the existence of a (procedural) means of recourse. It includes rights originating from directives that have been implemented in national legal systems. Practical and legal obstacles – such as a lack of knowledge or financial means, as well as restrictive procedural conditions – may equally stand in the way of the justiciability of those rights.

[11] Case C-414/16 *Egenberger v Evangelisches Werk Diakonie und Entwicklung eV* EU:C:2018:257, paras 78–79.

[12] F Cafaggi and P Iamiceli, 'The Principles of Effectiveness, Proportionality and Dissuasiveness in the Enforcement of EU Consumer Law: The Impact of a Triad on the Choice of Civil Remedies and Administrative Sanctions' (2017) 25 *European Review of Private Law* 575, 580.

[13] *Finanmadrid* (n 2).

[14] M González Pascual, 'Social Rights Protection and Financial Crisis in Europe: The Right to Housing, a Cautionary Tale' (2016) 9 *Inter-American and European Human Rights Journal* 260, 269–72.

for instance, in The Netherlands (section IV), where Article 47 is less visible. I conclude this chapter with a plea for 'open constitutionalisation' in order to raise further awareness about the importance of effective judicial protection in consumer cases and the (added) value of Article 47 in this respect.

II. ARTICLE 47 AND ORDERS FOR PAYMENT ISSUED AGAINST CONSUMERS IN SPAIN

In the wake of the 2007/2008 financial crisis, many creditors in Spain resorted to special expedited procedures for the collection of outstanding debts. One of these so-called 'privileged procedures'[15] is the order for payment procedure (*proceso monitorio*), aimed at granting creditors easy and rapid access to justice for uncontested pecuniary claims up to €250,000.[16] Compared to the ordinary model of adversarial court proceedings with corresponding procedural safeguards, the court only plays a limited role. The creditor must provide prima facie evidence of the claim, ie, the existence of a debt. The burden is placed on the defendant to initiate a contentious debate. If the defendant does not dispute the claim, it will only be ascertained whether the formal requirements are met. As it transpired, this was problematic where consumers were involved, who were seen as regular debtors, but often did or could not stand up for their own rights.

In *Banesto*, which pertained to the same order for payment procedure as *Finanmadrid*, the CJEU had already found there was a significant risk that consumer-debtors would not lodge an objection due to the short (20–day) period provided for that purpose, the costs of legal proceedings in relation to the debt, a lack of knowledge and/or the incomplete nature of the information available to them. This meant that creditors could deprive consumers of the protection intended by the UCTD by simply requesting an order for payment, whilst counting on the consumer's passivity and thus circumventing judicial control.[17] The CJEU held that the national court must therefore assess of its own motion – ie, *ex officio* – whether the claim is based on contractual terms that are unfair.[18] In 2014, two years after *Banesto*, the referring court in *Finanmadrid* raised a follow-up issue by reference to Article 47 of the Charter: the order for payment was no longer given by a judge, but by a court registrar (Secretario Judicial, presently called Letrado de la Administración de Justicia). Decision-making was removed from the judicial realm, whereas the order for payment had the same status as a judicial decision for the purposes of enforcement. Even though creditors still needed leave to

---

[15] H Díez García, 'Igualdad de Armas y Tutela Judicial Efectiva En El Art. 695.4 LEC Tras El Real Decreto-Ley 11/2014, de 5 de Septiembre: Crónica de Una Reforma Legislativa Anunciada (de Los AATC 70/2014, 71/2014, 111/2014, 112/2014 y 113/2014 a La STJUE de 17 de Julio de 2014)' (2014) *Derecho Privado y Constitución* 230; M Aguilera Morales, '¿Quo vadis "jura de cuentas"? ¿Quo vadis Europa? El estatus y función de los Secretarios Judiciales a examen por el TJUE' (2017) 41 *Revista General de Derecho Procesal* 3.

[16] Articles 812–816 of Ley 1/2000, de 7 de enero, de Enjuiciamiento Civil (LEC). See further I Díez-Picazo Giménez, 'Civil Justice in Spain: Present and Future, Access, Cost, and Duration' in A Zuckerman (ed), *Civil Justice in Crisis: Comparative Perspectives of Civil Procedure* (Oxford, Oxford University Press, 1999) 410; J Picó i Junoy, 'Requiem por el proceso monitorio' (2015) 2 *Justicia* 523, 524.

[17] Case C-618/10 *Banco Español de Crédito, SA v Joaquín Calderón Camino* (*Banesto*) EU:C:2012:349, paras 54–55. See also O Gerstenberg, 'Constitutional Reasoning in Private Law: The Role of the CJEU in Adjudicating Unfair Terms in Consumer Contracts' (2015) 21 *European Law Journal* 599, 610.

[18] *Banesto* (n 17) para 57. On the compensatory role of courts in this respect, see, eg, Micklitz and Reich (n 7) 803–04; JM Bech Serrat, 'Cláusulas suelo y autonomía procesal en la Unión Europea: ¿por qué no hacer una excepción a la cosa juzgada?' (2018) *InDret* 55; A Beka, *The Active Role of Courts in Consumer Litigation: Applying EU Law of the National Courts' Own Motion* (Cambridge, Intersentia, 2018) 129.

enforce the title they had obtained against the debtor, there was no (full) judicial review or examination on the merits, let alone unfair terms control.

In essence, *Finanmadrid* revolved around four problems. First, the court registrar could only check whether the formal admissibility requirements were met. The matter would only come before a court when the documents suggested that the claimed amount was incorrect or when the debtor contested the claim.[19] Second, the order was endowed with effects analogous to those of a judicial decision. Third, adjudicative competences – ie, decision-making powers – were outsourced to a court registrar, who is not an independent judicial authority and does not enjoy the same constitutional status as courts. And, fourth, there appeared to be procedural defects in the case at hand, which cast doubt on the defendants' possibility to exercise their rights of defence guaranteed by Article 47 of the Charter. There were three guarantors along-side the main debtor; for two of those, it was unclear whether they had actually been notified of the pending procedure against them.

The CJEU only dealt with the first and second problems. It held that the court ruling on enforcement of the order must have the power to perform *ex officio* control as a last resort.[20] In the words of Advocate General Szpunar, a balance must be struck 'between the notion that a court should compensate for a procedural omission on the part of a consumer who is unaware of his rights and the notion that it should make up fully for the consumer's total inertia'.[21] The mere fact that the consumer has not challenged the claim (in time) cannot justify the complete absence of judicial review. Moreover, time limits must be sufficient in practical terms to enable the concerned parties to prepare and bring an action.[22] The referring court had also mentioned the additional obstacle of mandatory legal representation, but the CJEU did not take this into consideration.

The question regarding Article 47 remained unanswered, which could be considered a blind spot. From the perspective of the UCTD's effectiveness, the possibility of judicial control at the enforcement stage might be sufficient. However, it neither addresses a potential violation of the rights of defence in the preceding stage, nor does it diminish the fact that disputes are resolved in a procedure of a (quasi-)judicial nature *outside* the judicial system. As Advocate General Kokott has pointed out in *Margarit Panicello*, the pressure that the very existence of an enforceable title exerts on consumers to discharge their (alleged) payment obligations must not be underestimated.[23] Consumers may not be able to tell the difference between a real judicial decision and an order for payment issued by a court registrar. In *Margarit Panicello*, a court registrar questioned his own competence to exercise judicial tasks by reference to Article 47. Paradoxically, this was precisely why the CJEU declared the case inadmissible: the court regis-trar was not a tribunal within the meaning of Article 267 of the Treaty on the Functioning of the European Union (TFEU).[24]

---

[19] Articles 815.3, 816.1 and 818 LEC (*Banesto* had not yet been implemented).

[20] *Finanmadrid* (n 2) paras 46 and 55.

[21] Case C-49/14 *Finanmadrid EFC SA v Jesús Vicente Albán Zambrano and Others*, Opinion of AG Szpunar, EU:C:2015:746, para 43. The term 'inertia' misleadingly implies an indifference that does not correspond with the notion of over-indebted and vulnerable consumers; it should not be equated with a renouncement of rights: Beka (n 18) 298–99.

[22] Case C-8/14 *BBVA SA v Peñalva López and Others* EU:C:2015:731, para 29.

[23] Case C-503/15 *Ramón Margarit Panicello v Pilar Hernández Martínez*, Opinion of AG Kokott, EU:C:2016:696, paras 136–37.

[24] Case C-503/15 *Ramón Margarit Panicello v Pilar Hernández Martínez* EU:C:2017:126, para 35. See also Aguilera Morales (n 15) 13, 16; J Bonet Navarro, 'La necesaria reforma de la mal llamada "jura de cuentas"' (2017) *Revista de Derecho UNED* 73, 100; MJ Garot, 'Acerca del concepto de "independencia judicial" en la reciente jurisprudencia del Tribunal de Justica de la Unión Europea' in M Aguilera Morales (ed), *Tribunal de Justicia de la Unión Europea, justicia civil y derechos fundamentales* (Pamplona, Thomson Reuters Aranzadi, 2020) 202.

In *Finanmadrid*, the signalling function of Article 47 clearly emerges in the request for a preliminary ruling. The referring court was well aware of the constitutional dimension of the case, accentuated by an explicit reference to Article 47:

> All this could constitute a violation of Directive 93/13/EEC, where judicial *ex officio* control of unfair terms is not allowed – neither in the decision-making phase nor in the enforcement. It could also be contrary to the right to effective judicial protection recognised in Article 47 of the Charter of Fundamental Rights, because the order for payment procedure without opposition is a procedure in which the court does not intervene.[25]

Article 47 signalled the lack of court involvement in the procedure at issue. This must be read against the background of the institution of a new Judicial Office (Oficina Judicial) in 2009. Court registrars were attributed decision-making powers in matters 'collateral to the jurisdictional function' – eg, to assess the admissibility of a case – for the purpose of stream-lining civil and administrative proceedings.[26] The court registrar is not a judge, but a public servant who supports the court in its task to adjudicate cases in a timely manner. Pursuant to Article 117 of the Spanish Constitution, justice must be administered by independent judges and magistrates who are members of the judiciary, and the exercise of judicial authority is vested exclusively in courts and tribunals foreseen by law. The process of 'dejudicialisation'[27] deprived courts of their jurisdictional competence, and parties of their access to an inde-pendent tribunal. Therefore, it could be a problem from the perspective of Article 47 of the Charter as well.[28]

Furthermore, the referring court in *Finanmadrid* found that the course of the proceedings jeopardised the defendants' right to be heard. Their only opportunity to contest the claim was in the order for payment procedure itself, where legal representation was mandatory. They needed to exercise their right to be heard within 20 days, otherwise an order would be issued. And if they did not lodge an objection, they could no longer claim restitution.[29] In its written observations about the case, the European Commission noted that a violation of Article 47 could have occurred in respect of the two defendants who had not been duly notified.[30] As Advocate General Szpunar observed, there might be a violation in cases where the defendant did not have access to an effective remedy due to, for example, a restrictive calculation of the time period for lodging an objection, the prohibitive costs of the procedure or the absence of recourse against an order adopted without the defendant's knowledge.[31] This can be framed as an infringement of the rights of defence, or as a restriction of the right of access to court or an effective remedy, understood as a procedural means of recourse. Actual access to a court is a necessary prerequisite for judicial protection. Indeed, any judicial intervention is based on the

---

[25] Juzgado de Primera Instancia No 5 de Cartegena, order of 23 January 2014 in case no 352/2013, para 56 (not published; copy obtained from the court upon request). Translated from Spanish: 'Todo esto podría suponer una vulneración de la Directiva 93/13/CEE, no se permite el control judicial de oficio sobre las cláusulas abusivas – ni en fase declarativa ni en ejecución. Además podría ser contrario al derecho a tutela judicial efectiva reconocido en el artículo 47 de la Carta de Derechos Fundamentales, pues el proceso monitorio sin oposición es un procedimiento en el que no interviene el Juez, sin embargo su resolución final produce efectos de cosa juzgada.'

[26] Ley 13/2009, de reforma de la legislación procesal para la implantación de la nueva Oficina judicial, preamble II.

[27] F Gascón Inchausti, 'Procesos judiciales para tutela de los consumidor' in S Díaz Alabart (ed), *Manual de Derecho de consumo* (Madrid, Editorial Reus, 2016) 138.

[28] Aguilera Morales (n 15) 5–6; Bonet Navarro (n 24) 90.

[29] Article 816.2 LEC.

[30] See the Commission's written observations of 19 May 2014 (sj.c(2014)1686122), para 33. The Commission also concluded that the court registrar could not be considered as an 'independent and impartial tribunal, established by law' (para 67).

[31] Opinion of AG Szpunar (n 21) para 95.

premise that a case can be, and is, brought before a competent court by one of the parties.[32] Excessively restrictive procedural conditions may constitute a violation of Article 47 of the Charter, as four more recent preliminary rulings in cases originating from Poland confirm.[33]

The problems with the procedure at stake in *Banesto* and *Finanmadrid* were subsequently addressed by the Spanish legislature and the Constitutional Court. As a result, the character of the order for payment procedure has fundamentally changed, at least in consumer cases.[34] In 2015, Spanish procedural law was changed to the extent that the court should perform unfair terms control (*ex officio*) at the enforcement stage.[35] A right to be heard was introduced for both parties in the order for payment procedure itself; legal representation was no longer required and the decision can now be appealed. The legislative reforms were meant to prevent a denial of justice (*indefensión*) in the sense of Article 24 of the Spanish Constitution, which could be seen as the national equivalent of Article 47 of the Charter.[36] The reference to the Charter in *Finanmadrid* thus resonates with national constitutional language. In 2016, the Spanish Constitutional Court held that a complete lack of judicial review of decisions of court registrars is unconstitutional, because it amounts to jurisdictional immunity.[37]

All of this did not have a direct impact on the outcome in *Finanmadrid*, where the referring court did perform unfair terms control in the end.[38] That does not make the case any less interesting. The diverging solutions show that how the problem is framed – either as an unfair terms issue or as a signal of unconstitutionality – defines how it is perceived. This could also be seen as a dichotomy between a functional approach to ensure the effectiveness of EU (consumer) law and the application of fundamental rights across the board.[39]

III. A SIGNAL OF UNCONSTITUTIONALITY

The case of *Finanmadrid* demonstrates that a reference to Article 47 may highlight systemic issues that transcend individual cases, such as the outsourcing of adjudicative competences. Insofar as these issues arise in cases covered by the UCTD, the fundamental rights guaranteed by the Charter are applicable.[40] The UCTD provides the connection with EU law, but these

---

[32] Case C-147/16 *Karel de Grote – Hogeschool Katholieke Hogeschool Antwerpen VZW v Susan Romy Jozef Kuijpers*, Opinion of AG Sharpston, EU:C:2017:928, para 32.

[33] *Profi Credit Polska* (n 2); Case C-266/18 *Aqua Med sp z oo v Irena Skóra* EU:C:2019:282; *Kancelaria Medius* (n 2).

[34] Picó i Junoy (n 16) 525–26; MP Calderón Cuadrado, 'Derechos, proceso y crisis de la justicia' (2015) 37 *Revista General de Derecho Procesal* 43; L Gómez Amigo, 'Control de las cláusulas abusivas y garantías procesales en los procesos con técnica monitoria, a la luz de la jurisprudencia reciente' (2019) *Revista General de Derecho Procesal* 11.

[35] Articles 552.1 and 815.4 LEC; Ley 42/2015, de reforma de la Ley de Enjuiciamiento Civil.

[36] See, eg, Case C-869/19 *L v Banco de Caja España de Inversiones*, request for a preliminary ruling from the Tribunal Supremo (currently pending before the CJEU). See also, eg, Audiencia Provincial de Barcelona (Sección 15ª), judgment no 407/2014 of 15 December 2014, JUR\2015\86196 (in the national proceedings following *Aziz* (n 2)); Audiencia Provincial de Madrid (Sección 10ª), order no 452/2016 of 22 December 2016, JUR\2017\25699.

[37] Tribunal Constitucional, judgment no 58/2016 of 17 March 2016, ES:TC:2016:58; see also Bonet Navarro (n 24) 101; P Concellón Fernández, 'Dialogando con Luxemburgo: Los órganos jurisdiccionales españoles y la cuestión prejudicial (1986–2017)' (PhD thesis, Universidad de Oviedo, 2018) 57–58, http://digibuo.uniovi.es/dspace/handle/10651/46902. In 2019, the Constitutional Court declared a similar type of procedure (*jura de cuentas*) to be unconstitutional due to the lack of judicial review: Tribunal Constitucional, judgment no 34/2019 of 14 March 2019, ES:TC:2019:34.

[38] Juzgado de Primera Instancia No 5 de Cartagena, order of 23 January 2014 in case no 352/2013 (not published).

[39] See also E Frantziou, 'The Horizontal Effect of the Charter of Fundamental Rights of the EU: Rediscovering the Reasons for Horizontality' (2015) 21 *European Law Journal* 657, 665–66.

[40] See, most recently, *Profi Credit Polska* (n 2) para 54.

issues are more fundamental than the Directive's effectiveness. Procedural difficulties may deter or prevent consumers from going to court. This is especially problematic when they are the defendant, and the possibility of judicial intervention depends on them lodging an objection against (the enforcement of) a claim. *Ex officio* control is only part of the solution; it neither removes procedural obstacles, such as time limits or costs, nor does it remedy an infringement of the right to be heard. Article 47 has its own identity and rationale.[41] It not only pertains to the effective enforcement of EU (consumer) rights, but also to the concept of EU citizenship and expectations of a fair and efficient justice system.[42] It reflects the importance attached by the EU legal order to court-based justice for EU citizens, who have individually enforceable rights that must be upheld by courts.[43] Access to court comes with procedural guarantees, such as judicial independence, and ensures the application of national and EU law.[44] Moreover, due process could be viewed as an end in itself.[45]

The fundamental right to effective judicial protection is not absolute, but it may not be denied altogether either.[46] In this respect, a differentiation could be made between, on the one hand, rules that obstruct (access to) an effective judicial remedy and thus impinge on the core components of Article 47, and, on the other hand, rules that merely regulate (and complicate) legal proceedings.[47] Not all procedural issues are fundamental rights issues. The fact that consumers must take certain steps to assert their rights does not automatically mean they do not enjoy effective judicial protection. If procedural rules preclude consumers from exercising their rights or prevent courts from protecting them, it may nevertheless become a fundamental rights issue. Pursuant to Article 52(1) of the Charter, the essence of Charter rights must always be respected; Dougan refers to 'an irreducible core of protection'.[48] Tridimas and Gentile argue that EU fundamental rights have their own identity (essence) that

---

[41] See, eg, Case C-69/10 *Brahim Samba Diouf v Ministre du Travail, de l'Emploi et de l'Immigration*, Opinion of AG Cruz Villalón, EU:C:2011:102, para 39; S Prechal and R Widdershoven, 'Redefining the Relationship between "Rewe-Effectiveness" and Effective Judicial Protection' (2011) 4 *Review of European Administrative Law* 31, 50; M Safjan and D Düsterhaus, 'A Union of Effective Judicial Protection: Addressing a Multi-level Challenge through the Lens of Article 47 CFREU' (2014) 33 *Yearbook of European Law* 3, 37–38; J Krommendijk, 'Is There Light on the Horizon? The Distinction between Rewe Effectiveness and the Principle of Effective Judicial Protection in Article 47 of the Charter after Orizzonte' (2016) 53 *Common Market Law Review* 1395, 1405.

[42] M Tulibacka, 'Europeanization of Civil Procedure: In Search of a Coherent Approach' (2009) 46 *Common Market Law Review* 1527, 1535; E Storskrubb, *Civil Procedure and EU Law: A Policy Area Uncovered* (Oxford, Oxford University Press, 2008) 83.

[43] HW Micklitz, 'The Consumer: Marketised, Fragmentised, Constitutionalised' in D Leczykiewicz and S Weatherill (eds), *The Images of the Consumer in EU Law: Legislation, Free Movement and Competition Law* (Oxford, Hart Publishing, 2016) 41; H Collins, 'The Constitutionalization of European Private Law as a Path to Social Justice?' in HW Micklitz (ed), *The Many Concepts of Social Justice in European Private Law* (Cheltenham, Edward Elgar, 2011) 156–57.

[44] See, eg, Case C-284/16 *Slovak Republic v Achmea BV* EU:C:2018:158, paras 42 and 50; Case C-64/16 *Associação Sindical dos Juízes Portugueses v Tribunal de Contas* EU:C:2018:117, paras 37–38 and 41.

[45] See also A Östlund, *Effectiveness versus Procedural Protection. Tensions Triggered by the EU Law Mandate of Ex Officio Review* (Baden-Baden, Nomos, 2019) 250, 290; N Półtorak, *European Union Rights in National Courts* (New York, Wolters Kluwer, 2015) 11–12; Z Vernadaki, 'Civil Procedure Harmonization in the EU: Unravelling the Policy Considerations' (2013) 9 *Journal of Contemporary European Research* 298, 310; I Benöhr, *EU Consumer Law and Human Rights* (Oxford, Oxford University Press, 2013) 96.

[46] Prechal and Widdershoven (n 41) 36; H Ellingsen, 'Effective Judicial Protection of Individual Data Protection Rights: Puškár' (2018) 55 *Common Market Law Review* 1879, 1893.

[47] J Nowak, 'Considerations on the Impact of EU Law on National Civil Procedure: Recent Examples from Belgium' in V Lazić and S Stuij (eds), *International Dispute Resolution: Short Studies in Private International Law* (The Hague, TMC Asser Press, 2018) 34–35; Krommendijk (n 41) 1413.

[48] M Dougan, 'The Vicissitudes of Life at the Coalface: Remedies and Procedures for Enforcing Union Law before the National Courts' in P Craig and G de Búrca (eds), *The Evolution of EU Law* (Oxford, Oxford University Press, 2011) 431.

signals a minimum of protection and serves as a limitation on legislative discretion. They observe a strong signalling effect of constitutional language, paying tribute to the rule of law.[49] A similar signalling function is ascribed to fundamental rights in (European) private law, which may indicate that an essential social issue is at stake and incite a desired legal development.[50] According to Mak, fundamental rights may mediate between the legal and the political sphere, where they raise policy questions or make the deliberation of policy choices more explicit. The interplay between fundamental rights and private law may help to 'open up' fixed or established rules that do not provide satisfactory solutions.[51] Fundamental rights may thus be used by courts as a check on law-making powers and processes where national (procedural) law is deemed to offer insufficient protection.[52]

The reference to Article 47 as a signal of unconstitutionality in *Finanmadrid* is not an isolated instance; other Spanish courts have picked it up as well. They have acknowledged that Spanish civil procedure is very rigid and should be made more flexible following the CJEU's case law on the UCTD.[53] To the extent that there was a missing link between the substantive and procedural protection of consumers, Article 47 empowered courts to step in.[54] Another example is the case of *Sánchez Morcillo*. The referring court brought up Article 47 to point out that creditors enjoyed an unjustified procedural advantage in mortgage enforcement proceedings, because consumer-debtors could not bring an appeal under the same conditions.[55] This seems to have been a response to the Constitutional Court's formalistic interpretation of access to court.[56] The CJEU held that, as long as the case concerned unfair terms, the proceedings were subject to the requirements of effective judicial protection under Article 47, read in conjunction with the UCTD.[57] It found the asymmetric right of appeal to be contrary to the principle of equality of arms or procedural equality.[58] The provision was subsequently changed.[59]

The signalling function of effective judicial protection as an EU fundamental right also resonates with the meaning of rights and 'rights talk' as a discursive framework.[60] There is a difference between fundamental rights protection by means of structural (legislative and policy) reforms and adjudication on a case-by-case basis. Civil courts may be hesitant to

---

[49] T Tridimas and G Gentile, 'The Essence of Rights: An Unreliable Boundary?' (2019) 20 *German Law Journal* 794, 815–16. See also D Farber, 'Rights as Signals' (2002) 31 *Journal of Legal Studies* 83, 84.

[50] JM Smits, 'Constitutionalisering van het vermogensrecht' in *Preadviezen uitgebracht voor de Nederlandse Vereniging voor Rechtsvergelijking* (Deventer, Kluwer, 2003) 51, 65.

[51] C Mak, *Fundamental Rights in European Contract Law* (Alphen aan den Rijn, Kluwer Law International, 2008) 282, with reference to D Kennedy, *A Critique of Adjudication* (Cambridge, MA, Harvard University Press, 1997) 319–20.

[52] D Wielsch, 'The Function of Fundamental Rights in EU Private Law' (2014) 10 *European Review of Contract Law* 365, 365, 368, 382; Półtorak (n 45) 50.

[53] Tribunal Supremo (Sala de lo Civil), judgment no 1916/2013 of 9 May 2013, ES:TS:2013:1916; Audiencia Provincial de Barcelona (Sección 15ª), judgment no 407/2014 of 15 December 2014, JUR\2015\86196; Audiencia Provincial Toledo (Sección 2ª), order no 297/2018 of 12 December 2018, JUR\2019\72784, with reference to art 47 of the Charter.

[54] See, eg, the above-mentioned order of the Audiencia Provincial de Toledo (n 53); Audiencia Provincial de Castellón (Sección 3ª), order no 171/2014 of 29 July 2014, JUR\2015\10598, ES:APCS:2014:55A; Audiencia Provincial de Madrid (Sección 10ª), order no 223/2015 of 9 July 2015, JUR\2015\186525.

[55] Audiencia Provincial de Castellón (Sección 3ª), order of 2 April 2014, JUR\2014\179524.

[56] See, eg, Tribunal Constitucional, order no 70/2014 of 10 March 2014, ES:TC:2014:70A; Díez García (n 15) 225. See also Mak, van Duin and Burgers (n 9) 875.

[57] *Sánchez Morcillo* (n 2) paras 25 and 35.

[58] ibid paras 50–51.

[59] Article 695.4 LEC, as amended by Real Decreto-ley 11/2014, de medidas urgentes en materia concursal.

[60] B Oomen, 'The Contested Homecoming of Human Rights in the Netherlands' (2013) 31 *Netherlands Quarterly of Human Rights* 41, 72.

directly interfere in the law-making process on the basis of fundamental rights, but a reference to those rights in judicial decisions can indirectly play a role in public discussions about rights implementation. In Spain, courts were seen as the 'last trench'[61] to provide protection against the enforcement of claims that were based on unfair terms or otherwise unfounded.[62] They questioned the balance struck between the creditors' interests and those of consumer-debtors in light of their weaker position.[63] Procedural inequalities – in terms of knowledge or financial means, or a difference in procedural rights – exacerbated the contractual imbalance between the parties. Some courts conceived this as a constitutional problem, which highlighted short-falls that were more profound than a failure to perform unfair terms control (*ex officio*) – in particular, a lack of (access to) judicial remedies and procedural safeguards for consumers, which could result in a denial of justice. This cannot be justified by reference to the creditor's interest in a swift recovery of the debt or the efficient administration of justice.[64] As we have seen in, for example, *Finanmadrid* and *Sánchez Morcillo*, it can be problematic if consumer debt collection cases are dealt with only summarily, especially when the claim is based on unfair terms or there are procedural defects which cannot be remedied in appeal or subsequent proceedings on the merits. Expedited procedures should not turn into an avenue for depriving consumers of effective judicial protection.

The Spanish experience shows that unfair terms control may be a stepping stone for courts to exercise extra scrutiny with regard to procedural guarantees. Article 47 inserts a vertical dimension in the adjudication of horizontal disputes between consumers and their professional counterparts.[65] It amplifies their duty to counterbalance the weaker position of consumers, which extends into the procedural realm.[66] In addition, Article 47 authorises them – as protectors of the subjective rights of EU citizens, here in the capacity of consumers[67] – to call out errors or omissions in the procedural framework.[68] Whereas a

---

[61] J Álvarez and LF Rodríguez, *La última trinchera* (Madrid, Planeta, 2016) 107.

[62] In this respect, Beka has rightly noted that there is a fundamental distinction between a debt that is owed but the consumer is unable or unwilling to pay, and a debt that results from an unfair term and/or consumer protection legislation not having been observed: Beka (n 18) 252.

[63] F Gómez Pomar and K Lyczkowska, 'Spanish Courts, the European Court and Consumer Law: Some Thoughts on Their Interaction' in F Cafaggi and S Law (eds), *Judicial Cooperation in European Private Law* (Cheltenham, Edward Elgar, 2017) 116.

[64] Gómez Amigo (n 34) 8. The creditor's expectations to get away with a breach of EU (consumer) law can hardly be classified as legitimate and worthy of protection: see P Rott, 'The Court of Justice's Principle of Effectiveness and its Unforeseeable Impact of Private Law Relationships' in D Leczykiewicz and S Weatherill (eds), *The Involvement of EU Law in Private Law Relationships* (Oxford, Hart Publishing, 2013) 198. See also *Merkantil Car Zrt v Hungary and Four Other Applications* App No 22853/15 (ECtHR, 20 December 2018), para 66.

[65] C Mak, 'Rights and Remedies: Article 47 EUCFR and Effective Judicial Protection in European Private Law Matters' in HW Micklitz (ed), *The Constitutionalization of European Private Law* (Oxford, Oxford University Press, 2014) 242; O Cherednychenko, 'The EU Charter of Fundamental Rights and Consumer Credit: Towards Responsible Lending?' in H Collins (ed), *European Contract Law and the Charter of Fundamental Rights* (Cambridge, Intersentia, 2017) 145.

[66] M Medina Guerrero, 'Derecho a la vivienda y desahucios: la protección del deudor hipotecario en la jurispruden-cia del TJUE' (2015) *Teoría y Realidad Constitucional* 261, 273.

[67] M Ebers, *Rechte, Rechtsbehelfe Und Sanktionen Im Unionsprivatrecht* (Tübingen, Mohr Siebeck, 2016) 123–24; G Soler Solé, 'Las ejecuciones hipotecarias en España, ante la cuestión prejudicial europea' (2013) *Revista Xuridica Galega* 25, 30; JH Sahián, 'Dimensión constitucional de la tutela de los consumidores. Progresividad y control de regresividad de los derechos de los consumidores' (PhD thesis, Universidad Complutense de Madrid 2017) 455, https://eprints.ucm.es/43562.

[68] H Collins, 'The Revolutionary Trajectory of EU Contract Law towards Post-national Law' in S Worthington, A Robertson and G Virgo (eds), *Revolution and Evolution in Private Law* (Oxford, Hart Publishing, 2018) 327; HW Micklitz, 'The ECJ between the Individual Citizen and the Member States: A Plea for a Judge-Made European Law on Remedies' in HW Micklitz and B de Witte (eds), *The European Court of Justice and the Autonomy of the Member States* (Antwerp, Intersentia, 2012) 363.

reference to Article 47 does not necessarily change the outcome of a case, it has discursive or rhetorical value: it underlines the seriousness of the issue as well as the urgency of remedying it. As such, it may incite a debate on the need for procedural reforms. In Spain, this debate has been largely court-driven, but courts do not 'make law' by prescribing structural solutions. The judicial protection of consumers can be characterised as a continuous interaction between the legislature and the judiciary, with Article 47 as one of the parameters in the 'trialogue' – as Cafaggi has aptly called it[69] – between courts, law-makers and the CJEU about an upgrade of national (procedural) law.[70] In this respect, the signalling function of Article 47 can be said to have institutional[71] and transformative aspects as well.[72]

IV. ARTICLE 47 AND ARBITRATION CLAUSES IN THE NETHERLANDS

Spanish civil courts have contributed significantly to the constitutionalisation of consumer protection under the UCTD, ie, the integration of fundamental rights reasoning – and more specifically the Charter – in the adjudication of unfair terms cases. It could even be said that they have been catalysts of the development of the CJEU's case law in this respect.[73] What happened in Spain is not unique: procedural bottlenecks have also surfaced in other Member States. In the Netherlands, EU consumer law provided a reason for civil courts to exercise more scrutiny in consumer debt collection cases as well. However, Article 47 of the Charter plays a much less visible role than in Spain. An important difference is that the Netherlands does not have a constitutional tradition.[74] Dutch civil courts might see no need to refer to Article 47 if the required level of protection can be achieved via other means, in particular consistent interpretation of existing norms. But it could also be that they fail to recognise the discursive value of Article 47, as exemplified by its signalling function. This would be a missed opportunity; a reference to Article 47 may enhance the visibility of procedural inequalities and show awareness of the fundamental rights at stake.

There is no separate order for payment procedure under Dutch law. However, creditors – especially if they are 'repeat players' that bring large numbers of claims – may count on the fact that many (consumer-)debtors do not contest the claim, which could undermine the protection of consumer rights and lead to the enforcement of unfounded claims. Dutch civil courts have become more (pro)active in default proceedings, ie, in case the defendant does not appear in court.[75] They try to put a check on opportunistic debt collection practices by

[69] F Cafaggi, 'On the Transformations of European Consumer Enforcement Law: Judicial and Administrative Trialogues, Instruments and Effects' in F Cafaggi and S Law (eds), *Judicial Cooperation in European Private Law* (Cheltenham, Edward Elgar, 2017) 228, 237.

[70] N Reich, 'The Principle of Effectiveness and EU Private Law' in U Bernitz, X Groussot and F Schulyok (eds), *General Principles of EU Law and European Private Law* (Alphen an de Rijn, Kluwer Law International, 2013) 305–07.

[71] F Cafaggi, 'Towards Collaborative Governance of European Remedial and Procedural Law?' (2018) 19 *Theoretical Inquiries in Law* 235, 257.

[72] Gerstenberg (n 17) 603, 613.

[73] JA Mayoral Díaz-Asensio, D Berberoff Ayuda and D Ordóñez Solís, 'El juez español como juez de la Unión Europea' (2013) *Revista española de derecho europeo* 127, 129.

[74] T Barkhuysen, AW Bos and F Ten Have, 'Een verkenning van de betekenis van het Handvest van de grondrechten van de Europese Unie voor het privaatrecht. Deel 2: De verhouding van het Handvest tot het EVRM en de meerwaarde van het Handvest' (2011) *Nederlands Tijdschrift voor Burgerlijk Recht* 547, 547.

[75] JML van Duin and C Leone, 'Doubling down on debt? Legal responses to private debt as a business model in the Netherlands' in C Stănescu (ed), *Regulation of Debt Collection in Europe* (London/New York, Routledge, 2022) 119.

asking the creditor to provide specific information. They dismiss the claim when it is not sufficiently substantiated or they issue a higher cost order on the basis of abuse of process. The situation differs from *Finanmadrid*, because the case is adjudicated by a court and the defendant has an opportunity to challenge the claim on the merits. Still, there are a few parallels: it is not only about *ex officio* control in the event of default on the part of consumers, but also about the balance between the procedural position of both parties as well as the deterrent effect of costs.[76]

The persuasive power of Article 47 as to the rationale of judicial protection in this context becomes clear when courts are sidelined altogether. Creditors have resorted to arbitration as an extrajudicial route for debt collection, because it is easier, faster and cheaper than the judicial system.[77] This may cause tension with the effective judicial protection of consumer-debtors, which has emerged as a fundamental rights issue in cases about arbitration clauses that exclude consumers' right to take legal action or exercise any other remedy. Before arbitration clauses were placed on the 'blacklist' of standard terms and conditions in consumer contracts in 2015,[78] two Dutch courts of appeal referred to Article 47 of the Charter as a factor in the (substantive) unfairness assessment.[79] In a way, this could be seen as an instance of the signalling function: a call for blacklisting arbitration clauses ahead of legislative change. Both courts held that such clauses withhold from consumers the protection of the courts, often without having been the subject of contractual negotiations and without consumers being aware that access to court is precluded. There are no equivalent safeguards for the independence of the arbitral tribunal – notwithstanding its presumed expertise – or the application of national and EU law. A similar point was made by Advocate General Trstenjak in *Asturcom*, who found that courts must always be able to assess the validity of an arbitration clause to fully guarantee the judicial impartiality required in a state governed by the rule of law.[80] The Dutch Supreme Court recently confirmed that the fundamental nature of the right of access to court entails that when a court is requested to grant leave for enforcement of an arbitral award, it should check whether the award is based on a valid arbitration clause.[81] This means that consumers must have been given a period of at least one month from the moment an arbitration clause is invoked against them to decide whether they prefer to go to court instead. If not, enforcement of the award must be refused. The question whether and to what extent consumer arbitration is acceptable is a sensitive one.[82] In my view, there is a crucial difference between cases where consumers are the claimant and where they are the defendant. In respect of the latter, it should

[76] See further JML van Duin, 'Wie betaalt de rekening? De kostenveroordeling in de context van het EU-consumentenrecht' (2018) *Tijdschrift voor Consumentenrecht en handelspraktijken* 177.
[77] E van Gelder, 'Online Dispute Resolution: een veelbelovend initiatief voor toegang tot het recht?' (2018) *Maandblad voor Vermogensrecht* 262.
[78] Article 6:236 sub (n) of the Dutch Civil Code (Burgerlijk Wetboek).
[79] Gerechtshof Leeuwarden, 5 July 2011, NL:GHLEE:2011:BR2500; Gerechtshof Amsterdam, 17 April 2012, NL:GHAMS:2012:BX3835.
[80] Case C-40/08 *Asturcom Telecomunicaciones SL v Cristina Rodríguez Nogueira*, Opinion of AG Trstenjak, EU:C:2009:305, para 66. See also N Reich, 'Party Autonomy and Consumer Arbitration in Conflict: A "Trojan Horse" in the Access to Justice in the EU ADR-Directive 2013/11?' (2015) 4 *Penn State Journal of Law & International Affairs* 290, 320.
[81] Hoge Raad, 8 November 2019, NL:HR:2019:1731. The Supreme Court had already held that the fundamental nature of the right of access to court entails that the question whether a valid arbitration agreement has been concluded must ultimately be answered by a court: Hoge Raad, 26 September 2014, NL:HR:2014:2837.
[82] See also C Mak, 'Judgment of the Court (First Chamber) of 6 October 2009, *Asturcom Telecomunicaciones SL v Cristina Rodríguez Nogueira*, Case C-40/08' (2010) 6 *European Review of Contract Law* 437, 443; H Schebesta, 'Does the National Court Know European Law? A Note on *Ex Officio* Application after *Asturcom*' (2010) 18 *European Review of Private Law* 847, 871.

be noted that Article 47 is put forward as a *legal* argument for judicial protection; it is not solely a matter of policy or politics, but a signal in a broader debate on the role of courts in the light of EU (consumer) law.

These developments are reminiscent of what happened in Spain, to the extent that there is a wider scope for courts to intervene in consumer cases. At the same time, the justiciability of consumer rights appears to be less of a problem in the Netherlands than in Spain. Restrictive procedural conditions that affect the core components of Article 47 appear to be non-existent, so there is no need to make legislative changes. Unlike their Spanish counterparts, Dutch civil courts do not question the applicable rules themselves; they find ways within the system to achieve effective judicial protection for consumers. A failure to perform unfair terms control in a concrete case is not the same as the structural inability to do so. However, Dutch civil courts should not shy away from the constitutional dimension of consumer adjudication, which may get obfuscated by an exclusive focus on *ex officio*. Like their Spanish counterparts, they have a responsibility to address not only situational but also systemic issues, especially as regards extrajudicial enforcement.[83] Referring to Article 47 is a way to make such issues more visible.

V. A CALL FOR 'OPEN CONSTITUTIONALISATION'

The cases discussed in this chapter illustrate a signalling function of Article 47 in consumer debt collection cases. Courts may use Article 47 to deliberate about (perceived) tensions between the requirements of EU law and fundamental rights on the one hand, and national (procedural) law on the other. As Sieburgh has noted, judicial reasoning in a discursive manner is important where national law meets EU law; conflicts and discrepancies should be openly discussed to motivate why and on what basis a certain path is chosen.[84] The question whether or not there is a violation of Article 47 is not black and white; Article 47 has discursive value. In my PhD thesis I discuss other functions that exemplify this, such as a reconciliatory function where Article 47 operates as a hinge between EU and national exigencies.[85] Again in Spain, courts have resolved the alleged conflict between *ex officio* control and the so-called dispositive principle[86] by reference to Article 47 and the right to be heard. Indeed, it could be argued that there is no conflict at all, as long as both parties have the opportunity to present their views and adapt their arguments if necessary.[87]

---

[83] See further JML van Duin, 'Effectieve rechtsbescherming van consumenten door de civiele rechter: een procesrechtelijk perspectief' (2019) *Tijdschrift voor de Procespraktijk* 138.

[84] CH Sieburgh, 'Legitimiteit van de confrontatie van Europees recht en burgerlijk recht van nationale origine' in WJM Voermans, MJ Borgers and CH Sieburgh (eds), *Controverses rondom legaliteit en legitimatie* (Deventer, Kluwer, 2011) 240.

[85] See also H Schebesta, 'Procedural Theory in EU Law' in K Purnhagen and P Rott (eds), *Varieties of European Economic Law and Regulation: Liber Amicorum for Hans Micklitz* (Cham, Springer, 2014) 862; Bech Serrat (n 18) 12.

[86] That is the principle that the subject matter of the case is delimited by the parties: Case C-618/10 *Banesto*, Opinion of AG Trstenjak, EU:C:2012:74, para 33. See also E Arroyo Amayuelas, 'No vinculan al consumidor las cláusulas abusivas: del Derecho civil al procesal y entre la prevención y el castigo' in E Arroyo Amayuelas and A Serrano de Nicolás (eds), *La Europeización del Derecho privado: cuestiones actuales* (Madrid, Marcial Pons, 2016) 71–72; V Pérez Daudí, *La protección procesal del consumidor y el orden público comunitario* (Barcelona, Atelier, 2018) 161.

[87] AF Carrasco Perera and MC González Carrasco, 'La doctrina casacional sobre la transparencia de las cláusulas suelo conculca la garantía constitucional de la tutela judicial efectiva' (2013) *Revista CESCO de Derecho de Consumo* 150–52; J Nieva Fenoll, 'La actuación de oficio del juez nacional europeo' (2017) *Justicia* 181, 204–05. An example can be found in the above-cited judgment of the Audiencia Provincial de Barcelona of 15 December 2014 (n 36).

How far the judicial protection of consumers should go in light of EU law and fundamental rights is far from settled. Open questions concern, inter alia, the scope of protection, the extent to which Article 47 entails positive obligations, limitations to (CJ)EU interference in the decentralised enforcement of EU rights, and limitations to the role of courts in providing (access to) justice. Insofar as there is still a 'civil justice gap', Article 47 is not a universal remedy. However, it may provide a source of inspiration for the ongoing discourse on effective judicial protection under EU (consumer) law. It does not impose specific solutions from above, but it empowers courts (and litigants) from below to expose potential fundamental rights issues. The (added) value of Article 47 is in the eye of the beholder: it is ultimately determined by the meaning attached to it by courts themselves, as reflected in their decisions. In its signalling function, a reference to Article 47 is a first step towards 'open constitutionalisation', which can clarify where the threshold is put and/or how the balance between competing rights and interests is struck. We need courts to show awareness about when effective judicial protection as an EU fundamental right is at stake. Otherwise, when there is a real issue with the justiciability of EU (consumer) rights, we may remain in the dark.

10

Judicial and Administrative Protection Intertwined

The Right to an Effective, Proportionate and Dissuasive Remedy

FABRIZIO CAFAGGI*

I. THE RISE OF ADMINISTRATIVE PROTECTION AND THE TRANSFORMATION OF ENFORCEMENT

T HE ENFORCEMENT GAP has been the focus of EU legislative and policy interventions in the last 20 years. The awareness that rights were hardly and unevenly enforceable across and within Member States has driven many attempts to improve the European institutional architecture towards a more effective coordination among national enforcers. Progress has been made but the gap persists, and the more recent events related to the pandemic have increased it.

The last quarter of the previous century was the time of judicial empowerment. National judges in the domain of civil remedies were provided with new instruments to become enforcers of EU law. The first quarter of this century has been the time of administrative empowerment. Independent administrative authorities have been given new and more effective powers to monitor violations and to handle both cross-border and domestic disputes related to the application of EU law.[1]

* This chapter builds on several presentations given as part of the 'Judges and Utopia' project and previously the 'REJUS' project. I would like to thank Paola Iamiceli, Raffaele Sabato, Chantal Mak, Betül Kas, Sandra Lange, Markus Thoma and Bostjan Zalar for very stimulating conversations over the years, which forced me to think over some of the ideas presented in this chapter. Responsibility is exclusively mine.

[1] I use the terms 'administrative enforcement' and 'judicial enforcement', and refrain from using the more conventional distinction between public and private enforcement. They do not coincide and the choice is conceptual and not terminological. It is beyond the scope of this chapter to compare the conceptual framework underlying this approach and the more conventional one. Suffice to say that the focus is on the public institutions, administrative authorities and courts that enforce rules and provide individuals and communities legal protection. The analysis tries to answer the question whether a distinction between administrative and judicial enforcement remains and, if so, what that is.

Administrative protection has risen in the last 20 years as the potential response to the enforcement gap.[2] Administrative enforcement encompasses sanctions, commitments and remedies. The substantive dimension includes a right to an effective administrative remedy.[3] In particular, administrative enforcement has been deployed in relation to cross-border infringements, where administrative cooperation has been regulated at the EU level to ensure concentration of powers and effective monitoring and sanctioning.[4] The extra-territorial effects of administrative decisions over firms' conducts have been regulated to ensure that remedies administered by national independent authorities can have effects throughout the EU and, to a more limited extent, even in third countries.[5] But the rise of administrative protection is not limited to cross-border infringements; rather, it permeates the full range of violations, including domestic ones. It has occurred in many areas from competition to consumer, from data protection to the environment, from financial services to utilities. The thesis presented in this chapter is that administrative protection has not risen at the expense of but rather as a complement to judicial protection.[6] We shall explore how and why they complement each other.

EU legislation has been enacted to confer new powers to independent administrative authorities (IAAs) and to public administrations involved in monitoring and enforcing rules.[7] They monitor and sanction violations of firms against consumers, and violations of individuals towards other individuals (for example, in data protection). In theory, according to the principle of procedural autonomy, the choice between administrative and judicial enforcement is left to the Member States.[8] In practice, the positive bias towards administrative enforcement of the new Regulations is clear in EU legislation and it has not yet been challenged before the Court of Justice of the European Union (CJEU) as a violation of procedural autonomy.

---

[2] Administrative protection is the combination of remedies for the victims and sanctions for the infringer deployed by administrative authorities and is subject to judicial review according to art 47 of the EU Charter of Fundamental Rights.

[3] See, eg, art 77 of the General Data Protection Regulation (GDPR) (Regulation (EU) 2016/679, [2016] OJ L119/1), which clearly defines a right to an effective remedy before the administrative authorities when it refers to the right to lodge a complaint.

[4] The competition regime established by Regulation 1/2003 ([2003] OJ L1/1) was the prototype, which was followed by the Regulation on consumer protection cooperation 2006/2004 ([2004] OJ L364/1), repealed by Regulation 2017/2394 ([2017] OJ L345/1) and, in the field of data protection, Regulation 2016/679 repealing Directive 95/46/EC ([2016] OJ L119/1). Similar phenomena have occurred in financial, banking, telecoms and electricity regulation.

[5] Interestingly, the effects of administrative remedies outside the EU are still limited, whereas the worldwide effects of court orders in the field of information provider services, regulated by Directive 2000/31/EC on electronic commerce ([2000] OJ L178/1), have been recognised in some instances. See Case C-18/18 *Eva Glawischnig-Piesczek v Facebook Ireland Ltd* EU:C:2019:821; Case C-507/17 *Google LLC, Successor in Law to Google Inc v Commission nationale de l'informatique et des libertés (CNIL)* EU:C:2019:772; Case C-311/18 *Data Protection Commissioner v Facebook Ireland Ltd and Maximillian Schrems* EU:C:2020:559, para 11. See M Szpunar, 'The Territoriality of Union Law in the Era of Globalization' in D Petrlík, M Bobek, J Passer and A Masson (eds), *Évolution des rapports entre les ordres juridiques de l'Union européenne, international et nationaux, Liber Amicorum Jiří Malenovský* (Louvain-la-Neuve, Bruylant, 2020).

[6] See F Cafaggi, 'The Great Transformation. Administrative and Judicial Enforcement in Consumer Protection: A Remedial Perspective' (2009) 21 *Loyola Consumer Law Review* 496; see also F Cafaggi, 'Tutela amministrativa, tutela giurisdizionale e principio di effettività' in P Iamiceli (ed), *Effettività delle tutele e diritto europeo. Un percorso di ricerca per e con la formazione giudiziaria* (Trento, Università degli Studi di Trento, 2020) 51.

[7] In the field of data protection, see Regulation 2016/679; in the field of consumer protection, see Regulation 2017/2394; and in the field of competition, see Regulation 1/2003, later Directive 2014/104/EU ([2014] OJ L349/1) and Directive 2019/1 ([2019] OJ L11/3).

[8] With the notable exception of competition law, where the complementarity has been an explicit EU choice with Regulation 1/2003 and in more detail with Directive 2014/104. In the field of data protection, complementarity has been the choice in Regulation 2016/679 as well.

The rise of administrative enforcement cannot reduce the level of protection.[9] A right to an effective administrative remedy should therefore be recognised as part of the general principle of good administration. Hence, the party protected with administrative instruments would enjoy a similar level of protection as the one warranted by judicial protection.

Effective sanctions and remedies presuppose enforcement coordination. Specific coordination rules between different enforcement instruments are missing.[10] The right to an affective judicial protection and the states' obligation to provide effective remedies provide the grounds for institutional coordination. Such a failure may profoundly affect the effectiveness of both consumer and data protection, and violates Article 19 of the Treaty on European Union (TEU) and Article 47 of the EU Charter of Fundamental Rights (EUCFR).[11] Thus, such rules of coordination are required by both provisions.[12]

Complementarity between administrative and judicial enforcement requires institutional and substantive coordination to ensure compliance with fundamental rights, including the right to effective judicial protection regulated by Article 19 TEU, Article 47 EUCFR and by Article 13 of the European Convention on Human Rights (ECHR). The right to an effective judicial protection should be complemented by a right to an effective administrative protection to warrant that the institutional architecture is conforming to fundamental rights and principles.[13]

---

[9] See in the field of data protection the judgment of the CJEU in Case C-132/21 *Budapesti Elektromos Művek* EU:C:2023:2 at para 43: 'Regulation 2016/679 requires, inter alia, the competent authorities of the Member States to ensure a high level of protection of the rights guaranteed in Article 16 TFEU and Article 8 of the Charter (see, to that effect, judgment of 15 June 2021, *Facebook Ireland and Others*, C-645/19, EU:C:2021:483, paragraph 45).'

[10] The general principle stated at both the EU level and according to national legal traditions is that the principle of judicial independence requires that judges cannot be bound by administrative decisions. See Case C-189/18 *Glencore Agriculture Hungary Kft v Nemzeti Adó- és Vámhivatal Fellebbviteli Igazgatósága* EU:C:2019:861 and AG Bobek's Opinion in that case, EU:C:2019:462, para 74.

[11] See S Prechal, 'Article 19 TEU and National Courts: A New Role for the Principle of Effective Judicial Protection?' in M Bonelli, M Eliantonio and G Gentile (eds), *Article 47 of the EU Charter and Effective Judicial Protection* (Oxford, Hart Publishing, 2022) 9 ff; S Prechal, 'Effective Judicial Protection: Some Recent Developments – Moving to the Essence' (2020) 13 *Review of European Administrative Law* 175; K Lenaerts, 'The Role of the Charter in the Member States' in M Bobek and J Adams-Prassl (eds), *The EU Charter of Fundamental Rights in the Member States* (Oxford, Hart Publishing, 2020) 19, 25; K Gutman, 'The Essence of the Fundamental Right to an Effective Remedy and to a Fair Trial in the Case-Law of the Court of Justice of the European Union: The Best is Yet to Come?' (2019) 20 *German Law Journal* 884; M Safjan and D Düsterhaus, 'A Union of Effective Judicial Protection: Addressing a Multi-level Challenge through the Lens of Article 47 CFREU' (2014) 33 *Yearbook of European Law* 3; S Prechal and R Widdershoven, 'Redefining the Relationship between "*Rewe*-Effectiveness" and Effective Judicial Protection' (2011) 4 *Review of European Administrative Law* 31.

[12] See the CJEU in *Budapesti Elektromos Művek* (n 9) stating at para 58 that 'Article 77(1), Article 78(1) and Article 79(1) of Regulation (EU) 2016/679 of the European Parliament and of the Council of 27 April 2016 on the protection of natural persons with regard to the processing of personal data and on the free movement of such data, and repealing Directive 95/46/EC (General Data Protection Regulation), read in the light of Article 47 of the Charter of Fundamental Rights of the European Union, must be interpreted as permitting the remedies provided for in Article 77(1) and Article 78(1) of that regulation, on the one hand, and Article 79(1) thereof, on the other, to be exercised concurrently with and independently of each other. It is for the Member States, in accordance with the principle of procedural autonomy, to lay down detailed rules as regards the relationship between those remedies in order to ensure the effective protection of the rights guaranteed by that regulation and the consistent and homogeneous application of its provisions, as well as the right to an effective remedy before a court or tribunal as referred to in Article 47 of the Charter of Fundamental Rights.' It is contended that not only art 47 EUCFR but also art 19 TEU require that coordination between administrative and judicial enforcement ensures effective protection.

[13] The right to an effective administrative remedy is part of the right to good administration, which is a principle of EU law. See Case C-219/20 *LM v Bezirkshauptmannschaft Hartberg-Fürstenfeld* EU:C:2022:89, paras 37, 42. This is an independent right from the right to effective judicial protection that is related to judicial enforcement, including judicial review of administrative decisions.

How has administrative enforcement been broadened? The role of IAAs includes both advisory and enforcement powers. Advisory powers refer to *ex ante* activities, performed in collaboration with the regulated entities.[14] *Ex ante* enforcement powers concern detection and monitoring compliance. *Ex post* enforcement powers include commitments, remedies and sanctions.[15]

The expansion of the advisory powers represents a paradigm shift within administrative enforcement and a distinguishing feature from judicial enforcement.[16] The possibility for regulated entities to seek advice over practices in consumer and data protection allows firms to learn and comply, thereby reducing the administrative burden of compliance monitoring. Advice is usually not binding, but it is extremely rare that administrative authorities contradict the advice by sanctioning *ex post* a conduct recommended *ex ante*.

Furthermore, regulated entities (traders) infringing rules are given the possibility to make commitments that eliminate or reduce the consequences of violations.[17] This opportunity is provided for the less serious infringements, whereas serious violations require sanctions.

The relationship between commitments, remedies and sanctions reflects a broader approach to administrative enforcement called the pyramidal approach.[18] The enforcer first tries soft and cooperative enforcement and, only when that fails, turns to hard and punitive instruments. This enforcement model applies not only to cross-border infringements but also to violations whose effects remain within the borders of Member States.

Why has administrative enforcement been broadened? Several concurring reasons have caused the rise and expansion of administrative enforcement.[19]

The effectiveness gap of judicial protection emerged in the traditional model, where rights were defined at the EU level and remedies at the Member State level.[20] The gap was related to the costs of accessing justice and the lack of administrative sanctions often leading to under-deterrence. This explains the EU intervention together with the need for more uniformity in Member States enforcement practices dealing with identical or similar violations.

Uneven enforcement practices across Member States have undermined EU policies and objectives.[21] The link between internal market and effective enforcement has driven the EU institutions to improve the enforcement architecture by increasing and broadening the powers of independent administrative authorities. The very limited EU competence in the criminal field and the difficulty to regulate civil judicial cooperation among Member States have also contributed to the upsurge of administrative protection. This sheds light on the modes of EU intervention.

The third (and possibly the most important) reason for the development of administrative protection is related to incentives, powers and resources.[22] Administrative authorities, unlike judges who act individually and in response to claims brought by private parties, can define an enforcement strategy with dedicated financial and human resources. Administrative enforcers

---

[14] Article 58 of Regulation 2016/679.

[15] Article 9 of Regulation 2017/2394.

[16] See art 58 of Regulation 2016/679 in the field of data protection.

[17] In the field of consumer law, see art 9 of Regulation 2017/2394 concerning authorities' minimum powers.

[18] See I Ayres and J Braithwaite, *Responsive Regulation* (Oxford, Oxford University Press, 1992).

[19] See C Scott, 'Consumer Law, Enforcement and a New Deal for Consumers' (2019) 27 *European Review of Private Law* 1279.

[20] See W van Gerven, 'Of Rights, Remedies and Procedures' (2000) 37 *Common Market Law Review* 501; C Mak, 'Rights and Remedies: Article 47 EUCFR and Effective Judicial Protection in European Private Law Matters' in HW Micklitz (ed), *Constitutionalization of European Private Law* (Oxford, Oxford University Press, 2014) 236.

[21] See recitals of Regulation 2016/679 and Regulation 2017/2394.

[22] ibid.

operate also or primarily *ex officio* and address violations that would not be brought before a court by private litigants. They have monitoring, investigative and enforcement powers subject to the principles of proportionality.[23] Hence, their enforcement strategy: (1) can be determined by the authority and does not depend on the parties' resources and objectives; (2) permits the exercise of investigative powers in relation to complex and sophisticated violations; (3) makes it possible to engage in a cooperative relationship with the infringer before and after the infringement to prevent future misconducts and mitigate the consequences of the violation.

While the horizontal coordination among administrative authorities is certainly more effective than that of national courts, the vertical dialogue with the CJEU is still precluded to administrative authorities. Courts can submit preliminary references concerning remedies and sanctions and their conformity with EU law. Administrative authorities cannot. However, administrative authorities have a duty of conforming interpretation and disapplication similarly to courts.[24]

The analysis below focuses on remedies and sanctions, but it is important to realise that sanctioning is only part of the administrative enforcement toolkit, a model that includes cooperative and hierarchical modes. Such a combination provides authorities with the power to select the most effective enforcement strategy within which sanctioning and remedies represent only one route.

The chapter proceeds as follows. Section II describes the differences between administrative and judicial enforcement. Section III examines the complementarity between administrative and judicial enforcement. Section IV analyses the function of the right to an effective remedy and its impact on the architecture of enforcement in EU law. Concluding remarks follow.

II. THE RELATIONSHIP BETWEEN ADMINISTRATIVE AND JUDICIAL PROTECTION AND THE ENFORCEMENT TRIANGLE

Regulating the relationship between administrative and judicial protection represents one of the most daunting challenges for the institutional design of EU enforcement policies.[25] They are part of the enforcement triangle that also encompasses alternative dispute resolution systems, often associated with either judicial or administrative protection.[26] They compose an enforcement triangle whose sides are all (albeit with different lengths and weights) important.[27]

---

[23] See Case C-466/19 P *Qualcomm, Inc and Qualcomm Europe, Inc v European Commission* EU:C:2021:76.

[24] See Case C-198/01 *Consorzio Industrie Fiammiferi (CIF) v Autorità Garante della Concorrenza e del Mercato* [2003] ECR I-8055. The duty to disapply national legislation which contravenes Community law applies not only to national courts, but also to all organs of the state, including administrative authorities (see, to that effect, Case C-103/88 *Fratelli Costanzo SpA v Comune di Milano* [1989] ECR 1839, para 31), which entails, if the circumstances so require, the obligation to take all appropriate measures to enable Community law to be fully applied (see Case C-48/71 *European Commission v Italian Republic* [1972] ECR 529, para 7).

[25] See Cafaggi (n 6). In that article, possible criteria to distinguish and combine administrative and judicial protection were suggested. Thus far in the EU, the only area where legislation has been enacted is competition law, where Directive 2014/104 has regulated damages and the interaction between administrative and judicial authorities dealing with the same violation. More recently, the issue has been legislated in representative actions in consumer law by EU Directive 2020/1828 ([2020] OJ L409/1). For an analysis of the interplay between administrative and judicial enforcement in light of judicial dialogue, see F Casarosa and R Sabato, 'The Impact of Judicial Interactions on the Interplay between Administrative and Judicial Enforcement' in F Casarosa and M Moraru (eds), *The Practice of Judicial Interaction in the Field of Fundamental Rights: The Added Value of the Charter of Fundamental Rights of the EU* (Cheltenham, Edward Elgar, 2022) 324.

[26] See F Cafaggi, 'Towards Collaborative Governance of European and Remedial and Procedural Law?' (2018) 19 *Theoretical Inquiries in Law* 235.

[27] In the field of data protection, see art 79 of Regulation 2016/679. On the issue of complementarity of remedies, see *Budapesti Elektromos Művek* (n 9) where the CJEU examined a preliminary reference from an Hungarian court

The rise of administrative protection has not reduced the role of judicial protection, but it has certainly rebalanced their relationship. Are they alternative or complementary modes of protecting rights? The answer, based on EU law, is clearly institutional complementarity.

Complementarity exists where objectives and instruments of enforcement differ and complement each other. Hence, in order to explain complementarity, differences need to be shown. Administrative enforcement focuses on the infringers, while judicial enforcement focuses on the victims.

Institutional complementarity refers not only to the institutions (eg, the choice between administrative authorities and the judiciary) but also to the instruments (eg, the combination between sanctions and remedies). Traditionally the distinction was based on the idea that administrative authorities (and criminal judges) administer sanctions, whereas judicial bodies administer remedies. As we shall see, this is no longer the case.

Administrative protection deploys both remedies for the victims and sanctions for the infringers.[28] Judicial protection deploys primarily remedies and, to a very limited extent, civil sanctions (*ammendes civiles*).[29]

It used to be the case that remedies focused exclusively on the injured, whereas sanctions focused exclusively on the injurer.[30] The EU has moved from a dichotomous architecture, where sanctions belonged to administrative enforcement and remedies were the domain of judicial enforcement, to a mixed architecture, where both enforcement bodies can exercise both sanctioning and remedial powers, but in different proportions and with different objectives.[31]

Administrative enforcers usually target the infringers. A limited role is played by individual victims, especially when they lodge complaints before administrative authorities.[32] Judicial proceedings are driven by private actors, usually the victims of the infringement or associations that represent their interests.

Complementary modes of enforcement can operate when the objectives and/or the instruments differ or diverge. There is a radical alternative when both the objectives and instruments of enforcement differ or a limited alternative when instruments differ while objectives are similar or identical. In both instances, complementary occurs. As we shall demonstrate, the functions of administrative and judicial enforcement remain rather different, despite the incremental coming together of administrative and judicial protection.

---

asking whether administrative enforcement should be given priority to judicial enforcement or whether they can proceed on parallel tracks with the possibility of reaching conflicting results. The CJEU, making specific reference to art 47 EUCFR, held that the remedies can be sought independently and concurrently. It is for the Member States to define the modes of complementarity as long as they comply with art 47 EUCFR.

[28] In the field of data protection, see art 58 of Regulation 2016/679. Interestingly the Regulation defines the possibility that sanctions are both complementary or alternative to corrective powers: 'The competent authority has the power to impose an administrative fine pursuant to Article 83, in addition to, or instead of measures referred to in this paragraph, depending on the circumstances of each individual case.'

[29] In a broad sense, judicial protection includes judicial review of administrative protection. Hence, judicial protection is made up of two areas: direct protection and judicial review of administrative protection.

[30] The term 'sanctions' includes several categories that are not always consistently deployed by EU legislation. Pecuniary sanctions are at times called 'penalties' and at other times 'fines'. See, for example, the term 'penalty' used by art 13 of the Unfair Commercial Practices Directive 2005/29 ([2005] OJ L149/22), art 8(a) of the Unfair Terms Directive 93/13 ([1993] OJ L95/29), art 23 of Directive 2008/48 ([2008] OJ L133/66) and art 84 of Regulation 2016/679. The principles of effectiveness, proportionality and dissuasiveness are at times referred to as applying to penalties, at times to sanctions, at times to fines.

[31] This change is mainly driven by the principle of procedural autonomy that leads the EU legislator to leave Member States the choice between administrative and judicial enforcement.

[32] See F Cafaggi, 'The Right to an Effective Administrative Remedy: The Principle of Good Administration and the Institutional Architecture', on file with the author.

Hence, the institutional question is not whether the instruments of protection are complementary, but rather what kind of complementarity. The rise of administrative enforcement has not cancelled the differences with judicial enforcement. Differences remain and constitute the basis of complementarity. The differences between administrative and judicial protection clearly emerge in relation to the *ex ante* advisory function and, then, to the *ex post* cooperative enforcement through, for example, commitments.

Administrative authorities can provide advice about the fairness of a practice or of a contractual term. The advisory function through recommendations characterises administrative protection and coordinates with both *ex post* administrative and judicial enforcement.

A second, and very important distinguishing feature, is monitoring compliance. Administrative authorities have monitoring tasks.[33] They have to detect violations and prevent them from occurring. Judicial protection occurs ex post, only if parties act, but there is no duty of the civil judges to monitor compliance with EU law without the parties' active role. A different perspective characterises criminal courts, but an analysis of criminal law is beyond the scope of this chapter.[34]

A third distinction between administrative and judicial enforcement concerns commitments by the infringers. Administrative authorities can authorise commitments instead of sanctions and have the power to enforce them or to terminate them and re-open the proceedings to issue sanctions.[35]

It should be clarified at the outset that the distinction between administrative and judicial protection does not coincide with that between sanctions and remedies. As will become clear, both sanctions and remedies may be available within both the administrative and the judicial domains.

Complementarity becomes more intricate in relation to the sanctioning power and to remedies like injunctions and restitution that can be administered by both IAAs and courts, albeit to a different degree in the various Member States. How complementarity operates here is not always clear-cut and there are often overlaps and even competing functions between the two modes of enforcement.

Fourth, the rise of administrative enforcement is also justified by the differences concerning the effects of decisions. In administrative enforcement the effects of remedies ordered by the authority may go beyond the requests of the claimant(s) who brought the claim before the authority. For example, an injunction issued by an IAA may have general effects and all the consumers affected by the unfair practice may benefit from the injunction regardless of whether they were parties to the administrative proceedings. The same is true for restitution. In the event of an unfair commercial practice, the administrative order upon the infringer to pay sums back can apply to all consumers who have been victims of that practice, regardless of whether they were parties to the administrative proceedings.[36] In judicial protection the effects are usually limited to the parties of the dispute and cannot apply ultra vires, except for collective actions concerning injunctions. Clearly when injunction and restitution are brought in the context of collective actions, they also have general effects and apply to all the consumers potentially involved in the practice. Injunctions prohibiting the use of unfair

---

[33] See Case C-362/14 *Maximillian Schrems v Data Protection Commissioner* EU:C:2015:650 para 47.

[34] The analysis does not include criminal judicial enforcement.

[35] Article 5 of Regulation 1/2003 expressly enables national competition authorities to adopt decisions accepting commitments when applying arts 101 and 102 TFEU. See also ECN recommendation on commitment procedures, www.ec.europa.eu/competition/ecn/ecn_recommendation_commitments_09122013_en.pdf.

[36] See, for example, Italian Council of State (Consiglio di Stato), Sezione VI, 24 February 2020, no 1368; Tribunal of Milan (Tribunale di Milano), 20 July 2021, no 6327 (unpublished) and 14 October 2021, no 8267 (unpublished).

terms or the engagement in unfair trade practices tend to have *erga omnes* effects.[37] They differ from compensatory collective actions where the European approach is usually but not always based on the opt-in mechanism and does not produce effects on those who 'decide' to stay out.

III. THE COORDINATION AND COMPLEMENTARITY OF ENFORCEMENT MECHANISMS

In order to comply with the right to an effective administrative and a judicial remedy, complementarity requires coordination: coordination between courts and administrative authorities, and, in cross-border infringements, coordination both among administrative authorities and courts, and between administrative authorities and courts. Coordination among enforcers is required and regulated by the principles of mutual recognition, mutual trust and sincere cooperation. Coordination should apply not only to cross-border infringements but also to domestic infringements with identical or similar content. Both remedies and sanctions have to be coordinated among national authorities to ensure effective protection across Member States. Coordination can operate in different ways and the degree of centralisation of enforcement power at the EU level is deeply connected to the architecture of enforcement and the respect of fundamental rights.[38]

Weak coordination leaves the individual enforcers of each Member State with significant discretion. Strong coordination often concentrates the power on a lead authority on the basis of guidelines usually defined by the European network of authorities.

A relevant facet of coordination is represented by institutional dialogue: dialogue between the courts, including vertical dialogue with the CJEU and horizontal dialogue among national courts, and dialogue among administrative enforcers. The latter, like the former, features both a horizontal and a vertical dimension. What is still missing is a proper system to regulate trilogues between national enforcers and EU enforcers.[39]

Coordination entails both procedural and substantive dimensions.[40] It affects the right of defence, the right to a fair proceeding and the right to use evidence. Often, for example, the consumer is not a party to the administrative proceedings, but can be a party to the litigation before the court. Hence, the right to defence can only be protected before the court, but the party's interests might have been prejudiced in the administrative proceeding by not issuing an injunction or not ordering restitution.

The same infringement should allow evidentiary transplants when the violation has been found by one authority whilst it is the subject of a dispute before another authority of a different Member State. If an administrative decision in one Member State has declared the existence of an unfair commercial practice, it should be possible to rely on that decision when

---

[37] Some legal systems allow courts to issue remedies with general effects beyond the litigants. See, for example, Poland discussed in Case C-119/15 *Biuro podróży 'Partner' Sp z oo, Sp komandytowa w Dąbrowie Górniczej v Prezes Urzędu Ochrony Konkurencji i Konsumentów* EU:C:2016:987 and, earlier in Hungary, Case C-472/10 *Nemzeti Fogyasztóvédelmi Hatóság v Invitel Távközlési Zrt* EU:C:2012:242.

[38] See below, section IV.

[39] See F Cafaggi, 'On the Transformation of European Consumer Enforcement Law: Judicial and Administrative Trialogues, Instruments and Effects' in F Cafaggi and S Law (eds), *Judicial Cooperation in European Private Law* (Cheltenham, Edward Elgar, 2017) 223.

[40] Procedural autonomy leaves Member States with a wide discretionary space. In relation to representative actions, see, for example, Recital 12 of Directive 2020/1828 on representative actions.

bringing an action before a court for damages and/or for restitution. Institutional coordination requires rules concerning the suspension of proceedings and prescription.[41] But coordination also concerns the combination of both sanctions and remedies in the light of the common principles of effectiveness, proportionality and dissuasiveness (the triad).[42] Their application differs in relation to sanctions and remedies; coordination to ensure consistency is necessary.

Complementarity between administrative and judicial enforcement related to sanctions and remedies can take different forms: simultaneous and sequential. In the former, both an administrative and a judicial remedy can be sought at the same time by the authority when it acts *ex officio* or as a response to a claim lodged before the administrative authority and/or a court. In the latter case, either the law or the practice may define a sequence where one mode of enforcement is conferred temporal priority over the other.

The Member States' choice between simultaneous or sequential enforcement regimes has a significant impact on the degree and the effectiveness of protection; it affects both the costs of enforcement and the efficiency of the system. This choice is constrained by the compliance with the right to an effective remedy and in particular by Article 47 EUCFR.[43]

The simultaneous or sequential structure of enforcement generates strategic interactions both between enforcement authorities and between the enforcers and the private parties.[44] Rules concerning enforcement coordination could limit the negative effects of strategic interactions and ensure consistency between enforcement decisions taken by administrative authorities and courts. Well-designed coordination can induce cooperation and ensure legal certainty and more effective protection. Lack of coordination may cause to inconsistency and legal uncertainty, leading to lower protection.

Typically, in sequential enforcement, administrative authorities act first and courts follow on. This is usually the case in consumer harm associated with violations of competition law where judicial compensatory claims follow administrative sanctions and remedies.[45] Article 9 of Directive 2014/104/EU has introduced the rule that the administrative decision may partially influence the court required to decide about damages. A valid administrative decision concerning the infringement generates a presumption of the violation before the judge who decides on the follow on compensatory claim.[46]

---

[41] See art 15 of Directive 2020/1828.

[42] See F Cafaggi and P Iamiceli, 'The Principles of Effectiveness, Proportionality and Dissuasiveness in the Enforcement of EU Consumer Law: The Impact of a Triad on the Choice of Civil Remedies and Administrative Sanctions' (2017) 3 *European Review of Private Law* 575.

[43] See Case C-73/16 *Peter Puškár v Finančné riaditeľstvo Slovenskej republiky and Kriminálny úrad finančnej správy* EU:C:2017:725; *Budapesti Elektromos Művek* (n 9).

[44] In game-theoretical terms, the simultaneous interaction between enforcers can only be based on the expectation of what the other enforcer might do. Instead, in sequential interaction, expectation is replaced by observation. The second enforcer observes what the first enforcer did and acts on the basis of the information acquired by the decision taken by the first enforcer. Sequential interaction can be modelled in different ways securing various degrees of dependence between the two enforcement proceedings. The decision to pursue both administrative and judicial enforcement and the temporal sequence have great strategic significance for the parties. See Ayres and Braithwaite (n 18); and from a different perspective M Polinsky and S Shavell, 'The Economic Theory of Public Enforcement' (2000) 38 *Journal of Economic Literature* 45.

[45] See Directive 2014/104 and Directive 2019/1. Recital 34 of Directive 2014/104 states: 'To ensure effective private enforcement actions under civil law and effective public enforcement by competition authorities, both tools are required to interact to ensure maximum effectiveness of the competition rules. It is necessary to regulate the coordination of those two forms of enforcement in a coherent manner, for instance in relation to the arrangements for access to documents held by competition authorities. Such coordination at Union level will also avoid the divergence of applicable rules, which could jeopardise the proper functioning of the internal market.' See H Ullrich, 'Private Enforcement of the EU Rules on Competition – Nullity Neglected', Max Planck Institute for Innovation and Competition, Research Paper 2021/09.

[46] This mechanism prevents not only the judge but also the defendant from bringing evidence to verify the existence of an infringement of competition law. This mechanism has been questioned for the potential violation of the right to defence. However, the possibility for the defendant in a suit for damages to seek judicial review before

However, Directive 2014/104 does not provide general principles of coordination between administrative sanctions ordered by the competition authorities and the remedies administered by courts, including but not limited to actions for compensation.

A new provision, related to coordination in the field of representative actions, has been introduced by Directive 2020/1828. According to Article 15, the parties can use the judgment or the administrative decision finding the infringement as evidence for other claims, such as compensation and restitution.[47] The legislative innovation is that regardless which authority acts first, be it the administrative authority or the court, the enforcer that follows can use the evidence produced in the other proceeding.[48] Hence, it applies to both simultaneous and sequential enforcement mechanisms. This is an important step forward to coordinate both administrative and judicial protection and collective and individual remedies.

Coordination among national administrative authorities has been regulated at the EU level.[49] The use of common positions has characterised the operations of networks of administrative authorities for example in the *Dieselgate* scandal.[50] The legislative approach requires to identify a lead authority that can carry out the investigation with the consensus of the other involved authorities.[51] It is a move towards a form of soft functional centralisation to avoid inconsistencies among national enforcers and to increase effectiveness. Participation of the other administrative authorities is necessary and various mechanisms are in place to ensure voice both in the case of action and of inertia by the lead or the competent national authority.[52]

When the infringement is cross-border and produces effects on several Member States, a question arises about the possibility that several administrative authorities proceed on a parallel track and fine the same enterprises for the same infringement. The possibility that several administrative national enforcers proceed against the same infringement has been allowed if they do not violate the *ne bis in idem* principle and operate in conformity with Article 50 of the EU Charter.[53] The CJEU applies the *ne bis in idem* principle not only to criminal proceedings but also to administrative proceedings before independent administrative authorities, when the administrative sanctions have a criminal nature.[54] The violation of the *ne bis in idem* principle occurs when there is both factual and legal coincidence, since no one can be punished twice for the same offence. Parallel proceedings are not in violation of Article 50 of the Charter if they pursue complementary aims.

---

an administrative court has been considered a sufficient guarantee for the infringer thereby excluding a violation of art 47. A different issue under national laws concerns the legitimacy of administrative pre-emption of judicial power when deciding about compensation. Rules concerning priority of administrative enforcement have always be respectful of judicial independence.

[47] See art 15 of Directive 2020/1828.

[48] Clearly the implementation of this provision will have to be carefully designed because the production of evidence in administrative proceedings follows different rules from those in judicial proceedings.

[49] See arts 56, 60 and 61 of Regulation 2016/679; arts 15 ff of Regulation 2017/2394; and Directive 2019/1. On the mechanisms of collaboration in the field of data protection, see Case C-645/19 *Facebook Ireland Ltd and Others v Gegevensbeschermingsautoriteit* EU:C:2021:483.

[50] See the Declaration of the Consumer Protection Cooperation (CPC) network on the use of defeat device software by Volkswagen Aktiengesellschaft (VW), 23 July 2021.

[51] See arts 56, 60 and 61 of Regulation 2016/679; and arts 15 ff of Regulation 2017/2394.

[52] Notice the difference between data protection and consumer protection and the possibility of exit in consumer protection regulated by art 18 of Regulation 2017/2394. In the context of data protection, see *Facebook* (n 49).

[53] The issue arose in relation to competition law and was decided by the CJEU in Case C-151/20 *Bundeswettbewerbsbehörde v Nordzucker and Sudzucker* EU:C:2022:203.

[54] ibid.

Complicated issues arise in relation to judicial review and what national courts can do when the injured parties are not satisfied with the results of administrative enforcement. An open issue is whether courts in Member States other than that of the lead authority can exercise any judicial review or whether the centralisation of administrative protection brings along that of judicial protection at least as far as judicial review is concerned.[55]

Coordination among national courts, administering remedies for the same infringement, is still missing, except for some important yet limited procedural aspects. Coordination among national administrative authorities and courts at the EU level is also missing.[56] Lack of coordination creates serious consistency problems for cross-border infringements, which are very frequent in competition and data protection and, increasingly, in consumer protection. The inconsistencies generated by a failure to coordinate may decrease protection and potentially violate Article 19 TEU and Article 47 EUCFR.

The shortcomings determined by a failure to coordinate increase at the EU level for cross-border infringements, where consistency between the 27 authorities and the 27 courts is needed. Despite common criteria, the applications by national authorities show very different approaches, as exemplified in consumer protection by the *Dieselgate* case and in data protection by the *Facebook* case.[57] The amount of the fines ordered in relation to the *Dieselgate* case differs significantly across Member States,[58] and the coordination between sanctions and other remedies like restitution and compensation differs to an even greater extent.[59] Administrative cross-border cooperation in dealing with the same infringements shows significant shortcomings despite the improvements with the new Consumer Protection Cooperation (CPC) Regulation 2017/2394 and the General Data Protection Regulation (GDPR)

---

[55] In data protection the issue is the interpretation of art 79 of Regulation 2016/679 in the light of art 47 EUCFR. See also *Facebook* (49).

[56] However, see in the field of data protection art 81 of Regulation 2016/679.

[57] In *Dieselgate*, national authorities have ordered sanctions of significantly different amounts for the same violations; see n 58 below.

[58] BEUC Report, 'Five Years of Dieselgate: A Bitter Anniversary. 2015–2020: A Long and Bumpy Road towards Compensation for European Consumers', available at www.beuc.eu/publications/beuc-x-2020-081_five_years_of_dieselgate_a_bitter_anniversary_report.pdf, at 6: 'The Italian Competition and Market Authority imposed a €5 million fine on Volkswagen AG and Volkswagen Italia in 2016 for unfair commercial practices. In November 2017, the Dutch Authority for Consumers and Markets also fined VW €450,000. Volkswagen appealed, and the case is currently reviewed by the Rotterdam Court. In December 2019, the Rotterdam Court decided to suspend the proceedings to wait for the CJEU decision in case C-693/18 seeking clarifications on the notion of "defeat device". In January 2020, the Polish Office of Competition and Consumer Protection (UOKiK) imposed a €27 million (PLN 120 million) fine against Volkswagen Poland for issuing false information in advertising materials.'

[59] Consider the different amounts received in settlements or in court judgments related to *Dieselgate*. On the different actions for compensations that have been initiated, see A Biard, 'Retour sur 6 ans de Dieselgate en Europe du point de vue des consommateurs' (2021) *Droit de la consommation – Consumentenrecht (DCCR)* 3. The field is still very dynamic, with actions and appeals pending in various Member States. Illustrative of the different amounts of compensation are the settlements in Germany, Italy and the UK. In Germany, the Federation of German Consumer Organisations and Volkswagen reached an agreement in 2020 to compensate consumers. This agreement resulted in almost 240,000 consumers being compensated, receiving between €1,350 and €6,257 depending on the model and age of their vehicles. In total, Volkswagen paid out almost €750 million in compensation (see the website of the consumer organisation: www.musterfeststellungsklagen.de/vw). In Italy, Altroconsumo launched a group action against Volkswagen. In July 2021, the court in Venice ordered Volkswagen to pay a total of approximately €200 million to 63,000 consumers involved, up to a maximum compensable amount of €3,300 EUR each. An appeal is currently pending (see the website of the consumer organisation: www.altroconsumo.it/auto-e-moto/automobili/news/altroconsumo-contro-volkswagen). In the UK, it has been recently reported that Volkswagen has agreed to pay £193 million to settle 91,000 legal claims in England and Wales. The claimants will each receive average payments of more than £2,100. After the settlement, the High Court in London dismissed the proceedings (see J Jolly, 'Volkswagen Settles Initial "Dieselgate" Claims with £193m Payout', *The Guardian* (25 May 2022), www.theguardian.com/business/2022/may/25/volkswagen-settles-uk-dieselgate-claims-with-193m-payout).

2016/679. Enforcement coordination is necessary to comply with the fundamental right to an effective judicial remedy enshrined in Article 47 EUCFR and with the right to an effective administrative remedy enshrined in the right to good administration.[60]

IV. THE RIGHT TO AN EFFECTIVE REMEDY AND THE COORDINATION BETWEEN ADMINISTRATIVE AND JUDICIAL PROTECTION

Effective protection should be warranted in both judicial and administrative enforcement. The right to effective judicial protection should therefore be combined with the right to effective administrative protection.

Fundamental rights have come to play a paramount role in making administrative and judicial protection effective.[61] An increasing institutional component of fundamental rights combines the conventional individual dimension with a collective and an organisational facet. Institutional choices concerning the national architectures of enforcement affect the effectiveness of rights' protection and should be subject to judicial scrutiny with deference to the political discretion belonging to national legislators.

Article 19(1) TEU and Article 47 EUCFR define the obligations of Member States and the rights of individuals and organisations to an effective judicial remedy.[62] Their impact varies depending on whether sanctions and remedies have criminal nature.[63] Article 47 EUCFR corresponds but does not coincide with Articles 6 and 13 ECHR.[64] It is directly applicable.[65] Its relationship with the principle of effectiveness is still disputed, but the CJEU has established continuity between the two.[66] National constitutions contain a similar principle.[67] When the administrative or civil sanctions have a penal nature with a dominant punitive component, procedural guarantees for the application of Article 6(2) and (3) ECHR increase.[68] Directive 2020/1828 has broadened the collective right to a remedy both before

---

[60] See, for example, Recital 19 of Directive 2020/1828.

[61] See Prechal, 'Effective Judicial Protection: Some Recent Developments' (n 11); R Mastroianni, 'Sui rapporti tra Carte e Corti: nuovi sviluppi nella ricerca di un sistema rapido ed efficace di tutela dei diritti fondamentali' (2020) 5 *European Papers* 493.

[62] See Case C-64/16 *Associação Sindical dos Juízes Portugueses v Tribunal de Contas* EU:C:2018:117. See more specifically the judgments on judicial independence and the right to effective judicial protection. Compare, for example, two recent judgments concerning the appointment of judges to the Supreme Court, one related to Poland and the other to Malta: Case C-896/19 *Repubblika v Il-Prim Ministru* EU:C:2021:311 and Case C-824/18 *AB and Others v Krajowa Rada Sądownictwa and Others* EU:C:2021:153, respectively. On this issue, see Lenaerts (n 11) 19; Prechal, 'Article 19 TEU and National Courts' (n 11) 9 ff, particularly 20.

[63] Case C-481/19 *DB v Commissione Nazionale per le Società e la Borsa (Consob)* EU:C:2021:84, para 42.

[64] See ibid paras 36–37. See Prechal, 'Effective Judicial Protection: Some Recent Developments' (n 11); K Gutman, 'Article 47: The Right to an Effective Judicial Remedy and the Right to Fair Trial' in Bobek and Adams-Prassl (n 11) 371; P Iamiceli, 'Effettività delle tutele e diritto europeo: il ruolo del giudice nel prisma della Carta dei diritti fondamentali' in Iamiceli (n 6) 1.

[65] See Case C-556/17 *Alekszij Torubarov v Bevándorlási és Menekültügyi Hivatal* EU:C:2019:626, para 56.

[66] See Prechal and Widdershoven (n 11); Safjan and Düsterhaus (n 11); E Navarretta, *Costituzione, Europa e diritto privato. Effettività e drittwirkung ripensando la complessità* (Turin, Giappichelli, 2018); Iamiceli (n 64). See also *Torubarov* (n 65) para 55.

[67] Article 13 of the Belgian Constitution; art 29 of the Croatian Constitution; art 24 of the Italian Constitution; arts 19 and 103 of the German Constitution; art 28 of the Hungarian Constitution; art 24 of the Spanish Constitution.

[68] See *Menarini Diagnostics SRL v Italy* App No 43509/08 (ECtHR, 27 September 2011), CE:ECHR:2011:0927JUD004350908; *Grande Stevens v Italy* App Nos 18640/10, 18647/10, 18663/10, 18668/10, 18698/10 (ECtHR, 4 March 2014), CE:ECHR:2014:0304JUD001864010; *A and B v Norway* App Nos 24130/11, 29758/11 (ECtHR, 15 November 2016), CE:ECHR:2016:1115JUD002413011; and *Gestur Jónsson and Ragnar Halldór Hall v Iceland* App Nos 68273/14, 68271/14 (ECtHR, 22 December 2020), CE:ECHR:2020:1222JUD006827314, where art 6 ECHR is applied to administrative proceedings.

administrative and judicial enforcers.[69] The right to a collective redress should be interpreted in the light of Article 47 EUCFR.

In the domain of administrative protection, Article 41 of the Charter, concerning the right to good administration, is only applicable to EU institutions, but the principle of good administration applies to the institutions of the Member States.[70] It includes both a procedural and a substantive dimension, as does Article 47 EUCFR.

Whether the protected right is fundamental or not might affect the content of the right to an effective remedy.[71] The procedural dimension encompasses the right to a fair and an impartial administrative proceeding, the right to judicial review, the right to defence, the right to participation, the right to be heard and the right to access documents.[72] Participation in the administrative proceedings constitutes the conceptual premise of the other rights and it parallels standing and the rights to access court and to a fair trial.

These rights differ depending on the criminal nature of the administrative sanctions.[73] When administrative sanctions of a criminal nature can be administered, the principles of *nulla poena sine lege* and *ne bis in idem* apply. The differences concerning the position of the potentially sanctioned party are significant. For example, the infringer has a right to remain silent if the sanction is of a criminal nature, whereas has a duty to cooperate and contribute to the identification of relevant facts if the prospective sanction does not have a criminal nature.[74]

Procedural guarantees differ depending on whether sanctions or remedies are at stake. In relation to remedies, the right of defence operate for both plaintiffs and defendants, and guarantees the equality of arms during administrative proceedings and during trial.[75] When both administrative sanctions and remedies are potentially involved, the most protective procedural regime should be in place.

Private claimants whose rights have been violated have a right to seek remedies before the administrative enforcer, especially when the administrative enforcer has to precede judicial enforcement in the context of sequential enforcement. It is not within the discretion of the administrative body to decide whether administering the remedy when the legal system

[69] See Recital 19 of Directive 2020/1828 on representative actions. Since both judicial proceedings and administrative proceedings could effectively and efficiently serve to protect the collective interests of consumers, it is left to the discretion of the Member States whether a representative action can be brought in judicial proceedings, administrative proceedings, or both, depending on the relevant area of law or the relevant economic sector. This should be without prejudice to the right to an effective remedy under art 47 of the Charter, whereby Member States are to ensure that consumers and traders have the right to an effective remedy before a court or tribunal, against any administrative decision taken pursuant to national measures transposing this Directive. This should include the possibility for a party in an action to obtain a decision ordering the suspension of the enforcement of the disputed decision, in accordance with national law. See also A Biard and S Voet, 'Collective Redress in the EU: Will it Finally Come True?' in A Uzelac and S Voet (eds), *Class Actions in Europe: Holy Grail or a Wrong Tail?* (Cham, Springer, 2021) 287. On Directive 2020/1828 and its relationship with the GDPR, see Case C-319/20 *Meta Platforms Ireland Ltd v Bundesverband der Verbraucherzentralen und Verbraucherverbände – Verbraucherzentrale Bundesverband eV* EU:C:2022:322.

[70] See DU Galetta, 'Il diritto ad una buona amministrazione nei procedimenti amministrativi oggi (anche alla luce delle discussioni sull'ambito di applicazione dell'art. 41 della Carta dei diritti UE)' (2019) *Rivista italiana di diritto pubblico comunitario* 165.

[71] For example, the right to data protection is a fundamental right, but the right to consumer protection is not.

[72] See, for example, Case T-791/19 *Sped-Pro SA v European Commission* EU:T:2022:67, para 23.

[73] See M Lickova, 'The Elusive Shape of the *Ne Bis in Idem* Rule' in Bobek and Adams-Prassl (n 11) 385; and M Bergstrom and H Sundberg, '*Ne Bis in Idem*: A Continuing Judicial Dialogue' in Casarosa and Moraru (n 25) 395.

[74] See *DB v Consob* (n 63).

[75] See *Biuro* (n 37). For a more detailed analysis of the positions of consumers and traders, see JML van Duin, *Effective Judicial Protection in Consumer Litigation: Article 47 of the EU Charter in Practice* (Cambridge, Intersentia, 2022).

precludes the use of the judicial system until all administrative remedies are exhausted.[76] The discretionary power concerns not the 'if', but the 'how', for example, the selection and the content of the remedy.[77] In the case of inertia or inaction of the administrative authority, the claimant has a right to go before a court and seek administrative action or ask that the judicial authority replaces the administrative authority.[78]

Both the right to a fair trial and to effective judicial protection, and the principle of good administration impose procedural guarantees related to both the defendant and the plaintiffs. However, these guarantees differ, depending on: (1) whether the proceeding is administrative or judicial; and (2) whether it concerns remedies or sanctions.

Whereas the procedural dimension of the principle of good administration has been fully analysed and both the CJEU and national courts have identified the various aspects of the principle, the substantive dimension has not. It is beyond the scope of this chapter to provide a full comparative examination of how Article 47 EUCFR and the principle of good administration affect the right to an effective remedy in administrative and judicial protection.

It is contended here that there is a right to an effective administrative remedy that private claimants can plead before IAAs for violations committed by private parties or by other public institutions.[79] When the consumer or the data subject in data protection seeks redress by requiring injunctive relief, an order of cessation, or removal from websites, they exercise a right to an effective administrative remedy.[80] Unlawful rejection of such a remedy may constitute a violation of the principle of good administration. In a similar fashion to what is stated in Article 19 TEU and Article 47 EUCFR regarding the judicial remedy, administrative remedies also relate to rights whose violation by the administrative authority can be subject to judicial review.

Yet, in the field of data protection, the GDPR goes even further. Not only does the party have a right to claim an effective remedy before a supervisory authority, but it also has a right to lodge a complaint before a court in the event of inaction by the administrative authority.[81] Clearly there is a right to judicial review of the administrative decision, which is included in the right of effective judicial protection.[82]

The relationship between the right to an effective judicial remedy and the right to an effective administrative remedy is related to the broader theme of coordination outlined

---

[76] This conclusion can be derived from *Puškár* (n 43).

[77] See Joined Cases C-293/12 and C-594/12 *Digital Rights Ireland Ltd v Minister for Communications, Marine and Natural Resources and Others and Kärntner Landesregierung and Others* EU:C:2014:238, para 68: '[T]he *control, explicitly required by Article 8(3) of the Charter, by an independent authority of compliance with the requirements of protection and security* is an essential component of the protection of individuals with regard to the processing of personal data (see, to that effect, Case C-614/10 *Commission v Austria* EU:C: 2012:631, paragraph 37)'.

[78] See *Facebook Ireland and Schrems* (n 5) paras 110–12.

[79] An explicit example is provided by art 77 of Regulation 2016/679. On the correlation between the principle of good administration and the right to effective remedy, see Cafaggi (n 32).

[80] The features of administrative remedies were defined by the CJEU in *Puškár* (n 43), para 62, when it was asked if a national legislation is compatible with art 47 EUCFR if it precludes access to judicial remedies until administrative remedies are exhausted. The administrative proceedings and remedies have to respect the essence of the right and are subject to the principle of proportionality.

[81] Articles 77 and 79 of Regulation 2016/679. On this issue and the relationship between the two provisions, see Advocate General Bobek in Case C-645/19 *Facebook Ireland Ltd and Others v Gegevensbeschermingsautoriteit*, EU:C:2021:5, para 103, referring to *Facebook Ireland and Schrems* (n 5) para 110; and Recitals 141 and 143 of Regulation 2016/679 and more recently *Budapesti Elektromos Művek* (n 9).

[82] See Article 79 of Regulation 2016/679, headed 'Right to an effective judicial remedy against a controller or processor'. See *Torubarov* (n 65) para 57.

above: the relationship between effective remedies and the optimal centralisation of enforcement power.[83] Does decentralisation of enforcement mechanisms through national authorities increase or decrease the effective protection of rights? To what extent can the principle of procedural autonomy and the enforcement choices made at the national level be limited by the compliance with the right to effective judicial and administrative protection?[84] The scope of procedural autonomy and its relationship with fundamental rights clearly concerns administrative protection and the relationship between the lead supervisory authorities and the other administrative authorities. But it also concerns courts. Despite a lack of coordination among court proceedings, the issue of coordination, especially in the case of representative actions, also concerns effective judicial protection. The architecture of EU administrative and judicial cooperation strongly relates to the right to effective judicial and administrative protection.[85]

As was underlined earlier, judicial review, which is part of the right to an effective judicial remedy, is deeply affected by the mechanisms of coordination at the EU level; there might be a persistent enforcement gap between the empowerment of administrative authorities and the absence of effective judicial review mechanisms related to the (failure of) cooperation among various enforcers.[86] Failure to cooperate may lead to the violation of effective judicial protection if judicial review is not accessible to those harmed by the violation of the right to an effective administrative remedy.

An important dimension of the right to an effective remedy is related to the institutional architecture of EU enforcement. The CJEU has established a connection between Article 47 EUCFR and the relationship between administrative and judicial enforcement.[87] Member States can choose the forms of complementarity between the two enforcement

---

[83] The issue is discussed at length by Advocate General Bobek in *Facebook* (n 81) paras 91 ff, where the idea that connects the plurality of enforcers with a higher level of protection of data subjects is questioned. The final judgment of the CJEU recognises the right of the national administrative authority not exercising leading functions to go before its national court.

[84] The limits of the right to effective judicial protection are also defined by respecting the essence of that right which might not be undermined by the principle of procedural autonomy. See Case C-497/20 *Randstad Italia SpA v Umana SpA and Others*, Opinion of AG Hogan, EU:C:2021:725, para 69: 'A limitation on the right to an effective remedy before a tribunal within the meaning of Article 47 of the Charter can therefore be justified, in accordance with Article 52(1) of the Charter, only if it is provided for by law, if it respects the essence of that right and, subject to the principle of proportionality, if it is necessary and genuinely meets objectives of general interest recognised by the EU or the need to protect the rights and freedoms of others. See, to that effect, judgment of 15 September 2016, *Star Storage and Others* (C-439/14 and C-488/14, EU:C:2016:688, paragraph 49).'

[85] See Cafaggi (n 39) 223.

[86] On this issue, see the recent preliminary reference of the Italian Council of State (Consiglio di Stato), 7 January 2022, no 68, concerning *Dieselgate* and the coordination between criminal sanctions and administrative sanctions of criminal nature issued in two different Member States for the same unfair commercial practice. In the preliminary reference the Italian Council of State asked whether the sanctions for an unfair trade practice, including pecuniary and non-pecuniary ones, have a criminal nature and in the event of this being the case, whether there would be a violation of the *ne bis in idem* principle if the legal person had already been sanctioned with a criminal sanction in a different Member State. See Case C-27/22 *Volkswagen Group Italia SpA, Volkswagen Aktiengesellschaft v Autorità Garante della Concorrenza e del Mercato* (pending).

[87] *Puškár* (n 43): '1. Article 47 of the Charter of Fundamental Rights of the European Union must be interpreted as meaning that it does not preclude national legislation, which makes the exercise of a judicial remedy by a person stating that his right to protection of personal data guaranteed by Directive 95/46/EC of the European Parliament and of the Council of 24 October 1995 on the protection of individuals with regard to the processing of personal data and on the free movement of such data, has been infringed, subject to the prior exhaustion of the remedies available to him before the national administrative authorities, provided that the practical arrangements for the exercise of such remedies do not disproportionately affect the right to an effective remedy before a court referred to in that article. It is important, in particular, that the prior exhaustion of the available remedies before the national administrative authorities does not lead to a substantial delay in bringing a legal action, that it involves the suspension of the limitation period of the rights concerned and that it does not involve excessive costs.' See also *Budapesti Elektromos Művek* (n 9)

mechanisms and the sequences according to the principle of procedural autonomy. However, this choice is constrained by the necessity to respect the right to an effective judicial remedy.[88]

In relation to the right of an effective administrative remedy, the European architecture of enforcement is also very important. The allocation of responsibility among national authorities and the role of the lead supervisory authority (LSA) in the case of cross-border infringements impinges on the right to an effective administrative remedy and the principle of good administration. In particular, how enforcement powers are distributed among national authorities and which coordination mechanism is in place may strongly affect the right to an effective administrative and judicial remedy. The mechanisms of cooperation among administrative authorities set out in Regulation 2016/679 related to data protection should be interpreted in such a way as to enhance the right to an effective remedy and never lower the level of protection. Hence, not only do fundamental rights influence the combination of administrative and judicial protection, but they also affect the modes of cooperation among national administrative and judicial authorities.[89]

There is a theoretical question related to the optimal level of power concentration in the hands of the LSA in cross-border enforcement, which is similar to the problem examined above for Member States. Does concentration of power in a lead authority enhance or undermine the right to an effective administrative remedy?[90] Regardless of the difficult answer to this question, the current regimes combine the identification of lead authorities with sharing responsibilities among national authorities.[91] The shared responsibilities of administrative authorities have an impact on the right to an effective administrative remedy.[92] Hence, the definition of cooperative mechanisms among administrative enforcers should consider the respect of that right. The choice of the sharing method should enhance the enforceability of the right to an effective administrative remedy.[93] The shape of the institutional architecture influences the protection of that right. As such, disagreement or conflicts among administrative authorities cannot delay the delivery of a remedy to the claimant.[94] When administrative cooperation is effective, it increases the level and quality of protection. When cooperation fails, it reduces the level of protection and institutional responses are needed. Negligent failure to cooperate among administrative enforcers constitutes a violation of the right to an effective remedy both before the administrative enforcer and before a court.

V. CONCLUSIONS

The chapter has described two important institutional changes in the enforcement strategies at the EU level: (1) the rise of administrative enforcement in a framework of complementarity with judicial enforcement; and (2) the role of fundamental rights, particularly of effective protection in the design of the institutional architecture of enforcement.

---

on the relationship between the right to lodge a complaint before administrative authorities and the right to effective judicial remedies.

[88] *Puškár* (n 43) identifies which dimensions of the sequence have to be regulated in order to comply with art 47.

[89] See *Facebook* (n 49) para 68, in relation to the 'one-stop shop' mechanisms. See also *Budapesti Elektromos Művek* (n 9).

[90] For a more detailed analysis, see Cafaggi (n 32).

[91] See *Facebook* (n 49) and specifically Advocate General Bobek's Opinion (n 81) at para 111.

[92] On the relationship between administrative cooperation among administrative authorities and the right to an effective judicial protection, see *Facebook* (n 49). The correlation is explicit in Recitals 123 and 141 of Regulation 2016/679.

[93] See Cafaggi (n 32).

[94] The conflict among administrative authorities is expressly regulated by art 65 of Regulation 2016/679.

Complementarity of enforcement refers to both objectives and instruments. Institutional complementarity highlights the differences between administrative and judicial enforcement. The former presents a much wider set of instruments, ranging from advisory to sanctioning power that allows a combination of cooperative and hierarchical enforcement. Advisory powers and commitments belong only to administrative enforcement. Administrative enforcement has progressively adopted a cooperative approach between enforcer and injurer. Hence, the rise of administrative enforcement also reflects its transformation. Judicial enforcement is still mainly defined by the parties' litigation strategy, even if *ex officio* powers have been broadened by the principle of effectiveness and the right to effective judicial protection; lately changes have also been introduced in relation to representative actions. Administrative enforcement mechanism is predominantly authority-driven; judicial enforcement is, instead, driven by the parties.

The vast majority of Member States have chosen the complementarity between administrative and judicial protection. Two dimensions of complementarity were identified and analysed: institutional complementarity between administrative authorities and courts; and instruments' complementarity among commitments, remedies and administrative sanctions. Sanctions and remedies are common to both administrative and judicial protection.[95] What varies among Member States implementing EU law are the forms of complementarity.

The complementarity reflects the different incentives and objectives of litigation. Administrative enforcement often operates where incentives and costs to litigate are too high for private parties. Costs may be high compared to the benefits when claims are small. Costs may also be high when there is uncertainty over the causal correlation between infringements and harms. Judicial enforcement provides the victims of infringement with redress they would be unable to obtain via administrative enforcement, especially when losses are idiosyncratic.

The principles of effectiveness, proportionality and dissuasiveness apply to both sanctions and remedies.[96] On the procedural side, sanctions – especially those of a criminal nature – differ from remedies. The rights for the accused in administrative proceedings are regulated by the principle of good administration and to the extent that Article 6 ECHR and Article 47 of the Charter are applicable by those of the right to fair trial. The rights of the victims are guaranteed in judicial proceedings by Article 47 EUCFR and Article 13 ECHR.

Administrative sanctions can only be ordered by administrative authorities. The category of civil sanctions is still on the move. Administrative sanctions, within which a relevant distinction concerns their criminal nature, and remedies are often complementary and sometimes overlapping.

---

[95] According to the principle of procedural autonomy, it is for each Member State to determine whether they prefer administrative, judicial enforcement or a combination of both.

[96] See Case C-205/20 *NE v Bezirkshauptmannschaft Hartberg-Fürstenfeld* EU:C:2022:168, stating that the principles of effectiveness, proportionality and dissuasiveness have direct effect if they are unconditional and sufficiently precise. Hence, even when Member States do not transpose the rule stating that sanctions have to be effective, proportionate and dissuasive, national enforcers (both administrative and judicial) have to apply those principles. Paragraph 17 states that: 'It follows from the settled case-law of the Court that, whenever the provisions of a directive appear, so far as their subject matter is concerned, to be unconditional and sufficiently precise, they may be relied upon before the national courts by individuals against the State where the latter has failed to implement the directive in domestic law by the end of the period prescribed or where it has failed to implement the directive correctly (judgment of 6 November 2018, *Max-Planck-Gesellschaft zur Förderung der Wissenschaften*, 684/16, EU:C:2018:874, paragraph 63 and the case-law cited).' On the principles and their applications to remedies and sanctions, see Cafaggi and Iamiceli (n 42).

Remedies can be administered by both IAAs and courts. Parties have a right to an effective judicial remedy and a right to an effective administrative remedy. This conclusion is consistent with the choice given to Member States to select administrative or judicial protection or a combination of both, according to the principle of procedural autonomy.[97] If the choice of administrative protection would undermine the level of guarantees for the potentially injured party, there would be a violation to the right to effective protection.

Judicial coordination in the EU is primarily vertical through the preliminary reference procedure, whereas it is still very weak horizontally among national courts. The *Dieselgate* litigation shows that no judicial coordination is taking place and remedies differ significantly across Member States. Administrative coordination is strong, at least on paper, horizontally among national administrative authorities, but weak vertically with the CJEU, since they cannot submit preliminary references. However, there is a difference between instruments of coordination in EU administrative enforcement, for example, the European Data Protection Board and the CPC network in consumer matters.

Such coordination among national enforcers and between authorities and courts should occur in the light of the principles established by the CJEU in its interpretation of Article 47 in the *Puškár* case and its follow-up.[98] The case law grounds the institutional dimension of fundamental rights related to enforcement. Article 47 EUCFR and the principle of sound administration not only affect the degree of the centralisation of enforcement power at the EU level, but also the intensity and modes of coordination among administrative and judicial enforcers.

A coordinated application of sanctions and remedies for the same violation is needed to avoid overlapping and inconsistencies among enforcers.[99] The application of the principles of effectiveness, proportionality and dissuasiveness requires an integrated approach when the functions of sanctions and remedies are homogeneous, and a coordinated approach when the functions are heterogeneous.[100] Both dimensions suggest that better legislative coordination among enforcers is needed in order to improve effectiveness. Differences concern instruments of coordination among Member States and between the EU and the Member States.

To conclude, the right to an effective remedy is protected both before the administration and before the courts. Such protection has also constitutional grounds. The right to an effective judicial protection under Article 47 EUCFR and the right to an effective administrative remedy under the principle of good administration influence the scope and modes of procedural

---

[97] See Recital 12 of Directive 2020/1828 on representative actions: 'In line with the principle of procedural autonomy, this Directive should not contain provisions on every aspect of proceedings in representative actions. Accordingly, it is for the Member States to lay down rules, for instance, on admissibility, evidence or the means of appeal, applicable to representative actions. For example, it should be for Member States to decide on the required degree of similarity of individual claims or the minimum number of consumers concerned by a representative action for redress measures in order for the case to be admitted to be heard as a representative action. Such national rules should not hamper the effective functioning of the procedural mechanism for representative actions required by this Directive. In accordance with the principle of non-discrimination, the admissibility requirements applicable to specific cross-border representative actions should not differ from those applied to specific domestic representative actions. A decision to declare a representative action inadmissible should not affect the rights of the consumers concerned by the action.'

[98] *Puškár* (n 43).

[99] See Recital 14 of Directive 2019/2161: 'Member States could lay down the appropriate coordination mechanisms for actions at national level regarding individual redress and penalties.'

[100] See Cafaggi, 'Tutela amministrativa, tutela giurisdizionale e principio di effettività' (n 6) 51 ff.

autonomy exercised by Member States when they choose and apply the enforcement mechanisms. Both the choice between administrative and judicial enforcement and the coordination between the two by Member States have to comply with the right to an effective remedy. Failure to define coordination mechanisms at the national level may constitute a violation of Article 47 EUCFR and of the right to an effective administrative remedy that is part of the principle of good administration.

Part IV

Representation

11

Representing Future Generations Through European Private Law Climate Change Litigation

LAURA E BURGERS

I. INTRODUCTION

D EMOCRATIC SYSTEMS ARE short-term biased and fail to properly take into account the needs of future generations. Can this be solved by resorting to the judiciary? In a number of climate cases brought before courts in European private law, the claimants aim to defend the rights and interest of future generations. Hence, this chapter investigates the representation of future generations in European private law climate change litigation.[1]

I understand European private law as civil law and civil procedural law in the EU, whether enacted at the national or the European level.[2] Climate change litigation is defined as cases brought before courts to establish legal responsibility for the catastrophic consequences of global warming.[3] This phenomenon is widespread: over 1,800 climate cases have been launched worldwide, before national, regional and international fora, using administrative, criminal, national, regional and international law.[4] Thus, the relevance of this chapter's observations might exceed the European private law realm.

Whereas several private law climate cases target private parties like oil corporations, this chapter studies cases that use private (procedural) law against governmental authorities. Three cases are analysed because they each contribute important insights into how environmentalist claimants and courts treat the issue of representation of future generations: the *Urgenda* case before the Dutch civil courts; the so-called *People's Climate Case* before the Court of Justice of the European Union (CJEU), based on, inter alia, non-contractual liability of the EU under Article 430 of the Treaty on the Functioning of the European Union (TFEU); and the Norwegian *Arctic Oil* case, based on Norwegian civil procedure.

---

[1] The chapter is based on Chapter III of my PhD thesis 'Justitia, the People's Power and Mother Earth: Democratic Legitimacy of Judicial Law-Making in European Private Law Cases on Climate Change' (University of Amsterdam, 11 November 2020), www.dare.uva.nl/search?identifier=0e6437b7-399d-483a-9fc1-b18ca926fdb5, which analyses how future generations are addressed in all European private law climate cases.

[2] Civil law referring to legal fields traditionally regulating relationships between private parties, like contract, tort and property; civil procedural law referring to the procedural law regulating such disputes, and in which the two parties are treated as equals by the court.

[3] Thus excluding 'unsexy' cases; see K Bouwer, 'The Unsexy Future of Climate Change Litigation' (2018) 30 *Journal of Environmental Law* 483.

[4] See the database of the Grantham Research Institute on Climate Change and the Environment, www.climate-laws.org.

Section II looks at the transnational and intertemporal challenges of climate change and establishes that future generations are legally relevant. Section III studies problems identified in political theory with regard to representation of future generations. Section IV showcases how these problems re-emerge in the three case-studies. The chapter concludes that courts have a duty to consider future generations that they do not always observe.

II. CLIMATE CHANGE AND FUTURE GENERATIONS

A. Climate Justice

Climate change demonstrates par excellence, first, the artificiality of state borders and, second, the problematic short-termism of most legal-political systems. Both problems are captured under the call for 'climate justice'.

The artificiality of state borders becomes clear when considering climate change; no matter where greenhouse gases are emitted, they will contribute to *global* warming. Still, national boundaries prove to be real obstacles to formulate an effective answer to climate change. That is, measures to reduce greenhouse gas emissions come with financial costs, which make it unattractive, regarding a nation's economic competitiveness, to take such measures outside an international cooperative scheme.[5]

To calculate how much each state should fairly reduce is not easy, inter alia because nations that, since the Industrial Revolution, contributed the most to global warming – largely the 'Global North' – also benefited the most from this revolution. Moreover, they are politically amongst the most powerful and economically the most entrenched in the use of fossil fuels. Meanwhile, nations who contributed least – largely the 'Global South' – will suffer most from climate change, and lack the political and financial resources to address it.

To date, an international agreement articulating reduction obligations for each state could not be reached. Hence, the 2015 Paris Agreement called upon the parties to the United Nations Framework Convention on Climate Change (UNFCCC) to formulate their own 'nationally determined contributions'.[6] Sadly, adding up all the submitted nationally determined contributions, the reduction in greenhouse gas emissions is not enough to keep global warming below the dangerous average of 1.5-2°C.[7]

People who are not yet born have not contributed to climate change at all, but will suffer more than past and current generations. Indeed, the short-term bias of political systems poses an obstacle to effective climate regulation. There is a delay between emissions and warming. Global warming and its effects today result from greenhouse gas emissions from the 1970s and 1980s, and we know for a fact that the worst consequences of climate change are yet to come. Politicians accountable in short election cycles hardly feel the urgency of the problem and fail to implement long-term solutions. True, climate laws have been adopted in an increasing number of countries,[8] but even these will not prevent the globe from warming more than 1.5°C or even 2°C.[9]

---

[5] See SM Gardiner and DA Weisbach, *Debating Climate Ethics* (Oxford, Oxford University Press, 2016).

[6] See arts 3 and 4 of the Paris Agreement.

[7] See United Nations Environment Programme (UNEP), 'Emissions Gap Report' (December 2020), www.unep.org/emissions-gap-report-2020.

[8] See LSE Grantham Research Institute on Climate Change and the Environment, 'Climate Change Laws of the World', www.climate-laws.org.

[9] UNFCCC, '"Climate Commitments Not on Track to Meet Paris Agreement Goals" as NDC Synthesis Report is Published', www.unfccc.int/news/climate-commitments-not-on-track-to-meet-paris-agreement-goals-as-ndc-synthesis-report-is-published.

Indeed, scholarship submits that politics should become inclusive towards people from other nations and future generations.[10] This chapter focuses on future generations (but analysing the Norwegian case, it becomes clear how the temporal and national boundaries of legal-political systems are inextricably linked).[11] Several political theorists have submitted that democratic systems should enfranchise the unborn, making their voices heard today and making politics more future-oriented.[12] For example, Read proposed introducing 'guardians of the future' in an extra chamber of Parliament, who could discuss and veto future-impairing legislation;[13] whilst Dobson suggested to reserve seats in the existing Parliament for representatives of future generations to be chosen by a 'proxy-electorate' consisting of environmentalists.[14] This, in turn, has added an extra boost to the theoretical debate on the question of whether it is conceptually possible to 'represent' future generations (see section III below).

In several states, the representation of interests of future generations has actually been institutionalised. Hungary, for example, installed an ombudsman for future generations in 2008, who may advise the public authorities, interfere in environmental legal proceedings and bring pieces of legislation to the attention of the constitutional court.[15] Likewise, Wales has instituted a Future Generations Commissioner, to whom law-makers must justify that their legislative proposals are future-proof.[16] Germany, Finland and Malta have parliamentary commissions checking legislative proposals on its future dimensions, and outside Europe similar institutions exist in Canada, for example.[17] In the UK, the initiative All Party-Parliamentary Group on Future Generations aims to foreground the interests of future generations in Parliament.[18] However, these institutions have softer powers than the proposals made in political theory; they cannot impose binding decisions.

B. Future Generations are Legally Relevant

There are legal sources reflecting the importance we attach to the generations after us. To protect future generations is an aim of the UNFCCC.[19] This is echoed by, inter alia, the Paris Agreement, which calls for 'intergenerational equity'.[20] Correspondingly, an increasing number of national constitutions refer to intergenerational justice[21] – for example, the Norwegian Constitution (see section IV.C below).

---

[10] And to non-humans; see A Dobson, 'Representative Democracy and the Environment' in WM Lafferty and J Meadowcroft (eds), *Democracy and the Environment* (Cheltenham, Edward Elgar, 1998); JS Dryzek and J Pickering, *The Politics of the Anthropocene* (Oxford, Oxford University Press, 2018); as well as the Global Network on Human Rights and the Environment's Declaration on Human Rights and Climate Change www.gnhre.org/declaration-human-rights-climate-change.

[11] See below, section IV.C.

[12] For an oversight of such proposals, see D Zwarthoed, 'Political Representation of Future Generations' in M Düwell, G Bos and N van Steenbergen (eds), *Towards the Ethics of a Green Future: The Theory and Practice of Human Rights for Future People* (Oxford, Routledge, 2018) 90–93.

[13] R Read, *Guardians of the Future: A Constitutional Case for Representing and Protecting Future People* (Weymouth, Greenhouse, 2012).

[14] Dobson (n 10).

[15] See www.ajbh.hu/web/ajbh-en/the-role-of-the-ombudsman.

[16] See www.futuregenerations.wales.

[17] See, eg, 'Network of Institutions for Future Generations', www.futureroundtable.org/en/web/network-of-institutions-for-future-generations/roundtable.

[18] See www.appgfuturegenerations.com.

[19] Preamble and art 3(1) UNFCCC, signed 1992, entered into force 1994.

[20] Preamble to the Paris Agreement, signed 2015, entered into force 2016.

[21] JC Tremmel, 'Establishing Intergenerational Justice in National Constitutions' in JC Tremmel (ed), *Handbook of Intergenerational Justice* (Cheltenham, Edward Elgar, 2006).

Future generations emerge in the most important international environmental political documents of the twentieth century. The 1972 Stockholm Declaration mentions future generations three times.[22] The 1987 UN report entitled *Our Common Future* (the Brundtland Report) coined the notion of 'sustainable development', which became leading in international environmental law and politics. Sustainable development was defined as development that 'meets the needs of the present without compromising the ability of future generations to meet their own needs'.[23] This emphasis on future generations also appeared in Principle 2 of the 1992 Rio Declaration:

> 'The right to development must be fulfilled so as to equitably meet developmental and environmental needs of present and future generations.'

The UN still operate the well-known Sustainable Development Goals, an agenda serving as 'a shared blueprint for peace and prosperity for people and the planet, now and into the future'.[24]

The Treaty on European Union (TEU) in turn stipulates in Article 3 that the EU shall contribute to 'the sustainable development of the Earth' and reiterates the importance of sustainable development in Article 21(2)(f). In the TFEU, this notion is present in Article 11: 'Environmental protection requirements must be integrated into the definition and implementation of the Union's policies and activities, in particular with a view to promoting sustainable development.' Implicitly, the needs of future generations can thus be read into the constitutive treaties of the EU as well, since the definition of sustainable development refers to the needs of future generations. The Charter of Fundamental Rights of the European Union (CFREU) even explicitly states in its preamble that: 'Enjoyment of these rights entails responsibilities and duties with regard to other persons, to the human community and to future generations.'[25]

Likewise, in its preamble and Article 1, the 1998 Aarhus Convention on Access to Information, Public Participation in Decision-Making and Access to Justice in Environmental Matters refers to a right to the environment to be protected for the benefit of future generations. This convention has been ratified by all EU Member States, by the EU itself and some Asian states.

Also, the international environmental *principle of prevention* is future-oriented; states have a duty to prevent transboundary pollution and environmental harm resulting from activities within their jurisdiction or control.[26] This duty is not absolute; it only comes into play with a considerable amount of pollution or harm that may be qualified in different ways. The preventive principle is included in so many international agreements that it is considered a principle of customary international law.[27] It is laid down in the laws of the EU and in many national legal systems as well.[28]

The preventive principle is applicable when risks are relatively certain, whereas the *precautionary principle* dictates that the absence of certainty on risks should not lead to postponing

---

[22] Principle 1 of the Stockholm Declaration, 16 June 1972.

[23] World Commission on Environment and Development, *Our Common Future* (Oxford, Oxford University Press, 1987) s 3.27.

[24] See https://sdgs.un.org/goals.

[25] The CFREU also mentions sustainable development in the Preamble and art 37.

[26] PW Birnie, AE Boyle and C Redgwell, *International Law and the Environment* (Oxford, Oxford University Press, 2009) 137.

[27] N de Sadeleer, 'The Principle of Prevention' in *Environmental Principles: From Political Slogan to Legal Rules* (Oxford, Oxford University Press, 2002) 66.

[28] ibid 68–72.

precautionary measures.[29] No agreed definition exists of the latter principle.[30] It is laid down in, inter alia, Principle 15 of the Rio Declaration and Article 191(2) of the TFEU. The precautionary principle is thought to have a procedural dimension; the environment is said to be given 'the benefit of the doubt':[31] absence of risk rather than the existence of the risk has to be proven.

In short, there is widespread recognition at the international, European and national level that future generations are legally relevant. This is confirmed by a recent judgment by the German Constitutional Court.[32] I do not cover it here since it is not a European private law judgment, though constitutional interpretation issued by this court can have a significant influence on the increasingly constitutionalised private law.[33] Suffice it to say that the Court deemed the German Climate Change Act unconstitutional because it lacked specified measures for after 2030 – the Court said that this was contrary to Article 20a of the German Constitution, which stipulates that the state 'protects the environment also in its responsibility for future generations'.[34]

III. POLITICAL THEORY PROBLEMATISES THE REPRESENTATION OF FUTURE GENERATIONS

Boosted by theoretical proposals for enfranchising future generations in democratic systems, a debate emerged on the question of whether it is possible to represent future generations. Several objections were raised. First, the so-called 'plurality problem' indicates that future generations will consist of a plurality of individuals who might have different wants and needs, so that it is not evident what representatives today should stand for.[35] Second, the literature raises the 'non-identity problem', reasoning that today's policies are determining the future, so that without today's policies, particular future people will simply not be there in the same way as otherwise.[36]

To the latter two problems, one may reply that 'most advocates of future generations would call for representation of whoever will live (regardless of their identities) and not representation of all possible people'.[37] In other words, the forecasted effects of specifically global warming are so disastrous that we may assume that future generations would want to live with a stable climate, regardless of their exact identity. Therefore, they are likely to favour preventive and precautionary measures today.

---

[29] ibid 75.

[30] ER de Jong, *Voorzorgverplichtingen: Over Aansprakelijkheidsrechtelijke Normstelling Voor Onzekere Risico's* (The Hague, Boom Juridisch, 2016) ch 5; EB Weiss, 'Intergenerational Equity: A Legal Framework for Global Environmental Change' in EB Weiss (ed), *Environmental Change and International Law: New Challenges and Dimensions* (Tokyo, United Nations University Press, 1992).

[31] See Birnie, Boyle and Redgwell (n 26) 156–57.

[32] German Constitutional Court (Bundesverfassungsgericht), 24 March 2021–1 BvR 2656/18, 1 BvR 78/20, 1 BvR 96/20, 1 BvR 288/20 ('*Klimaschutz*').

[33] The constitutionalisation of private law refers to the increasing influence of fundamental rights on private law; see, eg, C Mak, *Fundamental Rights in European Contract Law: A Comparison of the Impact of Fundamental Rights on Contractual Relationships in Germany, the Netherlands, Italy and England* (Alphen aan den Rijn, Kluwer Law International, 2008).

[34] *Klimaschutz* (n 32).

[35] Touched upon in, eg, I Gonzalez-Ricoy and F Rey, 'Enfranchising the Future: Climate Justice and the Representation of Future Generations' (2019) 10 *WIREs Climate Change* 3.

[36] ibid.

[37] KK Jensen, 'Future Generations in Democracy: Representation or Consideration?' (2015) 6 *Jurisprudence* 535, 538.

Third, the indeterminacy of climate change's exact implications (when, where and how?) are raised as problematic in the context of representation of future generations.[38] I do not find this particularly convincing: any kind of policy is necessarily based on an indeterminate future (one knows that raising the maximum speed leads to more deaths, but not who will die when, where or how).

Fourth, the 'authorisation problem' is raised: since future generations cannot authorise their representative today, the latter can merely *advocate for their interests*, but not represent them: 'I can talk *about* future generations, even though I cannot speak *for* them because I cannot act with their authorisation'.[39] Similarly, it has been remarked that it is impossible to determine of which particular individuals the future generations will be composed, so that representing them is 'a matter of promoting a view on what is best for the future', and that we can at best *consider the interests* of future generations, but not 'genuinely' represent them, ie, give them a political voice today as subjects rather than consider their interests as objects.[40] Whereas 'genuine' representation presumes meaningful communication with future generations, with advocacy we consider future generations because of who we ethically want to be ourselves.[41]

Analogously, it is argued that affectedness as the trigger for democratic inclusion should merely be understood in a legal sense – to be subjected[42] – meaning that future generations do not need to be included in today's democratic deliberations.[43] They are not subjected to today's laws, as they have the democratic liberty to change the law regulating them. However, this last argument I find little convincing: today's laws now do have at the very least a factual ability to subject future people to climatic harms.

In part responding to objections like the above, alternative models of representation were developed within the framework of deliberative democracy. Instead of conceptualising representation as a three-tiered model of a *representative* being *authorised* by a *constituency*, Saward understands representation as 'claim-making'.[44] This involves five elements: a maker of representations (M) puts forward a subject (S) which stands for an object (O) that is related to a referent (R) and is offered to an audience (A). Simplifying this model, it places legitimacy of representation not in the constituency's authorisation, but in the acceptability of the representative claim with the audience. Indeed, Rehfeld proposed a theory of political representation simply 'explaining' representation 'by reference of a relevant audience accepting a person as such'.[45] For instance, if the lifeguard at the pool agrees with Lucy and James' mother that at 3 pm, the children need to get out of the water, Lucy and James' mother is accepted as their representative, regardless of whether they agree.

Saward's model encompasses representation in general, ie, it goes beyond representation by elected representatives in Parliament. We can well use it in this chapter to reconstruct the

[38] L Meyer et al, 'Risk and Rights: How to Deal with Risks from a Rights-Based Perspective' in Düwell, Bos and van Steenbergen (n 12).

[39] H Schweber, 'The Limits of Political Representation' (2016) 110 *American Political Science Review* 382, 394.

[40] Jensen (n 37) 538, 548.

[41] I follow the distinction between *morality*, resulting from universally applicable norms about what is right, and *ethics*, resulting from norms that are specific to one entity (ie, one human being, one organisation, one state) about what is good. For reflections on the ethical dimension, see D Townsend, 'Taking Dignity Seriously? A Dignity Approach to Environmental Disputes before Human Rights Courts' (2015) 6 *Journal of Human Rights and the Environment* 204.

[42] See also J Karlsson Schaffer, 'Affected and Subjected: The All-Affected Principle in Transnational Democratic Theory' (2006) Discussion Paper SP IV 2006-304, Wissenschaftszentrum Berlin für Sozialforschung.

[43] L Beckman, 'Democracy and Future Generations: Should the Unborn Have a Voice?' in JC Merle (ed), *Spheres of Global Justice: Fair Distribution – Global Economic, Social and Intergenerational Justice*, vol 2 (Dordrecht, Springer, 2013).

[44] M Saward, *The Representative Claim* (Oxford, Oxford University Press, 2010).

[45] A Rehfeld, 'Towards a General Theory of Political Representation' (2006) 68 *Journal of Politics* 1.

climate cases. There, the claim-maker (M) is the lawyer, who puts forward the subject (S), being an environmental non-governmental organisation (NGO), which stands for an object (O), namely the needs of future generations, related to the referent (R) future humans, and offered to the audience (A), which primarily consists of the judges on the court and secondarily of other people who follow the case. In Rehfeld's conception as well, it is likely to be the court that forms the relevant audience.[46] If the representative claim is accepted by the audience, it may be said that we can deliberate with the represented (future generations) through the representative (the lawyer/the NGO).

Building on work of Saward and Rehfeld, Karnein has proposed 'surrogate representation' of future generations. That is, whilst acknowledging the problems of authorisation, accountability and plurality, she reasons that there are principles on the basis of which representatives of future generations may make decisions: 'future generations could not possibly agree to be treated with less regards for their well-being than we display for our own'.[47] Such principled reasoning should be combined, she proposes, with robust institutions employing people with expertise on matters like climate change and future narratives.[48]

In short, when delving deeper into the debate about representation of future generations, not all objections are convincing. More importantly, there are authors who submit that deliberative democracy theory *does* allow for future generations to be legitimately represented.

IV. FUTURE GENERATIONS IN THREE EUROPEAN PRIVATE LAW CLIMATE CASES

How do courts respond as primary assessors of representative claims on behalf of future generations? Below, I analyse three European private law cases, investigating: what representative claim is made; how the defendant responds to this; and whether the courts accept it.

I deem the *Urgenda* case (see section IV.A below) to pertain to the area of European private law as it addresses a governmental tort and the proceedings were based on civil procedural law. The so-called *People's Climate Case* against the EU (see section IV.B below) I deem part of European private law because the claimants brought forward – echoing the *Urgenda* case – the non-contractual liability of two EU institutions, a legal basis originating in tort law. Lastly, the Norwegian *Arctic Oil* climate case (see section IV.C below) can reasonably be classified as a constitutional/administrative case, but I discuss it because it was led by civil procedural law.[49] All three cases are fascinating in many respects – here I focus on the representation of future generations.

A. The *Urgenda* Case

i. First Instance

'This case concerns us and (our heritage to) our children and the future generations of the Dutch people', the Urgenda Foundation put forward in its 2013 summons, suing the State of

---

[46] As also suggested by Gonzalez-Ricoy and Rey (n 35) 4–5.

[47] A Karnein, 'Can We Represent Future Generations?' in I González-Ricoy and A Gosseries (eds), *Institutions for Future Generations* (Oxford, Oxford University Press, 2016) 93.

[48] ibid 94.

[49] The 2005 Act Relating to Mediation and Procedure in Civil Disputes, §1-5 Act of 17 June 2005 no 90 relating to mediation and procedure in civil disputes (The Dispute Act), unauthorised translation at www.wipo.int/wipolex/en/text.jsp?file_id=372075.

the Netherlands.[50] Urgenda submitted that the state had committed a tort by having lowered its emission reduction goal for 2020 from 30% to 20% compared to 1990 levels. The issue in this case was not the state's obligation to fight climate change, but rather how fast the path towards net-zero emissions should go: Urgenda said in 2020 at least 25% should be reduced, while the state wanted to do less before and more after 2020.

In its summons, Urgenda claimed to have standing on behalf of future generations. Thus, Urgenda argued that 'her interest' (determining whether the Foundation has enough interest to bring an admissible claim to the court) concerned the collective interests of the current '*and future generations to whom she gives a voice*' (emphasis added).[51] Moreover, the summons relied on all the legal sources described above in section II.B: it argued that the state's obligations under the European Convention on Human Rights (ECHR) should be understood in light of the prevention and precautionary principles; and it invoked the Aarhus Convention, the UNFCCC and its subsequent agreements, the relevant provisions in the EU treaties, etc.[52]

Interestingly, at first instance, the state did not challenge the Urgenda Foundation's standing on behalf of future generations *as such*; it only challenged the standing on behalf of future generations *from other nations*.[53] The Hague District Court observed that Urgenda's by-laws state that the Foundation strives for a sustainable society,[54] and that 'sustainable society' has an intergenerational dimension, as is clear from the Brundtland Report.[55] Thus, the Court ruled that Urgenda had standing on behalf of future generations.[56] This looks very much like a claim of 'genuine' representation, not mere advocacy of interests,[57] which was fully accepted by the Court.

The outcome of this judgment is well known: based on a state's duty of care to prevent hazardous negligence read into Article 6:162 of the Dutch Civil Code, the Hague District Court issued an injunction against the Dutch state, ordering a reduction of emissions of at least 25% by 2020 compared to 1990 levels. The Court denied Urgenda's claim based directly on Articles 2 and 8 ECHR, but did use these provisions to interpret the rather open norm of hazardous negligence.

ii. Appeals

On appeal, the state challenged the judgment on every possible point. It argued that the interests of Dutch (and foreign) future generations 'into infinity' were not sufficiently concrete for standing under the Dutch Civil Code.[58] This emphasis on 'infinity' expressed the state's scepticism about the usefulness of the notion of future generations, coming close to the plurality problem discussed in section III above.

The Court of Appeal deemed it unnecessary to delve into this issue, noting that it was undisputed that Urgenda had standing on behalf of the current generation of Dutch people. Therefore, the state had no interest in its complaint about standing; Urgenda had standing

---

[50] *Urgenda* claim, para 43, https://www.urgenda.nl/wp-content/uploads/Translation-Summons-in-case-Urgenda-v-Dutch-State-v.25.06.10.pdf.

[51] ibid para 58.

[52] Unofficial translations available at www.rechtspraak.nl/Bekende-rechtszaken/klimaatzaak-urgenda.

[53] See, eg, Court of First Instance The Hague (Rechtbank Den Haag), 24 June 2015, *Stichting Urgenda/Staat der Nederlanden*, NL:RBDHA:2015:7145 ('*Urgenda*'), para 3.3.

[54] ibid para 4.7.

[55] ibid para 4.8.

[56] ibid.

[57] See section III above.

[58] More specifically, arts 303 and 305a of Book 3 of the Dutch Civil Code; *Urgenda* (n 53) para 4.7.

anyway.[59] So, in contrast to the Court of First Instance, which *had* allowed standing to Urgenda on behalf of future generations, the Court of Appeal did not. On the other hand, the Court of Appeal *did not* say that this would *not* be possible.

The Court of Appeal *did* explicitly reject the state's argument that Urgenda was representing an interest so large that it encompassed people who did not want to be represented by Urgenda.[60] This is an interesting objection by the state, because it echoes the theoretical objections against representation of future generations: there is no *authorisation* to legitimise representation, and there is a *plurality* problem at play (ie, future generations will be so diverse that their representative cannot determine one coherent standpoint).[61] Yet the Court of Appeal was not convinced, basing itself on the parliamentary minutes of the Dutch Civil Code: 'Regarding the idealistic interests it does not matter whether every member in society attaches as much importance to these interests.'[62]

The largest contrast with the first instance is that the Court of Appeal agreed with Urgenda that the ECHR could be directly invoked in this case. Therefore, the Court extensively addressed how the ECHR is indeed aimed at the *prevention* of violations, as the Urgenda Foundation had argued. It observed that states have positive obligations under Articles 2 and 8 ECHR to prevent future infringements.[63] Such positive obligations should not imply an impossible or disproportionate burden. Yet when the government knows that real and immediate threatening dangers exist, it must take preventive measures to avoid infringement as much as possible.[64]

The Court continued to observe that the dangers of climate change are real (something on which the parties agreed) and that they create a serious risk that the *current* generation of Dutch people will be confronted with a loss of life or a disturbance of their family life.[65] Based on international climate science and international policy documents signed by the Dutch state, the Court subsequently found that a developed country like the Netherlands is not respecting its positive obligations under Articles 2 and 8 ECHR when less than 25% of greenhouse gas emissions would be reduced by 2020.[66]

The state also argued that it is uncertain in science when, where and how dangerous climate change will materialise[67] – an objection present in the theoretical literature discussed above in section III as well. The Court of Appeal rejected this argumentation based on the precautionary principle, pointing out that the uncertainties also imply that the situation can turn out to be worse than expected: 'Hence the circumstance, that there is a lack of full scientific certainty about the effectiveness of the reduction scenario ordered, does not mean that the State can justifiably refrain from taking further measures.'[68]

In their initial 2013 summons, the claimants still declared that they felt tempted to scream before the court, because the interests of future generations are so important, but so unheard and unseen.[69] The Court of Appeal in the *Urgenda* case was decided five years later, in 2018. It appears as if the generations who were deemed 'future' in 2015 when the District Court issued

---

[59] Court of Appeal of The Hague (Hof Den Haag), 9 October 2018, *Urgenda v State of the Netherlands*, NL:GHDHA:2018:22591, para 37.

[60] Appeal by the State ('Memorie van Grieven'), para 11.3.

[61] See section III above.

[62] *Urgenda* (n 59) para 38.

[63] ibid para 41.

[64] ibid para 43.

[65] ibid para 45.

[66] ibid paras 46–53.

[67] Appeal by the State ('Memorie van Grieven'), paras 12.41–43.

[68] *Urgenda* (n 59) para 63.

[69] *Urgenda* claim (n 50), para 422.

its decision became present generations before the Court of Appeal when the Court delivered its judgment in 2018. In other words, the Court no longer deemed it necessary to justify its order to the state pointing to the interests of future generations and weighing in their damage, as the interests of the current generation would suffice. The Supreme Court upheld this reasoning.

Remarkably, the Hague Court of First Instance delivered another climate change judgment on 26 May 2021, this time against the oil giant Royal Dutch Shell, again allowing standing on behalf of Dutch future generations to the environmentalist claimants, even if the interests of current generations would suffice for their standing.[70] Space constraints preclude an analysis of this judgment here. Suffice it to say for now that seemingly, the Court of First Instance is determined to reaffirm its stance that future generations can be represented in court and thus pushes back slightly on the more cautious approach of the Court of Appeal and Supreme Court in the *Urgenda* case.[71]

B. The *People's Climate Case* against the EU

In 2018, the *People's Climate Case*[72] was brought to the CJEU. The applicants argued that the EU's climate goal for 2030 – laid down in two regulations and a directive – was contrary to higher-ranking subjective rights and objective legal principles. The defendants, the European Parliament and the European Council, objected that the case should be declared inadmissible. The General Court agreed in its Order of 8 May 2019. The claimants appealed, but the CJEU upheld the General Court's findings in March 2021.[73]

The claim of the *People's Climate Case* was concerned mostly with children rather than the unborn. It referred to 'generations to come' in the context of the alleged intergenerational element of the right to equality enshrined in Article 21 CFREU, but also here it concluded with a reference to merely children when summarising that the intergenerational element is 'warning against the postponement of measures to later years, when today's *children* will be adults and dangerous climate change (avoidable by earlier action) will already have occurred' (emphasis added).[74] In short, there is no real representative claim on behalf of the unborn, only on behalf of already living children.

This choice makes sense when considering the strict admissibility requirements before the CJEU, known as the *Plaumann* test, upon which the claim also failed on both instances before the CJEU. After all, these requirements – to be directly and individually concerned – cannot be met by the unborn. That is, we can speak of them only as a group and not as particular individuals who could be concerned in a way distinguishable from other (unborn) individuals. This means that the unborn would never stand a chance before the CJEU, for a reason that neatly echoes the theoretical problem of *plurality* discussed in section III above: we cannot know the *individual* needs of future humans.

As such, the *Plaumann* test reflects the delicate balance between law and politics. That is, its requirements suggest that EU legislation is in principle thought to be brought about

---

[70] See Court of First Instance, The Hague (Rechtbank Den Haag), 26 May 2021, *Milieudefensie et al/Royal Dutch Shell*, NL:RBDHA:2021:5337, para 4.2.4.

[71] See Laura Burgers, 'The Minimum Principle' *Völkerrechtblog* (19 January 2022), www.voelkerrechtsblog.org/the-minimum-principle.

[72] See www.peoplesclimatecase.caneurope.org.

[73] Case C-565/19 P *Armando Carvalho and Others v European Parliament and Council of the European Union* EU:C:2021:252.

[74] *The People's Climate Case* claim, section H1.e197, http://climatecasechart.com/wp-content/uploads/sites/16/non-us-case-documents/2018/20180524_Case-no.-T-33018_application.pdf.

in a democratically legitimate manner, meaning it is not for the *legal* institution of the court to reconsider whether European *politics* have done a good job, with the exception of where certain individuals are directly affected by a piece of legislation. In other words, it is the task of the court to refrain from the political domain, and exceptionally to protect individual rights against a democratic majority.[75]

Yet, the problem with the people who are affected most by climate change – in particular future generations, including children – is that *they are not a minority.* On the contrary, they consist of a very large group. The claim in the *People's Climate Case* precisely argued that the rights of children and of unborn future generations have not sufficiently been considered in the political process resulting in this legislation; their interests are overruled by the democratic majority as if they were a minority. The claim aimed to repair this problem by advancing the rights of particular *children* before the CJEU – inter alia, two children from Fiji. Yet this attempt failed because both instances of the Court ruled that even these children did not meet the criteria of the *Plaumann* test, which is premised on the legitimacy of EU legislation and thereby makes it impossible to launch a collective environmental action before the CJEU.

On appeal, the claimants provided a number of arguments to depart from the *Plaumann* test, which, they argued, was not inherent to the text of the relevant treaty provision.[76] The claimants said it was 'paradoxical, or even illogical, to find that, where a failure by the EU to fulfil its legal obligations has far-reaching consequences, no individual can demonstrate individual concern'.[77] The Court, however, agreed with the defendants that such a deviation of the *Plaumann* test would go against even the textual interpretation of Article 263 TFEU.[78]

C. The Norwegian *Arctic Oil* Case

The Norwegian *Arctic Oil* case was instigated by Greenpeace Nordic, the youth organisation Natur og Ungdom (Nature and Youth) and Besteforeldrenes klimaaksjon (Grandparents' Climate Campaign). The claimants argued against the 2016 decision of the Norwegian government to invite 13 companies to search for and produce oil and gas (petroleum) in parts of the Barents Sea. Their most important objection was that this Licensing Decision violated §112 of the Norwegian Constitution:

(1)   Every person has the right to an environment that is conducive to health and to a natural environment whose productivity and diversity are maintained. Natural resources shall be managed on the basis of comprehensive long-term considerations which will safeguard this right for future generations as well.

The claimants invoked §112 on behalf of themselves – children and youngsters – and on behalf of their grandchildren – again, living children. They are also concerned with the unborn: 'This case … concerns the integrity of Norway's commitments to the international community and its duty of care to our children, our grandchildren and generations to come.'[79] Thus, they make

---

[75] See also M van Wolferen, 'To Justifie the Wayes of God to Men: Limits to the Court's Power of Interpretation' (PhD thesis, Groningen University, 2018) 299.
[76] See *Carvalho and Others* (n 73) para 54.
[77] ibid para 56.
[78] ibid paras 71–72.
[79] *Arctic Oil* claim, 18 October 2016, opening summary (on file with author).

a 'genuine' representative claim and they do so well-founded; after all, it is the Norwegian Constitution that recognises future generations as rights-holders to a healthy environment.

The claimants argued that the Licensing Decision was incompatible with the obligation under the UNFCCC and the Paris Agreement to take measures against climate change; this decision 'has the opposite effect: it facilitates petroleum production that will contribute extremely high CO2 emissions where petroleum is used, far into the future'.[80] Further, the claimants submitted that the Decision was contrary to the principle of prevention,[81] and to the national and international precautionary principle, which they read as embedded in §112 of the Norwegian Constitution.[82]

The Norwegian state contested all these arguments, saying inter alia that §112 was not even a justiciable norm. Thereby, the state implicitly refuted the representative claim made by the environmental organisations on behalf of future generations, understanding the Constitution as perhaps containing ethical aspirations regarding future generations, but surely not enforceable rights of the unborn.

I find it significant to note that Norway has a green self-image, illustrated by its active engagement in international climate politics and its swift ratification of the Paris Agreement. At the same time, its almost unequalled national wealth depends heavily on its petroleum revenues. The issue 'to drill, or not to drill' therefore is seen as existential to the Norwegian identity.[83]

Perhaps unsurprisingly then, the claimants lost on first instance, on appeal and before the Supreme Court. As a small victory, all three courts agreed that §112 of the Norwegian Constitution is a 'rights provision', ie, a justiciable norm invocable against the state before the Norwegian courts.[84] Yet all three courts allowed the Licensing Decision. Only the Court of Appeal engaged truly with the Norwegian Constitution's right to a healthy environment for future generations.

i. First Instance

The Court of First Instance noted that neither international climate law nor Norwegian law creates an obligation to account for emissions resulting from exported petroleum being burnt abroad. Norway is only responsible for environmental harm abroad resulting from CO_2 emissions occurring within its national boundaries.[85] Consequently, the Court only considered the extra emissions occurring within Norway as a result of the Licensing Decision, ie, the emissions resulting from searching for petroleum and pumping it up. Thus, the Court calculated that the harm would be marginal to the total load of emissions caused by petroleum activities, and judged that the Licensing Decision was not unconstitutional. Regrettably, the Court did not engage with the right to a healthy environment for future generations enshrined in the Norwegian Constitution.

---

[80] ibid para 6.1.

[81] ibid para 6.4.4.

[82] ibid para 9.2.3.

[83] Perhaps more than justified; see Marius Gulbranson Nordby, 'Olje' *Naturpress* (20 November 2017), www.naturpress. no/2017/11/20/olje.

[84] However, the Supreme Court understands § 112 as a significantly weaker test than the other two courts, saying it can only be used where the Norwegian Parliament (the Storting) has 'grossly disregarded' its duties; see Supreme Court of Norway (Noregs Høgsterett), 22 December 2020, *Natur og Ungdom & Greenpeace Norge v Staten* ('Arctic Oil'), case no 20-051052SIV-HRET, para 142.

[85] Oslo District Court (Oslo Tingrett), 4 January 2018, *Natur og Ungdom & Greenpeace v Staten* ('Arctic Oil'), case no 16-166674TVI-OTIR/06.

ii. Appeal

In contrast, the Oslo Court of Appeal explicitly recognised the democratic deficit from which future generations are suffering:

> [T]he second sentence of the first paragraph of §112 stipulates that natural resources are to be managed in a way 'that will safeguard this right for future generations as well'. The fact that the right is to be safeguarded across generations has an aspect of the concern for democracy, in that future generations cannot influence today's political process.[86]

In line with this, the Court found – for the sake of future generations – that Norway is responsible for the combustion of exported petroleum under §112. It remarked quite to the point that 'for the effect on the climate, including the climate in Norway, it does not matter whether the emissions occur during the production or the combustion, nor whether the petroleum is burned in Norway or abroad'.[87]

This step in the Court's reasoning should not be under-estimated. Indeed, under international climate change law, states are only obliged to report on those emissions coming from their own territory. The Court of Appeal thus emphasised the *constitutional autonomy* of Norway by interpreting §112 of the Norwegian Constitution this way. Moreover, it took seriously the duty to 'safeguard this right for future generations as well', accepting the claim of genuine representation. Through its innovative interpretation, it overcame the plurality problem, the non-identity problem and the uncertainty problem. This is what 'surrogate representation' suggested by Karnein can look like: when treating future generations with equal regard for their well-being as we display for our own, we must acknowledge that atmospheric emissions do not stop at national borders, and thus that it is nonsensical to have nations hide behind national boundaries from their responsibility to fight global warming.

However, despite this innovative take, the Court of Appeal's ultimate finding was remarkably conservative: it found that the Licensing Decision violated neither §112 Norwegian Constitution nor Articles 2 and 8 ECHR, because the emissions under scrutiny were only 'marginal' in comparison with the global whole.[88] Given the fact that Norway is one of the world's largest petroleum exporters, I find this an incomprehensible assessment, but that is for another paper.[89]

iii. The Supreme Court

The judgment of Norway's Supreme Court is split into a majority opinion written by Justice Høgetveit Berg, supported by 10 other justices, and a dissenting opinion written by Justice Webster, supported by three justices.[90] The majority view in particular is disappointing.[91]

---

[86] Oslo Court of Appeal (Borgarting Lagmannsrett), 23 January 2020, *Natur og Ungdom & Greenpeace Norge v Staten* ('Arctic Oil'), case no 18-060499ASD-BORG/03, para 2.2.

[87] ibid para 2.4. Importantly, these future generations concern only Norwegians and not *foreign* future generations, as becomes clear when the Court underlined that the Constitution codifies a solidarity principle across generations, but not a solidarity principle across nations.

[88] ibid para 3.3.

[89] In 2023, I intend to write with Tim Bleeker on the amount of emissions enough for climate liability.

[90] Supreme Court of Norway, *Arctic Oil* (n 84) paras 289–301.

[91] The dissenting opinion (ibid paras 254–88 of the judgment) held that the environmental impact assessment of the Licensing Decision should have included an assessment of the emissions resulting from the combustion of exported Norwegian petroleum and that, contrary to the majority view, this assessment could not be postponed to a later stage. These considerations were largely based on case law of the CJEU concerning the effectiveness of environmental impact assessments, but also on the effectiveness of §112 of the Norwegian Constitution, which contains a right to

Not only does it regress away from the innovative reasoning of the Court of Appeal, but it also manifestly errs on a number of occasions.[92] Below, I focus on the Court's lack of consideration for future generations.

Echoing the Court of Appeal, the Supreme Court said that, even if '§112 of the Constitution only protects the environment in Norway', there is 'no doubt that global emissions will also effect Norway',[93] which means that Norway's capability to influence those global emissions would fall within the scope of §112.[94] Yet one page later, the Supreme Court gave up the autonomy of the Norwegian Constitution, stating that 'it must be accepted' that the Norwegian Parliament and government base their climate policy on a division of responsibilities resulting from international agreements, and that '[a] clear principle applies here that each state is responsible for the combustion that occurs on its own territory'.[95] To my mind, whether this indeed 'must' be accepted is debatable. After all, international legal obligations constitute minimum but not always maximum norms – for example, Norway also offers more public health protection than is required under international human rights law. Future generations are not mentioned at all in the extensive interpretation of §112 by the Supreme Court.

In what follows, the Supreme Court considered whether the Licensing Decision might be contrary to Articles 2 and 8 ECHR. Going over case law of the ECtHR, it observed that establishing a violation of Article 2 would require an 'actual and imminent risk',[96] but that such could not be established because 'the possible effect [of the Licensing Decision] for the climate is a good deal into the future'.[97] For a violation of Article 8, the Supreme Court observed that a 'direct and immediate' threat is needed and, as such, it deemed it 'clear' that 'the possible future emissions' resulting from the Licensing Decision did not fall under Article 8 either.[98]

The Supreme Court dismissed the claimant's invocation of the *Urgenda* case in this regard. That is, the Court highlighted some differences between the Norwegian case and the *Urgenda* case,[99] but rather confusingly overlooked the relevant similarity, namely the question of whether Articles 2 and 8 ECHR contain positive obligations for states to fight climate change, which was answered in the affirmative by the Dutch courts.[100]

Thus, the Supreme Court failed to engage with the fact that the Norwegian Constitution regards future generations as rights-holders, and that a wide range of environmental legal sources (see section II.B above) call for consideration for future generations – sources that

---

[92] information in its second paragraph. The dissenting opinion concluded that the Licensing Decision was invalid. This reasoning seems crystal-clear, but I am surprised that the dissenting Justices did not oppose more of the majority view's findings, eg, those enumerated in the next footnote.

[92] Perhaps its lowest point is the judgment citing a decade-old document questioning whether climate change is anthropogenic; see Supreme Court of Norway, *Arctic Oil* (n 84) para 132. The decision also errs in stating that 'an individual right to an environment or climate has not been established by any convention' in para 92, whereas the African Charter of Human and Peoples' Rights *does* contain an individual right to an environment in art 24. Also, the Inter-American Court of Human Rights *did* recognise a human right to a healthy environment as part of the right to life enshrined in the Inter-American Convention of Human Rights, in its 15 November 2017 Advisory Opinion requested by the Republic of Colombia, no OC-23/17. Lastly, though admittedly formulated as a governmental duty rather than an individual right (yet still relevant), art 37 CFREU calls for a high level of environmental protection. The judgment of Norway's Supreme Court also mistakenly called the *Urgenda* decision a 'declaratory judgment' in para 172, whereas the Dutch courts chose *not* to deliver a declaratory judgment, but instead issued a binding injunction.

[93] Supreme Court of Norway, *Arctic Oil* (n 84) para 155.

[94] ibid para 149.

[95] ibid para 159.

[96] ibid para 166.

[97] ibid para 168.

[98] ibid paras 170–71.

[99] Namely, that the *Urgenda* case concerns a general reduction goal rather than a specific administrative decision; see ibid para 173.

[100] By the Hague Court of Appeal and the Dutch Supreme Court; see section IV.A above.

could have led a forward-looking interpretation of Norway's obligations under the ECHR. Instead, the Court deemed the impairment of the environment of these generations irrelevant because they were too distant into the future. We can read this as a variant of the indeterminacy problem identified in section III above. This is hard to reconcile with the scientific certainty that emissions today result in harms to people in the future (and already now).

The more convincing argumentation of the Supreme Court lies in its observations that the Norwegian Parliament had, on several instances, considered Norway's climate policy in general and in connection to petroleum explorations.[101] Though the primary function of fundamental rights is to protect the preconditions of democracy against majoritarian decision-making, and thus do create operational space for the judiciary to stand up against governmental decisions, to go against the seemingly clear intention of the Parliament and government is a far-reaching step that can only be made if judges feel backed up by support expressed in society-wide deliberations.[102] In the Norwegian public debate, there has been heavy pushback against the *Arctic Oil* case.[103]

Interestingly, a few months after the Supreme Court's ruling, the International Energy Agency advised to stop searching for new sources of fossil fuels because burning available fossil fuels will already mean exceeding the globally available carbon budget.[104] Yet the Norwegian Prime Minister Erna Solberg has said Norway will continue to drill for oil and gas.[105]

V. CONCLUDING REMARKS

Looking at the case law discussed above, it is clear that courts deal differently with representative claims on behalf of future generations. Much depends on the legal system at hand. The strict accessibility requirements of the so-called *Plaumann* test make it hard to imagine that the CJEU would ever allow a claim on behalf of future generations. After all, future generations can by definition not be affected 'individually', as this test requires. Even the claim of living children was declared inaccessible due to an alleged failure to meet this requirement in the so-called *People's Climate Case*. Thus, the problem of plurality seems part and parcel of the *Plaumann* test, not only for future generations but also for any pluriform group.

This contrasts sharply with the Dutch legal system, where a collective action or an action in a public interest is rendered possible in private law. Pointing to this possibility, the Court of Appeal in the *Urgenda* case was able to dismiss variations of the plurality problem and the authorisation problem invoked by the state arguing that Urgenda represented a group that was so large that it must have included people who did not want to be represented. Under Dutch private law, it is simply allowed to sue someone in a public interest, provided that some conditions are met.[106]

---

[101] Norwegian Supreme Court, *Arctic Oil* (n 84) paras 236–38.

[102] See L Burgers, 'Should Judges Make Climate Change Law?' (2020) 9 *Transnational Environmental Law* 55.

[103] eg B Braanen, 'Klimasøksmål' *Klassekampen* (18 November 2017), https://arkiv.klassekampen.no/article/20171118/ ARTICLE/171119962; Editorial board led by T Eilertsen, 'Aftenposten Mener: Domstolene Skal Ikke Styre Klimapolitikken' *Aftenposten* (25 October 2016) www.aftenposten.no/article/ap-0AvaG.html; H Skartveit, 'Domstolenes Makt Og Politikernes Avmakt' *VG* (29 October 2016), www.vg.no/i/6xdx8.

[104] International Energy Agency, 'Net Zero by 2050', www.iea.org/reports/net-zero-by-2050.

[105] R Milne, 'Norway's Prime Minister Erna Solberg Says Oslo Remains Committed to Oil and Gas' *Financial Times* (19 July 2021), www.ft.com/content/91c54cf9-4545-4bfe-9445-92fbf048fbd9.

[106] See art 3:305a of the Dutch Civil Code.

Similarly, the precautionary principle was invoked by the Dutch Court of Appeal to dismiss the indeterminacy argument invoked by the state: it had pointed to a level of uncertainty in climate science as to when, where and how the risks of climate change will materialise. Uncertainty of risk cannot lead to the postponement of precautionary measures, stated the Court, following the (international) environmental law principle of precaution.

In contrast, the dismissal by the Norwegian courts of the *Arctic Oil* case cannot be fully explained when looking at the rules at hand. The ruling of the Supreme Court in particular is surprising in this regard. It uses a variation of the indeterminacy argument about climate change to dismiss the application of Articles 2 and 8 ECHR, reasoning that these provisions respectively require 'imminent' and 'immediate' risks, and that the government's Licensing Decision could not be said to pose such risks in terms of climate change-related harms to the Norwegian people. This is surprising, especially in light of, first, the assessment of the Dutch Courts that (a lack of) climate policy does now pose such risks to current and future citizens, and, second, the Norwegian Constitution dictating a special attention for future generations. If anything, consideration for future generations should make us aware of risks that will materialise, in the words of the Norwegian Supreme Court, 'a good deal into the future'.

Instead, the attitude of the Norwegian courts can best be understood as cautiousness in terms of overstepping the boundaries of judicial discretion within the separation of powers principle. The Norwegian Parliament has, on a number of occasions and in a variety of forms, approved of the search for extra petroleum. Interestingly, one can also read the CJEU's *Plaumann* test in this way; it presumes that the European legislature already sufficiently takes the public interest into account and therefore only individually affected people can complain before the European Court. To accept an interest that surpasses the private legal sphere to form the basis for a claim would mean that the CJEU would have to redo the assessment of the public interest that was made by the legislature – that is, the rationale of the *Plaumann* test.

Yet, the problem with parliaments in most constitutional democracies is that they are biased towards the present, as explained above in section II.A. We can conclude that this issue cannot be fully solved by relying on the judiciary, despite the creative claims brought by environmentalists and the attempts to aptly respond by the Hague Court of First Instance and the Norwegian Court of Appeal.

12

The Case of the Ilva Steel Plant
A Never-Ending Battle between Health, the Environment and Employment

LUCA ETTORE PERRIELLO

I. THE TRAGEDY BEHIND ILVA

ILVA IS ONE of the largest steel plants in Europe. Its name is not an acronym, but the Latin for Elba, an island where large amounts of iron were extracted to power the first blast furnaces in the late nineteenth century. It extends on an area of 1,500 hectares, equipped with a 200 km railway and six piers, employs 12,000 people, and has a €6 billion annual turnover. Its headquarters are located in the coastal city of Taranto, in the southern Italian region of Apulia, where Ilva has been in operation since 1965. As many other industries depend on its steel, Ilva's impact on the whole Italian economy is undeniable. Its shutdown would bring about horrific consequences, with GDP and employment shrinking, the balance of trade worsening, and the Italian dependence on foreign steel escalating. Ilva's production is of such strategic importance that its managers have been granted immunity from criminal prosecution and financial penalties.

At first blush, it seems that Ilva is a classic tale of the social redemption of southern Italy, set in an age of unconditional economic progress and a lack of concern with its dark effects, but, on closer inspection, Ilva tells a much more modern story of environmental protection, sustainable development and social responsibility. Over the years, Ilva has been responsible for severe pollution, caused by the transportation of raw material from the harbour to the factory (with toxic powder depositing on the seabed and the road used for transportation), the storage in above-ground areas and the production itself, releasing dioxins and other pollutants in the surrounding area. Scientific reports have shown that the death rate for cancer, as well as cardiovascular, respiratory and digestive diseases in the Taranto area (which includes around 30 municipalities and almost 600,000 inhabitants) is higher than in the rest of the region, and exposure to Ilva's emissions increases the risk of miscarriage and autism.[1] Ilva is also reported to have compromised the food chain by contaminating meat with dioxins.

---

[1] For an overview of the scientific reports on the health damages caused by Ilva, see *Cordella and Others v Italy* App Nos 54414/13 and 54264/15 (ECtHR, 24 January 2019) CE:ECHR:2019:0124JUD005441413.

Faced with massive pollution coming from Ilva and the alarming data on the health of Taranto's residents, it did not take long for local courts to order the seizure of the plant. At the outset, this measure appeared to be problematic. It should not be assumed that criminal law is best positioned to tackle environmental disasters and that private law has no role to play. Arguments have been made that just a few violations of criminal law are found and many of these few are not even prosecuted, which leads to low expectations of punishability;[2] also, criminal fines are costly, because the threshold for their application is higher than that established by administrative law.[3]

Above all, the seizures gave rise to further conflict between the judiciary and the government, which – quite understandably – could not accept that a judicial measure stopped a strategic factory from working and resulted in the dismissal of thousands of employees. In reaction, the government enacted a series of 'save-Ilva decrees' which, notwithstanding the seizures, made it possible for Ilva to remain open, provided that it complied with the permit establishing the best available techniques to reduce pollution.[4] What originated as a dispute between the residents of a coastal town in southern Italy and the main economic actor therein escalated into a wider conflict, affecting a delicate balance between the right to health, the right to work and the environment.

This chapter will address how these rights have been balanced in the Italian and European legal debate. A critical stance will be taken against the scholarly and judicial opinions that do not facilitate 'reflected' environmental damages. As with many losses that individuals suffer in their life, health and property remain unaddressed by the current framework, this chapter will explore whether civil liability may play a role in repairing them. Drawing on the unilateral prevention of accidents and the irrelevance of a regulatory compliance defence, it will argue that reflected environmental damages should be awarded compensation through a strict rule of liability. Finally, it will articulate some policy suggestions as to the most effective model for regulating environmental disasters.

II. BALANCING THE RIGHTS AT STAKE

Soon after the first 'save-Ilva decree' was enacted, a criminal court in Taranto challenged it before the Italian Constitutional Court, which refused to declare it unconstitutional and took the view that it did not unleash a conflict between politics and the judiciary.[5] While letting Ilva stay in the steel business, the decree did not abolish the crime and did not halt the ongoing criminal investigation, nor did it prevent citizens from taking legal action to protect their rights. It is true that the judiciary has the power to ascertain crimes and prosecute them, but it does not have the power to define the regime and restrictions of the industrial policy of the country through measures that may interrupt the steel production and have catastrophic consequences on both the local and the national economy.[6]

---

[2] M Faure, 'Economic Approaches to Environmental Governance: A Principled Analysis' in D Fisher (ed), *Research Handbook on Fundamental Concepts of Environmental Law* (Cheltenham, Edward Elgar, 2016) 133–34.

[3] AI Ogus and C Abbott, 'Sanctions for Pollution: Do We Have the Right Regime?' (2002) 14 *Journal of Environmental Law* 283.

[4] The series started with law decree no 207 of 3 December 2012, converted into law no 231 of 24 December 2012, but many others followed.

[5] Corte costituzionale, 9 April 2013, no 85 (2014) *Foro italiano* I 441.

[6] V Onida, 'Un conflitto fra poteri sotto la veste di questione di costituzionalità: amministrazione e giurisdizione per la tutela dell'ambiente. Nota a Corte costituzionale, sentenza n. 85 del 2013', *Rivista AIC* (20 September 2013) 1, https://www.rivistaaic.it/it/rivista/ultimi-contributi-pubblicati/valerio-onida/un-conflitto-fra-poteri-sotto-la-veste-di-questione-di-costituzionalit-amministrazione-e-giurisdizione-per-la-tutela-dell-ambiente-nota-a-corte-costituzionale-sentenza-n-85-del-2013.

However, at the heart of the decision lies the balance between two fundamental rights, namely the right to health of the people living in Taranto and the right to work of Ilva's employees. According to the Constitutional Court, the protection of fundamental rights shall be systemic and not split up into a series of provisions that may be uncoordinated and in potential conflict. No right shall be a tyrant over the others and the fact that the Constitution classifies the right to health as 'fundamental' is not a sufficient ground to hold it as prevailing over all the others.[7] The Court went on to uphold the balancing technique adopted by the 'save-Ilva decree', based on the pollution permit setting the emission standards (*autorizzazione integrata ambientale*), ie, a public (it is issued by the Ministry of Environment), collaborative (all the stakeholders take part in its definition), dynamic (it is reviewed on a regular basis) and sanctioned measure. The permit is thought to be an effective way to balance the conflicting rights at stake.

This reasoning is quite weak. The judgment subjugates politics to technological standards, considering these standards to be value-neutral and to remain silent on how to balance rights and interests.[8] However, compliance with public standards shall not provide a release from civil liability,[9] because standards are not neutral (the recipients are often the same industries that have articulated them), are incomplete (they may not cover all kinds of emissions) and tend to be obsolete (they do not always reflect the outcomes of scientific and technological progress). Should Ilva strictly comply with the standards laid down in the pollution permit, a (significant) residual risk would still remain, which not even a stricter permit would remove.

It is surprising that the Constitutional Court, while maintaining that all rights should be weighed against each other, focused on a couple of rights only (ie, health and work) and concluded that there was no conflict under the circumstances of the case. By contrast, it did not consider freedom of enterprise, which, under Article 41 of the Italian Constitution, cannot run contrary to social utility. The idea is gaining currency, even at the European level (the Treaty on the Functioning of the European Union, as redrafted after the Lisbon Treaty), that freedom of enterprise is not a fundamental right per se, but it is functional to other objectives, both economic (promotion of employment, price stability, research and technological development) and not (adequate social protection, social inclusion, high level of education, protection of human health, peace, freedom, safety, justice, fight against discrimination etc).[10] However, it is disputable that Ilva is a champion of sustainable development when its activities are supervised by local authorities preventing children from playing outside or compelling farmers to put down cattle. Had the Court considered freedom of enterprise and its social function,[11] the outcome of the case might have been the opposite.

---

[7] See G Bucci and S d'Albergo, 'L'Ilva e gli embrioni di uno Stato neo-corporativo' (2014) *Marx ventuno* 107, 114, claiming that, while endorsing the 'tyranny of values' theory of German philosopher Karl Schmitt, the Court seems to downplay the innovative strength of the values and principles of the most advanced constitution of Western Europe, which clearly prioritises 'employment' over 'market'.

[8] P Carrozza, 'Conclusioni (molto provvisorie …)', *federalismi.it* (17 July 2013), https://www.federalismi.it/nv14/articolo-documento.cfm?artid=22885, 1, 4.

[9] F Santonastaso, 'Tutela della salute, tutela dell'ambiente ed evoluzione della "governance" nelle imprese di interesse strategico nazionale (il caso Ilva); un'applicazione dell'art. 41 Cost. per uno "statuto d'impresa"?' (2014) *Rivista del diritto commerciale e del diritto generale delle obbligazioni* 183, 204.

[10] M Libertini, 'A "Highly Competitive Social Market Economy" as a Founding Element of the European Economic Constitution' (2011) *Concorrenza e mercato* 491. But see Case C-426/11 *Mark Alemo-Herron and Others v Parkwood Leisure Ltd* EU:C:2013:521, where the European Court of Justice held that freedom to conduct a business (art 16 of the Charter of Fundamental Rights of the European Union) is a 'fundamental right'. The decision was critically commented on by S Weatherhill, 'Use and Abuse of the EU's Charter of Fundamental Rights: On the Improper Veneration of "Freedom of Contract"' (2014) 10 *European Review of Contract Law* 167.

[11] Defining art 41 of the Italian Constitution the 'most developed example' of the social recognition of freedom of business, because 'it is *not* classified as a fundamental principle, but is regarded as a *social function*': F Dorssemont, 'Values and Objectives' in N Bruun, K Lörcher and I Schömann (eds), *The Lisbon Treaty and Social Europe* (Oxford, Oxford University Press, 2012) 55.

The Constitutional Court instead took the view that the right to health is not really 'fundamental' as the Constitution says, and it is not compromised when balanced with the right to work of Ilva's employees. This reasoning is treacherous, because it is quite impossible to strike a balance between health and work. There is no right to work that does not entail a right to work in safe conditions and without prejudice to the health of other individuals; similarly, Taranto's residents do have the right to have a job in and to live in a healthy environment. In disputes between private actors, in which both may rely on fundamental rights protection, the Constitutional Court's task should be to lay down the conditions under which persons could *fully* exercise their fundamental rights in harmony. Accordingly, it is not really a matter of denying the fundamental character of the right to health and narrowing down its content through the balance with the right to work, but reconciling both rights while not impairing their content.[12]

III. THE ANTHROPOCENTRIC PROCEDURALISATION OF THE ENVIRONMENT

The Constitutional Court's decision did not put an end to the Ilva case. Dozens of citizens took the matter into their own hands and applied to the European Court of Human Rights (ECtHR), claiming that the Italian state had failed to adequately protect their health and the environment from Ilva's emissions, thereby infringing their rights to life, respect for private and family life, and an effective remedy (Articles 2, 8 and 13 of the European Convention on Human Rights (ECHR)).[13] The facts behind *Cordella v Italy* differed from those of *Smaltini*, in which a woman, diagnosed with leukaemia, alleged that her illness had been caused by the emissions from the plant.[14] While *Smaltini* focused on the causal link between the harmful emissions and the applicant's illness, *Cordella* addressed the Italian state's failure to take the necessary measures to protect the applicants' health and the environment in which they lived.

Cordella is quite a conservative judgment. The ECtHR upheld the 'anthropocentric' theory, which rejects a right to the environment per se, but considers it as a means to the end of fulfilling human rights, namely the right to life, health or respect for private and family life. The environment is thought to exclusively support living and healthy humans. It could not be cast as a right, because individuals could not appropriate it as their own, thereby using it as they wish or even destroying it.[15] The Court elucidated that neither Article 8 ECHR nor any other provision affords a specific protection to the environment in itself, so a violation of Article 8 could not consist in general environmental degradation, but requires adverse consequences on private or family life.[16]

However, while the opposite 'ecocentric' theory – which turns nature into a legal person with its own rights – is questionable due to its tendency to disregard poor and vulnerable individuals,[17] the ECtHR could have acknowledged a right to a healthy and balanced

---

[12] M Meli, 'Ambiente, salute, lavoro: il caso Ilva' (2013) *Le nuove leggi civili commentate* 1017, 1028.

[13] *Cordella* (n 1).

[14] *Smaltini v Italy* App No 43961/09 (ECtHR, 16 April 2015) (unpublished). The Court concluded that no evidence could be established that a causal link existed between the disease of the applicant and the harmful emissions coming from the plant.

[15] See DL Shelton, *Human Rights and the Environment* (Cheltenham, Edward Elgar, 2011) ix; M Anderson, 'Human Rights Approaches to Environmental Protection: An Overview' in M Anderson and A Boyle (eds), *Human Rights Approaches to Environmental Protection* (Oxford, Clarendon Press, 1996) 1.

[16] *Cordella* (n 1) paras 100–01.

[17] C Gearty, 'Do Human Rights Help or Hinder Environmental Protection?' (2010) 1 *Journal of Human Rights and the Environment* 7, 21.

environment, without construing it as instrumental to other human rights. Under this different formulation of the anthropocentric theory, individuals and states remain the subjects and holders of a freestanding right to environment, but this could be protected regardless of its impact on human life and health.[18] And the right-holders would have responsibilities too.

In fact, it is often the case that the ECtHR calls on the states to adopt adequate measures to protect the rights enshrined in the ECHR. Hence, while refusing to afford a freestanding right to the environment, the 'proceduralisation' of existing rights seeks to protect the environment by imposing a series of positive obligations on the states (eg, the duty to conduct Environmental Impact Assessments, inform the population, establish adequate administrative and judicial procedures),[19] whose violation triggers liability. Accordingly, it is quite striking that the ECtHR in *Cordella* – while finding that the Italian authorities had failed to protect the applicants' right to respect for private and family life (paragraph 173) and had violated their right to an effective remedy (consisting in the depollution of the areas affected by Ilva's emissions) (paragraph 174)[20] – refused to award damages on the ground that the finding of the ECHR violations amounted to sufficient reparation for the moral damages suffered by the applicants (paragraph 187).

So, this begs the question: is civil liability the ultimate loser? In the following sections, several aspects will be discussed: the notion of reflected damages, the nature of environmental liability and the problem of establishing a causal link between conduct and harm. The chapter will conclude with some remarks on the suitability of civil liability for cases concerning environmental damages.

IV. 'REFLECTED' ENVIRONMENTAL DAMAGES

The relevant damages in *Cordella* were not the environmental damages *tout court*, affecting natural resources and the utility thereof, but the environmental damages *sensu lato*, also known as individual or reflected damages, that is, the losses that individuals suffer in their life, health, property or other rights as a result of an environmental damage as such. While denying redress for these damages, the ECtHR did not consider that reflected damages may sometimes offer the only possibility for compensation of victims. This section will argue that the criticism levelled against reflected damages is unwarranted and the current legal framework may well be interpreted to offer more comprehensive reparation to the victims.

Directive 2004/35/CE on environmental liability is not concerned with individual damages, as it is left to Member States to determine the regime applicable to personal injuries, damages to private property or any economic losses, and the rights regarding these types of damages (Recital no 14). The Italian Environmental Code makes provision for reflected damages, affording individuals the right to claim compensation for personal injuries or property damages resulting from environmental misconduct (Article 313(7) of legislative decree no 152 of 2006).

---

[18] See N Bryner, 'A Constitutional Human Right to a Healthy Environment' in D Fisher (ed), *Research Handbook on Fundamental Concepts of Environmental Law* (Cheltenham, Edward Elgar, 2016) 169, arguing that 'inasmuch as the content of the right is defined in reference to an ecological balance or a "healthy environment", it diverges from an exclusively anthropocentric view, by recognising ecological integrity as valuable to human dignity, irrespective of the degree to which the natural environment is instrumental to meeting or supporting human needs and development'.

[19] For an analysis of the 'proceduralisation' of ECHR rights in environmental matters, see L Ferraris, '*Smaltini v Italy*: A Missed Opportunity to Sanction Ilva's Polluting Activity within the ECHR System' (2016) 13 *Journal for European Environmental & Planning Law* 82, 87.

[20] The Court of Justice of the European Union too has recently ruled that Italy has failed for years to comply with EU standards for air quality: Case C-644/18 *European Commission v Italian Republic* EU:C:2020:895.

Notwithstanding the unequivocal wording of the Environmental Code, some argue that reflected damages shall not be compensated on the ground that individuals neither hold a right to environment nor have personal standing to claim compensation for those damages before the courts.[21] While natural resources belong to the community as a whole and fulfil pecuniary and non-pecuniary interests (eg, a clean sea benefits both tourists willing to swim therein and the owners of hotels and holiday homes nearby), individuals cannot claim a right to own them exclusively. Thus, where the sea is polluted and, consequently, tourists stay away, the hotel owner could not lament that his right of ownership was hindered, for the reflected damage resulting from marine pollution is legally immaterial.[22]

Should all the affected individuals be allowed to reach the polluter's assets, the polluter may become insolvent and no longer afford to repair the natural resource.[23] The legal system is allegedly concerned with granting effective protection for direct damages only, which would no longer be feasible if reflected victims had 'compensatory' recourse against the polluter's assets.[24] To this end, one person only – in Italy the Ministry of Environment – is given standing to bring an action against the polluter and claim reparation in kind rather than a compensatory measure (Articles 311 and 313 of the Environmental Code),[25] thereby repairing the social utilities the natural resource provides the community with (eg, a measure seeking to increase fish stocks in the sea affected by an environmental disaster).[26] As the special and 'reparatory' regime of environmental liability takes priority over the general and 'compensatory' regime of civil liability contained in the Civil Code, Article 313(7) of the Environmental Code may be intended as having vertical effects, that is, in the relationship between the state and the individual, who would be entitled to claim damages whenever public authorities take no action or the action taken is inadequate.[27]

It seems that the arguments put forward by this scholarship are not persuasive. By denying compensation for reflected damages to property,[28] the logical consequence would be that even reflected personal injuries would receive no compensation, yet these injuries not only involve constitutional rights but can also hardly ever be repaired in kind. Since reparation in kind of personal injuries is almost impossible, and compensation in environmental liability is not an

---

[21] U Salanitro, 'L'evoluzione dei modelli di tutela dell'ambiente alla luce dei princípi europei: profili sistematici della responsabilità per danno ambientale' (2013) *Nuova giurisprudenza civile commentata* 795, 808.

[22] ibid 808–09, claiming that the same applies to (de facto) damages that the owner suffers as a result of damages sustained by a neighbour (eg, a beautiful private garden is destroyed, but the neighbouring hotel owner is not entitled to claim damages for the loss of the view). On the contrary, the hotel owner could claim compensation where a public authority has unlawfully ordered him to close down for a while, for in this case his business is *directly* affected by the order.

[23] ibid 810.

[24] ibid 809, arguing that in the event of the destruction of a neighbour's garden (n 22 above), the owner only shall be given standing, because he is the only subject to have the power to repair the garden, thereby returning the utilities it provides the community with.

[25] The polluter must take the measures to repair the natural resource himself or bear the costs for recovery anticipated by the public authorities. The Ministry of the Environment can bring an action to claim compensation equivalent to the loss only 'if necessary' (art 311(1) of the Environmental Code). By making monetary compensation a means of last resort, the Environmental Code clearly prioritises reparation in kind: M Meli, 'Il risarcimento del danno ambientale' (2011) *Nuova giurisprudenza civile commentata* 848, 850; C Castronovo, *Responsabilità civile* (Milan, Giuffrè, 2018) 854–55, claiming that environmental liability shall not be classified as a form of civil liability given the lack of compensation.

[26] See Salanitro (n 21) 810–12, contending that it is true that by increasing the fish stocks and refusing to compensate the damages, there might be old fishermen unwilling to carry on their business, who would not benefit from the reparation in kind of the environment, but this result would be consistent with the nature of the rights that the fishermen have on the environment, which are not rights of ownership and could not be compensated.

[27] ibid 812–13.

[28] Indeed, all the examples made by Salanitro concern damages to property.

option, personal injuries would be given no protection whatsoever. In the Ilva case, Taranto's residents suffering from irreversible health conditions caused by the emissions would have no remedy, given that the damage to their health would be classified as reflected.

Moreover, it appears that the line between direct and reflected damages is very fine. Even when it comes to damages to property, it is not sufficiently clear why the damage suffered by the hotelier due to the pollution that keeps tourists at bay should not be considered as directly affecting his right of ownership and freedom of business. Evidently, Taranto's court did consider this kind of damage as direct when it awarded compensation for the loss of value of people's homes due to the exposure to Ilva's emissions.[29] The court remarked that the damage to property results regardless of the owner's decision to put his home on the market (given, for instance, that he may struggle finding access to credit by providing his home as collateral).

The downsides of granting reflected damages do not appear so severe that they should not be made available. Allowing compensation for reflected damages opens the floodgates to the compensation for damages other than those to health and property (although these are the only rights mentioned by Article 313(7) of the Environmental Code), including damages that do not consist in the breach of a given right, but still run contrary to individual personality (Article 2 of the Italian Constitution), such as fear of getting sick[30] affecting citizens of a polluted area, or a dramatic change in living habits. Individuals would have standing to claim compensation for these damages, for there are no compelling reasons against a horizontal application of Article 313(7) of the Environmental Code, ie, extending to the relation between the polluter and the victims. The wording of the Article does not support a reading narrowed down to the action brought by the individual against the public authorities. It is true that potentially hundreds of victims may have recourse against the polluter's assets and expose him to bankruptcy, but this problem concerns any mass torts and may be addressed through a variety of solutions (eg, insurance) other than merely ruling out civil liability.

By this time, a discrepancy shows up in the standing against the polluter. While the individual has standing to claim compensation for reflected damages, he has no standing to claim reparation in kind of the environmental damage as such. This approach clearly results from Article 6 of Directive 2004/35/CE and Article 311(1) of the Italian Environmental Code. It is consistent with a construction of environment as a 'public asset' for the benefit of the whole community, thereby requiring 'public remedies' in order to be protected that could be relied on by public authorities only. However, in Italy new insights may come from the recent class action reform (law 12 April 2019 no 31, which entered into force on 19 May 2021), which allows persons – not only groups or associations but also single members belonging to the class – representing 'individual homogeneous rights' to bring a class action against the wrongdoer.

---

[29] Tribunale di Taranto, 15 January 2014, no 72, commented on by A Buonfrate, 'Caso Ilva: danno ambientale e tutela risarcitoria dei cittadini' (2015) *Ambiente & sviluppo* 355. The court allowed the preventive injunction under art 844 of the Civil Code along with the liability action under art 2043 of the Civil Code, given that the emissions from Ilva had exceeded the normal tolerability and determined a depreciation of the plaintiff's home. The award of damages was based on a previous unappealable judgment of the Court of Cassation that had found that Ilva had committed an environmental crime. The causal link between the depreciation and the emissions was established through an expert report, but the Court determined the amount of damages on an equitable basis, given the objective difficulty in isolating concurrent factors that may have affected the loss of value.

[30] The Seveso disaster case is emblematic here. In 1976, an industrial accident occurred in the ICMESA SpA plant in the Lombardy region of Italy and, as a result, thousands of people were exposed to high levels of dioxins. Due to the lack of reliable scientific information, in the aftermath of the event, local residents were forced to undergo medical examinations seeking to study the possible effects of dioxins on human health. When a group of residents took legal action, the Court of Cassation acknowledged the damage arising from fear of getting sick, irrespective of any other personal injuries or damages to property: Corte di cassazione, Sezioni unite, 21 February 2002, no 2515 (2003) *Giurisprudenza italiana* 691; Corte di cassazione, 13 May 2009, no 11059 (2010) *Giustizia civile* 1467.

Environmental lawyers will have to clarify whether those 'individual homogenous rights' include not only rights to health and property, so as to claim reflected damages, but also rights to a healthy and balanced environment, so that any persons, whether individually or through associations, might bring a class action to claim restoration in kind for environmental damages as such.

V. LIABILITY WITHOUT FAULT

What is the nature of this 'reflected' environmental liability? Is it based on fault or not? A law and economics perspective may give some insights into these questions, thereby showing that issues of environmental liability may be addressed through a multi-faceted approach, drawing on non-economic reasons (inter alia, human rights) *and* legal-economic standards of efficiency.

It may be argued that a negligence rule better serves the deterrent function of civil liability because, once the polluter has complied with the standards set out in the pollution permits, he will escape liability. Accordingly, a negligence rule would create incentives for polluters to comply with the due care requirement, thereby leading to an optimal internalisation of the negative externalities.[31] Also, a negligence rule would make contributory negligence relevant, so the victim's blameworthy conduct might be taken into account to reduce the amount of damages owed by the polluter.

However, in the event of environmental damages, what a negligence rule overlooks is the distinction between unilateral and bilateral prevention.[32] When the injurer only can prevent the accident – as is the case with reflected environmental damages caused by Ilva's emissions – a strict liability rule would be the most efficient, because the victim could not avoid the accident under any circumstances. The deterrent function of a negligence rule implies that the injurer is given incentives to take optimal care (indeed, if he is diligent, he is immune from liability), while the victim is given incentives to take the measures necessary to minimize the damage that could still result from the injurer's diligent conduct. But if prevention of the accident is unilateral, it would make no sense to burden the victim with the damage resulting from the injurer's diligent conduct in order to provide that victim with incentives to minimise that damage, because the victim is simply not in a position to take measures that would avoid or contain the accident.[33]

A negligence rule may determine the optimal level of care, but not the optimal level of production. If the polluter is diligent, whether he releases one gram or one ton of dioxins makes no difference: either way, he releases himself from liability by staying within the permits.[34] However, under EU law, pollution permits are not supposed to play such an 'exculpatory' role. First, permits usually restrict *emissions* but say nothing of *immissions*, ie, interferences with individual rights to life, health and property. Second, Ilva cannot exonerate itself from liability by claiming that its *activity* has been authorised. Directive 2004/35/CE does make provision for

---

[31] Faure (n 2) 118–19, 127–28.

[32] This distinction dates back to S Shavell, *Economic Analysis of Accident Law* (Cambridge MA, Harvard University Press, 1987) 7.

[33] See PG Monateri, 'La responsabilità civile' in R Sacco (ed), *Trattato di diritto civile* (Turin, Utet, 1998) 37, claiming that strict liability is the most efficient model whenever the prevention of damage is unilateral, the damages owed match the loss sustained and, finally, the role of the potential tortfeasor and the victim are known before the accident takes place.

[34] See Faure (n 2) 128, contending that strict liability 'provides incentives to adopt both efficient care as well as efficient activity levels'. In his opinion, this is the most important difference between strict liability and negligence, whereas both models tend to perform a deterrent function.

an exemption from liability, but this concerns authorised *emissions*. More exactly, the exclusion of liability requires that the polluter shows that the authorities have duly authorised a specific emission and that 'he was not at fault or negligent' (Article 8(4)(a) of Directive 2004/35/CE). Although the wording is inaccurate, the basic idea behind the Directive is that, notwithstanding an express authorisation of a given emission, the polluter is held liable if he had knowledge of or should have had knowledge of the environmental damage by taking the relevant standard of care.[35] Yet, it seems that Ilva could not benefit from the exemption, because its activity as a whole (not a specific emission) was authorised and, even if a specific emission were authorised, Ilva would be in a position to have knowledge of the environmental risk.

These brief remarks show that liability for environmental reflected damages should be classified as strict. Assuming that Ilva runs a dangerous activity – given the strong likelihood of damage or the severity thereof – the applicable rule under Italian law might well be Article 2050 of the Civil Code,[36] which holds liable whoever causes injury to another in the performance of a dangerous activity. The hazard posed by the activity at stake is made relevant by the Environmental Liability Directive too, which imposes a strict regime on any operators if damage is caused by any of the hazardous activities listed in Annex III (Article 3(1)(a) of Directive 2004/35/CE), whereas liability is based on fault if the operator does not run a hazardous business.[37]

It is true that Article 2050 of the Civil Code makes it possible for the injurer to escape liability if he proves that he has taken all suitable measures to avoid the accident, but this exculpatory proof should not be over-emphasised. On the one hand, under living law it has been given a narrow interpretation and mostly identified with a fortuitous event. In other words, once the activity has been classified as hazardous, courts tend to set aside the proof that all suitable measures to avoid the accident were taken, so that the injurer may escape liability only by showing that his activity is not hazardous or providing evidence of a fortuitous event (but this may be a hard task).[38]

On the other hand, even if it is accepted that the injurer may really be released from liability if he discharges the burden of proof that he has taken all suitable measures to avoid damage,[39] this raises the question of determining the magnitude of these in environmental matters, considering that overly expensive measures may cause the polluter to go bankrupt and make the victims rely on public assistance.[40] Yet, the Environmental Code has replaced the yardstick of 'excessive costs' (set forth in the previous legislation) with that of 'reasonable conditions' (Article 5(l-*ter*)(2)); thus, the polluter may be now required to take measures that are costly but reasonable. The legal change was anticipated by a decision of the Italian Constitutional Court illustrating that no measure is excessive where it is required to protect human health. As such, a measure may be found excessive only once the threshold of human protection has been met.[41]

---

[35] See Salanitro (n 21) 802 fn 13, pointing out that the Directive does not hold the emission permit sufficient for the purposes of the exclusion of liability, thereby showing that the administrative authorisation may have shortcomings (eg, due to lack of information or 'regulatory capture').

[36] Italian courts have ruled that producers of toxic waste (in the case at issue, special industrial waste) are subject to the strict liability rule on hazardous activities under art 2050 of the Civil Code: Corte di cassazione, 1 September 1995, no 9211 (1996) *Nuova giurisprudenza civile commentata* 358.

[37] Praising the distinction between hazardous and 'safe' activities in the Environmental Liability Directive, giving rise to strict and fault liability respectively, see Faure (n 2) 130.

[38] See, lately, Corte di cassazione, 12 March 2019, no 7007 (2019) *Massimario Giustizia civile*.

[39] Arguing this way, see G Alpa, 'La responsabilità oggettiva' (2005) *Contratto e impresa* 959, 969. This view, however, does not seem to be endorsed by the Italian courts.

[40] Monateri (n 33) 903.

[41] Corte costituzionale, 7–16 March 1990, no 127 (1991) *Regioni* 525.

The Court, as if anticipating the Ilva case, went on to say that costs are not relevant where the measures concern particularly polluted areas.

VI. ESTABLISHING THE CAUSAL LINK

Even in its strict pattern, civil liability requires that a causal link be established between the environmental damage and the act or failure of the identified polluter. This may be quite complicated when it comes to reflected damages,[42] due to the variety of concurrent causes or alternative factors that may cause them (eg, cigarette smoke),[43] the toxic effects that may not be immediate but cumulative and show up in the long run,[44] the multitude of victims and injurers, and the scientific uncertainty around certain kinds of damages.[45]

Accordingly, the ECtHR has at times ruled that a causal link cannot be established in the event of diffuse pollution.[46] Scholars too fear that relaxing the standard of proof would encourage frivolous litigation and impinge on the court system.[47] Indeed, the Environmental Liability Directive itself states that liability is 'not a suitable instrument for dealing with pollution of a widespread, diffuse character, where it is impossible to link the negative environmental effects with acts or failure to act of certain individual actors' (Recital no 13 of Directive 2004/35/CE). It appears that the Directive leaves out of its scope of application the most interesting cases of environmental liability, ie, diffuse pollution arising from disasters.[48]

In any case, the problem of causation in environmental liability should not be overstated. On the one hand, it is now acknowledged that both causation and damage can be established through presumptions (eg, the factory's proximity to the disaster; the match between the toxins found and the materials used by the operator in connection with its activities; the high rates of disease; an infringement proceeding commenced by public authorities; and probably even media exposure or special legislation tackling the disaster).[49]

---

[42] *cf* PG Monateri, 'Il futuro della responsabilità civile per danni all'ambiente in Italia' in B Pozzo (ed), *La responsabilità ambientale. La nuova direttiva sulla responsabilità ambientale in materia di prevenzione e riparazione del danno ambientale* (Milan, Giuffrè, 2005) 137–38, claiming that what is problematic to prove is not the link between the action and the event, but between the event and all the damages ensuing therefrom; Castronovo (n 25) 854–55. In US scholarship, arguing that 'the only clear observation in toxic tort litigation is the unparalleled dilemma of establishing a cause and effect relationship between a toxin and a plaintiff's injury': D Conway-Jones, 'Factual Causation in Toxic Tort Litigation: A Philosophical View of Proof and Certainty in Uncertain Disciplines' (2002) 35 *University of Richmond Law Review* 875, 878.

[43] GW Boston, 'A Mass-Exposure Model of Toxic Causation: The Content of Scientific Proof and the Regulatory Experience' (1993) 18 *Columbia Journal of Environmental Law* 181, 301.

[44] DA Farber, 'Toxic Causation' (1987) 71 *Minnesota Law Review* 1219, 1228.

[45] See Note, 'Causation in Environmental Law: Lessons from Toxic Torts' (2015) 128 *Harvard Law Review* 2256, 2261.

[46] See *Smaltini* (n 14) para 60, where the Court, based on the scientific knowledge available at the time of the case, but without prejudice to the findings of future studies, concluded that the applicant (a citizen of Taranto diagnosed with leukaemia) had not shown that the government had failed to protect her right to life. Yet, the Court did leave 'open the possibility for future claims arising out of the situation in Taranto': J Harrison, 'Significant International Environmental Law Cases: 2018–19' (2019) 31 *Journal of Environmental Law* 1, 2. In fact, see *Cordella* (n 1) paras 163–66, for new scientific evidence showing that a causal link exists between Ilva's emissions and a variety of diseases.

[47] JC Mosher, 'A Pound of Cause for a Penny of Proof: The Failed Economy of an Eroded Causation Standard in Toxic Tort Cases' (2003) 11 *NYU Environmental Law Journal* 531, 594–96.

[48] Monateri (n 42) 140.

[49] *cf* Case C-378/08 *Raffinerie Mediterranee (ERG) SpA, Polimeri Europa SpA and Syndial SpA v Ministero dello Sviluppo economico and Others* [2010] ECR I-1919, paras 56–57. Italian courts too have accepted presumptions of damage; see Corte di cassazione, 13 May 2009, no 11059 (pain and suffering arising from the Seveso disaster); Tribunale di Taranto, 6 March 2014, no 708 (2015) *Ambiente & sviluppo* 355 (damages to properties in Taranto arising from limitations to the possibility of opening the windows, the accumulation of powder on the balconies and the plants, and the impossibility of hanging laundry outside).

On the other hand, causation in environmental liability tends to require not certainty, but probability that a given accident results from an antecedent cause.[50] Indeed, in industrialised societies, it would be almost impossible to single out causes of events with absolute certainty; if causation implied certainty, then many victims would be left with no judicial protection at all. An argument to the contrary could be made that a probability test would pave the way for any claims in generic connection with sources of pollution, which are in ever greater numbers in modern societies.[51] However, scientific criteria may be used to differentiate frivolous claims from serious ones.[52] If a science-based probability test is accepted, Ilva's victims will be successful if they can show, based on scientific evidence, that it is highly likely that their conditions result from the plant's emissions and it is highly unlikely that alternative factors may have caused them.

VII. SOME POLICY REMARKS

The above analysis has attempted to show that the decisions of the Italian Constitutional Court and the ECtHR are more politically than legally sound and, in particular, the ECtHR's refusal to award compensation for reflected environmental damages is not justified. On a policy level, concerns may arise as to whether civil liability really is the best model to tackle reflected environmental damages. Certainly, it is not the only one. Pollution is a negative externality, ie, an adverse effect of the activity that the polluter imposes on society without conferring any benefits. If polluters are not forced to pay for the externalities they create, they are not encouraged to take preventive measures and may be in a position to offer goods and services at too low a price, that is, a price that does not really reflect the social costs of the activity. Consumers will demand too many goods and services that determine high costs for society in terms of pollution. In this respect, pollution is also a market failure.[53]

Faced with this failure, the self-regulating capacity of the market should not be overestimated. There have been cases where environmental disasters have been handled through settlements (such as *Seveso*), but contract works where transaction costs are low[54] and the payoffs may still depend on structures and concepts drawn from tort law.[55] Hence, a legal model stronger than 'regulating through contract' is in demand to correct the market failure, but it is questionable whether the best rule is civil liability.

Some advocate for a public regulatory intervention that would fix the market failure by putting a price on the environment, thereby forcing businesses to curb overproduction and pollution, and balancing the private and social costs in the production process.[56] Underpinning

---

[50] See Corte di cassazione, Sezioni unite, 11 January 2008, no 581 (2008) *Responsabilità civile e previdenza* 827, highlighting the different threshold of probability in criminal and civil procedure. While the former requires proof beyond reasonable doubt, the latter accepts the 'more likely than not' rule, given the different positions between prosecution and defence in the criminal trial, and the equal positions between the plaintiff and the defendant in the civil trial.

[51] Ferraris (n 19) 91–92.

[52] F Piraino, 'Il nesso di causalità' (2018) *Europa e diritto privato* 399, 446–447.

[53] Faure (n 2) 114–15.

[54] Monateri (n 33) 904–05, mentioning the settlement on the damages arising from the Seveso disaster, signed by the Italian state and the Lombardy region, and Icmesa and Givaudan companies. Monateri believes that it is not necessarily true that where damages are widespread, transaction costs are high and would thus make litigation desirable. On the contrary, litigation may be more costly, and the many victims of a single accident tend to group together, thereby reducing transaction costs. However, if those victims can bring a class action, then tort law would regain its priority over contract law.

[55] Monateri (n 42) 139.

[56] Meli (n 12) 1039.

this proposition is a note of scepticism about the judicial power's ability to adjudicate environmental disasters. Courts are thought to have trouble understanding technical and scientific data, to make decisions based on the information provided by the litigants only, to decide different cases similarly and similar cases differently, thereby creating uncertainty.[57] Some courts may be even reluctant to strike down legislative or executive actions that threaten the environment due to concerns about the principle of separation of powers.[58]

A variety of legislative measures may be envisaged, but they all have greater or lesser shortcomings. Taxation is seen as an efficient deterrent to prompt businesses to abate pollution, as well as a flexible instrument, because it does not dictate the optimal level of production, but leaves polluters with the leeway to determine how to internalise the negative externality. However, taxation should relate to the cost of pollution, but quantifying this cost may be extremely difficult or may still require structures of tort law. Moreover, monitoring and enforcement systems are often costly.[59] An alternative regulatory approach is setting emission standards, but these may prevent new firms from entering the market and raise the profits of the existing ones, thereby hampering competition.

Lately, arguments have been increasingly made for the nationalisation of Ilva. State intervention has attracted criticism as it purports to save Ilva from bankruptcy while preserving the private ownership and letting it keep polluting for the sake of profit. Public regulation has never sought to fix the market failure by holding Ilva accountable for the social costs inflicted upon the community. On the contrary, nationalising Ilva and internalising the externality would make Ilva's survival possible for the benefit of the whole community and not just the owners.[60] Yet, it is hard to argue that the state has the skills to run a steel company. There have been times when Ilva was owned or at least run by the state, but this did not sort out its problems – it actually made them worse.

The upside of a private law system such as tort law is that it is a flexible measure, because it is administered by the courts on a case-by-case basis. It also involves distributional aspects. Ilva should be held liable because it runs a risky business[61] and it would be unfair and unequitable to exempt it from the adverse consequences it inflicts upon the community. Most importantly, unlike other instruments, liability is capable of performing several functions. The recovery of damages is just one of them, probably not even an essential one. As the ECtHR refused to award compensation, but urged the Italian state to take all the measures necessary to protect the environment and the health of the people, it clearly showed this 'polyfunctionality'.

If the scope of liability were only to transfer the loss from the victim to the polluter, there would probably be less costly instruments than setting up trials and adding the costs

---

[57] These arguments are often made in product liability scholarship, but they may apply to environmental liability too; *cf* JA Henderson Jr, 'Judicial Review of Manufacturers' Conscious Design Choices: The Limits of Adjudication' (1973) 73 *Columbia Law Review* 1531, 1532–33; SG Lindvall, 'Aircraft Crashworthiness: Should the Courts Set the Standards' (1986) 27 *William & Mary Law Review* 371, 401.

[58] Bryner (n 18) 178. Reflecting the tension between politics and courts in climate change litigation, see the Dutch decisions in *Urgenda*, with a brilliant comment by L Burgers, 'Should Judges Make Climate Change Law?' (2020) 9 *Transnational Environmental Law* 1. The final decision in *De Staat der Nederlanden v Stichting Urgenda* was delivered by the Supreme Court of the Netherlands – see Hoge Raad, 20 December 2019, NL:HR:2019:2006.

[59] Faure (n 2) 117. On the contrary, supporting environmental taxation, see AC Pigou, *A Study in Public Finance*, 3rd edn (London, Macmillan, 1951).

[60] See Meli (n 12) 1040; Bucci and d'Albergo (n 7) 111.

[61] According to the business risk theory, liability should fall on the entrepreneur who created a risk within society while running his business; see the pioneering work of P Trimarchi, *Rischio e responsabilità oggettiva* (Milan, Giuffrè, 1961). See also Alpa (n 39) 1005, contending that a system based on business risk is a paradigm of strict liability, because the entrepreneur is best positioned to internalise the externalities that its activity generates within the environment and the community, insure himself and incorporate the cost of insurance into the sale price.

of litigation to the costs of the accidents. But what really makes civil liability desirable is its ability to create incentives to avoid the accident.[62] Effective deterrence requires that liability should fall on the 'cheapest cost-avoider', that is, the party that can avoid the accident in the cheapest way, based on a cost-benefit analysis whereby the costs of the accident exceed the costs of its prevention.[63] Ilva seems to meet this threshold. This is not to say that 'regulation through litigation' is the best system or the only way to address reflected damages, but it is an effective instrument when used alongside public regulation and contract law.

---

[62] Castronovo (n 25) 852 points out that the title of Directive 2004/35/CE ('environmental liability with regard to the prevention and remedying of environmental damage') epitomises the compensatory and deterrent function of civil liability. See also Faure (n 2) 134, contending that 'in order to deter the violation of an environmental rule, there needs to be the expectation of a substantial penalty or sanction to convince the potential perpetrator to comply'. On the punitive function of environmental liability *tout court*, where compensation is not connected to the loss, because it reflects the public interest that the environment shall not be contaminated, see Monateri (n 42) 138. In case law, see Corte di cassazione, 17 April 2008, no 10118 (2008) *Giurisprudenza italiana* 2708.

[63] See the masterpiece of G Calabresi, *The Costs of Accidents: A Legal and Economic Analysis* (New Haven, Yale University Press, 1970). See also R Posner, 'A Theory of Negligence' (1972) *Journal of Legal Studies* 29, 32, arguing that the cost of prevention consists of measures making the activity safer or the benefit foregone by curtailing or eliminating the activity: 'If the cost of safety measures or of curtailment – whichever cost is lower – exceeds the benefit in accident avoidance to be gained by incurring that cost, society would be better off, in economic terms, to forgo accident prevention.'

13

The Causal Link in Tort-Based Climate Change Litigation

A Challenge for the Courts

MONIKA HINTEREGGER

I. INTRODUCTION

T HE PROBLEM OF climate change is one of the hot topics of our time. There are no
easy solutions for the problem and it is up to every branch of science and scholarship
to consider what contribution it can make in order to tackle the problem. This also
applies to tort law. The question of compensability of climate change damage has already
attracted the attention of a considerable number of legal writers[1] and, primarily in the US,
several cases have already been brought to court.[2]

For tort law the picture is, however, rather ambiguous. Tort law has undoubtedly some
interesting properties for tackling climate change: it is a commonly available instrument for
the compensation of losses with significant preventive effects. Unlike instruments of administrative law or tax law, it covers cross-border damage and relies less on the initiative of public

---

[1] For the discussion in legal literature, see, for instance, J Spier, 'Legal Aspects of Global Climate Change and
Sustainable Development' (2006) 2 *InDret: Revista para el Análisis del Derecho* 1; R Abate, 'Automobile Emissions and
Climate Change Impacts: Employing Public Nuisance Doctrine as Part of a "Global Warming Solution" in California'
(2008) 40 *Connecticut Law Review* 591; D Grossman, 'Warming up to a Not-So-Radical Idea: Tort-Based Climate
Change Litigation' (2003) 28 *Columbia Journal of Environmental Law* 1; J Salzmann and D Hunter, 'Negligence in the
Air: The Duty of Care in Climate Change Litigation' (2007) 155 *University of Pennsylvania Law Review* 101; M Duffy,
'Climate Change Causation: Harmonizing Tort Law and Scientific Probability' (2009) 28 *Temple Journal of Science,
Technology and Environmental Law* 185; M Faure and M Peeters (eds), *Climate Change Liability* (Cheltenham,
Edward Elgar, 2011); R Lord et al (eds), *Climate Change Liability: Transnational Law and Practice* (Cambridge,
Cambridge University Press, 2011); D Kysar, 'What Climate Change Can Do about Tort Law' (2011) 41 *Environmental
Law Reporter* 1; G Munro, 'The Public Trust Doctrine and the Montana Constitution as Legal Bases for Climate
Change Litigation in Montana' (2012) 73 *Montana Law Review* 123; M Gerrard and J MacDougald, 'An Introduction
to Climate Change Liability Litigation and a View to the Future' (2013) 20 *Connecticut Insurance Law Journal* 153;
J Ellis, 'The Sky's the Limit: Applying the Public Trust Doctrine to the Atmosphere' (2014) 86 *Temple Law Review* 807;
E Pöttker, *Klimahaftungsrecht* (Tübingen, Mohr Siebeck, 2014); M Lee, 'Climate Change Tort' (2015) Adjudicating
the Future: Climate Change and the Rule of Law, London, 17–19 September 2015, www.ssrn.com/abstract=2695107;
J Peel and HM Osofsky, *Climate Change Litigation* (Cambridge, Cambridge University Press, 2015).

[2] An overview of climate change litigation in the US is provided by the Sabin Center for Climate Change Law of
Columbia Law School at www.climatecasechart.com.

authorities that often fail to address environmental problems adequately.[3] There is no doubt that the enforcement of liability claims against emitters of greenhouse gases could have its merits. It must be stressed, however, that plaintiffs will have to deal with the high cost of litigation and that the clarification of actual and quite serious legal uncertainties will make such trials an arduous task for plaintiffs and defendants alike. There is thus no doubt that the application of tort law to climate change damage will most likely be limited to actionist trials by non-governmental organisations (NGOs) in order to raise awareness of the public for the perils of climate change. As such trials attract a great deal of public attention, they are well suited to affect the behaviour of emitters of greenhouse gases beyond the individual case. Since companies tend to avoid negative publicity, this may even be the case when the claim is not successful.

From a theoretical point of view, tort law claims against emitters of greenhouse gases encounter fundamental difficulties. One of the many obstacles (applicable causes of action, proof of unlawfulness respectively fault under fault-based liability, the concept of recoverable damage and the high cost of litigation) is the proof of a direct causal link between the emission of greenhouse gases by one specific emitter and the harm sustained. The reasons for this lie in the characteristic properties of greenhouse gases. Gases like carbon dioxide, methane and nitrous oxide do not directly affect plaintiffs, but cumulate in the atmosphere and over time cause the temperatures of the earth to rise. Direct cause of the harm is actually a natural event (storm, heat, rainfall, drought etc) triggered by the accumulation of these substances. The other fundamental difficulty lies in the specific nature of climate change damage because harm caused by climate change that is caused by human emissions can very often not be distinguished from harm caused by pure natural events. In these cases only part of the damage, namely the part of the damage caused by the increase in the occurrence of such incidents or by the increase in their intensity, is of human origin. A good example for such a causality scenario is the formation of hurricanes. Hurricanes are a natural phenomenon, but climate science shows that global warming makes them more frequent and more destructive. This argumentation was brought forward in the case of *Comer v Murphy Oil*,[4] where victims of Hurricane Katrina sued a number of energy companies for compensation for the damage caused by the hurricane. They argued that the defendants had contributed considerably to global warming by emitting greenhouse gases, thereby increasing the destructive power of Hurricane Katrina.

It is thus not surprising that until now no claim based on tort law against an emitter of greenhouse gases for compensation of climate change damage has been successful. The State of California which sued the six major American car manufacturers for damages caused by the emissions of greenhouse gases by the manufactured cars dropped the lawsuit after losing the suit at first instance.[5] The claims in *Comer v Murphy Oil*[6] and *Kivalina v ExxonMobil*[7] were dismissed by the courts holding that: (i) climate change matters are not judicial, but rather political questions that must be resolved by Congress and the government (the 'political question doctrine'); and (ii) that the claimants could not establish a sufficient causal link between their damage and the defendant's emissions. The inability to show causation was

---

[3] For a comprehensive analysis, see M Hinteregger, 'Civil Liability and the Challenges of Climate Change: A Functional Analysis' (2017) 8 *Journal of European Tort Law* 238.

[4] *Comer v Murphy Oil* 585 F3d 855 (5th Cir 2009).

[5] *California v General Motors Corp* No C06-05755 MJJ, 2007 WL 2726871 (ND Cal 2007).

[6] *Comer v Murphy Oil* 585 F3d 855 (5th Cir 2009).

[7] *Native Village of Kivalina v Exxon Mobil Corp* 696 F3d 849 (9th Cir 2012), cert denied, 569 US 1000 (2013). The inhabitants of the Inuit village of Kivalina in Alaska claimed monetary damages from the energy industry for the destruction of their village by flooding caused by climate change.

also the reason why the German Regional Court of Essen dismissed the damage claim of the Peruvian farmer and mountain guide Saul Luciano Lliuya against the German energy corporation RWE.[8] Lliuya was claiming a share of the costs which are necessary to protect his village in the Peruvian Andes from flooding by Lake Palcacocha, which is constantly rising due to glacial meltdown. Lliuya sued RWE for 0.5% of the costs of a protective dam (€17,000) because RWE has been responsible for about 0.5% of the worldwide greenhouse gas emissions from human activity since the beginning of industrialisation. The case is now being assessed on its merits by the Higher Regional Court of Hamm.

In the following discussion I will examine the significance of the requirement of causation for tort law claims. I will show that the traditional methods of establishing causation, the 'but for' test of the common law and the *conditio sine qua non* formula applied in the civil law systems, have inherent weaknesses which require additional deliberations to ensure fair results for the individual case. I will first describe the strategies courts traditionally apply in order to meet the structural deficits of the 'but for' test, and then I will highlight some cases where courts developed even more far-reaching strategies when victims encountered typical and unsurmountable difficulties in proving causality. From this I will try to draw some conclusions for climate change damage.

II. THE 'BUT FOR' TEST AND THE *CONDITIO SINE QUA NON* FORMULA

Civil liability requires a sufficient causal link between the defendant's activity and the harm sustained by the victim. This requirement is stressed both by legal doctrine and the economic theory of law. For any legal doctrine, the causality requirement is a question of justice as it would be utterly unfair to burden a person with a loss to which this person has no sufficient connection. This is complemented by the economic deliberation that in order to pursue the optimal allocation of resources, it is essential to allocate damage costs to the person who is in the best position to minimise these costs (the cheapest cost avoider), which requires that the liable person is able to influence the cost of potential damage by his behaviour, namely by the applied level of care.

Legal doctrine provides that the causal link is established according to the 'but for' test (common law) or the *conditio sine qua non* formula (civil law), which qualifies any circumstance as the cause of the damage if the damage would not have occurred without it. This method of damage attribution has a long tradition and enjoys widespread recognition.[9]

The 'but for' test is a suitable instrument for the attribution of damage in most causality scenarios. For climate change damage, it is essential to see that it even ensures appropriate damage attribution when damage is caused by the *synergistic effects* of two or more interacting substances. Such effects can be of a different nature. If the harmful effect is only created because of the interaction of otherwise harmless substances, the 'but for' test indicates full causation by both substances (and therefore joint and several liability, provided that the incident is covered by an applicable cause of action). The same solution applies if the noxiousness of a substance is only triggered by its reaction with the natural environment or a natural

---

[8] For information on the case, see www.germanwatch.org/en/huaraz; A Kling, 'Die Klimaklage gegen RWE – Die Geltendmachung von Klimafolgeschäden auf dem Privatrechtsweg' (2018) 2 *Kritische Justiz (KJ)* 213; HJ Ahrens, 'Außervertragliche Haftung wegen der Emission genehmigter Treibhausgase?' (2019) 11 *Versicherungsrecht (VersR)* 645; G Wagner, *Klimahaftung vor Gericht* (Munich, CH Beck, 2020).
[9] R Zimmermann, 'Comparative Report' in B Winiger et al (eds), *Digest of European Tort Law, Volume 1: Essential Cases on Natural Causation* (Vienna, Springer, 2007) 99.

substance, and also in case of the chemical or physical interaction of two harmful substances. In all these constellations the application of the 'but for' test shows that the damage would not have occurred without the emission of these substances into the natural environment.

Things get a bit more complicated when the interaction of two harmful substances has a *progressive effect*, that is, when the common effects of the harmful interacting substances are greater than the sum of the individual effects of any of them. Here the result of the 'but for' test indicates the part of damage that was caused by each substance and, in addition, the common increase in damage. Again, given that there is an applicable cause of action, this can lead to the joint and several liability of each polluter or, if the damage is divisible, liability can be split according to the shares. This would mean that each emitter is severally liable for the individual share and has to bear joint liability for the common increase.[10]

All tort law systems traditionally provide for diverse strategies to cope with specific cases where the causal link does not pass the 'but for' test. Typical constellations are the cases where: (i) two or more separate acts cause harm to a third party without the possibility of apportionment (*concurrent causation*); (ii) two or more separate acts cause harm when each would have been in itself sufficient to cause the harm (*cumulative causation*); or (iii) it cannot be established whether the harm was caused by the tortious act of person A or person B (*alternative causation*). In most jurisdictions the answer to such causality constellations is joint and several liability of each tortfeasor.[11] The defendant who has compensated the victim has a right of recourse against the other defendants. However, when one cause has taken effect before the other (*intervening causation*), it is predominantly held that only the person who caused the damage first is liable.[12] For the case of *minimal causation*, another causality constellation which is traditionally discussed by tort law theory, causation cannot be established according to the 'but for' test, but needs further considerations in order to avoid unjust results. When damage is caused by a large number of people, the 'but for' test works for the whole group, because it correctly indicates that all the members of the group caused the damage, but it is not appropriate for the adequate attribution of damage to the individual members of the group. Due to the minimal effects of each contribution on the development of the damage, the 'but for' test would in most cases lead to the conclusion that no member of the group has caused the damage. As causation by the whole group is, however, a proven fact, this result is apparently not correct. From a theoretical point of view, minimal causation constitutes a special subcategory of concurrent causation. The fact that not only two or several persons, but also a multitude of persons contributed to the damage makes it difficult, or even impossible, to determine the individual share of each contributor, which, according to the theory of concurrent causation, would lead to the finding of joint and several liability for each contributor. It is again apparent that this result is disproportionate to the detriment of the individual tortfeasor and thus not justifiable. Therefore, in legal doctrine, it is generally accepted that the 'but for' test is not suitable for cases of *minimal causation*. When a large number of people cause specific damage, doctrine suggests that each contributor should only be liable for a part of the damage. If the individual case gives no further indications for the determination, or at least an

---

[10] M Gimpel-Hinteregger, *Grundfragen der Umwelthaftung* (Vienna, Manz, 1994) 199; Pöttker, (n 1) 140.

[11] See, for instance, Austria: § 1302 ABGB; Germany: §§ 830 (1) (2), 840 (1) and 426 (1) BGB; Greece: art 926 of the Astikos Kodikas; Italy: art 2055 of the Codice Civile; Portugal: arts 490 and 497 of the Código Civil; Ireland: pt III of the Civil Liability Act 1961; the Netherlands: art 6:102 of the Burgerlijk Wetboek. See J Spier (ed), *Unification of Tort Law: Causation* (The Hague, Kluwer Law International, 2000); Winiger et al (n 9).

[12] See the discussed cases in Winiger et al (n 9) 479 and 505.

estimation, of the individual share, the incurred damage must be equally divided among the members of the group.[13]

However, a look at various legal systems, shows that courts find even more sophisticated solutions when the causality situation becomes more complex and plaintiffs encounter structural problems with respect to the proof of causality.

III. SPECIFIC COURT SOLUTIONS FOR COMPLEX CAUSALITY CONSTELLATIONS

A. DES Cases and Beyond

In the famous *Sindell v Abbott Laboratories* case,[14] the Supreme Court of California created the theory of market share liability. In this case, the plaintiffs could show that their harm was caused by a specific drug (Diethylstilbestrol (DES)) prescribed to their mothers during pregnancy in order to prevent miscarriage. What the plaintiffs could not ascertain was the relationship between the individual plaintiff and the defendant because the product was generically marketed by several manufacturers and there was no way for them to show which company had produced or distributed the drug taken by the individual plaintiff's mother. In *Sindell* the court referred to the doctrine of alternative liability in the case of *Summers v Tice*,[15] where the court held that the burden of proof is upon the tortfeasors. Where the conduct of two actors is tortious, and it is proven that the harm has been caused to the plaintiff by only one of them, but there is uncertainty as to which one of them has caused it, the burden is upon each such actor to prove that he has not caused the harm. This solution for cases of alternative liability, as was shown above, is shared by many other jurisdictions. In *Sindell* the court expanded the theory of alternative liability to the constellation that not only two but several tortfeasors could have caused the harm in question. It held that the burden of proof shifts to the defendants if the plaintiff joins manufacturers of a substantial share of the DES produced and marketed in the relevant area, and if the plaintiff is able to prove a prima facie case on every element of the cause of action except identification of the direct tortfeasor. It is then up to the defendants to prove that they did not cause the plaintiff's injuries, and those defendants failing in this proof are held liable for the percentage of damages approximating their share of the relevant market. This means that each defendant's share of the damages would approximate the probability that it caused the plaintiff's injuries.

In *Sindell* the court thus set up several requirements for the application of the theory of market share liability. These requirements are as follows: (i) the defendants in court must constitute substantially all of the market; (ii) all the defendants must have been in the market within the critical timeframe; (iii) the marketed products must be of the same composition and thus interchangeable; and (iv) it must not be the plaintiff's fault that the individual tortfeasor cannot be identified.

Subsequent court decisions concretised the burden of proof for the defendants. In *Martin v Abbott Labs*[16] the Washington Supreme Court supported the plaintiffs with regard to their

---

[13] See art 3:105 of the Principles of European Tort Law. The Principles are a proposal by a group of academics for a comprehensive system of tort law. They are published in: European Group on Tort Law, *Principles of European Tort Law* (Vienna, Verlag Österreich, 2005). B Koch, 'Comparative Report' in Winiger et al (n 9) 541 indicates that case law dealing with this problem is scarce.

[14] *Sindell v Abbott Laboratories* 607 P2d 924 (Cal 1980).

[15] *Summers v Tice* 199 P2d 1 (Cal 1948).

[16] *Martin v Abbott Labs* 689 P2d 368 (Wash 1984).

obligation to join defendants with a substantial share of the market in the action by introducing the presumption that all the defendants who cannot exculpate themselves (by showing that DES ingested by the individual mother did not come from their production) have equal shares of the market ('presumptive share liability'). It is then up to the individual defendant to prove a lower share. This approach was also adopted by the Florida Supreme Court in *Conley v Boyle Drug Co.*[17]

In *Collins v Eli Lilly & Co*[18] the Wisconsin Supreme Court went an important step further. Because of the practical difficulty of defining and proving market share, the court allowed the plaintiff to bring a cause of action against one single defendant and, in full application of the alternative liability rule in *Summers v Tice*, it shifted the burden of proof as to causation fully to the defendant.[19] The defendant was thus obliged to show that it did not produce the DES taken by the plaintiff's mother. In order to justify this, the court referred to the Wisconsin Constitution, which provides in Article I, section 9 that: 'Every person is entitled to a certain remedy in the laws for all injuries, or wrongs which he may receive in his person, property, or character.' This allows the courts 'to fashion an adequate remedy' 'when an adequate remedy or forum does not exist to resolve disputes or provide due process'. The Wisconsin Supreme Court therefore came to the conclusion that 'the interests of justice and fundamental fairness' mean that the producers of the drug should bear the cost of injury. It assumed that the drug company is in a better position than the victim to absorb the cost of the injury and that the cost of damages awards will act as an incentive for drug companies to adequately test the drugs they make available to the public.

The New York Supreme Court adopted an even broader market share theory in *Hymowitz v Eli Lilly*[20] by relating to the risk a defendant created in the national market ('national market theory'). In this case, the Court dispensed with the requirement of an individual causal relationship between the plaintiff and the defendant. According to this theory, the plaintiff must only show that she ingested DES and that her injuries resulted from the use of DES. Defendants can evade liability only by proving that they did not manufacture or market DES for pregnancy use.

It must be stressed that the doctrine of market share liability is only used in a minority of US states. In the majority of states, liability still requires that the specific product alleged to have caused the injuries is identified with particularity. Efforts to expand the market share approach beyond DES cases have been mostly rejected by US courts. In *Becker v Baron Brothers*[21] the Supreme Court of New Jersey declined to apply the market share approach to an asbestos case because asbestos products – unlike DES – are not uniformly dangerous; they have a varying degree of toxicity and can therefore not be treated as a monolithic group.[22] In *Santiago v Sherwin Williams Co*[23] and *Skipworth v Lead Indus Association*[24] the courts rejected market

---

[17] *Conley v Boyle Drug Co* 570 So2d 275 (Fla 1990).
[18] *Collins v Eli Lilly & Co* 342 NW2d 37 (Wis 1984).
[19] The court obliged the plaintiff to allege 'that the plaintiff's mother took DES; that DES caused the plaintiff's subsequent injuries; that the defendant produced or marketed the type of DES taken by the plaintiff's mother; and that the defendant's conduct in producing or marketing the DES constituted a breach of a legally recognised duty to the plaintiff. In the situation where the plaintiff cannot allege and prove what type of DES the mother took, as to the third element the plaintiff need only allege and prove that the defendant drug company produced or marketed the drug DES for use in preventing miscarriages during pregnancy'. ibid 50 ff.
[20] *Hymowitz v Eli Lilly* 539 NE2d 1069 (NY 1989).
[21] *Becker v Baron Brothers* 649 A2d 613 (NJ 1994).
[22] See also *Robertson v Allied Signal, Inc* 914 F2d 360, 379–80 (3d Cir 1990).
[23] *Santiago v Sherwin Williams Co* 3 F3d 546 (1st Cir 1993).
[24] *Skipworth v Lead Indus Association* 690 A2d 169 (Pa 1997).

share liability for personal injury caused by lead paint because the plaintiffs were not able to show the defendants' contribution to the market in the relevant period of time which spanned over several decades. The defendants were also not the actual manufacturers of the hazardous product, but only the bulk suppliers of the raw material. The only judicial decision to date allowing the plaintiff in a lead pigment case to proceed under market share theory is *Jackson v Glidden Co.*[25] The theory of market share liability was also rejected in several rulings in cases concerning products containing the HIV virus,[26] but in *Methyl Tertiary Butyl Ether*,[27] market share liability was applied in an environmental liability case concerning the contamination of groundwater in Orange County, California, by various oil companies. The companies used the gasoline additive methyl tertiary butyl ether in underground storage tanks, from where it leaked into the groundwater.

For European lawyers, the 'market share liability' doctrine has inspired many theorists of tort law over the last few decades. However, Dutch and French courts, when deciding DES cases, did not follow the market share theory of the Californian Supreme Court, but found different, even more far-reaching solutions in favour of the victims. The Dutch Supreme Court[28] reduced the burden of proof of causation for the victims and held all the defendant drug producers jointly and severally liable. In 2009[29] and 2010[30] the French Supreme Court also ruled in favour of the plaintiffs. It came to the conclusion that the plaintiffs in DES cases only need to show that the victim's bodily injury was caused by prenatal exposure to DES. Causation is already established if medical expertise asserts that the victim suffered from a disease (eg, a cancerous tumour) that typically results from exposure to DES and if there are no indications that the victim has been exposed to other risk factors for the development of the disease. It is then up to the defendant pharmaceutical companies who put the substance on the market to prove that their product did not cause the damage. If they fail to do so, they are jointly and severally liable for the sustained harm.

B. The 'Increased Material Risk of Harm' Test of the UK Supreme Court

In *Fairchild v Glenhaven Funeral Services Ltd*[31] the House of Lords (since 2009 'The Supreme Court') had to deal with compensation claims of workers who had been exposed to asbestos at three different workplaces. The workers suffered from mesothelioma, a specific kind of cancer which is typical for exposure to asbestos, but unlike asbestosis (another asbestos related disease) not dependent on the amount of fibre ingested which, taken to the extreme, means that one inhaled fibre can already trigger the disease. Accordingly, the claimants could show that their illness was caused by exposure to asbestos at the workplace, but could not say which employer was the most likely source of the asbestos fibre which caused the harm. The court held that in a case where causation cannot be established because of a lack of scientific knowledge, the application of the 'but for' test would lead to the inherently unfair

---

[25] *Jackson v Glidden Co* 647 NE2d 879 (Ohio App 1995). The appeal was rejected in 868 NE2d 680 (Ohio 2007).
[26] *Ray v Cutter Labs* 754 F Supp 193 (MDFla 1991); *Morris v Parke, Davis & Co* 667 F Supp 1332 (CDCal 1987); *Smith v Cutter Biological, Inc* 823 P2d 717 (Haw 1991).
[27] *In re Methyl Tertiary Butyl Ether (MTBE) Products Liability Litigation* 859 F3d 178 (2d Cir 2017).
[28] Hoge Raad, 9 October 1992, NL:HR:1992:ZC0706, Nederlandse Jurisprudentie (NJ) 1994, 535.
[29] Cour de cassation 1re civ, 24 September 2009, no 08-16.305, Bulletin 2009, I, no 187.
[30] Cour de cassation 1re civ, 28 January 2010, no 08-18.8307, Bulletin 2010, I, no 22.
[31] *Fairchild v Glenhaven Funeral Services Ltd* [2002] UKHL 22, [2003] 1 AC 32.

result of leaving the claimant without any remedy. In such cases, it must be sufficient for the proof of causation that the claimants can show that the defendant's actions constituted a breach of duty and that this breach of duty had a material effect on the likelihood of injury. Accordingly, the House of Lords held that all the employers were jointly and severally liable for the damage.

This 'increased material risk of harm' test was also applied in the mesothelioma case of *Barker v Corus (UK) Ltd*[32] with the difference that the House of Lords decided not for joint, but only for several liability according to the increase in risk caused by the individual defendant. For victims of mesothelioma (but not for other constellations), this ruling was reversed by the legislator that provided in section 3 of the Compensation Act 2006 for joint and several liability of each tortfeasor. In *Sienkiewicz v Greif (UK) Ltd*[33] the *Fairchild* rule was even applied in a mesothelioma case against one single defendant. The Supreme Court held the defendant employer liable for the full loss, although the evidence did not show that the defendant increased the risk of harm by more than 50% (as would be required by the evidentiary standard of the common law), but, according to the judge on the facts, only by a smaller amount, concretely by 18% over the general environmental exposure.

C. Proportional Liability

Many jurisdictions allow under certain circumstances for the finding of proportional liability. A very prominent example is the theory of loss of a chance (*perte d'une chance*). This theory does not solve the causality problem as such, but rather opens the way to circumventing the problem of causation by recognising the loss of an opportunity as compensable damage. Many jurisdictions accept this theory for compensation under tort and/or contract law, especially in cases concerning compensation for medical malpractice and against lawyers for loss of procedural chances.[34] In these cases the defendant's breach of contract or, under tort law, negligent activity was not the cause of the harm itself (the illness or the legal problem), but only deprived the claimant of the opportunity to obtain a benefit or avoid a loss (eg, the chance to recover from an illness or to win a lawsuit). In most jurisdictions, especially in France where this theory has a long tradition, the recognition of the theory allows for partial compensation of the incurred harm in proportion to the reduction of the chances not to suffer the loss.[35]

A concept with comparable results is applied by Austrian courts who, in application of the theory of alternative causation, find for proportional liability in some exceptional cases where it cannot be established whether the harm (eg, personal injury) was caused by the defendant's tortious behaviour (eg, the doctor's medical malpractice) or by a fact in the claimant's own sphere (eg, genetic predisposition).[36]

---

[32] *Barker v Corus (UK) Ltd* [2006] UKHL 20, [2006] 2 AC 572.

[33] *Sienkiewicz v Greif (UK) Ltd* [2011] UKSC 10, [2011] 2 AC 229.

[34] According to a comparative study concerning Europe, the theory is accepted in France, Italy, Portugal Spain, The Netherlands, Ireland and Slovenia; see H Koziol, 'Comparative Report' in Winiger et al (n 9) 589.

[35] See F Terré et al, *Droit civil. Les obligations*, 12th edn (Paris, Dalloz, 2018) 1005.

[36] B Koch, 'Proportional Liability for Causal Uncertainty' in M Martin-Casals and D Papayannis (eds), *Uncertain Causation in Tort Law* (Cambridge, Cambridge University Press, 2016) 67.

D. Compensation Despite Scientific Uncertainty: Hepatitis B Vaccinations and the French Courts

In the last two decades, the French Supreme Court (Cour de cassation) was confronted with a series of compensation claims brought by persons who developed a demyelinating disease (especially multiple sclerosis) after having been vaccinated against hepatitis B. Some of these claims were based on compensation rules for work accidents, but most were product liability cases filed against the producer of the vaccine.[37] At the beginning, the court dismissed the claims due to a lack of sufficient scientific evidence that the plaintiffs' harm was actually caused by the vaccination, although the lower courts had stressed the fact that science was not able to show that the vaccinations were not the cause of the disease either.[38] After the Conseil d'État, the highest French administrative court, accepted causation in cases where the disease appeared within three months after vaccination provided that there were no other plausible causes for the disease,[39] the Supreme Court changed its position. It came to the conclusion that the question of causation is a matter of fact which must be decided by the lower courts. It further held that this decision cannot be based on probabilistic evidence alone, but must be decided by the lower courts according to the facts of the individual case.[40] Since these rulings of the Supreme Court, several lower courts have delivered decisions in hepatitis B cases. The rulings are diverse, but in most cases the courts have ruled that the causal link cannot be established.[41]

IV. CAUSATION AND CLIMATE CHANGE DAMAGE

A. The Problem

There is no doubt that the establishment of causation for climate change damage is very difficult and a true challenge for any court. In the context of climate change damage, all thinkable causality scenarios culminate at the same time. Damage is caused by multiple emitters. Emitters and injured parties are located far from each other. There is a considerable time lag between emissions and the harm, and there is the influence of synergistic effects between the various emitted substances on the one hand, and between those substances and the natural environment on the other hand. However, at least from a theoretical point of view, one can say that the matter of causation for climate change damage is difficult, but not totally unsolvable. As outlined before, tort law theory provides for some useful instruments that can also have some merits for the adequate attribution of climate change-related damage. Traditional tort law is even able to offer well-balanced solutions for the problems of synergistic and progressive effects of noxious substances.

---

[37] For a comprehensive account of these cases, see JS Borghetti, 'Litigation on Hepatitis B Vaccination and Demyelinating Diseases in France' in M Martin-Casals and D Papayannis (eds), *Uncertain Causation in Tort Law* (Cambridge, Cambridge University Press, 2016) 11.

[38] Cour de cassation 1re civ, 23 September 2003, no 01-13.063, Bulletin 2003, I, no 188.

[39] Conseil d'État, 9 March 2007, no 267635, no 278665, no 283067, no 285288.

[40] Cour de cassation 1re civ, 22 May 2008, no 05-20.317, Bulletin 2008, I, no 148; Cour de cassation 1re civ, 22 May 2008, no 06-10.967, Bulletin 2008, I, no 149. This reasoning was accepted by the Court of Justice of the European Union in Case C-621/15 *NW and Others v Sanofi Pasteur MSD SNC and Others* EU:C:2017:484, a preliminary ruling upon request of the Cour de cassation on the interpretation of art 4 of Council Directive 85/374/EEC of 25 July 1985 on the approximation of the laws, regulations and administrative provisions of the Member States concerning liability for defective products [1985] OJ L210/29.

[41] See Borghetti (n 37) 11, 26 f.

B. Possible Solutions

i. The Concept of Minimal Causation

First of all, when discussing causality with respect to climate change damage, it is necessary to emphasise the fact that climate change leads to different types of damage and that not all types of climate change damage raise the same problems of causation.[42] For those events which can be directly attributed to the large-scale rise of the temperature of the atmosphere, like the rise of sea levels or the gradual melting of glaciers and polar ice caps, climate science can show that the causal link is actually quite clear: these events are predominantly caused by greenhouse gases emitted into the atmosphere due to human activities. The causal relationship between the emission of greenhouse gases and the consequences for the natural environment also includes the finding of actionable harm caused by those natural events to persons and property. Examples for such scenarios are the rebuilding cost for a village situated on a sea-cliff that has become uninhabitable, as in the *Kivalina* case, or the cost for a protective dam against the melting glacier water, as was alleged by the claimants in the *Lliuya* case. With respect to these scenarios, the problem for the establishment of causation lies not so much in the scientific proof of causation as such, but in the attributability of the incurred harm to specific polluters due to the long emission periods and the large number of polluters who, over the last 100 years, have been releasing greenhouse gases into the atmosphere.

For such constellations, causation theory can offer the theory of minimal causation. In such scenarios the mere application of the 'but for' test is not able to produce acceptable results because, due to the smallness of the contributions, it does not indicate the concrete share of the individual contributor. Although this cannot be established with any certainty for the individual emitter, it is legitimate to assume that each emitter actually caused a part (albeit a very small part) of the damage. According to legal doctrine, such scenarios can be qualified as cases of concurrent minimal causation. As the number of emitters is quite high and the shares that can be attributed to the individual emitters are quite low, the solidary liability of each emitter would be excessive and would lead to a result that is neither just nor, due to an extreme over-deterrent effect, economically efficient. It would therefore make much more sense to hold each emitter only liable for its share. As this share cannot be established with sufficient probability, it is fair and reasonable to estimate the share according to the overall amount of greenhouse gases which the individual contributor has emitted in the past.

However, the application of the theory of minimal causation to these types of climate change damage encounters the further problem that greenhouse gases only lead to climate change if they exceed a certain threshold. Greenhouse gases, especially carbon dioxide (and also methane and nitrous oxide, but not fluorinated gases), are part of natural processes and can be absorbed by the natural environment to a certain extent. It can therefore be assumed that emissions caused by a single person (breathing, driving a motor vehicle, heating the home) will never be sufficient to exceed this threshold. As these emitters do not even have the slightest potential to cause climate change damage, it would, already from a theoretical point of view, not be justifiable to subject those contributors to the theory of minimal causation. The idea to

---

[42] This was already stressed by W Frank, 'Climate Change Litigation – Klimawandel und haftungsrechtliche Risiken, Erwiderung auf Chatzinerantzis/Herz (NJOZ 2010, 594 = NJW 2010, 910)' (2010) 44 *Neue Juristische Online-Zeitschrift* (NJOZ) 2296; W Frank, 'Überlegungen zur Klimahaftung nach Völkerrecht' (2014) 11 *Neue Zeitschrift für Verwaltungsrecht Extra* 1, 5; W Frank, 'Zur Kausalitätsproblematik und Risikozurechnung bei Klimaschäden im Zusammenhang mit Entschädigungs- und Schutzansprüchen gemäß Völkerumweltrecht' (2015) 1 *Bonner Rechtsjournal* 42.

hold the average person liable for climate change damage would also constitute a perversion of the tort law system which is designed for the solution of conflicts between certain identifiable persons on a case-by-case basis. Such an approach would overwhelm the system both from a theoretical and, considering the enormous number of past and actual emitters of greenhouse gases, a practical viewpoint. Hence, the theory of minimal causation can at best be applied to the major emitters of greenhouse gases, such as the 'big players' in the energy-generating industry, who are responsible for the emission of enormous amounts of greenhouse gases over the last decades.

Under the condition that the concept of minimal causation is accepted for such large-scale emitters, the main problem for the allocation of the loss to the individual polluter is then not so much the matter of causation, but rather the need to find an applicable cause of action for the claim. Since liability for climate change damage is not yet covered by international treaties, climate change litigation must resort to national tort law. In absence of an applicable regime of no-fault liability for compensation claims against emitters of greenhouse gases, claimants must rely on fault-based liability.[43] The establishment of fault according to the civil law juris-dictions[44] or the breach of a duty of care under the tort of negligence of the common law both require a violation of a certain standard of conduct (unlawful behaviour or violation of a duty of care). For climate change damage, this assessment encounters some difficulties. The evaluation whether an emitter of greenhouse gases violated the required standard must be performed for the point in time when the emission was made and not when the damage occurred. With respect to climate change damage, this point of time can lie considerably in the past, which obliges the court to make extensive findings of the quantity of greenhouse gases emitted during specific time periods in the past. Moreover, for the allegation of fault, the emitters of greenhouse gases must have been aware of the risk at the time of the emission. However, this latter hurdle is not as big as it looks at the first moment because historical studies show that the risk of climate change has already been known since the end of the nineteenth century. The first scientific analyses of the warming effects of greenhouse gases go even back as far as 1861.[45] At least since the publication of the first IPPC report on climate change in 1990,[46] it can be assumed that industrial emitters of greenhouse gases must have had knowledge of the risk.

ii. The Concept of Proportional Liability for Cases of Mere Statistical Evidence

An even bigger challenge of climate change damage for legal doctrine is posed by those cases where it is only possible to establish statistical evidence between the rising temperatures on the planet and the sustained damage. Examples of this are the causation of property damage or personal injury by extreme weather events, like storms, floods or heatwaves. Such events occur

---

[43] For an account of applicable liability regime for environmental harm and climate change damage, see M Hinteregger, 'Environmental Liability' in E Lees and J Viñuales (eds), *The Oxford Handbook of Comparative Environmental Law* (Oxford, Oxford University Press, 2019) 1025; and M Hinteregger, (n 3).

[44] In the Germanic civil law tradition (Austria, Germany, the Netherlands and Switzerland) the notion of fault is split into two parts: (i) unlawfulness which relates to the assessment of the act of the damaging party; and (ii) fault in the strict sense which deals with the blameworthiness of the concrete actor. In the Romanic countries, like France and Spain, unlawfulness is not regarded as a separate requirement, but is absorbed by the criterion of fault.

[45] J Tyndall, 'On the Absorption and Radiation of Heat by Gases and Vapours, and on the Physical Connexion of Radiation, Absorption, and Conduction' (1861) 151 *Philosophical Transactions of the Royal Society of London* 1. For a comprehensive overview, see D Archer and R Pierrehumbert (eds), *The Warming Papers: The Scientific Foundation for the Climate Change Forecast* (Chichester, Wiley-Blackwell, 2011).

[46] Intergovernmental Panel on Climate Change (IPCC), 'Climate Change: The IPCC 1990 and 1992 Assessments' (1992), www.ipcc.ch/site/assets/uploads/2018/05/ipcc_90_92_assessments_far_full_report.pdf.

regularly even without climate change, but science shows that climate change increases their frequency and severity. In these cases the causal link between the emission of greenhouse gases and the incurred damage is not straightforward, but only of a statistical nature. In order to cope with such constellations under tort law, the question arises as to: (i) whether under these conditions full proof of causation can be dispensed with; and (ii) whether it can be justified to split the damage incurred by an individual person according to the percentage of the increase in probability of the occurrence of such damage or, respectively, according to the percentage of the increase in damage caused by the human emission of greenhouse gases.

Legal doctrine, as was shown before, is not altogether reluctant to award liability in cases where plaintiffs are confronted with scientific and structural problems for the proof of causation. These examples from court practice indicate that courts are ready to address the issue and to adjust their usual requirements for the establishment of the causal link in relation to the individual constellation. The applied solutions vary. Courts may accommodate the injured party by lowering the standard of proof for the individual case, as was done by the UK Supreme Court in the *Fairchild* and the *Sienkiewicz* cases and by the French courts with respect to the hepatitis B vaccination cases. Another method to address the plaintiff's evidentiary distress is the reversal of the burden of proof from the plaintiff to the defendant, like the courts did in the DES cases. Under both theories, courts may decide for only partial liability (as in the DES cases, where the courts applied the theory of market share liability, and the UK case of *Barker v Corus*) or even full liability (as in *Fairchild*, *Collins v Eli Lilly & Co* and the DES decisions of the Dutch and French Supreme Courts). Especially in medical cases, partial compensation of the actual damage in proportion to the reduction of the chances not to suffer the loss (theory of 'loss of a chance') increasingly gains recognition.

The solution to apportion compensation according to the statistical evidence of causation is also supported by tort law theory.[47] From a theoretical point of view, liability for the increase of risk is recommended because it leads to just and efficient results: liability for the statistical increase of risk allocates each emitter exactly the damage costs he or she has caused (the justice argument) and would induce him or her to reduce his or her future emissions to the efficient level (the economic argument). Whether jurisdictions are ready to accept such theories of proportionate liability is a matter of policy. To make emitters of greenhouse gases liable for an increase in damage which is only statistically verifiable is in any case a far-reaching measure that pushes tort law to its conceptual and factual limits. In these cases the causal connection between the individual emitter of greenhouse gases and the person who suffers specific climate change-related damage is very loose. The causal connection only then becomes more obvious when it is established between the respective groups: the group of emitters of greenhouse gases on the one side and the group of injured parties on the other side. Such an undertaking requires procedural instruments that allow for the aggregation of these persons to coherent groups. A good example of such a device is the class action of US law.[48] Another appropriate

---

[47] I Gilead et al (eds), *Proportional Liability: Analytical and Comparative Perspectives* (Berlin, De Gruyter, 2013); Winiger et al (n 9). For the application of proportional liability to climate change damage, see Kysar (n 1); and Duffy (n 1).

[48] In the US, class action is provided by r 23 of the Federal Rules of Civil Procedure. For the application of this procedural instrument on pollution damage, see, for instance, J Elrod, 'The Use of Federal Class Actions in Mass Toxic Pollution Torts' (1988) 56 *Tennessee Law Review* 243; K Rivlin and J Potts, 'Proposed Rule Change to Federal Civil Procedure May Introduce New Challenges in Environmental Class Action Litigation' (2003) 27 *Harvard Environmental Law Review* 519; J Betts, 'The Influence of Mass Toxic Tort Litigation on Class Action Rules Reform' (2004) 22 *Virginia Environmental Law Journal* 249; D Hensler, 'The Globalisation of Class Actions: An Overview' (2009) 622 *Annals of the American Academy of Political and Social Science* 7. For prominent cases, see *In re Agent Orange* 745 F2d 161 (2d Cir 1984); *In re Three Mile Island*, 87 FRD 433 (MD Pa 1980).

instrument would be the introduction of specific compensation funds that are fed by the greenhouse gas generating industry.

V. SUMMARY AND OVERALL CONCLUSION

Climate change is happening and there is no doubt that courts will increasingly be confronted with claimants seeking compensation for the damage resulting from climate change on the basis of tort law. Very often, these attempts will not primarily be motivated by the desire to actually obtain compensation for the incurred loss, but will rather serve as a vehicle to draw public attention to the problem in order to induce emitters of greenhouse gases to change their future behaviour. The compensability of climate change damage caused by greenhouse gas emissions on the basis of tort law raises fundamental legal issues that cannot be answered easily. A major problem for such claims is the need for the establishment of causation. All available bases of claims, whether fault-based or not, require the proof of causation. It is a well-founded doctrine of tort law that it is, in principle, up to the claimant to prove all the preconditions of liability required by the concrete cause of action. But an examination of the national tort law rules and court practice shows that the observation is also well founded that legislators and courts tend to lighten this burden of proof when claimants encounter unsurmountable problems beyond their control to meet this requirement. Tort law traditionally recognises specific constellations where the 'but for' test or the *conditio sine qua non* rule – the usual methods of the common law and the civil law to establish causation – are set aside. Textbook examples are the scenarios of concurrent, cumulative, alternative and intervening causation. However, it could be shown that under specific circumstances, courts are ready to transgress these traditional boundaries of tort law doctrine. This is especially so in cases concerning loss of life and personal injury sustained by consumers, patients and workers because of medical malpractice, the unknown risks of drug products (DES) or the exposition to asbestos at the workplace. In order to deal with the problem of causation, courts developed new causation theories, such as market share liability (in the US), the 'increased material risk of harm' test (in the UK) or the French theory of 'loss of a chance'. In some cases, courts even reversed the burden of proof from the claimant to the defendant, as was done by several US and European courts in the DES cases.

Victims of climate change also encounter such fundamental and unsurmountable obstacles for the proof of causation. Today this is seen by many tort lawyers rather as a reason to decline compensation for lack of proof of causality. However, this might not be the case for much longer. The greater the threat of climate change and the more frequent and severe the resulting damage, the more likely the courts will see the necessity to adapt tort law in order to serve 'the interests of justice and fundamental fairness', as the Wisconsin Supreme Court required in *Collins v Eli Lilly*. An important step would be to lighten the burden of proof for claimants and to develop specific causation theories for climate change damage. In order to do so, courts need not to start from scratch, but can rely on existing theories, namely the theories of minimal causation and proportionate liability.

Part V

Reflections

14

The Job of the Judge in the Supranational European Rule of Law

CASSANDRA CW LANGE*

Ubi ius, ibi remedium [Where there is a right, there must be a remedy].

I. INTRODUCTION

EVERYTHING GOOD IN life is about balance. It is no different for the rule of law. A division of the legislative, the executive and the judicial powers within the rule of law, and the checks and balances between them, are crucial for the good functioning of the rule of law.[1] In utopia[2] there would be a perfect balance between the three powers so that they can limit each other, avoiding abuses of power. In a society under the rule of law, equipped with well-trained professionals and where the powers within are perfectly balanced, these powers would strengthen each other to the benefit of all state powers. This would lead to high-quality legislation, good governance[3] and effective judicial protection for all parties concerned, including citizens and minorities. In real-life, finding and keeping this perfect balance proves to be quite a challenge that needs constant evaluation and adjustment. As in a happy marriage, the rule of law also requires constant nourishing. This is true for the national rules of law of the EU Member States, but even more so for the supranational, multi-layered European rule of law enshrined in Article 2 of the Treaty on European Union (TEU). At least, if we want to tackle the big challenges that the EU is facing in areas such as environmental protection,

---

* This chapter is written to conclude the 'Judges in Utopia. Judicial Law-Making in European Private Law' research project, led by Chantal Mak and funded by the Netherlands Organisation for Scientific Research (the NWO Vidi scheme). This aimed to inform practitioners, policy-makers, academics and law students of developments in European case law on private legal relationships, with a particular focus on the influence of fundamental rights and public policy. I would like to thank Chantal Mak, Betül Kas, Rosanne van der Straten and Ramona Grimbergen for their valuable comments on an earlier version of this chapter. All views expressed are mine.
[1] Montesquieu, *The Spirit of the Laws* (1748). Montesquieu distinguished three powers: a legislature, an executive and a judiciary, generally known as the *trias politica* model.
[2] See the 'Judges in Utopia. Judicial Law-Making in European Private Law' research project.
[3] According to the definition of the United Nations, good governance has eight major characteristics: it is participatory, consensus-oriented, accountable, transparent, responsive, effective and efficient, equitable and inclusive, and follows the rule of law. It ensures that corruption is minimised, that the views of minorities are taken into account and that the voices of the most vulnerable in society are heard in decision-making. It is also responsive to the present and future needs of society.

climate change, migration, consumer health and safety, and data privacy.[4] The EU has set high goals in these areas and it is of the utmost importance that Member States stay focused on and committed to these goals. Tim Koopmans, a former Judge of the Court of Justice of the European Union (CJEU), was quite right when he remarked that 'the Court of Justice is aware that lack of judicial interference may very well mean that nothing will happen at all'.[5] This is true in general. For instance, you can have the most wonderful recipe for a tasty apple pie, but if you don't actually use the prescribed ingredients and make sure the instructions are followed, then the tasty apple pie will remain a dream image.

So, for the proper functioning of the EU, it is essential that all judges in the EU play their part in relation to the European rule of law. But what part is that? If EU law does not apply, national judges work within their own national rule of law with their own constitutional traditions. Judges in every Member State face their own challenges in combining their tasks in both the European and the national rule of law. This chapter focuses on the meaning and influence that the right to effective judicial protection against infringement of EU rights and freedoms as laid down in Article 47 of the Charter of Fundamental Rights of the European Union (CFR) can have on the fulfilment of the job of the judge, both at a European and a national level.

II. THE JOB OF THE JUDGE IN THE DUTCH RULE OF LAW

Contrary to most other Member States, the Netherlands does not have a constitutional court or the ability for the judge to review statutory provisions against the Constitution. Article 120 of the Dutch Constitution (DC) prohibits the judge from reviewing the constitutionality of laws by Parliament and treaties. The responsibility for ensuring that no legislation in conflict with the DC is passed rests primarily with the legislature. This 'legislative supremacy' is seen as one of the main characteristics of the Dutch constitutional tradition. However, according to Article 93 DC, provisions of treaties and decisions of international organisations, such as the European Convention on Human Rights (ECHR), which have direct effect by virtue of their content, are legally binding. Furthermore, Article 94 DC stipulates that the judge is obliged to assess whether legislation is compatible with those universally binding (directly effective) provisions and may even set aside statutory provisions. Therefore, the Netherlands has a partly monist system. However, EU law has direct effect and is applicable regardless of the provisions of the DC.[6]

Within these (constitutional) boundaries, the job of the Dutch judge requires walking a fine line. On the one hand, the judge is not permitted to examine statutory provisions against the DC and the fundamental rights therein. On the other hand, the judge should uphold directly effective provisions of treaties, EU law and the fundamental rights contained in the CFR. Sometimes this causes friction between the powers of state in the Netherlands, in the sense that the judge is accused of carrying out too intrusive a review of fundamental rights or, on the contrary, of being too reticent. Examples of both extremes will now be given.

---

[4] See the interview with CCW Lange in the FRICoRe Newsletter No 4 of June 2020, https://www.fricore.eu/fc/news/newsletter-n-4-june-2020.

[5] As cited by TT Koncewicz, 'The Supranational Rule of Law: Taking Stock' *Verfassungsblog* (27 December 2019), www.verfassungsblog.de/the-supranational-rule-of-law-taking-stock.

[6] Since the landmark *Van Gend en Loos* (Case C-26/62 [1963] ECR 3) the direct effect of EU law was established and *Costa v ENEL* (Case C-6/64, [1964] ECR 1141) established the supremacy of the EU legal order. This legal order cannot be limited by the (constitutions of the) Member States.

A. The *Urgenda* Climate Change Case

In the ruling of the Dutch Supreme Court of 20 December 2019 in the *Urgenda* climate change case,[7] the effect of international law was at issue. The Supreme Court upheld the previous decisions of the District Court and the Court of Appeal, finding that the Dutch government has the (positive) obligation to urgently and significantly reduce CO_2 emissions in line with its human rights obligations stemming from Articles 2 and 8 ECHR. This ruling received acclaim, criticism and disbelief not only in the Netherlands, but from all over the world. Questions were raised as to whether the judiciary exceeded its powers with this ruling and sat on the chair of politics, the legislature and/or the executive power.[8] Some even accused the judiciary of 'dikastocracy' or 'rule by judges'.

B. The *Childcare Allowance Affair*

However, recently the opposite question was posed in cases that took place within the national legal order: Has the judge done enough to protect the litigant? This question arose in the so-called *Childcare Allowance Affair*, which led to the establishment of the Van Dam Parliamentary Interrogation Committee. This affair concerned around 26,000 parents, who were victims of false allegations of fraud between 2009 and 2019. Even if they committed minor offences, such as administrative errors, they were obliged to pay back the full amount of childcare allowance they had received from the government. Consequently, in many cases, whole families fell into severe poverty for many years. This was the result of a harsh law that lacked a hardship clause, with the objective of tackling fraud relating to public funding of childcare. This law was strictly executed by the Dutch tax authorities and (initially) strictly interpreted and applied by the judiciary. The Van Dam Committee presented a report entitled 'Unprecedented Injustice' on 17 December 2020. According to the Committee, fundamental principles of the rule of law had been violated. All three state powers were criticised for their actions in this affair. Also, the role of the Administrative Law Division of the Council of State, the last-instance court in these cases, was scrutinised. The committee also found that the administrative judiciary made a substantial contribution for years to the maintenance of the non-compulsory, harsh implementation of the childcare allowance scheme. According to the committee the judiciary had thus neglected its important function of (legal) protection of individual citizens. The *Childcare Allowance Affair* led to the fall of the Dutch government in January 2021.

In response to the Report from the 'Van Dam' Committee, the President of the Administrative Law Division of the Council of State announced a period of self-reflection on the Division's role in the *Childcare Allowance Affair*.[9] This led to a quite unique report from the Division entitled 'Lessons from the Childcare Allowance Cases' in November 2021.[10] The main conclusion was that the Division held on to the strict interpretation and application of the law for too long. It should and could have changed this case law sooner. By failing to do so, the Division has not been able to give parents the legal protection that they were entitled to and who got

---

[7] Judgment of the Dutch Supreme Court (Hoge Raad), 20 December 2019, NL:HR:2019:2006, also translated in English, NL:HR:2019:2007.

[8] See, for instance, G Boogaard, 'Urgenda en de rol van de rechter. Over de ondraaglijke leegheid van de Trias Politica' (2016) *Ars Aequi* 26–33; KJ de Graaf and AT Marseille, 'Van "waar bemoeit die rechter zich mee?" tot "res loquitur ipsa". De Urgenda-zaak bij de Hoge Raad' (2020) *Ars Aequi* 955–60.

[9] BJ van Ettekoven, 'Tussen wet en recht' (2021) *Nederlands Juristenblad* 100, afl 2, 98.

[10] Raad van State, 'Lessen uit de kinderopvangtoeslagzaken', www.raadvanstate.nl/reflectierapport.

into trouble because of this. The report concluded that this would not be allowed to happen again. The Division apologised for this. Also, more general lessons were learnt. One of them is that settled case law, containing strict interpretation and application of harsh laws, must leave room for a just outcome (in the sense of material justice) in the individual case. But how can a judge achieve this without going beyond his or her powers?

In the same period, and in line with the question raised above, the President of the Administrative Law Division of the Council of State also set in motion a Grand Chamber[11] to assess similar issues in other areas of law. In essence, the questions were about the job the judge has to fulfil in cases involving harsh laws without a hardship clause and to what extent the human dimension can be taken into account. The outcome shows that inspiration can be drawn from the principles in EU law in order to find answers to these questions. A more detailed explanation follows in section V, after the sections on the fundamental right to effective judicial protection under EU law.

III. SHAPING THE JOB OF THE JUDGE IN THE EUROPEAN RULE OF LAW

As mentioned earlier, the big challenges for the EU lie in areas such as environmental protection, climate change, migration, consumer health and safety, and data protection. It is obvious that these challenges must be met at the European level. The importance of the judiciary for the proper functioning of the EU as a whole gradually became clearer within the EU. More focus and attention were given to the role of judges in the European rule of law.

A. Constitutional Status of the Right to Effective Judicial Protection in Article 47 CFR

The granting of full legal effect to the CFR, with the entry into force of the Lisbon Treaty on 1 December 2009, was an important incentive for the further development of the role of the judge within the EU. The Charter became a source of primary EU law. The most important article concerning the role of the judge in the European rule of law is included in Chapter VI on Justice. Article 47 CFR[12] embodies the right to effective judicial protection against infringement of EU rights and freedoms:

> Right to an effective remedy and to a fair trial
>
> Everyone whose rights and freedoms guaranteed by the law of the Union are violated has the right to an effective remedy before a tribunal in compliance with the conditions laid down in this Article.

This article makes explicit an essential condition for the good functioning of the rule of law, namely *ubi ius, ibi remedium*, meaning that where there is a right, there must be a remedy.

---

[11] In the Netherlands there are four last-instance courts in administrative law. Besides the Administrative Law Division of the Council of State (Raad van State), there is the Supreme Court (fiscal chamber), the Administrative High Court (Centrale Raad van Beroep) and the Trade and Industry Appeals Court (College van Beroep voor het bedrijfsleven). Since 2013, it has been legally possible for these last-instance courts to hear cases with enlarged panels of five judges – so-called Grand Chambers – instead of three judges. Grand Chambers consist of full-time judges of one last-instance court and at least one judge who is a full-time judge at another last-instance court. The goal is the uniform application of general administrative law by the four last-instance courts.

[12] Similar principles are stipulated in arts 6 and 13 ECHR, which were already upheld in EU law before the entry into force of the CFR. See also the second subparagraph of Article 19(1) TEU, according to which Member States are obliged to provide 'the necessary' remedies for effective legal protection in areas governed by EU law, and its use as a rule of law provision in recent case law.

If EU rights cannot be enforced, the credibility of the EU is at stake. This would undermine the support for and trust in the EU and with that the goals it wants to achieve. So, the right to an effective remedy was officially promoted to a codified fundamental right.[13] Article 47 CFR therefore contains a very weighty task for the judge within the European rule of law. Contrary to the DC, where a similar article is missing,[14] with Article 47 the CFR gives substance to this task.[15] And positioning this task in the Charter gives the job of judge a constitutional status, thus empowering the judge to actually fulfil this job within the European rule of law. Naturally always with respect of the jobs of the other state powers.

B. Dialogues between Judges, Academics and Other Legal Practitioners

Another indispensable development for the shaping of the role of the judge in the European rule of law is the European judicial training projects on EU law and the CFR.[16] These projects brought together many judges, academics and other legal practitioners from all Member States. The participants became acquainted with each other's domestic legal systems and shared best practices on how to effectively apply EU law within their legal orders. They also shared difficulties they encountered in applying EU law within their national legal orders and solutions to overcome these problems. Not only is it inspiring to hear and learn from each other's experiences, but it is also crucial to meet and know each other in order to build mutual trust and understanding within the EU. Thus, judges are contributing to one of the pillars of the EU, namely the free movement of judgments, essential for the success of the internal market. With those projects, insights grew about the role of the judge in the supranational, multi-layered European rule of law and, more importantly, how to actually fulfil it.

The dialogue between judges, academics and other legal practitioners during some of these European projects about the implications of Article 47 CFR in the different areas of law turned out to be very fruitful. It allowed them to look beyond their borders, not only literally but also figuratively by comparing the effect of Article 47 CFR within the different areas of EU law. The spin-off of these interactions in academic literature,[17] but also in referrals to the CJEU,[18] is very valuable for the shaping of the role of the judge under EU law.

It goes without saying that the dialogue of national judges with the CJEU about the CFR was and still is crucial for the further development of the shaping of the role of the judge under EU law. Further exploration and clarification of the exact impact of Article 47 CFR on the job of judge within the EU would be very welcome.

---

[13] A second written legal basis for the principle of effective judicial protection is provided by art 19(1) TEU, which requires Member States to establish a system of legal remedies and procedures ensuring effective judicial protection in the fields covered by EU law.

[14] Constitutional amendments in this area are currently on the agenda of the House of Representatives in the Netherlands. Since August 2022 a new paragraph is added to article 17 DC about the right to a fair trial within a reasonable time before an independent and impartial judge.

[15] Manon Julicher, 'Nederlandse grondrechten: klaar voor de toekomst? Modernisering van grondrechten in de Grondwet in het licht van het EVRM en het EU-Grondrechtenhandvest' (PhD thesis, University of Utrecht, 2020).

[16] For instance, the ReJUS projects and the FRiCoRe project, led by Fabrizio Cafaggi and Paola Iamicelli.

[17] See, for instance, Anna van Duin, 'Justice for Both: Effective Judicial Protection under Article 47 of the EU Charter of Fundamental Rights and the Unfair Contract Terms Directive' (PhD thesis, University of Amsterdam, 2020).

[18] See, for instance, the referrals in Dutch asylum detention cases about the *ex officio* assessment of the criteria of detention for asylum seekers. The questions were also asked in response to the rulings of the CJEU in consumer law cases about *ex officio* assessment. These referrals are registered as joinedCases C-704/20 and C-39/21. The CJEU rendered judgment in these cases on 22 November 2022, see *Staatssecretaris van Justitie en Veiligheid (Examen d'office de la rétention)* EU:C:2022:858.

C. Independence of the Judiciary

Last but not least, the independence of the judiciaries within the Member States is of the essence for effective judicial protection[19] and also for the further shaping of the role and the job of the judge in the European rule of law. Without judicial independence, there is no room for contradiction between state powers. The possibility to contradict each other is the only way to keep a good balance between the state powers and to nourish and strengthen the rule of law. Contradiction can cause confrontations between the state powers, but when done with respect for each other's positions in the rule of law, it only adds to the quality of the respective state powers and thus of the rule of law.

IV. ARTICLE 47 CFR: *UBI IUS, IBI REMEDIUM*

So, with Article 47 CFR, the job of the judge in the European rule of law now has a constitutional status and effective judicial protection for individuals on a national level has become a (written) fundamental right of primary EU law.[20] But what does this mean for the role of the judge?

A. Large Impact in Theory

Three observations will be made about Article 47 CFR to begin with. The first concerns its scope of application. Whenever EU law comes into play, whether directly or indirectly, and Member States act within the scope of EU law, Article 47 CFR is applicable (Article 51 CFR). The CFR and therefore also Article 47 has a structuring function: it marks the borders between EU law and the national legal orders. If applicable, the scope of Article 47 CFR can be broader than the partly overlapping Articles 6 and 13 ECHR. Article 47 CFR is not limited to disputes concerning civil rights and obligations and criminal charges, but also covers the entire *acquis communautaire*, including administrative disputes.[21] Moreover, Article 47 CFR relates not only to the fundamental rights guaranteed by the Charter itself, but also to all the rights and freedoms of EU law.

Second, Article 47 CFR has direct effect.[22] If EU law is at stake, the judge has to offer effective judicial protection, regardless of the way in which the rule of law in the Member State is organised and of the constitutional traditions of the national legal order. So, the legal order of the Member State does not and must not stand in the way of the job the judge has to fulfil in order to provide effective judicial protection against infringement of EU rights and freedoms.

Third, the *Rewe*[23] principles of equivalence and effectiveness,[24] 'l'effet utile' and the principle of effective judicial protection[25] already existed under EU law before the CFR came into

---

[19] Case C-64/16 *Associação Sindical dos Juízes Portugueses v Tribunal de Contas* EU:C:2018:117, para 41; Case C-274/14 *Banco de Santander SA* EU:C:2020:17, paras 57–63.

[20] M Bonelli, 'Effective Judicial Protection in EU Law: An Evolving Principle of a Constitutional Nature' (2019) 12 *Review of European Administrative Law* 35.

[21] This is especially important in immigration law.

[22] Case C-414/16 *Vera Egenberger v Evangelisches Werk für Diakonie und Entwicklung eV* EU:C:2018:257, para 78.

[23] Case C-33/76 *Rewe-Zentralfinanz eG and Rewe-Zentral AG v Landwirtschaftskammer für das Saarland* [1976] ECR 1989.

[24] Based on the principle of sincere cooperation in art 4(3) TEU.

[25] Recognised as a general principle of EU law as it underlies the constitutional traditions common to the Member States. This principle is also laid down in arts 6 and 13 ECHR.

effect. Without getting into the differences between these three forms of effectiveness (if this is clear at all),[26] it is important to highlight the added value of Article 47 CFR for the job of the judge. Contrary to these principles of effectiveness, Article 47 CFR also sets a positive standard.[27] Not only must a national provision that fails to satisfy the requirements of the principles of effectiveness or of effective judicial protection be set aside in a concrete case; under Article 47 CFR, the judge also has to create a new remedy if needed.[28] So, Article 47 CFR does not only remove obstacles to protection, but also provides for a constitutional basis to actually safeguard specific EU law rights in a concrete case, preferably by using national remedies, but if necessary (and if possible) by creating a new remedy (see section IV.C). Thus, Article 47 CFR contains autonomous procedural safeguards relating to specific EU rules.[29]

B. Many Variables in Practice

This all sounds wonderful in theory, but at the end of the day, when and how can and should a judge actually give substance to Article 47 CFR in a concrete case? Logically this question only comes into play when a lack of effective judicial protection of specific EU rights or freedoms is at stake in a national procedure. Unfortunately, a straightforward instruction manual is not (yet) available. Many variables are at play.

How Article 47 CFR can be applied depends first of all on the context of the case the judge is facing, both at an EU level and at a national level. The specific EU rule must after all be embedded in the respective national legal order so that it can be enforced in court. Thus, not only are the specific EU rule at stake, its purpose and scope decisive, but also the national legal order in which the EU right has to be upheld. These variables are all part of the multi-layered rule of law. And it is the task of the judge not to get lost in translating the EU rule into the national legal order if he or she wants to offer effective judicial protection.

Another not to be underestimated variable is how the state powers within the Member States perceive their roles within their national rule of law. This depends largely on the constitutional background of the Member State. Dutch research in six Member States (Belgium, Germany, France and the Scandinavian countries, in particular Denmark, Norway and Sweden) and the UK[30] shows that in all the countries surveyed there is now some form of constitutional review of formal laws by judges. In the examined systems with a separate constitutional court (Belgium, Germany and France), the jurisdiction of those courts has gradually been extended, both by the constitutional legislator and the (special) legislator as in the practice of the relevant courts, who have begun to interpret their jurisdiction and their review mandate

---

[26] See, for instance, S Prechal and R Widdershoven, 'Redefining the Relationship between "Rewe-Effectiveness" and Effective Judicial Protection' (2011) 4 *Review of European Administrative Law* 31; R Widdershoven, 'National Procedural Autonomy and General EU Law Limits' (2019) 12 *Review of European Administrative Law* 5.

[27] Widdershoven (n 26) 19.

[28] Case C-432/05 *Unibet (London) Ltd and Unibet (International) Ltd v Justitiekanslern* [2007] ECR I-2271. In *Unibet*, para 72, the CJEU held that under the principle of effective judicial protection the national court has to be able to grant the interim relief necessary to ensure EU rights are respected, even though the possibility of giving such a remedy is uncertain under national law.

[29] Van Duin (n 17) 37 and 65. Van Duin mentions Case C-472/11 *Banif Plus Bank v Csaba Csipai and Viktória Csipai* EU:C:2013:88 para 29, as an example of the framing of (a lack of) effective judicial protection as a fundamental rights issue and thus as a move towards 'proceduralised constitutionalisation'.

[30] This research was conducted at the request of the Minister of the Interior and Kingdom Relations of the Netherlands by four (assistant) professors of Maastricht University: Monica Claes, Aalt Willem Heringa, Marijn van der Sluis and Maarten Stremler. This led to a report: 'Rechtsvergelijkend onderzoek constitutionele toetsing' (Comparative Law Research on Constitutional Review) (31 January 2021), https://cris.maastrichtuniversity.nl/ws/portalfiles/portal/63839879/Rechtsvergelijkend_onderzoek_constitutionele_toetsing.pdf.

more broadly. In those systems the researchers generally see a higher frequency of laws being declared unconstitutional (in the formal sense) than in countries where the ordinary court performs that function. The authority of the constitutional courts in Belgium, Germany and France has gradually grown and increased. This contributes to the intrusiveness of testing and frequency of unconstitutional rulings. The experiences in countries without a constitutional court, where the ordinary courts review the constitutionality of laws (Scandinavia and the UK), show that this judicial review is more reserved. According to the researchers, this reluctance to test the constitutionality of laws can perhaps be explained by the constitutional culture (the deep-seated constitutional views regarding the place of the judge in the *trias politica*), the (constitutional) provisions that institute judicial review for the ordinary courts and the fact that no separate body was established with the specific mandate to review the constitutionality of laws. Therefore, depending on their constitutional background, judges might perceive and fulfil the job they have under EU law and the CFR differently, even though with Article 47, the CFR gives everyone equally a fundamental right to effective judicial protection against infringement of EU rights and freedoms and to a remedy where there is a right. It is important for judges to realise that their national constitutional backgrounds may influence their perception of their job in the supranational European rule of law.

In her dissertation,[31] van Duin gives a striking example of how Article 47 CFR fulfils different roles within the judiciaries of two Member States while applying one and the same Directive, depending on the national legal framework at issue and their constitutional backgrounds. She researched the case law of the CJEU and of the courts in Spain and the Netherlands concerning the Unfair Contract Terms Directive.[32] In contrast to their Spanish colleagues, Dutch judges hardly made any preliminary references to the CJEU based on Article 47 CFR. This might have to do with the lack of a constitutional tradition in the Netherlands and/or maybe the judges did not see the need or the added value of Article 47 CFR in those cases. Van Duin distils five main categories of functions that are attributed to Article 47 CFR: (1) a legitimising, (2) a strengthening or empowering, (3) a signalling or transformative, (4) an eliminating and (5) a generative function.[33] She concluded that Article 47 CFR is a chameleon-like provision that changes colour depending on the context in which it is applied.

Judges in all Member States can draw inspiration from these categories in order to provide effective judicial protection in a concrete case in their national legal order. How Article 47 CFR is applied depends on the EU law instrument with which it is read in conjunction, the factual and legal framework, the constitutional background of the judge and the way in which an issue is framed by the judge. For instance, Article 47 CFR can be applied at the national level in order to eliminate an obstacle – or to create an effective remedy – to ensure substantive EU rights in a national procedure (the eliminating or generative function). Alternatively, Article 47 CFR can be applied in a signalling capacity at the European level to make a preliminary reference to the CJEU, in order to clarify the seriousness of the problem or the urgency of finding a solution in order to provide effective judicial protection (the signalling function).

Against this background, it is not surprising that it is difficult to give hard and fast rules on when and how a judge should apply Article 47 CFR in his or her national legal order.

---

[31] Van Duin (n 17) 58–76.

[32] Council Directive 93/13/EEC of 5 April 1993 on unfair terms in consumer contracts [1993] OJ L95/29.

[33] Van Duin (n 17) 300: the first function is the most similar to the principle of effectiveness; it legitimises the CJEU's intervention in national (procedural) law. The strengthening or empowering function goes further and explicitly recognises the constitutional dimension of a particular case or issue. The signalling or transformative function focuses on the seriousness of the problem and the urgency of finding a solution. The eliminative and generative functions express that art 47 has direct effect and, as such, offers an independent (autonomous) basis for setting aside existing national rules or creating new requirements. Unfortunately, the scope of this chapter does not allow for a further elaboration here.

That does not alter the fact that under EU law, a judge has to provide effective judicial protection if necessary. Another lesson of the *Childcare Allowance Affair* was that the outcome of a judgment in a concrete case should be materially just,[34] which means that the judge uses the law as a tool to reduce injustice and abuses of power, and thereby strives for a just outcome of a decision for the parties concerned in a concrete case. Under EU law, Article 47 CFR gives the judge not only the opportunity but also the task of actually offering effective judicial protection in concrete cases.

C. The Tasks of the Judge under Article 47 CFR

In principle, it is for the national courts to interpret procedural and substantive rules governing actions brought before them in such a way that those rules, wherever possible, are applied so that they contribute to ensuring effective judicial protection of an individual's rights under EU law.[35] Maybe the judge can interpret or bend the national rules at stake, whether or not with reference to Article 47 CFR, in a way that does justice in an effective way to the goals and purposes of the specific EU rules at stake. If so, then there is no problem. If not, the judge needs to be more activist and creative. A judge can, for instance, not validly claim that it is impossible to interpret a provision of national law in a manner that is consistent with EU law merely because that provision has consistently been interpreted in a manner that is incompatible with EU law.[36] But how activist and creative should the judge be in order to provide a remedy where there is an EU right? Is there a limit to what a judge can do under Article 47 CFR?

If EU law is not directly applicable, a judge should interpret a national substantive rule as much as possible in accordance with EU law. But if this results in an interpretation *contra legem*, EU law cannot be applied in the national legal order. For instance, if the national legislator, contrary to the Working Time Directive,[37] explicitly ruled out the payment of certain holiday days not yet taken in case of illness under the Civil Code, the judge cannot grant such a claim to an employee directly under the Directive.[38] Creating a new remedy is not an option under these circumstances. This should be resolved through compensation on the basis of state liability.[39]

But what if a procedural rule stands in the way of an effective remedy in a concrete case? Should the judge disapply this procedural rule and create another? Or, if a specific remedy does not exist under national law, can or should the judge create such a remedy? The CJEU indicated that if in a national legal system, no legal remedy exists which makes it possible to ensure respect (even indirectly) for an individual's EU law rights, then the Member State concerned must provide for a self-standing action to challenge the compatibility of a national provision

---

[34] Ruth de Bock, *Grip op kwaliteit: een model voor inhoudelijke kwaliteit van rechterlijke beslissingen, Handelingen Nederlandse Juristen Vereniging, 145ᵉ jaargang* (Deventer, Wolters Kluwer, 2015). De Bock describes a model for the substantive quality of judicial decisions. In short, there are three demands: those of craftsmanship, justice and effectiveness.

[35] Case C-379/18 *Deutsche Lufthansa AG v Land Berlin* EU:C:2019:1000, para 63; *Unibet* (n 28) para 44.

[36] See also *Deutsche Lufthansa* (n 35) para 63.

[37] Directive 2003/88/EC of the European Parliament and of the Council of 4 November 2003 concerning certain aspects of the organisation of working time [2003] OJ L299/9.

[38] See, for instance, the judgment of the Appeal Court of Amsterdam (Gerechtshof Amsterdam), 10 November 2009, NL:GHAMS:2009:BK4648. But there are exceptions – see, for instance, Case C-193/17 *Cresco Investigation GmbH v Markus Achatzi* EU:C:2019:43. In the case of infringement of a fundamental right (here art 21 CFR), provisions in a Directive can have direct effect in a horizontal dispute.

[39] Joined Cases C-6/90 and C-9/90 *Andrea Francovich and Danila Bonifaci and Others v Italian Republic* [1991] ECR I-5357.

with EU law.[40] What does this mean for the job of the judge in a concrete case? Under what circumstances should the judge be active in creating remedies and solutions in order to provide effective judicial protection in a concrete case? Should a judge wait for the legislature to take action and how would that relate to the adage *ubi ius, ibi remedium* – where there is a right, there must be a remedy?

There are more questions that arise when it comes to the content of job of the judge. For instance, what is the degree of judicial scrutiny a judge should exercise in an individual case on the basis of Article 47 CFR? Answers to these questions are also pivotal for the further shaping of the job of the judge. Widdershoven describes how Article 47 CFR is far more demanding than the *Rewe* principles of equivalence and effectiveness when it comes to the intensity of national judicial scrutiny of administrative decisions, leaving the national courts with hardly any discretion in this regard. The precise level of intensity of national judicial scrutiny depends on the EU rule at stake.[41]

A judge could also use the principle of proportionality to provide for effective protection in a concrete case. But the exact intensity of judicial review with respect to the principle of proportionality under EU law is not always completely clear. The CJEU applies the principle of proportionality in accordance with the three-step goal/means test: (1) suitability; (2) necessity; and (3) proportionality *stricto sensu* (in its narrow sense). In order to provide effective judicial protection under Article 47 CFR in a concrete case, how much leeway is there for the judge, for instance, to test a decision against proportionality *stricto sensu* when according to EU law, minimum standards apply? This question, in a case about a professional lorry driver who was refused the renewal of his driving licence to drive lorries, has recently been referred to the CJEU.[42]

All these questions need clarification. So, if a judge is not sure how to rule in accordance with Article 47 CFR in order to guarantee effective judicial protection of a specific EU rule in a concrete case, making a referral to the CJEU is the obvious next step. In doing so, the judge could make use of the functions that are attributed to Article 47 CFR, as discussed in section IV.B above. Thus, the CJEU is given the opportunity to further clarify the job of the judge in the supranational, multi-layered European rule of law under Article 47 CFR.

V. TOWARDS EFFECTIVE JUDICIAL PROTECTION UNDER THE DUTCH RULE OF LAW

A good example of how the European rule of law, specifically through the European principle of proportionality, influences the Dutch rule of law are the developments after the *Childcare Allowance Affair*. As already mentioned in section II.B above, the President of the Administrative Law Division of the Council of State set in motion a Grand Chamber to assess how jurisdiction containing strict interpretation and application of harsh laws can leave room for a just outcome (in the sense of material justice) in an individual case. Coming from a background where 'legislative supremacy' is seen as one of the main characteristics of the Dutch constitutional tradition, there was some concern that the judge would exceed his power if he deviated from (the strict execution of) harsh laws.

---

[40] *Unibet* (n 28) para 42.
[41] Widdershoven (n 26) 24.
[42] See the referral judgment of the Council of State (Raad van State), 16 November 2022, NL:RVS:2022:3273, Case C-703/22.

In February 2021 the President of the Administrative Law Division of the Council of State asked the advocates general of the Council of State – Widdershoven and Wattel – for an opinion on questions about: (1) the legal basis for assessing the proportionality of decisions based on laws without a hardship clause under EU law, the ECHR or national law respectively; (2) how intrusively the administrative judge should assess the proportionality of such a decision; and (3) which circumstances the judge should take into account. These questions provided food for thought. Would the answers to these questions differ according to the assessment framework under EU law, the ECHR or national law respectively? Would and should the job of the judge be different depending on this?

In their opinion delivered on 7 July 2021,[43] the advocates general were clear that there should be no difference in the assessment of proportionality under national or European law. They advised the Grand Chamber to abolish the 'two-extreme system' in which the Dutch judge under national law would only have two ways of testing decisions against the principle of proportionality: the marginal/reluctant assessment or the full/intrusive assessment (in the case of punitive sanctions). They supported a system where the intensity of the assessment varies continuously with the weight of the general and private interests involved, the degree of infringement of fundamental rights and the circumstances of the case. In short, they proposed that administrative judges apply the principle of proportionality as enshrined in Article 3:4, paragraph 2 of the Dutch General Administrative Law Act (GALA) in accordance with the three-step goal/means test used in EU law and employed when restricting ECHR rights, as already mentioned in section IV.C above.

In the judgment delivered on 2 February 2022,[44] the Grand Chamber followed the conclusion of the advocates general and abandoned the national 'two-extreme system'. It is beyond the scope of this chapter to go into too much detail on this. In short, the Grand Chamber, also inspired by EU law, ruled that in the future, administrative judges can test decisions against the national proportionality principle laid down in Article 3:4, paragraph 2 GALA in accordance with the European three-step goal/means test. The intensity of judicial review depends on so many factors that according to the Grand Chamber, it is a sliding scale to which all intensities between full and restrained must be able to be applied. The proportionality test therefore varies from case to case. The more important the interests, the more serious the adverse effects or the more serious the infringement on fundamental rights, the more intensive the judicial review will be.

This recent judgment shows that under the influence of the European proportionality principle, the job of the administrative judge in the Netherlands in domestic procedures becomes more active. While testing decisions against the (Dutch) principle of proportionality, judges will from now on have more leeway to take the human dimension into account. These developments can be seen as a direct result of the *Childcare Allowance Affair* and coincide perfectly with the objective to provide effective judicial protection, as referred to in Article 47 CFR.

VI. CONCLUSION

The good functioning of the European rule of law, like everything good in life, is all about balance. If the European legislator creates rights, then those rights must be executable and, if not, enforceable – otherwise, what is the use of creating those rights in the first place?

---

[43] Council of State (Raad van State), Opinion of the Advocates General, 7 July 2021, NL:RVS:2021:1468.
[44] Judgment of the Council of State (Raad van State), 2 February 2022, NL:RVS:2022:285.

The credibility of the European rule of law and the goals that the EU stands for depend on it. A cornerstone of the European rule of law is therefore the adage *ubi ius, ibi remedium* – in other words, 'where there is a right, there must be a remedy'. It is ultimately the job of the judge, the third state power in the rule of law, to provide this remedy. It is therefore essential for the good functioning of the European rule of law that judges (are able to) do their job well.

With the promotion of this adage in Article 47 CFR to binding EU primary law in 2009, the job of the judge was given a constitutional status under EU law. Contrary to the 'old' principles of effectiveness, Article 47 CFR also gives a positive standard. And it provides a constitutional basis for judges to create remedies for the effective judicial protection of specific EU law rights in a concrete case. The supremacy of EU law entails that any judge in any Member State is bound to ensure the effective judicial protection of individual parties before him or her in court against infringement of EU rights and freedoms, regardless of the 'constitutional background' in the domestic rule of law of his or her Member State, thus strengthening public confidence in the European rule of law.

The job of the judge seems perfectly clear in theory, but in practice the road to effective judicial protection in a concrete case can be rather foggy. EU rights are to be applied in the national legal orders of the Member States. It is not only the specific EU rule at stake, its purpose and scope that are decisive. Also, the national legal order in which the EU right has to be enforced is important. These variables are part of the multi-layered rule of law. The judge has to be careful not to get lost in translating EU rights into that national legal order if he or she wants to offer effective protection of these rights.

Also, the national constitutional culture and understanding of the rule of law can have an influence on how the judge perceives the job to be fulfilled under EU law. Research shows that the presence of a constitutional court in a Member State contributes to the intrusiveness of testing against fundamental rights in the constitution and also to the frequency of unconstitutional declarations of laws; however, the experiences in Member States without a constitutional court, where the ordinary courts review the constitutionality of laws, show that this judicial review is more reserved.

Article 47 CFR has a wide range and turns out be a chameleon-like provision that can change colour depending on the EU law instrument with which it is read in conjunction, the factual and legal framework, the 'constitutional background' of the judge and the way in which an issue is 'framed' by the judge. Thus, Article 47 CFR can be applied, both on a national and on a European level, in the capacity of the various functions attributed to this provision.

These are all variables of the supranational and multi-layered European rule of law to take into account while shaping the job of the judge in the European rule of law. Against this background, it is difficult to give hard and fast rules on when and how a judge should apply Article 47 CFR. This does not alter the fact that under EU law, a judge has to provide effective judicial protection if needed in a concrete case. The fulfilling of this job takes judicial cooperation, communication, wisdom, courage and skill.

The CJEU plays an important role in the shaping of the job of the judge – for example, by further clarifying the precise levels of intensity of judicial review of the EU rule at stake, and by further clarifying EU law and the circumstances under which the judge can disapply and/ or create a national procedural rule or create a substantive remedy in a concrete case. Also, the dialogue between judges, academics and other legal practitioners from all Member States are pivotal for the job of the judge and the nourishing of the European rule of law. Facilitating and supporting this dialogue through European judicial training projects and meetings at both a national and a European level is crucial in order to build mutual trust and understanding within the EU. And of course, the independence of the judiciary is vital for the development of the job of the judge in the European rule of law and, for that matter, in any rule of law.

In the Netherlands the influence of the European rule of law on the job of the administrative judge within the national legal order became quite evident after the *Childcare Allowance Affair*. In a judgment of 2 February 2022, the Grand Chamber of the Administrative Law Division of the Council of State, inspired by EU law, ruled that in the future, administrative judges can test decisions against the national proportionality principle in accordance with the European proportionality principle (the three-step goal/means test). This means that under the influence of the European proportionality principle, the job of the administrative judge in the Netherlands in domestic procedures becomes more active. In other words, the judge has more leeway to provide effective judicial protection in an individual case. This coincides perfectly with the adage *ubi ius, ibi remedium*, as enshrined in Article 47 CFR. The Dutch rule of law thus benefits from the European rule of law – in this case, by strengthening the job of the Dutch administrative judge in the domestic rule of law in order to be able to provide more effective judicial protection to citizens when the legislature enacts a harsh law and/or the executive enforces the law too strictly. In response, the Dutch legislator has amended the relevant law with a hardship clause. The balance between the state powers has thus been restored for the benefit of its citizens and of the (trust in the) rule of law.

This demonstrates the importance of the job of the judge for the balance between the state powers and the good functioning of the rule of law. It also shows the importance of Article 47 CFR as a supranational legal basis for judges to properly perform their jobs in concrete cases. This article can serve as a beacon for the judge to guide him or her towards the effective judicial protection of specific EU law rights in a concrete case. It should not come as a surprise that this cornerstone can also provide solutions for problems judges are facing in their national legal order as described above. After all, the adage *ubi ius, ibi remedium*, contains a universal truth for every rule of law.

15

Lights and Shadows of the Aziz *Case*

JOSÉ MARÍA FERNÁNDEZ SEIJO

O N 14 MARCH 2013, the Court of Justice of the European Union (CJEU) delivered its judgment in the *Aziz* case.[1] I was the judge who resolved the case in the first instance and from the beginning of the procedure I had the conviction that, with the application of the Spanish regulations, the protection of Mr Aziz would be very weak.

The judgment provided an answer to the preliminary reference concerning consumer protection in mortgage enforcement proceedings. Spanish procedural rules prevented consumer debtors from being able to challenge unfair contract terms prior to being evicted from their homes.

The judgment of the CJEU had a significant impact in Spain. It coincided with the most difficult moment of the financial crisis and had the effect of suspending thousands of foreclosure proceedings. The solution that the Court gave in the *Aziz* case was nevertheless to be expected. It was clear from previous judgments of the Court that consumers have to be protected in special expedited procedures as well.[2] Still, Spanish and European legal academics have analysed the *Aziz* case in depth (for instance, Hans-W Micklitz, Julio Banacloche Palao, Chantal Mak, Norbert Reich and many others).

The *Aziz* case forced a profound procedural reform in Spain and many civil judges found in the preliminary reference procedure before the CJEU an essential tool to protect millions of citizens affected by unfair terms included in financial contracts.

Despite the significant media attention and impact on the Spanish legal system, the case did not end so well for Mr Aziz. He was evicted from the house he bought and after a journey through a complicated judicial maze, his claims were finally rejected. Although the *Aziz* case may represent an important leap forward in the utopia of ensuring that the judiciary is effectively involved in the application of Article 47 of the Charter of Fundamental Rights of the European Union, the truth is that what Mr Aziz had to go through is, really, a complete dystopia.

Mohamed Aziz's story is an example of what happened to many workers in Spain. He bought an apartment in a small city on the outskirts of Barcelona. These were the years of an apparent boom when it was easy to access bank financing. He had to dedicate a very high percentage of his salary to paying the mortgage for many years. Within a few months, he lost his job and stopped paying the loan instalments, and the bank's requests for repayment started.

---

[1] Case C-415/11 *Mohamed Aziz v Caixa d'Estalvis de Catalunya, Tarragona i Manresa (Catalunyacaixa)* EU:C:2013:164.
[2] See Case C-618/10 *Banco Español de Crédito, SA v Joaquín Calderón Camino* EU:C:2012:349.

Soon after the bank initiated legal proceedings, the unpaid instalments increased, and the bank decided to terminate the loan contract early and claim the whole amount of the loan.

Mr Aziz didn't oppose the enforcement proceedings: the grounds for objection were very limited and he preferred to remain silent, remain in default and wait for his luck to improve, or reach some type of agreement with the bank.

The judicial enforcement proceedings were slow, but finally all the procedures were exhausted, and the court put Mr Aziz's home up for auction. In the absence of any bidders, the house was acquired by the bank itself, and the date and time for the eviction were determined. Mr Aziz was still silent. He was notified of the different stages and, finally, he knew the day and time when he would be irrevocably evicted from his home.

In despair, Mr Aziz decided to take legal action, not within the enforcement proceedings, where all opportunities were closed, but in a separate procedure, covered by the Spanish Law on General Conditions of Contract of 1998,[3] which transposed Council Directive 93/13/EEC of 5 April 1993 on unfair terms in consumer contracts.[4] He claimed that the loan agreement contained several clauses that could be considered unfair. This lawsuit was within the jurisdiction of the commercial court, which means that while the enforcement procedure was dealt with by a civil judge situated at the place where Mr Aziz lived, the lawsuit on the fairness of the terms of the consumer contract had to be resolved by a different judge situated in a different place.

The lawsuit itself was not far-reaching; the only thing that mattered to Mr Aziz was staying the enforcement in order to avoid the loss of his home. In the lawsuit, he did not assume any commitment to pay the outstanding debt, nor did he request to renegotiate the mortgage contract, but only interim relief that would prevent his eviction. He only asked that several clauses be annulled, without clearly defining how he would meet the contractual obligations and the outstanding debt.

The lawsuit was filed in February 2011, a few days before the eviction date scheduled by the court arrived. At that time, the Spanish Code of Civil Procedure allowed the mortgage debtor to object to the enforcement on only very limited grounds, which did not include a complaint on the basis of unfair terms. The Spanish rules were absolutely restrictive in excluding any other judicial intervention in the enforcement proceedings. The debtor could only start a declaratory procedure that did not suspend the enforcement, which meant that Mr Aziz would lose his home and enter a long and uncertain trajectory in which he could only be granted a reduction of the pending debt if the terms were found to be unfair, but he would not be able to return to his home.

The request for interim relief was rejected; the bank had not had an opportunity to be heard and insufficient security was offered for the damages that the bank could incur if the main claim would finally be dismissed. The request was thus unsuccessful due to serious procedural flaws that could no longer be fixed, and so Mr Aziz was evicted. Spanish procedural laws prevented the adoption of precautionary measures by the judge – who knew about the procedure due to the general conditions that were in place – if there was an execution in progress, which could not be suspended for any reason.

The declaratory procedure concerning the alleged unfairness of the contractual clauses was still in process, with an uncertain and ineffective outcome regarding the possibility of regaining possession of his home.

---

[3] Ley 7/1998, sobre condiciones generales de la contratación.
[4] Council Directive 93/13/EEC of 5 April 1993 on unfair terms in consumer contracts [1993] OJ L95/29.

Given the prospects of the case, it would have been complicated or impossible to suspend the eviction; maybe it would have made sense to refer the matter to the CJEU and ask whether interim measures to suspend the eviction should not be possible in order to avoid causing irreparable damage to Mr Aziz. However, it would have been complicated to obtain a suspensive interim ruling that would compromise the previous decisions of another judge, taken in a different procedure, in which Mr Aziz had decided not to defend himself.

There was no doubt about the shortcomings of the Spanish procedural system, which prevented the examination of the existence of possible unfair terms in enforcement proceedings and the effect of those terms on the enforcement. It was impossible to achieve the required level of protection by applying Spanish procedural law and it was also very complicated to find a European way to question the Spanish procedural law due to the principle of national procedural autonomy. Moreover, the procedural channels of the CJEU did not enable a simple way to achieve the suspensive effect that Mr Aziz was trying to achieve.

Once the request for interim relief was rejected, Mr Aziz didn't appeal and his lawyer continued with the course of the declaratory procedure, with his client already being on the street. The bank didn't consider it necessary to bring Mr Aziz to court to testify, so I wasn't given the opportunity to meet Mr Aziz personally.

An out-of-court settlement between Mr Aziz and the bank, under the conditions set by Spanish procedural law, turned out to be impossible, despite the bank being warned of a possible request for a preliminary ruling.

On 23 February 2011, Mr Aziz was evicted from his home. He still had to repay a large part of the loan, since the home was awarded to the bank for an amount significantly lower than the original mortgage. The property market in Spain had collapsed and the houses lost 25% of their value in a few months.

The unfairness examination in the declaratory proceedings would make it possible, at best, to reduce the outstanding debt, but not to recover the home.

When raising the question for a preliminary ruling before the Luxembourg Court, it was noted that the initiation of a declaratory procedure by Mr Aziz would not allow for effective judicial protection if the clauses were finally annulled, because the national court could not declare the enforcement procedure void retrospectively.

At the beginning of November 2012, the Advocate General of the CJEU published her conclusions, where she indicated that the Spanish procedural system for mortgage enforcement was contrary to the principle of effectiveness. It prevented the debtor, if he was a consumer, from defending himself against unfair terms in the enforcement proceedings, forcing him to resort to declaratory proceedings, in which the court cannot order to stop the enforcement proceedings.[5]

The Advocate General's opinion was already a trigger for the Spanish courts to halt most of the ongoing enforcement proceedings. This effect, which Mr Aziz had not achieved for himself and his family, was obtained for thousands of consumers without them having to undertake any legal action because the judges began to suspend enforcement proceedings *ex officio*, based on the doctrine established by the CJEU in the *Océano* case.[6]

The CJEU judgment in *Aziz* consolidated the criteria already announced by the Advocate General: Directive 93/13 must be interpreted in the sense that it precludes legislation of a

---

[5] *Aziz* (n 1), Opinion of AG Kokott, EU:C:2012:700.
[6] Joined Cases C-240/98–C-244/98 *Océano Grupo Editorial SA v Roció Murciano Quintero and Others* [2000] ECR I-4941.

Member State, which, while not providing, in the context of the enforcement proceedings, the possibility of raising grounds of objection based on the unfair nature of a contract terms that constitutes the basis of the enforcement, does not allow the judge who hears the declaratory procedure and who is competent to assess the unfair nature of that term to grant interim measures, including, in particular, the suspension of the enforcement proceedings, where granting such measures is necessary to guarantee the full effectiveness of the national court's final decision.

The ruling of the CJEU meant upholding the suspension of thousands of foreclosures in Spain. This suspension was maintained despite the legal reforms that had in the meantime been adopted by the Spanish government and that were again subjected to preliminary questions. Hence, the CJEU rendered new rulings in which a system of consumer protection in mortgage enforcement proceedings was outlined further.[7] The Spanish Constitutional Court in its judgment of 28 February 2019 has accepted and developed this European jurisprudence, enabling much more effective mechanisms for the protection of consumers in foreclosure procedures.[8]

Meanwhile, in Mr Aziz's case, a judgment was rendered in which the terms he denounced as unfair were annulled.[9] In that judgment there was no final ruling on the nullity of the enforcement proceedings, which Mr Aziz had not requested in his application. That issue was therefore left to be determined during a possible subsequent execution of the judgment.

The bank's lawyer appealed this judgment and the Court of Appeal of Barcelona revoked an important part of the first decision.[10] While it considered that some of the terms of the contract should be considered unfair, the terms at issue didn't warrant reversing the enforcement and enabling Mr Aziz to recover his home.

Mr Aziz's lawyer subsequently filed an appeal in cassation before the Supreme Court. The appeal was in fact suspended for several years because the Supreme Court waited until the CJEU ruled in March 2019 on the nullity of clauses allowing for the early termination of mortgage loan contracts (so-called acceleration clauses).[11]

The Supreme Court eventually did not find the cassation appeal to be admissible. It rejected it without going into the merits of the case on the grounds that the appeal had insurmountable procedural defects. The Court issued a simple resolution rejecting the appeal, without entering into any deeper reflection on the substance of the case. Therefore, Mr Aziz, who managed to blow up the Spanish mortgage enforcement system, has not enjoyed any of the advantages of his own initiative. Almost 10 years after entering into the maze of legal proceedings with which he was trying to regain his home, all his efforts remained meaningless. It is a paradox that is difficult to understand for those who don't know the law and its dark areas. The jurisprudence that developed after the *Aziz* case therefore leaves me with a bitter aftertaste.

---

[7] See, for instance, Case C-169/14 *Juan Carlos Sánchez Morcillo and María del Carmen Abril García v Banco Bilbao Vizcaya Argentaria SA* EU:C:2014:2099.

[8] See Tribunal Constitucional, judgment no 31/2019 of 28 February 2019, ES:TC:2019:31.

[9] Juzgado de lo Mercantil No 3 de Barcelona, judgment no 13/2011 of 2 May 2013, ES:JMB:2013:21.

[10] Audiencia Provincial Barcelona (Sección 15ª), judgment no 407/2014 of 15 December 2014, JUR\2015\86196 ES:APB:2014:14543.

[11] Joined Cases C-70/17 and C-179/17 *Abanca Corporación Bancaria SA v Alberto García Salamanca Santos and Bankia SA v Alfonso Antonio Lau Mendoza and Verónica Yuliana Rodríguez Ramírez* EU:C:2019:250.

Index

Ingram Content Group UK Ltd.
Milton Keynes UK
UKHW051949240723
425398UK00031B/201